Human Rights Interventions

Series Editors
Chiseche Mibenge
Stanford University
Stanford, CA, USA

Irene Hadiprayitno
Leiden University
Leiden, Zuid-Holland, The Netherlands

The traditional human rights frame creates a paradigm by which the duty bearer's (state) and rights holder's (civil society organizations) interests collide over the limits of enjoyment and enforcement. The series departs from the paradigm by centering peripheral yet powerful actors that agitate for intervention and influence in the (re)shaping of rights discourse in the midst of grave insecurities. The series privileges a call and response between theoretical inquiry and empirical investigation as contributors critically assess human rights interventions mediated by spatial, temporal, geopolitical and other dimensions. An interdisciplinary dialogue is key as the editors encourage multiple approaches such as law and society, political economy, historiography, legal ethnography, feminist security studies, and multi-media.

More information about this series at
http://www.palgrave.com/gp/series/15595

Huub van Baar • Ana Ivasiuc
Regina Kreide
Editors

The Securitization of the Roma in Europe

Editors
Huub van Baar
Justus Liebig University Giessen
Giessen, Germany

Ana Ivasiuc
Justus Liebig University Giessen
Giessen, Germany

Regina Kreide
Justus Liebig University Giessen
Giessen, Germany

Human Rights Interventions
ISBN 978-3-319-77034-5   ISBN 978-3-319-77035-2 (eBook)
https://doi.org/10.1007/978-3-319-77035-2

Library of Congress Control Number: 2018935401

© The Editor(s) (if applicable) and The Author(s) 2019
This work is subject to copyright. All rights are solely and exclusively licensed by the Publisher, whether the whole or part of the material is concerned, specifically the rights of translation, reprinting, reuse of illustrations, recitation, broadcasting, reproduction on microfilms or in any other physical way, and transmission or information storage and retrieval, electronic adaptation, computer software, or by similar or dissimilar methodology now known or hereafter developed.
The use of general descriptive names, registered names, trademarks, service marks, etc. in this publication does not imply, even in the absence of a specific statement, that such names are exempt from the relevant protective laws and regulations and therefore free for general use.
The publisher, the authors, and the editors are safe to assume that the advice and information in this book are believed to be true and accurate at the date of publication. Neither the publisher nor the authors or the editors give a warranty, express or implied, with respect to the material contained herein or for any errors or omissions that may have been made. The publisher remains neutral with regard to jurisdictional claims in published maps and institutional affiliations.

Cover image: Image (detail) of the public art installation "Safe European Home?" by Damian John Le Bas and Delaine Le Bas. Photograph by Damian James Le Bas

Cover design by Fatima Jamadar

Printed on acid-free paper

This Palgrave Macmillan imprint is published by the registered company Springer International Publishing AG part of Springer Nature.
The registered company address is: Gewerbestrasse 11, 6330 Cham, Switzerland

Foreword: On Multiplicity, Interstices and the Politics of Insecurity

Exploring the securitization of the Roma in Europe today necessarily makes for a bleak reading of both contemporary minority politics and how discrimination and violence are currently inscribed into European societies. The Roma have been a key target of intensifying xenophobia, racism, economic marginalization, social destitution and the hollowing out of citizenship. They are not the only group of people who have become a battleground for the institutionalization and contestation of who can legitimately and effectively claim which human, civil, social, economic and political rights. However, together with refugees and particular groups of immigrants, they are certainly at the heart of struggles and disputes over the distribution of rights in a Europe that is experiencing a severe crisis of European integration, a continuing marketization of life, increasing precarity and inequality, an intense contestation over the viability of multiculturalism and a revival of geopolitical nationalism. As the chapters in this book show, the Roma have been and continue to be subjected to severe discrimination in this conjuncture. Their rights claims and campaigns for the right to have rights have become very precarious indeed.

Political, socioeconomic and cultural securitizations of Roma play a central role in instituting discrimination and exclusion and the grounds for legitimizing them. One of the major contributions of this volume is its detailed analyses of the multiple processes through which the Roma are enacted as a source of insecurities. However, in this preface, I want to focus on this volume's contribution to the study of securitization, not just of minorities, but more generally. Although it may seem more comfortable to reflect on the academic question of how to study security than to engage the—in places—quite disturbing and violent realities that securitizations produce for the Roma, that is not the reason for drawing attention to the understanding of securitization. The approach to the question of security is important for a proper understanding of the predicament of the Roma in Europe, and also for understanding how to critically engage the processes of securitization.

The term 'securitization' was introduced into security studies in the 1990s to study insecurities as the product of discourses which articulate phenomena as existential threats to a society, state, community, individual or systemic entity. It refocused security analysis from the actions of those considered as posing a threat, to the actions of those who claim to defend against these threats. The latter are considered key for understanding how issues such as housing policies or border crossings become politicized as matters of security concern. The question is not whether the Roma are threatening or not, but rather what practices, and by whom, are framing the Roma as a matter of security, and what are the consequences of this? Such a take on insecurities creates reflective distance from the justification of security practices and their effects along the lines of, 'We know that security policies are not necessarily the ideal response and have possible negative side-effects, but we are not the ones posing a threat; we have a responsibility to defend the community, society, state against the threat'. By drawing attention to the active involvement of security practices in the production of insecurities, responsibility for its consequences shifts significantly to those claiming to defend and protect, whether vigilante, security agencies or politicians. As a result, the politics of security takes on a broader set of concerns as to how best to protect against a threat, including whether security methods and representations should be deployed at all.

The chapters in this book draw on this understanding of security, and share a critical disposition towards deploying security methods and representations of the Roma. The book is not, however, simply an application of securitization analysis to the Roma in Europe. It introduces a distinct take on the study of securitization. Between them, the chapters put forward the idea that, for understanding the securitization of the Roma, security studies need to move beyond focusing on security agencies and political speech. Nobody in this book argues that the latter are not important, but the securitization of the Roma involves significantly more than the application of coercive governmental methods by state security agencies and spectacular security statements by political leaders. The book multiplies the sites and processes that are significant, including urban gentrification, regional policies, entertainment culture, local vigilante groups, social media, social policy, border practices and criminalization. In doing so, it makes a strong case for understanding securitization as a more diffuse process that is enacted throughout societies. That may sound obvious, but analytically it is not so easy to pull off because it requires recognition that the securitization of the Roma is really multiple in terms of the kind of actors involved, the processes through which it is enacted and the differences in experiences at different sites. It also demands that the analysis retain the heterogeneity of securitization while nevertheless articulating that these multiple practices are related, but not necessarily in an aggregative way that would bring the diverse processes together into a systemic securitization of the Roma. One of the strengths of the volume is that it is quite careful in seeking to retain the multiplicity of minor processes—minor not in the sense of small scale or micro but in the sense of resisting integration into aggregated/aggregating systemic processes—while nevertheless giving a real sense of resonance between them in terms of the discriminations, exclusions and violence directed at Roma people. Although the concept of multiplicity is not explicitly deployed and developed by the authors, the book makes a strong case for pursuing methods and conceptual takes that sustain and develop securitization analyses which take multiplicity seriously.

Analysing the multiplicity of securitizations in itself does not, however, address a particular issue with securitization studies: as a mode of security studies, it tends to isolate or home in on the security dimensions of phenomena and practices; as a mode of disciplinary knowing, it always risks reifying the centrality of security in the processes of governing and politicizing. By approaching security sideways, this volume addresses the need to avoid that risk. Most of the chapters take as their focal point practices which are not, strictly speaking, security practices. They look at the marketization of government and social relations, the development logic enacted in minority politics, visual cultures enacted in reality TV shows and social media, border practices and policies, the use of governmental methods reminiscent of colonialism, the enactment of racism, urban gentrification and so on. They then analyse how these practices take on securitizing characteristics, intersect with security practices and sustain renditions of the Roma as the source of insecurity. However, it is always clear that the discriminations, exclusions and violence addressed to the Roma cannot be reduced to securitization. Coming to security sideways thus guards against explicit or implicit reductive readings. It allows for an interstitial approach to securitization in which the securitization analysis creates interstices between security and various other practices, issues and processes. It opens towards a more complex and heterogeneous understanding of how discrimination against and exclusion and subordination of the Roma are enacted, and the place of security discourses and techniques within that enactment. Taking such an approach leads to a better understanding of how situations are shaped for the Roma and the place of securitization in this process. It proposes a study of security that is not really a security study; indeed, in some places, it leads to analyses in which securitization seems more like a minor theme than a central force, and that is exactly what is valuable about deriving an understanding of the securitization of the Roma from the analysis of the multiple processes of governance and modes of representation and diffusion that are irreducible to security.

Combined with multiplying securitizations, this sideways approach to securitization contributes to a fracturing analysis of the securitization of the Roma and the discrimination, violence and stereotyping to which they are subjected. Rather than pulling all the chapters together into an aggregated statement at a macro-level on the process of securitization of the Roma, which does not really exist, the volume preserves a fractured landscape of securitizations, with the chapters, between them, allowing the reader to glimpse resonances across various sites and processes that do indeed imply a securitization of the Roma in Europe. In my understanding, this is a more accurate, but also more politically astute, approach to securitizations than tracing processes of securitization as such.

A related but distinct method of avoiding reifications of security is to move away from the understanding that securitization is depoliticizing, with depoliticizing understood as a technological or technocratic governing practice or an exceptionalist political practice. Several chapters do emphasize that insecurities and security practices always exist in contestations of rights, disputes over the right to have rights, claims of autonomy, protests, resistance and so on. However, in most of the chapters the bulk of the analysis remains focused on governing processes and modes of representation of the Roma. This is partly because security is primarily understood as securitization rather than as a politics of insecurity. Taking securitization as the driving analytical approach draws attention, in the first instance, to the social, cultural and political forces which structure situations into security situations. The place of disputes, conflicts, contestations, and appropriations of rights, identities, conceptions of acceptable practices and autonomy that are equally defining of the situation, but in a continuously changing rather than an entrenching way, then tend to be ignored, become an afterthought or are given only secondary attention. Embedding the study of securitizations within an analysis of the politics of insecurity gives these elements a front-row seat in the analysis. It foregrounds categories and methodologies that approach politicizations as fractured and multiple becomings which simultaneously configure and challenge the enactment of insecurities and their consequences. The disruptive claims to rights of the Roma, counter-cultures, appropriations in everyday life, mobilizations of understandings that rupture reproduced imaginaries and so on then become crucial practices for understanding the renditions of insecurities in relation to the Roma in Europe today. It does not necessarily produce a less depressing picture of the way the Roma are governed and understood, or of the subjugations they experience; it does, however, open towards a world with more possibilities. It introduces an understanding that situations of securitization are not shaped by processes but by disputes, controversies, contestations, struggles and misappropriations, which continuously create new possibilities.

The distinct approach to securitization that this book expresses matters politically. It emphasizes the heterogeneity and multiplicity of securitizing practices, and how discriminations and subordinations are produced at interstices between securitizing practices and various processes that are not reducible to security. If the discriminating processes are inherently fractured, and connect more through resonances than systemic aggregations, then the fractured political acts and possible resonances between them are key to creating possibilities in specific sites for changing the precarious situation of many Roma in Europe today. Such an approach to the securitization of the Roma gives value to minor practices which, from the aggregated level of the state or the EU, appear as insignificant, as not having any bearing on the political process. In doing so, the book opens towards the valuing of a broad array of political actions for challenging securitization and the continuing marginalization, silence and subjugation to which the Roma are subjected in Europe. Combined with the book's distinct approach to the study of securitization, this makes for a great and timely contribution to both security studies and Roma politics. It sets an example of how to assemble a study of securitization which captures its fractured but highly consequential reality by drawing together a group of researchers working, from multiple disciplinary angles, on how the lives of a particular group of people are rendered precarious today.

Queen Mary University of London Jef Huysmans
London, UK

Acknowledgements

A book such as this could not have been realized without the support of many people. First and foremost, we wish to express our appreciation for the authors who entrusted their work to this volume, giving it the form and quality of an ongoing and inspiring interdisciplinary conversation. We would also like to thank our colleagues from the research centre *Dynamics of Security: Forms of Securitization in Historical Perspective* at the Justus Liebig University in Giessen, the Philipps University in Marburg and the Herder Institute for Historical Research on East Central Europe in Marburg. We thank the German Research Foundation (DFG) which has, through grant SFB/TRR 138 (2014–17), financed the inspiring and open-minded context of research which includes our research project 'Between Minority Protection and Securitization: Roma Minority Formation in Modern European History'.

The vibrant intellectual exchange both within and beyond *Dynamics of Security* allowed us to engage in a number of very stimulating international debates. We would particularly like to thank Thierry Balzacq, Didier Bigo, Marieke de Goede, Beatrice de Graaf, Mark Duffield and Jef Huysmans for visiting our research centre and for the various inspiring discussions about and beyond security issues. We thank the Justus Liebig University in Giessen for hosting the international conference 'The Politics of Security: Understanding and Challenging the Securitization of Europe's Roma' (1–3 June 2016) which laid the ground for this volume. For their attendance and energizing participation in the discussions, we are grateful to, among many others, Ethel Brooks, Emile Julien Costache, Ulderico Daniele, Harika Dauth, Kenan Emini, Jan Grill, Theodora Müller-Balauru,

Mark Neocleous, Moritz Pankok, Dotschy Reinhardt, Zsuzsanna Vidra and Václav Walach.

We particularly want to thank very much Delaine and Damian John Le Bas for allowing us to use their artwork 'Safe European Home?' for the cover of this volume, and Damian James Le Bas for providing the photograph of the artwork. It was with great sorrow that we heard that, on 9 December 2017 and shortly before this book went into production, Damian John Le Bas suddenly died, at the age of 54. His death is a great loss for the international Roma art movement, and for the Roma social and civil rights movement generally.

We want to thank the editors of this series for providing us with the opportunity for this cooperation. At Palgrave Macmillan, we would like to thank Anca Pusca, Anne Schult and Katelyn Zingg for eloquently convening the trajectory towards this publication. We are grateful to the anonymous reviewers for their commentaries on the proposal that formed the basis for this volume. We also thank Peggy Birch for her careful and thorough reading of the entire manuscript, and Chris Engert for his thorough proofreading of the volume.

Yasmin Feltz, Emmanuel Ametepeh and Laura Kienzle have supported us with their organizational talents through the years; Angela Marciniak has been indispensable for her theoretical and organizational knowledge and her continued support. Last, but not least, we owe Marion Groh a debt of gratitude for the humorous and patient way she has dealt with all the different and unexpected problems which have occurred as we worked together as a team during this time.

Contents

1 The European Roma and Their Securitization: Contexts, Junctures, Challenges 1
Huub van Baar, Ana Ivasiuc, and Regina Kreide

Part I Mobility 27

2 The Securitization of Roma Mobilities and the Re-bordering of Europe 29
Nicholas De Genova

3 Crossing (Out) Borders: Human Rights and the Securitization of Roma Minorities 45
Regina Kreide

4 Domestic Versus State Reason? How Roma Migrants in France Deal with Their Securitization 67
Olivier Legros and Marion Lièvre

Part II Marketization — 89

5 The Invisibilization of Anti-Roma Racisms — 91
Ryan Powell and Huub van Baar

6 Security at the Nexus of Space and Class: Roma and Gentrification in Cluj, Romania — 115
Manuel Mireanu

7 The Entertaining Enemy: 'Gypsy' in Popular Culture in an Age of Securitization — 137
Annabel Tremlett

Part III Development — 157

8 From 'Lagging Behind' to 'Being Beneath'? The De-developmentalization of Time and Social Order in Contemporary Europe — 159
Huub van Baar

9 Illusionary Inclusion of Roma Through Intercultural Mediation — 183
Angéla Kóczé

10 Voluntary Return as Forced Mobility: Humanitarianism and the Securitization of Romani Migrants in Spain — 207
Ioana Vrăbiescu

Part IV Visuality — 231

11 Sharing the Insecure Sensible: The Circulation of Images of Roma on Social Media — 233
Ana Ivasiuc

12 The "gypsy Threat": Modes of Racialization and Visual
    Representation Underlying German Police Practices   261
    Markus End

13 Roma Securitization and De-securitization
    in Habsburg Europe   285
    Marija Dalbello

Index   311

Notes on Contributors

Marija Dalbello is an Associate Professor of Information Science in the School of Communication and Information at Rutgers University, New Jersey, in the USA. Her teaching and publications focus on the history of knowledge and history of the book applied to liminal phenomena and visuality. She has published on digital mediation, visual epistemology and immigrant literacies. She is the co-editor of *Visible Writings: Cultures, Forms, Readings* (2011) and *A History of Modern Librarianship: Constructing the Heritage of Western Cultures* (2015).

Nicholas De Genova has held academic appointments at King's College London, Goldsmiths, Columbia and Stanford, as well as visiting professorships and research positions at the Universities of Chicago, Amsterdam, Bern and Warwick. He is the author of *Working the Boundaries: Race, Space, and "Illegality" in Mexican Chicago* (2005), co-author of *Latino Crossings: Mexicans, Puerto Ricans, and the Politics of Race and Citizenship* (2003), editor of *Racial Transformations: Latinos and Asians Remaking the United States* (2006), co-editor of *The Deportation Regime: Sovereignty, Space, and the Freedom of Movement* (2010) and editor of *The Borders of "Europe": Autonomy of Migration, Tactics of Bordering* (2017).

Markus End is an independent scholar from Berlin, Germany, and the Chairman of the *Gesellschaft für Antiziganismusforschung* (GfA). He was awarded his Ph.D. in Education from the University of Bielefeld in Germany in 2017 and has published widely in the field of antigypsyism. He is the author of *Antiziganismus in der deutschen Öffentlichkeit* (2014) and the co-editor of *Antiziganistische Zustände: Zur Kritik eines* *allgegenwärtigen Ressentiments* (2009), *Antiziganistische Zustände 2: Kritische Positionen gegen gewaltvolle Verhältnisse* (2013) and *Antiziganism: What's in a Word?* (2015).

Jef Huysmans is a Professor of International Politics at Queen Mary University of London. After finishing his Ph.D. at the University of Leuven, Belgium, he was a Lecturer in International Relations and European studies at the University of Kent in Canterbury. Later, he moved to the Open University in Milton Keynes, where he taught politics and international relations and was Director of the Centre for Citizenship, Identities and Governance. He has published several books, including *The Politics of Insecurity: Fear, Migration and Asylum in the EU* (2006), *Security Unbound: Enacting Democratic Limits* (2014) and, with Xavier Guillaume, *Citizenship and Security: The Constitution of Political Being* (2013).

Ana Ivasiuc is an anthropologist and a postdoctoral researcher at the Institute of Political Science of the Justus Liebig University in Giessen, Germany, where she is carrying out research on the securitization of the Roma in Italy within the project *Dynamics of Security: Forms of Securitization in Historical Perspective*, funded by the German Research Foundation (2014–17). She was awarded her Ph.D. in Sociology from the National School for Political and Administrative Studies in Bucharest, Romania. She is the co-editor of *Roma Activism: Reimagining Power and Knowledge* (forthcoming in 2018).

Angéla Kóczé is an Assistant Professor of Romani Studies and Academic Director of the Roma Graduate Preparation Programme at Central European University (CEU) in Budapest, Hungary. Previously she was a Visiting Assistant Professor in the Women's, Gender and Sexuality Studies Program at Wake Forest University, Winston-Salem (North Carolina), the USA (2013–17). She was the principal investigator of the research project 'Institutionalization of Romani Politics After 1989 in Hungary', funded by the Hungarian Social Research Fund (2013–16). She is the co-editor of *The Romani Women's Movement: Struggles and Debates in Central and Eastern Europe* (forthcoming in 2018).

Regina Kreide is a Professor of Political and Social Theory and the History of Ideas at the Justus Liebig University in Giessen, Germany. She is the co-director of the Collaborative Research Centre *Dynamics of Security* and, together with Huub van Baar, leads the research project

'Between Minority Protection and Securitization: Roma Minority Formation in Modern European History', financed by the German Research Foundation (DFG). She is the author of *Die verdrängte Demokratie: Essays zur Politische Theorie* (2016) and *Globale Gerechtigkeit* (forthcoming in 2018), and the co-author of *Transformations of Democracy: Crisis, Protest, and Legitimation* (2015).

Olivier Legros is a geographer and senior lecturer at the University of Tours in France. Since working on the articulation between urban policies and social dynamics in the informal neighbourhoods of southern cities (e.g. Tunis, Dakar), he has focused his research on the policies towards Roma migrants in precarious situations in France. Legros is a founding member of URBA-ROM, the observatory of policies towards groups referred to as Roma/Gypsies. He oversees the Marginalization/Inclusion (MARG/IN) research programme devoted to policies aimed at Roma migrants and their effects on target populations in France, Italy and Spain. The French National Research Agency (ANR) finances this programme.

Marion Lièvre is a researcher at the Paul-Valéry University, Montpellier 3 in Montpellier, France. Previously, she was a postdoctoral researcher (2015–17) at the University of Tours, France, where she participated in the framework of the MARG-IN research programme, financed by the French National Research Agency (ANR). In 2013, she completed her Ph.D. thesis, entitled 'Ethno-Cultural Nationalism and its Relation to the Culture of Roma in Post-Communist and Multicultural Romania', at the Paul-Valéry University, Montpellier 3. Her research is dedicated to the analysis of the relationship between Roma migrant practices and public policies, with a specific focus on the role of the 'new social worker'.

Manuel Mireanu was awarded his Ph.D. in International Relations from Central European University (CEU), Budapest, Hungary, in 2015. He has conducted research on the security practices of vigilante groups in Europe. He is conducting research autonomously in Romania.

Ryan Powell is a Reader in Urban Studies in the Department of Urban Studies and Planning at the University of Sheffield in the UK, where he is also the Department's Director of Research. He previously worked at the Centre for Regional Economic and Social Research (CRESR) at Sheffield Hallam University. He has diverse research interests spanning urban marginalization, urban governance, citizenship and the stigmatization of 'outsider' groups.

Annabel Tremlett is a Senior Lecturer in Social Inclusion at the University of Portsmouth in the UK. Since gaining her Ph.D. in Cultural Studies from King's College London (2008), she has been awarded two external grants to continue her research into visual representations. Her research interests include investigating the differences between public and self-representations of minority or marginalized groups. She is particularly interested in how to challenge misleading representations to bring about social change and has extensive expertise in ethnographic and photo elicitation research.

Huub van Baar is an Assistant Professor of Political Theory at the Justus Liebig University in Giessen in Germany and a senior research fellow at the Amsterdam Centre for Globalisation Studies (ACGS) and at the Department of European Studies of the University of Amsterdam in the Netherlands. Together with Regina Kreide, he leads the DFG-funded research project 'Between Minority Protection and Securitization: Roma Minority Formation in Modern European History'. He is the author of *The European Roma: Minority Representation, Memory, and the Limits of Transnational Governmentality* (2011) and the editor of *Museutopia: A Photographic Research Project by Ilya Rabinovich* (2012).

Ioana Vrăbiescu is a postdoctoral researcher in the ERC project *SOLIDERE: The Social Life of State Deportation Regimes*, at the University of Amsterdam in the Netherlands. She was previously a Roma Initiative Office Fellow at the Open Society Institute (OSI) and a visiting scholar at the University Autonoma of Barcelona in Spain. She holds a Ph.D. in Political Science and has an academic background in gender studies and international relations.

List of Figures

Fig. 11.1	The iconic stranger. (Source: Facebook)	237
Fig. 11.2	'Bad people walking up and down'. (Source: Facebook)	238
Fig. 11.3	Rooting through containers. (Source: Facebook)	239
Fig. 11.4	Disposable body. (Source: Facebook)	241
Fig. 11.5	'Gypsy vans'. (Source: Facebook)	242
Fig. 11.6	'Abusive market'. (Source: Facebook)	243
Fig. 11.7	Smoke. (Source: Facebook)	244
Fig. 11.8	The protected 'Territory': condominiums. (Source: Facebook)	248
Fig. 11.9	The protected 'Territory': shops. (Source: Facebook)	249
Fig. 11.10	'Suspicious van'. (Source: Facebook)	250
Fig. 13.1	*Zigeunermädchen* (von Ihrer k. und k. Hoheit Erzherzogin Maria Dorothea). *Gypsy Girl*. Creative Commons licence by Austria-Forum (Bilder: *Kronprinzenwerk*, Band 23: 565). (Note: The painting is autographed 'María' and the engraving is signed 'Morelli G.F.I.')	295
Fig. 13.2	*Wanderzigeuner* (von Johann Greguss). *Nomadic Gypsies*. Creative Commons licence by Austria-Forum (Bilder: *Kronprinzenwerk*, Band 23: 567). (Note: The engraving is signed, 'Pásztori' (a personal name or a location in the Győr-Moson-Sopron area))	296
Fig. 13.3	*Zeltzigeuner und Zigeunerin* (nach Photographien in der Alcsuther Sammlung Seiner k. und k. Hoheit Erzherzog Josef). *Tent Gypsy man and woman*. Creative Commons licence by Austria-Forum (Bilder: *Kronprinzenwerk*, Band 23: 571). (Note: The engraving is signed, 'Morelli G.F.I.')	297

Fig. 13.4   *Lager von schnitzenden Zigeunern* (Johann Greguss). *A settlement with Gypsies carving.* Creative Commons licence by Austria-Forum (Bilder: *Kronprinzenwerk*, Band 23: 573). (Note: The engraving is signed 'Morelli G.F.I. Mésés K sc.')   298

Fig. 13.5   *Zigeunerhütten am Dorfende* (Johann Greguss). *Gypsy huts at the edge of town.* Creative Commons licence by Austria-Forum (Bilder: *Kronprinzenwerk*, Band 23: 574), unsigned   298

CHAPTER 1

The European Roma and Their Securitization: Contexts, Junctures, Challenges

Huub van Baar, Ana Ivasiuc, and Regina Kreide

Events and transformations in and of the world—terrorist attacks, the movements of migrants and refugees, violent conflicts in Ukraine, Syria, and elsewhere, climate change, and a changing world order beyond the bipolarity of the Cold War—are all, in one way or another, framed in terms of security and insecurity these days. We live in a world where threats to security are constant—at least, this is what the prevalent public and political discourses on security seem to want us to believe. But, as the diversity of the examples indicates, the question of *whose* security needs to be defended and guaranteed is not unambiguous. For some groups—minorities and migrants in particular—security discourses and practices have themselves turned into a kind of threat, as they have often become the targets and the objects of measures which—allegedly—are designed to bring about 'more security'. Security and its impact on minorities and migrants, and on the Roma in Europe in particular, are the central focus of this volume.

H. van Baar (✉) • A. Ivasiuc • R. Kreide
Justus Liebig University Giessen, Giessen, Germany
e-mail: Huub.van-Baar@sowi.uni-giessen.de; Regina.Kreide@sowi.uni-giessen.de

© The Author(s) 2019
H. van Baar et al. (eds.), *The Securitization of the Roma in Europe*, Human Rights Interventions, https://doi.org/10.1007/978-3-319-77035-2_1

During the Cold War and in traditional security studies, the term 'security' referred mostly to national security and the guaranteeing of the borders of territorialized nation states; hence, minorities were not a specific concern of these analyses. With the emergence of critical security studies in the 1990s, the alleged neutrality and objectivity of security and its conditions of possibility, as well as the methodological nationalism of traditional security analyses, have explicitly been questioned. Over the last two decades, a series of studies inspired by the linguistic and post-structuralist turns in modern philosophy has sought to understand why and how security discourses and mechanisms are created, and what the effects of the subsequent policy measures are on human lives. Among these studies are those pertaining to the 'Copenhagen School' (Buzan et al. 1998) and the 'Paris School' (Bigo et al. 2010; Bigo and Guild 2005; Huysmans 2006; Huysmans et al. 2006) of securitization.

For the Copenhagen School, speech acts uttered by political elites perform security with 'words' in a process called securitization. Speech acts invoke a semantic repertoire, a 'grammar of security' (Buzan et al. 1998: 33) through which a societal affair can be performed as a security 'problem'. Here, securitization involves defining something as a security problem, and thus triggering exceptional political measures to deal with it.

This approach has been criticized, most notably for its one-sided focus on the discursive dimension of securitization. The representatives of the Paris School, in particular, consider the speech-act approach to be too narrow, as it neglects both non-discursive practices of securitization and the ways in which a process of normalizing securitization is always already underway, for instance, through the practices and technologies used by security professionals which go beyond publicly uttered speech acts (profiling, satellite techniques, risk assessments, or the activities of Frontex). By asking who *accepts* the discourses on security, their approach focuses on the relationship between security measures, the actors discursively and non-discursively articulating security threats, and audiences who are, or are not, responsive to these threat renditions (Balzacq 2011). Understood in this way, securitization encompasses discursive and non-discursive ways of creating knowledge about the security techniques which change the governance of social, political, economic, cultural, and military affairs. Moreover, in this approach, practices of securitization come to the fore in a *dialectical* relationship in which the formation of security does not bring about a *more secure* world but only produces more insecurity (Ivasiuc, Chap. 11, this volume; Kreide, Chap. 3, this volume) through practices of normalization which distinguish, for example, between 'regular' citizens and migrants, and those who are rendered 'irregular' such as minorities and illegalized migrants. This dialectical, Foucault-based approach includes not only a reflection on the processes of discursive representation and construction but also a critical interrogation of the techniques and forms of expertise and knowledge formation involved in enacting, maintaining, reinforcing, or challenging aspects such as migration-related processes of securitization (Bigo et al. 2013; Huysmans 2006; van Baar 2011a, 2015).

Uniquely, this volume links critical security studies with minority studies and focuses on the Roma as a much discriminated-against, 'irregularized' transnational minority in Europe from the perspective of various intersections of security. The chapters in this book shed light on the question of what is implied by securitization, both conceptually and in practice, combining the approaches of both the 'schools' discussed. The authors illustrate—from a variety of perspectives—the process of securitization as a mechanism of exclusion: from territories, residence, citizenship, public services, humanity, and the egalitarian promise of citizenship.

The contributors discuss the position of the European Roma from the angle of how they and their practices have been considered to be a threat to public, social, or even national security or to themselves—the latter mostly in the context of human security—in various national and European contexts. While research regarding the securitization of the Roma has so far primarily focused on the nexus of security and mobility in the context of Roma migration from Central and Eastern to Western Europe, and in that of 'free movement' in an enlarging European Union (EU), this volume offers a notably more comprehensive approach: it situates Roma-related concepts, discourses, and practices of securitization in the broader context of their mutual interactions and intersections with mobility, development, marketization, and visuality. In so doing, we show not only how the processes and mechanisms of securitization significantly impact the everyday lives of the Roma throughout Europe but also how several programmes presented as solutions to 'their problems' are ambiguously related to the ways in which the Roma have been problematized as security threats. We do not understand securitization as a kind of master narrative or frame through which we can comprehensively understand the situation of the Roma in Europe; rather, we adopt it as an analytical tool which can illuminate the processes to which the European Roma are subjected, but always at the intersection with regimes of mobility, marketization, development, and visuality. Thus, we take a 'fractured' look at securitization (Huysmans, Foreword, this volume).

The book also sheds new light on how the securitization of the Roma and their practices can be questioned and challenged. Normatively, conceptually and empirically, this is not simply a matter of reframing or approaching them in the 'non-security' terms of human and minority rights, empowerment, inclusion, participation, or development more generally. In fact, our volume shows that this reframing and the correlated political interventions are often also problematic in different respects. The contributions to *The Securitization of the Roma in Europe* imply that any serious attempt at 'de-securitization' should thoroughly reflect on how the prevalent securitization of the Roma and their practices largely overlaps with regimes of mobility, marketization, development, and visuality. De-securitization is always linked to securitization and vice versa. Thus, there is no de-securitization without pre-existing securitization, and any process of securitization explicitly or implicitly has the potential to be unmasked, offset, and overcome.

In critical security studies, de-securitization has generally been conceptualized in binary opposition to securitization and as its normatively 'good' and 'desirable' counterpart (Aradau 2004; Hansen 2011a). Indeed, overly dramatized and exceptionalized issues can be brought back into the realm of 'politics as usual' through de-securitization. Following critiques of this view (e.g. Austin and Beaulieu-Brossard 2018), in this volume, we question both this binary opposition and the qualification of de-securitization as inherently normatively 'good'. In the case of the Roma, also given the historical continuity of their problematization as a threat, de-securitization is possible but not always easy to pinpoint empirically. While it often remains ambiguously interwoven with practices of securitization (Dalbello, Chap. 13, this volume), it can sometimes involve openings and alternative narratives. The power of de-securitization does not merely stem from an objective or normative strategy to reveal securitizing measures but, rather, from creative political counter-narratives to securitizing practices on an everyday basis requiring a micro-lens on tactics and the ordinary (Legros and Lièvre, Chap. 4, this volume). These creative 'counter-narratives' can become part of the orchestrated ways of political movements and resistance (Kreide, Chap. 3, this volume).

This book is structured in four parts, which discuss the securitization of Roma minorities in terms of mobility, development, marketization, and visuality. Discussing these intersections separately does not imply that they are *separated* from one another: these intersections form a *continuum* and mutually constitute one another.

Mobility

Since the fall of communism, the mobility of the Roma has primarily been approached in academic contexts and circles—but also and most extensively in political, public, and policy debates—in terms of their migration from Eastern to Western Europe rather than as socioeconomic mobility (but see Ivasiuc 2018; van Baar 2012). In most European countries, the migration of the Roma has been framed in terms of a problem of—or even a threat to—public order, public health, or the social security systems of the host countries. This problematization has led to the introduction of radical measures, such as stop-and-search practices, surveillance, police raids, eviction, and deportation. The reasons for this prevailing focus on the migration of the Roma as a threat are highly ambiguous. They relate, firstly, to the racializing subtext of the distinction between mobility and migration, secondly to the legacies of excluding the Roma through the irregularization of their mobility, and thirdly, to the often neglected role of the Roma's agency in debates about their mobility.

First, the shift of the debate from broader issues of mobility to a narrow focus on migration is problematic because of the way in which migration since the 1980s has increasingly become securitized (Huysmans 2006). According to one of the key principles of the EU, all EU citizens have the right of free movement within the Union, usually qualified as the *mobility* of EU citizens; indeed, its encouragement could even be considered to be one of the main driving forces behind the EU political project. But when it comes to those forms of intra-EU mobility that are considered problematic—such as the mobility of the Roma or that of Central and Eastern European citizens more generally—the EU citizens involved are considered to be *migrants* or even 'poverty migrants' or 'social tourists'. These discursive frames suggest that, in such cases, these 'migrant' EU citizens should be governed differently to their fellow EU citizens. This can be seen in the all too familiar cases of non-EU migrants deemed unwelcome in Europe, but who, in many cases, are nonetheless differentially included on the basis of ambiguous and often precarious and exploitative arrangements in the labour and housing markets, or even in detention centres across Europe (Jansen et al. 2015).

Meanwhile, unorthodox technologies of citizenship (Walters 2010; van Baar 2017a) such as those of surveillance, profiling, detention, eviction, and deportation are deemed to be prerequisites for dealing with the tensions in public opinion regarding migrants. Consequently, these technologies have rendered technical and normal the policy responses to non-EU migrants, as well as to European citizens such as the Roma. The fact that Romanian and Bulgarian Roma citizens who have 'migrated' to France continue to be deported back to their countries of origin is telling, not only of the limitations of EU citizenship but also of the *normalization* of illegitimate practices through populist politicization, administrative regularization, and public consent. The law plays an ambivalent role in this context: through an inscription of these practices into national legislation, the law *usually* functions *against* the Roma (Kreide, Chap. 3, this volume).

At the same time, the 'migrantization' (New Keywords Collective 2016: 29) and 'irregularization of migration' (Jansen et al. 2015) in contemporary Europe, in which the mobility of particular citizens is rendered 'naturally' irregular or illegal, reveal the neoliberal conditions under which mobility regimes in and at the borders of Europe have begun to function. This has become prominent in the recent contexts of the financial-economic crisis, the 'migrant'/'refugee' crisis, and, more generally, crisis-driven neoliberalization (Brenner et al. 2010; New Keywords Collective 2016; Walby 2015).

The securitization of mobility has thus gone hand in hand with new forms of racialization that qualify some forms of mobility in Europe as less desirable than others. Moreover, as the example of the ongoing deportations of Roma from France makes clear, we are dealing not only with a disqualification regarding the supposedly general EU right to mobility but also with regard to social, civil, human, and minority rights (Kreide, Chap. 3, this volume) and to those rights which Sandro Mezzadra (2004) brought together in his idea of 'the right to escape'. He uses this concept 'to highlight the elements of subjectivity which permeate the migratory movements and which must be kept in mind if one wants to produce an image of these movements as *social* movements in the full sense' (2004: 270). This is not meant to disregard the objective background to why people migrate but rather to 'underline the fact that for these migrations to exist, there must be an individual motion… of desertion from the field where those "objective causes" operate, a reclaiming precisely of a "right to escape"' (ibid.). The fact that many Roma who—for various objective *and* subjective reasons—have used their EU right to mobility have been faced with practices ranging from denial to removal implies that their right to escape has been seriously violated.

The second problem that we want to address with regard to the securitization of the mobility of the Roma relates to the long history of problematizing the mobility of the Roma along the lines of a threat. The various groups of Roma who live throughout Europe have often been portrayed as a people with a shared background of travelling through and beyond Europe (Mayall 2004; Willems 1997). They are characterized as being mobile by culture, a stereotype that has been so influential that some have suggested that 'the Gypsy is a nomad even when not travelling' (Liégeois 1986: 54). Yet the majority of people in Europe who are called or call themselves Roma[1]—particularly those who live in Central and Eastern Europe—have already lived sedentarily for a long time for various political and socioeconomic reasons, ranging from taxation policies in the Ottoman Empire and assimilation policies under Habsburg rule to renewed assimilation and labour-market policies in the former socialist states (see also Dalbello, Chap. 13, in this volume). Nevertheless, through a process of 'nomadization', they have often been stereotyped and differentially governed as a nomadic people who have no strong 'roots' in, but only loose 'routes' through, European cultures and societies (van Baar 2011b). For example, during the 1970s and 1980s, Western European states and European institutions frequently problematized their Roma citizens in terms of nomadism (Simhandl 2006).

Whereas post-war Western and Eastern European practices of governing through nomadization were initially used to regulate Roma minorities domestically, since 1989, they have increasingly been mobilized to manage newly emerged forms of mobility among the Roma within Europe's contested borders. Throughout Europe, this development has led to the emergence of a heterogeneous, ramified 'perpetual mobile machine of forced mobility' (van Baar 2015) in which many migrating Roma are confronted with their 'unwantedness', and with policy measures intended to govern, and thus 'nomadize' them through practices of repeated expulsion (De Genova, Chap. 2, this volume; Legros and Lièvre, Chap. 4, this volume; van Baar, 2011b, 2017a, Chap. 8, this volume; Vrăbiescu, Chap. 10, this volume).

A third aspect regarding the securitization of mobility addressed in this volume relates to the criminalization, victimization, or commodification of the Roma. If we suggest that all the mechanisms which have emerged to control and regulate their mobility have been successful in turning their subjects into 'docile (im-)mobile bodies', we overlook those practices that articulate the agency and subjectivity of the 'right to escape' and which—in the debates about the autonomy of migration, for example—have been qualified as the migrants' 'practices of appropriation' (Scheel 2015). The established regimes of migration and border control 'aim at de-politicizing migration', something which is achieved 'through reducing the migrants to their labour power, to needy victims, or to cunning criminals' (ibid.: 4).

A consideration of the 'subjective face' (Bojadžijev and Karakayalı 2007: 212) of mobilities, which is taken away through these reductions, helps to show both the limits of practices of securitization and the wider politics of security involved in the idea of the 'efficient' control and management of borders and migration. But this consideration also gives us an insight into how we could conceptualize practices of de-securitization, and thereby also those practices which question, disrupt, circumvent, or challenge the powerful dynamics of security involved in the securitization of the Roma. Practices of de-securitization relate to a variety of practices of appropriation and re-appropriation and politicization and re-politicization, and we should avoid understanding them too easily as binaries of power *versus* resistance. Indeed, we have seen an entire spectrum of practices of resistance situated between, at one end of this spectrum, open activist and artistic acts of protest (Aradau et al. 2013; Çağlar and Mehling 2013; van Baar 2013) and, at the other end, much more mundane, less visible, or even consciously invisibilized acts of appropriation which, *because of* the asymmetric power relations involved in managing mobilities, have to operate mostly by stealth (Legros and Lièvre, Chap. 4, this volume). All of the practices in this complex spectrum articulate that migration has to be acknowledged as an *autonomous* practice of resistance in the sense of a 'right to escape' or 'egress' (De Genova 2017; van Baar, Chap. 8, this volume). In the first part of this volume, we address the question of the 'politicality' of these practices of resistance: to what extent do these varied practices articulate important political moments, not only in addressing the limits of securitization but also in directing our societies and cultures towards alternative paths?

The three chapters in the first part of the book speak in various ways to the three discussed arguments that problematize the nexus of mobility and security. In Chap. 2, *Nicholas De Genova* takes up the debate about the Roma's nomadization to make the original argument that the situation of the 'stateless' and 'refugees' discussed so prominently by Hannah Arendt in the 1940s and 1950s can be compared to that of the Roma, particularly when it comes to the new forms of nomadization imposed on them which characterize their position in Europe today. De Genova suggests a relational history in which he mobilizes Arendt's work to examine the position of the Roma. Inspired by her analysis of the deprivation of rights suffered by the refugees, De Genova examines to what extent the

'Europeanized' Roma are 'pervasively exposed to the punitive and discriminatory recriminations that ensue not from the absence of a state's oversight but rather from an excess of superintendence by state power, and whose migrant mobility across the space of EU merely multiplies that exposure to state power and exacerbates their persecution'. This leads De Genova to argue that—EU citizenship notwithstanding—the securitization of the Roma has led to a 'harmonization' of their highly precarious status within the EU 'with their real (debased) status in their countries of origin'.

Regina Kreide continues this discussion in Chap. 3 and makes a similar argument regarding the ambiguous ways in which human rights in the EU both 'protect' the Roma and exclude them at the same time. She situates her discussion in the context of the ongoing Europe-wide debate about whether member states and the EU have 'a right to exclude', that is, a right to close their borders. Borders, Kreide argues, are multifaceted zones of infrastructure and expanding areas of securitization at the same time. As long as borders are imposed coercively, and through this imposition contribute to securitization, they are illegitimate. This becomes obvious through an analysis of Europe's external and internal border politics, the growing entanglement between the two, and the inherent power of securitization of borders. The Roma are a case in point when it comes to the politics of border securitization: being evicted and forced to move, the Roma make borders and practices of securitization visible and reveal how the materialization of closing borders inherently affects them negatively, rendering them 'irregular' and 'illegal' and thus denying them their fundamental and human rights.

In Chap. 4, *Olivier Legros* and *Marion Lièvre* focus on what they call 'the politics of Roma migrants' to theorize the ways in which the Roma who have migrated from Romania to France have articulated practices of appropriation which—despite the often overpowering reality of the management of their mobilities—help them to materialize some of their aims, desires, and dreams. On the basis of fieldwork in French urban contexts, Legros and Lièvre qualitatively distinguish different practices of appropriation. At the same time, they examine the 'politicality' of Foucauldian 'counter-conducts' and of what Michel de Certeau underscored with his notion of 'tactics'. Both refer to various practices of resistance, which question the mechanisms of securitization and the interrelated politics of security even though they do so mostly 'below the radar' with a mere simulation of compliance rather than by openly challenging the formal and informal rules, regulations, and norms of border and migration control (Scheel 2015: 10). By revealing these practices, Legros and Lièvre demonstrate that the Roma have created for themselves a horizon of opportunities which clearly, though mostly clandestinely, question the effectiveness of the apparatus of migration management.

Marketization

The forced mobility/immobility and reduced social mobility of the Roma, as well as their westward migration, are usually explained as a consequence of the fall of state socialism in Central and Eastern Europe coupled with the collapse of the agricultural and industrial sectors in which the Roma were traditionally employed; the shift to market economies and neoliberalism; and institutional and everyday anti-Roma racism. The second part of this volume focuses on the nexus of security and marketization, and discusses several of these issues, in their interrelated complexity, both in the context of Central and Eastern European 'transitions' and in the context of Western European neoliberalization.[2]

The three chapters which make up this part of the book demonstrate that marketization can be considered as a *lens* through which the different articulations and effects of the securitization of the Roma become discernible. To clarify how a differentiated reading and impact of securitization relate to marketization, we first explain the relation between marketization and neoliberalization; second, the ways in which marketization has been articulated differently in different regional contexts are explored; and third, we examine how, for us, a differentiated understanding of marketization goes hand in hand with acknowledging the varied impact of the nexus of marketization and securitization on processes of categorization along the intersectional lines of nationality, class, space, race, ethnicity, and gender.

In this volume, we understand neoliberalization and marketization along the same lines as a constructivist project embodying a specific rationale and specific technologies of governing. Wendy Brown's (2003) post-structuralist formulation is helpful here, in that neoliberalism is a constructivist endeavour which, rather than being an ontologically given and all-encompassing economic rationality, 'takes as its task the development, dissemination, and institutionalization of such a rationality' (ibid.: §9). She follows a Foucauldian conception of neoliberalism as a form of governmentality that actively produces market and enterprise models and tries to penetrate the whole of society 'so that competitive mechanisms can play a regulative role at every moment and every point to make its objective possible; that is to say, a general regulation of society by the market' (Foucault 2008: 145).

This reading of neoliberalization demonstrates that neoliberalism does not imply the rolling back of the state or its de-regulation at large; rather, we are dealing with practices of *re-regulation* in which the boundaries between state and society and between state and economy are blurred. There is thus much overlap between the concepts of neoliberalization and marketization, something which can also explain the renewed relationship to social security systems. From a neoliberal viewpoint, welfare regimes tend only to promote dependency culture because they keep significant parts of a population outside the labour force. Consequently, under neoliberal conditions, the unemployed are not only securitized as 'problem groups' that threaten the efficient functioning of markets through the inflation of governmental apparatus, such as the expensive over-administration generally associated with welfare regimes. The unemployed are also faced with a continuous stream of 'employability tests' in the material form of training and/or in the more symbolic form of public works, both of which are meant—at least officially—as prerequisites for access to the labour market. Access to work has thus also been significantly 'marketized' through mechanisms of securitization.

Marketization does not remain limited to the spheres of the economy and society, because it also affects the governing and 'responsibilization' of the self; the individual self is now conceptualized as an enterprise, and an investor not only of economic capital but also of human and social capital that should be responsibly 'activated' to improve its own 'marketability'. Yet, in combination with the usual qualification of the Roma as a 'problem group' or—in the newspeak of international organizations and national governments—as 'at risk' of unemployment, vulnerability, dependency, poverty, crime, or societal exclusion, this neoliberal approach to issues of social and human security has led to ambiguous and dubiously legitimized programmes of state and non-state intervention (Kóczé, Chap. 9, this volume; Legros and Lièvre, Chap. 4, this volume; van Baar, Chap. 8, this volume; Vrăbiescu, Chap. 10, this volume). For instance, the consequences of the introduction of active labour-market policies for the Roma across Europe have turned out to be highly ambiguous (Grill 2018; Messing and Bereményi 2017) and have led to racial practices of neoliberal governmentality (van Baar 2011a, 2012).

In pointing out these ambiguous outcomes of marketization *across* Europe, we are not implying that there is only one neoliberal programme, or that the effects of neoliberalization are more or less similar everywhere; rather, in its intersection with securitization, we understand marketization as impacting *heterogeneously* throughout Europe. We depart from the idea that there is a kind of blueprint or master narrative of neoliberalism which has, for example, been exported from its supposed heartland—generally seen as the United States—to other parts of the world, including Central and Eastern Europe (for such a view, see Sigona and Trehan 2009). The EU's introduction of a notion of the right to free movement, for example, qualifies as a neoliberal project from Europe's 'own soil' in which free movement is related to the profitable logic inherent in the flows of capital (goods, currency) and labour (services, humans). This idea and policy of free movement—or perhaps of 'un/free mobility' (Yıldız and De Genova 2017)—has been articulated differently across Europe, and the impact of these diverse mobility regimes has been different in different locations, as the case studies in this volume, from France (Legros and Lièvre), Italy (Ivasiuc), Romania (Mireanu), Slovakia (Powell and van Baar), Spain (Vrăbiescu), and the United Kingdom (Powell and van Baar), substantiate.

The third aspect that we want to address is the impact of the nexus of marketization and securitization on the way in which societies are differentially organized along various classifications. Three decades after the fall of state socialisms, the rethinking of marketization along the lines of its regional specificity also requires a critical reflection on the assumed logic behind 'transitional' states and societies. The region's changes have notably been driven and influenced by 'transregional', European, and global developments, such as the processes towards EU enlargement; the changing relations between world powers; global social movements; new violent conflicts within and outside Europe; and the emergence of novel regimes of security, citizenship, migration, media, and development. But the investigation of 'actually existing neoliberalism(s)' in the region must, to a considerable extent, also be analysed through post-socialism, as well as the legacies of socialism, instead of through an external or global understanding of neoliberalism (Stenning et al. 2010; van Baar 2011a). The continued use of the concept of transition as a category of analysis risks the 'causes' of neoliberalization being one-sidedly projected abroad or its supposed 'incompleteness' leading to calls for more marketization. An analysis of the region's marketization should take into account the fact that political, social, economic, cultural, and media neoliberalization processes clearly have their own regional traditions and roots, which relate to how recent and current elites and institutions have supported neoliberalization and even to how they have mobilized the 'spectre' of socialism to legitimize it (Chelcea and Druţă 2016). Importantly, this argument also relates to new societal divisions along the lines of class and race. While the middle classes are glorified 'as a rupture with the communist past', the poor—and the Roma in particular—are often represented—not least in the media—as dependent on government assistance and therefore 'as a vestige of the same socialist past and arrested development' (Chelcea and Druţă 2016: 525; Kóczé, Chap. 9, this volume; Mireanu, Chap. 6, this volume; van Baar 2017b, Chap. 8, this volume) and thus as a 'threat' to the nation and its 'post-socialist', 'future-oriented' development. These class differentiations have simultaneously been translated into new and re-shaped spatial, racialized, and nationalized or renationalized urban, and also rural, arrangements. For instance, market-led and often government-supported urban regeneration has securitized and negatively affected the Roma in various ways, mostly through processes of gentrification, suburbanization, eviction, ghettoization, policing, the privatization of social housing and other public services, and the financialization of debts.

Of particular relevance to an analysis of intersections of security and marketization is the commodification of 'Gypsy images' or, for that matter, of 'Roma celebrities', characterized by recently produced and often extremely popular and spectacular media shows across Europe. Some have suggested that the introduction of 'ordinary' people, members of minorities included, into television broadcasting has led to its 'demotic turn' (Turner 2010) and, thus, to a kind of media democratization. Yet, while this might be the case to some extent, 'a growing body of work looks at how these [popular media] shows are produced in increasingly governed and commercialized societies, and how they frequently use familiar, strong tropes of gender, ethnic, and class differences' (Tremlett 2014: 317). With regard to the Roma, several authors (Imre 2015; Szeman 2017; Tremlett 2014) have shown that it is the regional articulations of these global media arrangements, rather than demonstrating a demotic turn, which often 'lean towards the *demonic* through emphasizing such groups as spectacular, extraordinary, and above all, negatively different' (Tremlett 2014: 316). Re-fashioned traditional and stereotypical 'Gypsy' images tend to dominate these popular media, articulated, for instance, through performing normalized whiteness and 'modern' middle-class values *versus* the troublesome and backward 'Gypsy' masculinity and femininity suggested as threatening what the middle or upper classes stand for.

In Chap. 5, *Ryan Powell* and *Huub van Baar* show how regionally specific processes of securitization and neoliberalization have gone hand in hand with regionally specific practices of anti-Roma racism. They bring David Goldberg's work on racial neoliberalism into dialogue with that of Loïc Wacquant on the neoliberal government of social insecurity to argue that processes of neoliberalization and securitization have contributed to the de-politicization of the root causes of the societal problems with which many Roma have been confronted. Powell and van Baar explain how this de-politicization has led to a 'trend to "invisibilize" the racial and racializing dimensions of the precarious conditions under which many Roma live', and thus to the difficulty of adequately challenging present-day anti-Roma racisms. They utilize Wacquant's concepts of the 'hyperghetto' and the 'anti-ghetto' to articulate two different mechanisms of 'invisibilizing' the conditions under which Roma racialization and anti-Roma racism occur in contemporary Europe, in Slovakia and the United Kingdom in particular.

In Chap. 6, *Manuel Mireanu* focuses on a notorious case of Roma eviction to argue that, in the setting of post-socialist marketization in Romania, their securitization has intersected with their categorization not only along the lines of race but also along those of class, space, and national identity. Mireanu sets the eviction in the recent historical context of the drastic post-socialist privatization of the housing sector, market-led urban regeneration, and the re-shaping of Romanian national identity. During socialism, Roma such as those in Cluj-Napoca were often allowed to live in the abandoned, 'bourgeois' centres of historic towns and cities. Mireanu shows how the post-1989 rediscovery and reinvention of national cultural heritage and the revaluation of economically attractive urban centres have provoked the securitization of urban space at the radical expense of its original but allegedly unproductive, inadaptable, dirty, and intimidating Roma tenants.

In Chap. 7, *Annabel Tremlett* explores the relationship between popular culture and media practices of securitization. She argues that reality TV formats tend to 'have moved away from the flamboyant "other" denoted by the Gypsy celebrity, to the Gypsy as a threat, an "enemy" to the nation-state or national culture'. She examines the ways in which migrant Roma and UK travellers are represented in several highly popular and commercially successful British reality TV shows. She argues that initially, in productions such as *Big Fat Gypsy Weddings*, 'the Gypsy' was still celebrated, albeit through processes of classification and racialization. In later programmes, such as *Benefits Street*, and other productions qualified as 'poverty porn', Tremlett shows how media practices of securitization have contributed to turning 'the Gypsy' into a kind of 'entertaining enemy'. Tremlett's chapter deals not only with issues of Roma and 'Gypsy' representation but also, and importantly, with the ways in which, in the context of media neoliberalization, the makers of these popular programmes have produced and reproduced specific 'Gypsy images' and have managed to reach large audiences, making the exploitation of images of a 'Gypsy threat' highly profitable.

Development

While the fall of communism went hand in hand with the introduction of new *market* economies, it also instigated novel *moral* economies vis-à-vis the Roma. Soon after 1989, human rights organizations and activist networks played a crucial role in representing the situation of the Roma as a 'human emergency', and in bringing them onto Europe's institutional and human and minority rights agendas. At more or less the same time, in 1993, the EU made 'respect for and protection of minorities' a cornerstone of its foundational Maastricht Treaty. A report on the situation of Europe's Roma published in the same year by the High Commissioner on National Minorities of the CSCE—the forerunner of the Organisation for Security and Co-operation in Europe (OSCE)—perfectly illustrates the ambiguity of the then emerging and still prominent moral economies:

> The aim… should be to *improve the 'quality of life'* in *migration-producing countries*… for the sake of such improvements, but also for the *reduction in pressures on international migration*. In addition to commerce, investment, and development assistance leading to economic opportunity, efforts at addressing *the specific problems of the Roma*, including discrimination and violence against them, will contribute considerably to improving their 'quality of life'. Such efforts are likely *to encourage people to continue their lives where they already are*. (van der Stoel 1993: 11, our emphasis)

The lives of the Roma are thus problematized as lives to be protected through development assistance and simultaneously as a real or potential security threat to be protected against. To explain how development and security have merged in post-1989 Roma-related development agendas, discourses, and practices, we first situate their emergence in the broader global and post-colonial contexts and, second, show how Roma-related development programmes are interconnected with the ways in which 'life' (bios) and 'morals' have ambiguously entered the politics of the protection of the Roma.

The 'will to improve' the situation of the Roma, as well as the political and institutional commitment to their 'minority protection' through development programmes, is inherently related to what Huub van Baar (2011a) has called 'the Europeanization of the representation of the Roma', involving the post-1989 problematization of the Roma in terms of their 'Europeanness'; the classification of heterogeneous groups scattered all over Europe under the umbrella term 'Roma'; and the devising and implementation of large-scale and Europe-wide local, national, and regional development programmes dedicated to—most notably—their inclusion, rights, community and capacity building, empowerment, and societal participation. This third dimension of the Europeanization of Roma representation characterizes the rise of a post-1989 'institutional developmentalism' (van Baar 2017a) of which the scope and impact can only be adequately grasped in the broader global and post-colonial contexts.

In development, security, and post-colonial studies, as well as in global justice debates, much attention has been paid to a critique of post-colonial developmentalism (Chakrabarty 2000; Escobar 1995) and to the emergence of a new, problematic neoliberal nexus of development and security in the post-Cold War relationship between the 'Global North' and the 'Global South' (Duffield 2007; Pogge 2010). Yet, a fundamental critique of how Europe's major development project regarding the Roma represents an ambiguous continuation of Europe's developmentalist history—now *within* the contested borders of Europe—is mostly lacking. Consequently, the debates about Roma-related development programmes have so far remained fundamentally Eurocentric in scope and have failed to address the way in which the interrelated security-development nexus has contributed to a Roma-related articulation of a 'colour line' across Europe (van Baar 2017a, b).

Institutional developmentalism represents a neomodernist narrative and practice according to which, by means of various development rationales and initiatives dedicated to inclusion, participation, empowerment, human and minority rights, and community and capacity building, the 'underdeveloped' Roma will gradually join in with Europe's 'developed' majorities. Accordingly, this developmentalism is based on the *promise* of the Roma's full European citizenship and their social inclusion. Development interventions are envisioned and legitimized to fulfil this promise.

This developmentalism is situated within the broader post-Cold War trend to problematize the security-development nexus from a people- or human-centred perspective. The advent of programmes of *human* security and *human* development has frequently been perceived as the result of an evolving humanism within international relations and organizations, which would take into account internationally recognized human rights norms, acknowledge the role of individuals and communities in safeguarding their own security, and include threats to human life such as poverty, displacement, and disease. This view neglects how Roma-related development programmes are, at the same time, *governmentalizing technologies* which in practice do not necessarily, or even primarily, alleviate poverty but rather govern it in ways that often maintain a fragile status quo, create new relations of power and dependency, and serve the protection of majorities and their interests more than the lives of the Roma or their needs and rights.

Roma-related human security and development programmes more often than not represent a biopoliticization of development in which the focus is on the Roma and local, community-based, forms of development; on ways to 'activate' their citizenship and make them 'resilient' as regards daily hazards; and on social or community work that aims to facilitate their relation with various kinds of institutions, including municipalities, schools, health services, employment offices, the police, and creditors. Such development programmes are therefore often focused on the *biopolitical* conditions that would have to be fulfilled to improve the Roma's position yet fail to address the root causes of poverty and underdevelopment, territorializing and culturalizing Roma problems at the expense of broader political and socioeconomic issues and consequently contributing further to maintaining a racialized status quo in which the Roma continue to be confronted with marginalization and displacement.

The moment at which life enters the Roma-related politics of protection inherently goes together with the introduction of morals into that politics, something which has usually been understood as 'humanitarianism'. Humanitarian intervention, Didier Fassin (2007: 500–01) clarifies, represents both a biopolitics and what he qualifies as 'a politics of life' in which moral decisions about which lives need to be 'saved' and which ones 'risked' are the key consideration. This politics of life touches on a widespread contemporary situation in Europe in which humanitarian assistance offered to the Roma—be it in cases of violent conflict, of becoming victims of human trafficking, or in instances of their arrival abroad to request asylum or in search of better living conditions—has frequently gone hand in hand with a questioning of their motivation and with viewing their lives as causing trouble to their human and natural environment and thus with assessing the urgency of their protection as a lesser priority.

The three chapters that are brought together in the third part of this volume speak in closely related ways to how development and security problematically intersect in Roma-related developmentalism and humanitarianism. In Chap. 8, *Huub van Baar* combines the debate about institutional developmentalism he began recently with a reflection on how anti-Roma racisms have been addressed in the literature. He argues that the ways in which discourses and practices of anti-Roma racism have intersected with a variety of programmes officially dedicated to the improvement of the situation of the Roma have so far been underrepresented. He clarifies that, at the practical intersection of anti-Roma racisms with those development programmes, the latter have often become highly ambiguous: under biopolitical conditions, development-related governmentalities vis-à-vis the Roma tend to socially isolate them and to contribute more to governing their poverty than to structurally improving their living circumstances or ensuring their 'inclusion' in economic, social, public, and political infrastructures. He observes that, consequently, a 'de-developmentalization' currently tends to take place which is no longer based on the assumption that the Roma will gradually join in with their more developed fellow citizens, but rather on significantly reifying and racializing the Roma's status as representing a lower societal position. He ends his analysis by outlining several ways in which the Roma have tried to escape this situation.

In Chap. 9, *Angéla Kóczé* continues the debate about institutional developmentalism and confronts it with the example of the Council of Europe's post-1989 investment in what it conceives as 'Roma mediation programmes'. Particularly, she critically examines the rationale behind and the discourse of the large-scale mediation programme ROMED, which the Council of Europe and the European Commission conjointly designed and officially introduced throughout Europe for reducing the gap between Roma communities and public institutions, such as educational and health facilities, and local and regional administrations. By revealing the blatant neoliberal newspeak of individual and communal responsibilization in ROMED, Kóczé explains how it is fully complicit in a biopoliticization and securitization of development that tends to create new relationships of dependency and racialized, second-rank citizenship. Mediation thus conceived exemplifies a highly ambiguous institution between Roma communities and public bodies: while it should officially represent the Roma community involved, it primarily represents the authority of local institutions *in* this community, not unlike, she suggests, the colonial institution of native administration, now in its neoliberal incarnation.

In Chap. 10, *Ioana Vrăbiescu* focuses on the role of humanitarianism in the way that Spanish state authorities, mostly in private-public partnerships with NGOs, have introduced and legitimized practices of so-called 'voluntary return' in which EU migrants with a Roma background are encouraged and guided to return to Eastern Europe. Through an analysis of these schemes and how they function in practice, she illuminates how migration management through the securitization of Roma migrants is seamlessly linked with humanitarian interventions that present assistance and 'voluntary return' as benevolent policies. Vrăbiescu explains how the articulation of the humanitarian logic is fundamental to how, at the security-development nexus, both local evictions and transnational deportations of Roma migrants are carried out and justified. Rather than eliminating 'unwanted' migrants directly through punitive practices of deportation, she maintains, the Spanish authorities have invented mechanisms of 'soft deportation' (Kalir 2017) in which local administrators measure the ability of migrants to integrate and their degree of 'deservingness' to finally assess them, more often than not, in terms of 'failed subjects of integration' qualifying for 'voluntary return'.

Visuality

In the currently prevailing problematization of the Roma as a threatening, underdeveloped, excessively mobile, backward, and unruly population, the policy, political, and media lenses are often primarily trained on placing the Roma somewhere on the thin and sterile line from those 'at risk' to those considered as 'risky'. The correlated representations, images, and sensations which circulate on the Roma rely strongly on significantly limited ways of 'seeing' and 'imagining' them and on regimes of visuality that render them 'hypervisible' in terms of stereotypical representations of their supposed criminality, deviancy, and vulnerability. These culturally informed scopic regimes inextricably conjoining the Roma with negative attributes and notions of danger have deep historical roots (Dalbello, Chap. 13, this volume) and complex ramifications, intersecting, in their evolution, the axes of mobility, marketization, and development hitherto examined in the volume. This makes the dimension of visuality a particularly fitting one with which to conclude our argument, summing up the various strands opened by the previous lines of analysis.

Scholarly inquiry into representations of the Roma from a historical perspective has emphasized the role of the emergence and development of capitalism in the production of stigmatizing visions of the Roma (Bogdal 2011; Lucassen et al. 1998). Indeed, the Roma have been *seen* as running counter to everything embodied by the modern state and its economies: sedentarism, the harnessing of the labour force for the benefit of productivity, and notions of civilization and progress which have accompanied the state project since its inception as a form of sociopolitical organization in Western Europe. As a corollary, large corpuses of representations have emerged—exoticizing at best and negative at worst—with various interwoven strands depicting the Roma as deviant and dangerous. Even though these cultural products vary in the context of each particular project of European nation-building, the common traits of threat and deviance are striking across European landscapes and have maintained surprising continuities into contemporary representations of the Roma. One such representation of deviance is rooted in constructions of essentialized nomadism, and has ultimately led to devastating policies of segregation and exclusion at end of the twentieth century and the beginning of the twenty-first in Italy, which have progressively acquired clearer securitarian overtones in the last decade or two (Ivasiuc, Chap. 11, this volume).

On the axis of marketization, alongside the advancement of neoliberal projects, the Roma have been represented as unproductive and thus dangerous to a social order based on political economies for which disciplined and controlled wage labour is essential. The numerous anti-vagrancy laws targeting Roma and those stigmatized as 'Gypsies', coupled with repressive measures aimed at rendering them productive within prescribed economic schemes, attest to the obstinacy of state apparatuses and majority societies in their attempts to force the Roma to conform to dominant paths of social behaviour through assimilationist measures. Simultaneously, however, complex processes have, on the one hand, prompted many Roma to resist adherence to such economic and political hegemonies and, on the other hand, relied heavily on mechanisms of 'othering' which have maintained many Roma in a state of advanced marginality and led to the economic deprivation of many others. Representations of danger and vulnerability have thus converged, something which has amounted to concerted interventions aimed at governing the Roma through humanitarian apparatuses. These interventions, however, have always entailed visions of threat to others and to self. In turn, these representations, as well as their obstinate and ongoing circulation, have certainly accelerated with the advent of the mass media and then of social media, acquiring agency in structuring policies and practices aimed at containing the threat of the Roma embodied in these depictions; they become 'operational representations' which permeate institutions and frame interventions (van Baar and Vermeersch 2017). As such, they are highly consequential in terms of their security-centred governance.

Given the agency of these visions of threat and danger, the fourth part of the volume, which deals with visuality, is not limited to the representational dimension, but also encompasses issues beyond representation in a visual sense, seeking to examine the links between particular regimes of visuality and policymaking, political and public debates, practices of security such as neighbourhood patrols and police profiling, as well as visual culture more broadly. By using the term 'regimes of visuality', we aim at theorizing more broadly an ensemble of security-related practices which cannot be reduced to, nor explained by, mere visualizations but which involve a refined analysis of power, authority, community-making, the relaying of information, and the social relations underlying these processes. This section therefore transcends issues of 'visualizations', or analyses of 'visibility/invisibility', extending to a wider idea of regimes of visuality encompassing more than vision. Thus, taking a cue from Nicholas Mirzoeff's (2011) theorization of 'complex of visuality' as a set of ideas and organizing practices—engaging imagination, insight, and information and segregating rulers from ruled, legitimizing authority, and aestheticizing the status quo—we delve into the social relations spanning particular representations of the Roma as objects of policing in a broad sense of the word.

The three chapters in this final part of the volume focus, on the one hand, on the question of how such prevailing regimes of visuality have been produced and reproduced, and on the consequences of such representations in informing the security practices of formal and informal policing, and, on the other hand, on attempts to devise alternative visualities with possible de-securitizing effects. In Chap. 11, *Ana Ivasiuc* draws on a digital ethnography of material shared on social media by a neighbourhood patrol group in the peripheries of Rome, analysing the social relations underpinning representations of 'others' traversing the neighbourhood. While various figures of the 'other' are constructed as a threat at the intersection of race and class, security discourses and practices of informal policing produce 'vigilant visualities' (Amoore 2007), coagulating a community around notions of security and insecurity. In the process, insecurity is reproduced and exacerbated through the circulation of material on social media, and security becomes a principle of world-ordering social organization effectuating categorizations of subjects based on their ability to produce, demand, or impart security. The security practices and material circulated on social media betray their embeddedness in what Ivasiuc, building upon Mirzoeff's concept, calls the 'complex of securitarian visuality' grounded in operations of social categorization, separation of dangerous undesirables, and legitimation of the status quo.

In Chap. 12, *Markus End* discusses German police practices of portraying, applying, and communicating the 'gypsy threat' through racialized representations. Through the examination of police press statements, End points to the existence and the agency of an antigypsyist visual regime in which racialized stereotypes constructing a 'gypsy threat' are circulated as forms of 'expert knowledge'. This narrative, connected to the discourse intersecting migration and criminality, has the dual effect of structuring police action as the carrying out of data collection which is plainly illegal and of perpetuating the antigypsyist narrative of a 'gypsy threat'. But the jarring exhortation to call the police 'if you see a gypsy', which often accompanies police press statements, does more than perpetuate a stereotype; it alerts the public to a threat that it subsequently meticulously constructs through visual cues which function as racial markers. Thus, End shows how an antigypsyist visual regime with the remarkable ability to flexibly rearticulate and actualize definitions of 'the gypsy' has been widely disseminated through countless securitizing police statements.

Finally, in Chap. 13, *Marija Dalbello* examines the visualities of 'Gypsies' produced and circulated by means of an entry in a popular illustrated Habsburg encyclopaedia of the nineteenth century authored by Archduke Joseph Karl Ludwig of Austria. Dalbello articulates an analysis of the texts and images of the encyclopaedia entry with the examination of the Archduke's practices of ethnographic research and his project of colonization at his estate in Alcsuth and analyses these three sites of visibility and de-securitization. These sites appear as ambivalent strategies of de-securitization running counter to the time's prevailing regimes of visuality and to the assimilationist policies directed at the Roma in the Habsburg Empire but nevertheless captive in discourses producing difference as dangerous. Conceptually, she builds upon Lene Hansen's work on de-securitization, on the one hand (2011a), and on visual securitization, on the other (2011b), to show the ambiguities of de-securitization processes, narratives, and depictions underpinned by the rendition of Roma as both 'risky' and 'at risk'.

Notes

1. We take a constructivist stance to ethnicity and thus use 'Roma' as an umbrella term encompassing not only those who claim Roma ethnicity but also, importantly, those who are seen and treated as 'Gypsies'.
2. We use the term 'neoliberalization', rather than 'neoliberalism', to emphasize its processual character and its high degree of flexibility.

References

Amoore, L. 2007. Vigilant Visualities. *Security Dialogue* 38 (2): 215–232.
Aradau, C. 2004. Security and the Democratic Scene. *Journal of International Relations and Development* 7 (4): 388–413.
Aradau, C., et al. 2013. Mobility Interrogating Free Movement? In *Enacting European Citizenship*, ed. E. Isin and M. Saward, 132–154. Cambridge: Cambridge University Press.
Austin, J.L., and P. Beaulieu-Brossard. 2018. (De)Securitization Dilemmas. *Review of International Studies* 44 (2): 301–323.
Balzacq, T., ed. 2011. *Securitization Theory*. London: Routledge.
Bigo, D., and E. Guild, eds. 2005. *Controlling Frontiers*. Farnham: Ashgate.
Bigo, D., et al., eds. 2010. *Europe's 21st Century Challenge*. Farnham: Ashgate.
Bigo, D., S. Carrera, and E. Guild, eds. 2013. *Foreigners, Refugees or Minorities?* Farnham: Ashgate.
Bogdal, M. 2011. *Europa erfindet die Zigeuner*. Frankfurt am Main: Suhrkamp.
Bojadžijev, M., and K. Karakayalı. 2007. Autonomie der Migration. In *Turbulente Ränder*, ed. Transit Migration Forschungsgruppe, 203–209. Bielefeld: Transcript.
Brenner, N., J. Peck, and N. Theodore. 2010. After Neoliberalization? *Globalizations* 7 (3): 327–345.
Brown, W. 2003. Neoliberalism and the End of Liberal Democracy. *Theory and Event* 7 (1): 1–43.
Buzan, B., O. Waever, and J. De Wilde. 1998. *Security: A New Framework for Analysis*. Boulder, CO: Lynne Rienner.
Çağlar, A., and S. Mehling. 2013. Sites and Scales of the Law. In *Enacting European Citizenship*, ed. E. Isin and M. Saward, 155–177. Cambridge: Cambridge University Press.
Chakrabarty, D. 2000. *Provincializing Europe*. Princeton, NJ: Princeton University Press.
Chelcea, L., and O. Druţă. 2016. Zombie Socialism and the Rise of Neoliberalism in Post-Socialist Central and Eastern Europe. *Eurasian Geography and Economics* 57 (4–5): 521–544.

De Genova, N., ed. 2017. *The Borders of 'Europe': Autonomy of Migration, Tactics of Bordering.* Durham, NC: Duke University Press.
Duffield, M. 2007. *Development, Security and Unending War.* Cambridge: Polity.
Escobar, A. 1995. *Encountering Development.* Princeton, NJ: Princeton University Press.
Fassin, D. 2007. Humanitarianism as a Politics of Life. *Public Culture* 19 (3): 499–520.
Foucault, M. 2008. *The Birth of Biopolitics. Lectures at the Collège de France, 1978–1979.* New York: Palgrave Macmillan.
Grill, J. 2018. Re-learning to Labour? *Journal of the Royal Anthropological Institute.* https://doi-org.proxy.uba.uva.nl:2443/10.1111/1467-9655.12802.
Hansen, L. 2011a. Reconstructing Desecuritisation. *Review of International Studies* 38 (3): 525–546.
———. 2011b. Theorizing the Image for Security Studies. *European Journal of International Relations* 17 (1): 51–74.
Huysmans, J. 2006. *The Politics of Insecurity.* London: Routledge.
Huysmans, J., A. Dobson, and R. Prokhovnik, eds. 2006. *The Politics of Protection.* London: Routledge.
Imre, A. 2015. Love to Hate: National Celebrity and Racial Intimacy on Reality TV in the New Europe. *Television & New Media* 16 (2): 103–130.
Ivasiuc, A. 2018. Social Mobility and the Ambiguous Autonomy of Roma Migration. *Intersections* 4 (2): forthcoming.
Jansen, Y., R. Celikates, and J. de Bloois, eds. 2015. *The Irregularization of Migration in Contemporary Europe.* Lanham, MD: Rowman & Littlefield.
Kalir, B. 2017. Between "Voluntary" Return Programs and Soft Deportation. In *Return Migration and Psychosocial Wellbeing*, ed. R. King and Z. Vathi, 56–71. London: Routledge.
Liégeois, J.-P. 1986. *Gypsies: An Illustrated History.* London: Saqi Books.
Lucassen, L., W. Willems, and A. Cottaar. 1998. *Gypsies and Other Itinerant Groups.* Basingstoke: Macmillan.
Mayall, D. 2004. *Gypsy Identities 1500–2000.* London: Routledge.
Messing, V., and Á. Bereményi. 2017. Is Ethnicity a Meaningful Category of Employment Policies for Roma? *Ethnic and Racial Studies* 40 (10): 1623–1642.
Mezzadra, S. 2004. The Right to Escape. *Ephemera* 4 (3): 267–275.
Mirzoeff, N. 2011. *The Right to Look: A Counterhistory of Visuality.* Durham, NC: Duke University Press.
New Keywords Collective. 2016. Europe/Crisis: New Keywords of "the Crisis" in and of "Europe". *Near Futures Online* 1 (1). Available at: http://nearfuturesonline.org/europecrisis-new-keywords-of-crisis-in-and-of-europe-part-6/.
Pogge, T. 2010. *Politics as Usual.* Cambridge: Polity.

Scheel, S. 2015. Das Konzept der Autonomie der Migration überdenken? Yes, please! *movements. Journal für kritische Migrations- und Grenzregimeforschung* 1 (2): 1–15.
Sigona, N., and N. Trehan, eds. 2009. *Romani Politics in Contemporary Europe*. New York: Palgrave Macmillan.
Simhandl, K. 2006. "Western Gypsies and Travellers" – "Eastern Roma". *Nations and Nationalism* 12 (1): 97–115.
Stenning, A., et al. 2010. *Domesticating Neoliberalism*. Oxford: Wiley-Blackwell.
Szeman, I. 2017. *Staging Citizenship*. Oxford: Berghahn.
Tremlett, A. 2014. Demotic or Demonic? Race, Class and Gender in "Gypsy" Reality TV. *The Sociological Review* 62 (2): 316–334.
Turner, G. 2010. *Ordinary People and the Media*. London: Sage.
van Baar, H. 2011a. *The European Roma: Minority Representation, Memory and the Limits of Transnational Governmentality*. Amsterdam: F&N.
———. 2011b. Europe's Romaphobia: Problematization, Securitization, Nomadization. *Environment and Planning D: Society and Space* 29 (2): 203–212.
———. 2012. Socio-Economic Mobility and Neo-Liberal Governmentality in Post-Socialist Europe. *Journal of Ethnic and Migration Studies* 38 (8): 1289–1304.
———. 2013. Homecoming at Witching Hour: The Securitization of the European Roma and the Reclaiming of Their Citizenship. In *We Roma: A Critical Reader in Contemporary Art*, ed. D. Baker and M. Hlavajova, 50–73. Utrecht: BAK/Valiz.
———. 2015. The Perpetual Mobile Machine of Forced Mobility. In *The Irregularization of Migration in Contemporary Europe*, ed. Y. Jansen, R. Celikates, and J. de Bloois, 71–86. Lanham, MD: Rowman & Littlefield.
———. 2017a. Contained Mobility and the Racialization of Poverty in Europe: The Roma at the Development-Security Nexus. *Social Identities*. https://doi.org/10.1080/13504630.2017.1335826.
———. 2017b. Evictability and the Biopolitical Bordering of Europe. *Antipode* 49 (1): 212–230.
van Baar, H., and P. Vermeersch. 2017. The Limits of Operational Representations. *Intersections* 3 (4): 120–139.
van der Stoel, M. 1993. *Report on the Situation of Roma and Sinti in the CSCE Area*. The Hague: Conference on Security and Cooperation in Europe.
Walby, S. 2015. *Crisis*. Cambridge: Polity.
Walters, W. 2010. Imagined Migration World. In *The Politics of International Migration Management*, ed. M. Geiger and A. Pécoud, 73–95. New York: Palgrave Macmillan.
Willems, W. 1997. *In Search of the True Gypsy*. London: Frank Cass.
Yıldız, C., and N. De Genova, eds. 2017. Un/free Mobility: Roma Migrants in the European Union. Special Issue of *Social Identities*, https://doi.org/10.1080/13504630.2017.1335819.

PART I

Mobility

CHAPTER 2

The Securitization of Roma Mobilities and the Re-bordering of Europe

Nicholas De Genova

Minoritized 'Roma' communities within and across Europe have long been the target of processes of racialization and criminalization.[1] Contemporary processes of securitization with regard to Roma mobilities, and the concomitant state and extra-state coercive practices dedicated to their encampment and ghettoization, as well as their eviction and displacement, are inextricable from these well-established processes of Roma subordination. Inasmuch as many Roma people have been juridically re-inscribed over recent years as ostensible citizens of the EU, however, the securitization of their mobility within and across the area of the EU exemplifies a premier instance of their precisely *abject* relation to EU citizenship (Hepworth 2012, 2014, 2015). Simultaneously but uneasily inhabiting the socio-political conditions of 'citizens', 'migrants', and also 'refugees' (Bigo et al. 2013), Roma people repeatedly emerge as a kind of limit

---

Acknowledgments: I am grateful to Can Yıldız for her perseverance in familiarizing me with many of the defining disputes and key debates in scholarship concerning Roma communities, as well as to Huub van Baar for his gracious invitation to participate in this project and his careful and incisive engagement with earlier iterations of this text.

N. De Genova (✉)
Independent Researcher, Chicago, IL, USA

© The Author(s) 2019
H. van Baar et al. (eds.), *The Securitization of the Roma in Europe*, Human Rights Interventions, https://doi.org/10.1007/978-3-319-77035-2_2

figure, and their mobility therefore provides a particularly revealing site for the interrogation of the re-bordering of 'Europe' as such.

ABJECT MOBILITY AND NEO-NOMADIZATION

Roma people have perennially (and inordinately) been burdened by the pernicious ascription of racializing and criminalizing stigma to their mobility. The notorious construction of 'Gypsies' as nomads and the well-worn apparatus of suspicion and derision that has conventionally shadowed this allegedly unsettled condition have thus been purported to ensue from the unsettling, but supposedly intrinsic, mobility of the Roma themselves (Drakakis-Smith 2007; Hepworth 2012, 2015; van Baar 2011b). However, contemporary EU (statist) constructions of Roma 'nomadism' not only signal the most entrenched expressions of methodological and political sedentarism (Malkki 1995) but have also routinely served as desultory alibis for campaigns of eviction and deportation and hence as a protracted strategy of state-enforced mobility for the Roma (Fekete 2014; Hepworth 2012; Kóczé 2017; Clough Marinaro and Daniele 2011; Nacu 2012; van Baar 2011b, 2015, 2017b). Here, of course, it is likewise imperative to note the productivity of both sporadic pogroms and systematic violence, perpetrated by racist mobs or neo-fascist gangs, that have complemented and exacerbated the handiwork of the police (Clark and Rice 2012; Fekete 2016; Mirga 2009). Roma communities have hence been widely subjected to statist as well as extra-state strategies of both coercive *immobilization* (through segregated ghettoization and encampment) (see Sardelić 2017) and forced *mobilization* (through various forms of expulsion and displacement) (see Solimene 2017; van Baar 2017a). In short, it is crucial to underscore the extent to which *new forms of nomadization* are being coercively perpetrated by various formations of state power, serving to reinforce and reinvigorate the customary abjection of Roma mobility, and also cynically mobilizing the specter of Roma mobility to the ends of broadening the purview of their abjection and subjugation (van Baar 2011b, 2015). Indeed, as Roma migrants have arrived in places where they did not already occupy well-established positions within existing racial hierarchies as an automatically recognizable racialized category (see, e.g., Fox 2012; Fox et al. 2012; Grill 2012, 2017), these spectral (and increasingly spectacularized) projections of putative Roma 'nomadism'—which I designate as their *neo-nomadization*—serve to refortify the processes of 'Gypsy' re-racialization and criminalization.

The hegemonic EU political ideal of 'free movement' thus becomes riddled with 'a free movement across countries that is defined by social and security excesses and an imperative to contain them...[reconfiguring] free movement from an opportunity into a series of dangers' (Aradau et al. 2013: 138). The mobility of Europe's working poor, and particularly of the Roma, thus transmutes the free movement of presumably self-governing and responsible *individuals* (properly neo-liberal subjects) into a 'problem', perceived always as being a matter of unruly *collectivities*— (racial) formations of 'group' mobility—and as a result, is presented as 'a question of categorising those who can be legitimately mobile and those whose mobility needs to be restricted on grounds of security' (Aradau et al. 2013: 138; cf. van Baar 2017a). For Roma people and other poor migrants within and across the space of the EU, free movement—as an ostensible entitlement and distinguishing feature of EU citizenship—reveals itself to be a distinctly 'un/free mobility' (Yıldız and De Genova 2017).

Vexations of Citizenship

The abjection of the 'undesirable' mobility of Roma (EU) 'citizens' reveals a constitutive contradiction within the larger EU-ropean project (Riedner et al. 2016). Repeatedly and persistently, 'the Roma' paradoxically emerge as a (racialized) 'problem' precisely *because* of their EU citizenship and the consequent requirement for EU Member States to circumvent or subvert EU law in order to render Roma migrants 'irregular' and deportable (Çağlar and Mehling 2013: 173). This is a remarkable instance of the contradictions that can arise for mobile, ostensible citizens who, despite their EU passports, come to be effectively irregularized and thus 'migrantized' (Garelli and Tazzioli 2016; Tazzioli 2014; see also Riedner et al. 2016). This is particularly the case among Roma migrants, who tend to find little opportunity for employment other than in the informalized economy (often as day labor) and whose impoverished (and not uncommonly homeless) condition as the sometimes over-employed working poor must nonetheless be supplemented by begging, resulting in their being rendered deportable and subject to racially targeted policing (Yıldız and Humphris n.d.; cf. Hepworth 2014, 2015).

The contemporary condition of the Roma in Europe becomes more complex still, however, if we consider Roma mobility within the EU area not merely as 'migration' but also (not implausibly) as veritable refugee movements, in the sense that migration is often a form of escape from or desertion of one or another socio-political regime of subordination and persecution repudiated by the 'migrants' as intolerable and from which they flee (Mezzadra 2001, 2004). Given the abundant evidence to support the proposition that Roma people are indeed routinely subjected to systematic racist persecution and discrimination in their countries of origin, their ostensible (EU) citizenship consequently becomes riddled with the vexations of an officially impermissible and unspeakable putative oxymoron—that in Europe, 'citizens' become 'refugees' by virtue of the fact that certain EU Member States are culpable of abuses of the supposed civil or human rights of their own citizens and that, as citizens of the EU, members of these persecuted and minoritized communities might consequently be compelled to seek asylum within other EU countries. Furthermore, not unlike many other 'asylum-seekers' who are compelled to migrate to Europe as illegalized migrants (the great majority of whom are ultimately refused refugee status), we may discern in the condition of most of the Roma who cross borders within Europe a still more extreme perversion of the pretensions to human rights of the EU asylum regime: theirs is precisely the predicament of refugees who are systematically disqualified from any consideration for recognition as such and are preemptively rendered ineligible for any asylum process—presumptively disqualified from eligibility for the status of refugees by the mere fact of their EU citizenship—and reduced, in practice, to the status of virtually irregular and deportable 'migrants' whose putative right to mobility as citizens is negated by virtue of their marginalization and poverty (van Baar 2015, 2017a, b).

Once this uncanny fact becomes cognizable, however, we must go further and consider the perfectly reasonable proposition that 'the Roma' are not (and never were) truly 'citizens' in the first place. The juridical anomaly of their ostensible EU citizenship and the un/free mobility that it occasions, facilitating their efforts to travel as migrants to EU Member States other than the countries of their national citizenship, must then be subjected to extraordinary policing and exceptional measures to render them 'irregular', evictable, and deportable—in short, to harmonize their socio-political and juridical status within the larger constellation of the EU with their real (debased) status in their countries of origin. Furthermore, when they return 'home', to those (predominantly Eastern European) countries of origin where their citizenship was always already disavowed, they are further derided as 'undesirable' migrants for allegedly having blemished the reputations of these 'sending' countries and simultaneously stigmatized anew as 'failed' migrants, if not as 'criminal' deportees. They thus become double losers. In short, Roma migrants everywhere in the EU seem, sooner or later, to become *re*-racialized as 'Roma'—that is to say, they are produced anew as 'Roma', or, to put it more bluntly, they are re-Gypsified (Riedner et al. 2016). Their citizenship is consequently bedeviled, as it always is, by countless vagaries and vexations and seldom— if ever—suffices to counteract their actual lived experience of de facto statelessness.

Stateless Citizens

It is instructive here to return to the locus classicus of the theorization of statelessness: Hannah Arendt's much-celebrated chapter, 'The Decline of the Nation-State and the End of the Rights of Man' in *The Origins of Totalitarianism* (1968: 267–302). Arendt's meditation on 'the Rights of Man' (or what, in a less classical idiom, might be termed 'human rights') is, perhaps counter-intuitively, particularly resonant and pertinent here, because it is deeply preoccupied by precisely this question of *mobility*. Arendt confronts a crisis for 'human rights' instigated by the mass displacements of whole populations expelled from their natal lands and coercively set in motion, whereby 'rightlessness' presents itself as an inexorable effect of statelessness. The refugees whose predicaments she contemplates were mobilized by their expulsion into a kind of no-man's land between states.[2] Of course, the mobility of Roma migrants within the larger spatial arena of the EU may appear to present a striking contrast, inasmuch as their 'migrant' mobilities are predominantly self-activated and autonomous. In this regard, even with their historically specific and sociopolitically particular characteristics as virtual refugees, Roma migrants, like many other 'irregular' labor migrants, forfeit their natal countries (the states where they are most often juridically inscribed as citizens) and traverse the borders of nation states in order to more or less deliberately inhabit the no-man's land of protracted rightlessness that prevails under the bleak horizon of prospective expulsion (deportation). Notably, the mobile EU citizenship of Roma migrants confirms that such predicaments are not exclusively reserved for illegalized migrant non-citizens originating from non-EU 'third countries'. What, for Arendt, was a paradox of refugees whose mobility had been inflicted upon them like a curse, stripping them of the presumptive protections of any state, now appears as the banal and matter-of-fact racialized condition of Roma people, ostensible EU citizenship notwithstanding, pervasively exposed to the punitive and discriminatory recriminations that ensue not from the absence of a state's oversight but rather from an *excess* of state superintendence and whose migrant mobility across the space of the EU merely multiplies such exposure to state power and exacerbates their persecution.

The tumultuous succession of cataclysmic events that generated the defining features of the first half of the twentieth century is, in Arendt's (1968: 267) account, chiefly distinguished for having provoked the 'migrations of groups... who were welcomed nowhere and could be assimilated nowhere, [who] once they had left their homeland... remained homeless... [and] became stateless'. The resemblance here with the predicament of many Roma people is remarkable. Arendt is most directly concerned with the dilemma of the deprivation of civil rights suffered by dispossessed people and, following their forced displacement, the consequent transmutation of these initial travesties into the prolonged and irremediable condition of their veritable rightlessness. This conundrum, which surrounds the question of 'human rights', provides an instructive backdrop for my own questions with respect to the condition of the Roma. It is especially revealing, as Arendt incisively remarks, that this is the process which allowed totalitarian regimes (that of Nazi Germany in particular) to convert their victims into precisely what they had always already alleged them to be: namely, 'the scum of the earth' (1968: 267). That is to say, by means of an utterly and devastatingly effective 'factual propaganda', they were delivered across nation-state frontiers as 'unidentifiable beggars, without nationality, without money, and without passports' (1968: 269).We may therefore detect, at the heart of Arendt's prescient enquiry into the perplexities of human rights, a question about human mobility in an extreme form, which, despite its extremity, nonetheless bears a striking resemblance in the twenty-first century to the rather mundane plight of an ever-growing and increasingly prominent mass of restless denizens: irregularized migrants, presumptively susceptible to administrative detention and all manner of police measures, and with little or no recourse to any semblance of legal process—all existentially homeless, inassimilable, and prospectively deportable. And remarkably, perhaps even more than many other categories of (non-citizen, non-European) migrants, the Roma resurface as Europe's premier racialized internal alterity, now re-nomadized as 'migrants' (EU passports notwithstanding).

Deportation has long been a technique crucial to state power for the disposal of diverse populations of 'undesirables' (cf. Kanstroom 2007; Walters 2002), who are sometimes subjected to serial expulsions and displacements, as we are reminded by Arendt's discussion of statelessness. Furthermore, in Arendt's account, these serial expulsions never guarantee that those subjected to mass deportation could not otherwise be targeted for outright extermination. The problem in Arendt's era, of course, was what she astutely calls 'the undeportability of the stateless person' (1968: 283) and the perennial dilemma of *how to make refugees deportable* yet again (1968: 284). As Arendt (1968: 279) notes in her exposition of how the very concept of statelessness degenerated into one of mere 'displacement', the refusal to acknowledge the veritable statelessness of the so-called displaced persons 'always means repatriation, i.e., deportation to a country of origin, which either refuses to recognize the prospective repatriate as a citizen, or, on the contrary, urgently wants him back for punishment'.[3] These same vexations inevitably generated a more general crisis for the immigration and naturalization regimes in the receiving states and undermined the status of migrants who had been previously naturalized, such that 'living conditions for all aliens markedly deteriorated' (1968: 285). Confronted with those who had been stripped of their citizenship (de-nationalized) and ultimately deported by another state, these receiving states came increasingly to render an ever-wider cross section of their own lawfully resident aliens and citizens susceptible to de-naturalization or de-nationalization. Thus, these states became embroiled in the sorts of 'lawlessness organized by the police' which threatened them with a subtle but seemingly ever more inexorable 'danger of a gradual transformation into a police state' (1968: 288). In Arendt's (1968: 290) account, therefore, an incapacity 'to treat stateless people as legal persons and... the extension of arbitrary rule by police decree' fostered a 'temptation to deprive all citizens of legal status and rule them with an omnipotent police'.[4] It ought to be obvious here that whatever securitized abuses may be deployed against Roma people, these will inevitably tend to serve to render routine such excesses of state power, which are first authorized as 'exceptional' or 'emergency' measures but are increasingly extended to an ever-wider circle of other denizens and abject citizens, and thus become normalized.

Re-bordering 'European' Citizenship: Re-bordering 'Europe'

In the face of the newly reanimated 'pan-European racism' against the Roma, palpably enacted through the pervasive securitization of their mobilities and through exceptional measures against a phantasmatic (spectacularized) 'invasion' of destitute beggars and alleged welfare benefits 'tourists' and 'scroungers', re-racialized, re-nomadized Roma migrant citizens can only encounter Europe as something approximating to 'a huge open prison', as Liz Fekete has incisively argued (2014: 68). Once again, Arendt is strikingly relevant here. In her account, the perplexities of 'human rights' derive, in no small measure, from a peculiar consequence: the fact that 'whether we like it or not we really have started to live in One World' (Arendt 1968: 297). In other words, Arendt's paradox derived from the consolidation of what she deemed to be 'the new global political situation': 'a completely organized humanity' in which there is 'no longer any "uncivilized" spot on the earth'. Paradoxically, as this newly comprehensive degree of global integration became self-evident (largely as a consequence of European colonialism), there arose the conditions of possibility for millions of people to have been shorn not only of particular rights but of even the 'right to belong to some kind of organized community' such that 'the loss of home and political status became identical with expulsion from humanity altogether' (Arendt 1968: 297). By a curious and striking postcolonial inversion, with the unprecedented degree of comprehensive institutionalized juridical and socio-political harmonization that has been created with the EU—albeit with its inevitable unevenness and irreconcilable constitutive contradictions—and the consequent completely new political situation, corresponding to a 'completely organized' EU-rope, it is now European integration which has meant that the Roma now re-emerge as '*Europe's* largest ethnic minority' (see, e.g., European Commission 2010, 2011, 2013; cf. Guglielmo and Waters 2005; McGarry 2011; van Baar 2011a; Yıldız and De Genova 2017), a racialized 'minority' on a European scale, whose deprivation of the presumed rights of the citizen derives in no small measure from the fact that they now find themselves in 'One Europe'. Of course, this singular and fully unified 'Europe' remains, in very significant ways, both an incomplete project and a rather fragile and beleaguered ideological projection (De Genova 2016a, b). If 'Europe' remains, however, deeply contradictory and fundamentally incoherent—indeed, if 'Europe' remains in many ways an abstraction—it is nevertheless crucial to recognize it as a real abstraction (Sohn-Rethel 1978: 20), produced and continuously sustained by socio-political relations. We may even posit that, in the era of the EU, this real abstraction of 'Europe' is perhaps more real than ever before. And for the Roma—for Roma migrants in particular—who encounter analogous and partially coordinated efforts to securitize their abject mobility as ostensible EU citizens, the apt analogy of an open prison reminds us that the amorphous but cruel borders and boundaries of 'Europe' (De Genova 2017) not only trace an external perimeter or an externalized border zone extending outward but also assume the fractalized form of a centripetal proliferation of internalized, involuted, and increasingly securitized barriers which traverse the EU-ropean space (Riedner et al. 2016; van Baar 2014) and thus increasingly permeate the space of everyday life for those who find themselves racialized as 'Roma' (or 'Gypsies').

The consequences for the stateless in Arendt's account of 'a problem not of space but of political organization' (1968: 294), that is, their mass dislocation from the jurisdictions of particular ('national') states, were that they came to be represented in the abject figure of the stateless, rightless subjects of 'human rights' and nothing more. In other words, shorn of what Arendt deemed to be the more proper and substantial 'rights' of citizens, the stateless were abandoned to 'the abstract nakedness of being human and nothing but human' (1968: 297). For the Roma, confronted with an analogous problem not of space but of political organization, it is not so much their dislocation or forced expulsion from the precincts of one or another punitive nation state so much as their larger-scale, supranational subsumption within a juridical and socio-political framework which both facilitates their un/free mobility across the space of the EU and seems to partially subvert the national borders of its Member States, while at the same time abandoning them everywhere to the substantial condition of being despised as Gypsies and nothing but Gypsies, against whom the borders of national (welfare) state are repeatedly re-activated through exceptional security measures.

Even when they are fleeing violent persecution and desperate circumstances, the Roma are widely figured as 'bogus' refugees or 'illegitimate' asylum-seekers, and when they are thereby categorized as 'mere' migrants, they are pervasively denigrated as 'poverty migrants' and perniciously affiliated with the specter of 'benefit tourism' and 'abuse' of social welfare systems (Castañeda 2014). Alternately, the Roma are criminalized as a specifically 'itinerant' group whose alleged menace to the security of

EU-ropean society as a whole is amplified by its devious recourse to an essentialized and de-historicized 'nomadism', and thus exquisitely affiliated with a defining and intrinsically unsettling mobility (van Baar 2014: 91). The abjection of the mobility of the Roma thus contributes to a wider-ranging process of neo-nomadization. Moreover, to the extent that they are singled out for special policy consideration as a 'European minority' and presumed to be in need of developmental assistance, their separation tends to re-inscribe their re-racialization, segregation, and securitization (van Baar 2017a). In this respect, the very same juridical regime of 'human rights' norms and priorities which has been institutionalized at the EU level, and according to which the Roma in particular, as ostensible EU citizens, are repeatedly made to reappear as a 'problem' which the EU must solve, serves nonetheless to re-entrench their racialized minoritization and marginalization and hence tends to further mobilize them in a seemingly unrelenting quest to seek their fortunes as migrants across the space of the EU. In short, the EU-ropeanization of the Roma has not reduced them to the abstract nakedness of merely 'human' life, nor has it supplied them with the substantive entitlements or rights of 'citizenship', however much these may ultimately remain similarly abstract (and merely juridical). Instead, their encompassment within 'Europe', particularly as migrants, has reconfigured their de facto statelessness, now on a quasi-supranational yet multi-national (re-bordered) scale. Thus, with newly excessive and rather concrete forms of racial stigmatization, criminalization, securitization, and neo-nomadization, the EU-ropeanization of the Roma has reconstructed their subordination.

Finally, a crucial difference can be found here between the plight of the stateless refugees in Arendt's account and the predicament of most Roma refugees/migrants within the EU today, and that is the inherent ambiguity and instability which pertain to Roma mobilities—the veritable undecidability between a mobility that has been compelled (a refugee condition) and one which, because it has been self-activated as an act of flight and desertion, is a manifestation of the autonomy of migration. In this respect, we are reminded that, no matter how abject their citizenship, and no matter how effectively un/free their mobility, as EU citizens, many Roma migrants nonetheless appropriate their putative right to 'free movement' and migrate in order to realize their various aspirations and ambitions for a way of life free from the asphyxiating constraints of their racial subjugation 'at home'. Their securitized neo-nomadization, criminalization, and re-racialization as 'undesirable' Gypsies across the whole of the EU notwithstanding, Roma migrants nevertheless autonomously enact their mobility. They frequently confound the juridical regime of EU citizenship precisely because their freedom of movement is exercised first. Confronted, in other words, with the primacy and autonomy of Roma migration, the apparatuses of policing, eviction, and deportation are mobilized only in response, as reaction formations dedicated to rendering these presumptive citizens effectively 'stateless' yet again. In an objective sense then—even though their challenges do not always manifest themselves as overt defiance and often take only the modest and mundane form of a simple disregard for the mandates and machinations of a EU-ropean socio-political order which disparages them as loathsome vagabonds, unwanted beggars, and suspected criminals—Roma migrants incessantly confront the EU regime of un/free mobility as autonomous subjects with their own priorities and prerogatives and thereby expose the contradictions of their abject citizenship.

Notes

1. A note on terminology: I have opted here to use the term 'Roma' as both a noun (as is customary) and as an adjective, and I am thus deliberately choosing not to resort to the term 'Romani' as an adjective. This usage admittedly reflects the increasingly established normativity and ubiquity of the label 'Roma'—as a generic name for the heterogeneous (multi-lingual, plurinational, and culturally diverse) minoritized communities which variously call themselves Rom, Roma, Vlach Roma, Romany, Sinti, Ashkali, Bayash, Kalé, 'Egyptian', Gypsies, and so on—which has itself arguably been an effect of the larger processes of EU institutionalization (cf. Guild and Carrera 2013; Sigona and Trehan 2009; Simhandl 2006; van Baar 2011a). Consequently, my use of the phrase 'Roma people' entails what may seem to some readers to be an awkward redundancy. Nonetheless, inasmuch as the term 'Roma' has already acquired a thoroughly racialized salience, my usage intends to simultaneously acknowledge the saturation of the term with racial significance—without euphemizing it or retreating from it—while also seeking to emphatically re-humanize the people so described.
2. Elaborating the concept of 'frontier zones', Leanne Weber and Sharon Pickering (2011) have discerned analogous processes underway in the contemporary global regime dedicated to the 'management' of refugee and migrant mobilities, whereby states (such as Australia in their research) willfully produce a gap between international law and national sovereignty, as a result of which human mobility may be subjected to repressive violence and

coercion but is deprived of any legal protection (see also Heller and Pezzani 2017 and, more generally, Agier 2011).
3. Furthermore, the more vexed the predicament of such 'undesirables' and the states which did not desire them became, the more the internment camp emerged as 'the routine solution for the problem of domicile of the "displaced persons"' (Arendt 1968: 279); 'the only practical substitute for a non-existent homeland... the only "country" the world had to offer' them (284).
4. It seems indisputable that this transformation of deportation from the exception to a presumptive norm, across the intervening decades with which Arendt was concerned, owes a great deal to the general degradation of the global status of 'aliens' in light of the mass deportations and forced population movements of the era she describes (see De Genova 2013; De Genova and Peutz 2010; Fekete 2005; Hing 2006; Kanstroom 2007, 2012).

REFERENCES

Agier, M. 2011. *Managing the Undesirables: Refugee Camps and Humanitarian Government*. Cambridge: Polity.
Aradau, C., et al. 2013. Mobility Interrogating Free Movement? Roma Acts of European Citizenship. In *Enacting European Citizenship*, ed. E. Isin and M. Saward, 132–154. Cambridge: Cambridge University Press.
Arendt, H. 1968 [1951]. *The Origins of Totalitarianism*. New York: Harvest/Harcourt.
Bigo, D., S. Carrera, and E. Guild, eds. 2013. *Foreigners, Refugees or Minorities? Rethinking People in the Context of Border Controls and Visas*. Farnham: Ashgate.
Çağlar, A., and S. Mehling. 2013. Sites and Scales of the Law: Third-Country Nationals and EU Roma Citizens. In *Enacting European Citizenship*, ed. E. Isin and M. Saward, 155–177. Cambridge: Cambridge University Press.
Castañeda, H. 2014. European Mobilities or Poverty Migration? Discourses on Roma in Germany. *International Migration* 53 (3): 87–99.
Clark, C., and G. Rice. 2012. Spaces of Hate, Places of Hope: The Roma in Belfast. In *The Gypsy 'Menace': Populism and the New Anti-Gypsy Politics*, ed. M. Stewart, 167–190. London: Hurst & Company.
Clough Marinaro, I., and U. Daniele. 2011. Roma and Humanitarianism in the Eternal City. *Journal of Modern Italian Studies* 16 (5): 621–636.
De Genova, N. 2013. The Perplexities of Mobility. In *Critical Mobilities*, ed. O. Söderström et al., 101–122. London/Lausanne: Routledge/Presses Polytechniques et Universitaires Romandes.
———. 2016a. The "European" Question: Migration, Race, and Post-Coloniality in "Europe". In *An Anthology of Migration and Social Transformation:*

European Perspectives, ed. A. Amelina, K. Horvath, and B. Meeus, 343–356. New York: Springer.
———. 2016b. The European Question: Migration, Race, and Postcoloniality in Europe. *Social Text* 128: 75–102.
———., ed. 2017. *The Borders of 'Europe': Autonomy of Migration, Tactics of Bordering*. Durham, NC: Duke University Press.
De Genova, N., and N. Peutz, eds. 2010. *The Deportation Regime: Sovereignty, Space, and the Freedom of Movement*. Durham, NC: Duke University Press.
Drakakis-Smith, A. 2007. Nomadism a Moving Myth? Policies of Exclusion and the Gypsy/Traveller Response. *Mobilities* 2 (3): 463–487.
European Commission. 2010. Communication from the Commission to the European Parliament, the Council, the European Economic and Social Committee of the Regions: The Social and Economic Integration of the Roma in Europe, April 7. Available at: http://eur-lex.europa.eu/LexUriServ/LexUriServ.do?uri=COM:2010:0133:FIN:EN:PDF.
———. 2011. Communication from the Commission to the European Parliament, the Council, the European Economic and Social Committee of the Regions: An EU Framework for National Roma Integration Strategies up to 2020, April 5. Available at: http://ec.europa.eu/justice/policies/discrimination/docs/com_2011_173_en.pdf.
———. 2013. *EU and Roma* (last updated 5 November 2013). Available at: http://ec.europa.eu/justice/discrimination/roma/index_en.htm.
Fekete, L. 2005. *The Deportation Machine: Europe, Asylum, and Human Rights*. Special Issue of the *European Race Bulletin*, No. 51. London: Institute of Race Relations.
———. 2014. Europe Against the Roma. *Race & Class* 55 (3): 60–70.
———. 2016. Hungary: Power, Punishment and the "Christian-National Idea". *Race & Class* 57 (4): 39–53.
Fox, J. 2012. The Uses of Racism: Whitewashing New Europeans in the UK. *Ethnic and Racial Studies* 36 (11): 1871–1889.
Fox, J., L. Moroşanu, and E. Szilassy. 2012. The Racialization of the New European Migration to the UK. *Sociology* 46 (4): 680–695.
Garelli, G., and M. Tazzioli. 2016. *Tunisia as a Revolutionized Space of Migration*. Basingstoke: Palgrave Macmillan.
Grill, J. 2012. "It's Building Up to Something and It Won't Be Nice When It Erupts": Making of Roma Migrants in a "Multicultural" Scottish Neighborhood. *Focaal: Journal of Global and Historical Anthropology* 62: 42–54.
———. 2017. "In England, They Don't Call You Black!" Migrating Racialisations and the Production of Roma Difference Across Europe. *Journal of Ethnic and Migration Studies*. https://doi.org/10.1080/1369183X.2017.1329007.

Guglielmo, R., and T. Waters. 2005. Migrating Towards Minority Status: Shifting European Policy Towards Roma. *Journal of Common Market Studies* 43 (4): 763–785.

Guild, E., and S. Carrera. 2013. Introduction. International Relations, Citizenship and Minority Discrimination: Setting the Scene. In *Foreigners, Refugees or Minorities?* ed. D. Bigo, S. Carrera, and E. Guild, 1–29. Farnham: Ashgate.

Heller, Ch., and L. Pezzani. 2017. Liquid Traces: Investigating the Deaths of Migrants at the EU's Maritime Frontier. In *The Borders of 'Europe': Autonomy of Migration, Tactics of Bordering*, ed. N. De Genova, 95–119. Durham, NC: Duke University Press.

Hepworth, K. 2012. Abject Citizens: Italian 'Nomad Emergencies' and the Deportability of Roma. *Citizenship Studies* 16 (3–4): 431–449.

———. 2014. Encounters with the Clandestino/a and the Nomad: The Emplaced and Embodied Constitution of (Non-)Citizenship. *Citizenship Studies* 18 (1): 1–14.

———. 2015. *At the Edges of Citizenship: Security and the Constitution of Non-citizen Subjects*. Surrey: Ashgate.

Hing, B. 2006. *Deporting Our Souls: Values, Morality and Immigration Policy*. Cambridge: Cambridge University Press.

Kanstroom, D. 2007. *Deportation Nation: Outsiders in American History*. Cambridge, MA: Harvard University Press.

———. 2012. *Aftermath: Deportation Law and the New American Diaspora*. Oxford: Oxford University Press.

Kóczé, A. 2017. Race, Migration and Neoliberalism: Distorted Notions of Roma Migration in European Public Discourses. *Social Identities*. https://doi.org/10.1080/13504630.2017.1335827.

Malkki, L. 1995. Refugees and Exile: From 'Refugee Studies' to the National Order of Things. *Annual Review of Anthropology* 24: 495–523.

McGarry, A. 2011. The Roma Voice in the European Union: Between National Belonging and Transnational Identity. *Social Movement Studies* 10 (3): 283–297.

Mezzadra, S. 2001. *Diritto di fuga: Migrazioni, cittadinanza, globalizzazione*. Verona: Ombre corte.

———. 2004. The Right to Escape. *Ephemera* 4 (3): 267–275.

Mirga, A. 2009. The Extreme Right and Roma and Sinti in Europe: A New Phase in the Use of Hate Speech and Violence? *Roma Rights* 1: 5–9.

Nacu, A. 2012. From Silent Marginality to Spotlight Scapegoating? A Brief Case Study of France's Policy Towards the Roma. *Journal of Ethnic and Migration Studies* 38 (8): 1323–1328.

Riedner, L. et al. 2016. 'Mobility' in New Keywords Collective (edited by N. De Genova and M. Tazzioli) 'Europe/Crisis: New Keywords of "the Crisis" in and of "Europe"' *Near Futures Online* 1(1), New York: Zone Books. Available at:

http://nearfuturesonline.org/europecrisis-new-keywords-of-crisis-in-and-of-europe-part-6/. Accessed 1 Sept 2017.

Sardelić, J. 2017. In and Out from the European Margins: Reshuffling Mobilities and Legal Statuses of Roma Minorities Between the Post-Yugoslav Space and the European Union. *Social Identities.* https://doi.org/10.1080/13504630.2017.1335829.

Sigona, N., and N. Trehan. 2009. Introduction: Romani Politics in Neoliberal Europe. In *Romani Politics in Contemporary Europe: Poverty, Ethnic Mobilization and the Neoliberal Order*, ed. N. Sigona and N. Trehan, 1–20. New York: Palgrave Macmillan.

Simhandl, K. 2006. "Western Gypsies and Travellers" – "Eastern Roma": The Creation of Political Objects by the Institutions of the European Union. *Nations and Nationalism* 12 (1): 97–115.

Sohn-Rethel, A. 1978. *Intellectual and Manual Labour: A Critique of Epistemology.* London: The Macmillan Press.

Solimene, M. 2017. Challenging Europe's External Borders and Internal Boundaries: Bosnian *Xoraxané Xomá* on the Move in Roman peripheries and the Contemporary European Union. *Social Identities.* https://doi.org/10.1080/13504630.2017.1335828.

Tazzioli, M. 2014. *Spaces of Governmentality: Autonomous Migration and the Arab Uprisings.* Lanham, MD: Rowman & Littlefield.

van Baar, H. 2011a. *The European Roma: Minority Representation, Memory and the Limits of Transnational Governmentality.* Amsterdam: F&N.

———. 2011b. Europe's Romaphobia: Problematization, Securitization, Nomadization. *Environment and Planning D: Society and Space* 29 (2): 203–212.

———. 2014. The Centripetal Dimension of the EU's External Border Regime. *Etnofoor* 26 (2): 87–93.

———. 2015. The Perpetual Mobile Machine of Forced Mobility. In *The Irregularization of Migration in Contemporary Europe: Detention, Deportation, Drowning*, ed. Y. Jansen, J. de Bloois, and R. Celikates, 71–86. Lanham, MD: Rowman & Littlefield.

———. 2017a. Contained Mobility and the Racialization of Poverty in Europe: The Roma at the Development-Security Nexus. *Social Identities.* https://doi.org/10.1080/13504630.2017.1335826.

———. 2017b. Evictability and the Biopolitical Bordering of Europe. *Antipode* 49 (1): 212–230.

Walters, W. 2002. Deportation, Expulsion and the International Police of Aliens. *Citizenship Studies* 6 (3): 265–292.

Weber, L., and S. Pickering. 2011. *Globalization and Borders: Death at the Global Frontier.* London: Palgrave Macmillan.

Yıldız, C., and N. De Genova. 2017. Un/free Mobility: Roma Migrants in the European Union. *Social Identities*. https://doi.org/10.1080/13504630.2017.1335819.

Yıldız, C. and R. Humphris. n.d. 'De-valuable, Disposable, Deportable: Spatio-Racial Formations of Homeless Roma Migrants in Central London,' Unpublished paper, presented to the Workshop "The Roma in the Nexus of Homelessness, Begging and Racialisation," Sponsored by the Spatial Politics Research Domain, Department of Geography, King's College London (6 May 2016).

CHAPTER 3

Crossing (Out) Borders: Human Rights and the Securitization of Roma Minorities

Regina Kreide

In the summer of 2015, striking images depicting tired, desperate, and sometimes furious refugees at the border gates dominated the media in Germany. Chancellor Angela Merkel then took the dramatic decision to admit about a million of these people to Germany as asylum seekers, bypassing the controversial Dublin Accord, which it was by then obvious had failed. In interviews and press statements, Merkel explained her politically hazardous decision as a commitment to human rights, and in terms of responsibility for the victims of the so-called refugee crisis. While support for this policy from the public and politicians in Germany has not been negligible, it has also become the subject of fierce opposition and critique—both in Germany and in other Member States of the European

---

I am grateful to criticisms and observations by the many colleagues involved in the SFB research consortium *Dynamics of Security*, especially Huub van Baar, Ana Ivasiuc, and Andreas Langenohl. Special words of thanks are due to colleagues at the University of Washington, Seattle, among them Amos Nascimento, Bill Talbott, and Michael Forman. I am also indebted to Andreas Niederberger and colleagues, who participated in a conference at the University of Duisburg-Essen in November 2016, for helpful insights and suggestions.

R. Kreide (✉)
Justus Liebig University Giessen, Giessen, Germany
e-mail: Regina.Kreide@sowi.uni-giessen.de

© The Author(s) 2019
H. van Baar et al. (eds.), *The Securitization of the Roma in Europe*, Human Rights Interventions, https://doi.org/10.1007/978-3-319-77035-2_3

Union (EU). Political mobilization against the admission of migrants and refugees has become manifest, mainly because a security discourse where the newcomers are depicted as a threat to security and public order has begun to dominate public debate and media coverage. Open borders, and immigrants seeking access to Europe—be they refugees, asylum seekers, or immigrants—were and still are depicted as a major security problem. The threat, it seems, comes in the incarnation of an immigrant or refugee—or both.

But the more philosophical question is whether countries have a right to close their borders or, to put it another way, a right to exclude? This is most pressing for those states that claim to be legitimate, in the sense that they respect human rights and are democratically organized (Wellman and Cole 2011: 2). Clearly, borders are not just walls and fences, they do not just block the way by defining a territory, nor do they simply create obstacles to gaining membership; they are all of these. What's more, they are multifaceted zones of infrastructure and at the same time elements of securitization. As long as borders are imposed coercively and, through this imposition, contribute to securitization, I argue that they are illegitimate. The reason for this, as this chapter shows, is mainly because the power to securitize restricts people's qualified options: structurally, by literally blocking their escape from war zones, hunger, and economic deprivation, and interactionally, by making migrants invisible or depicting them as criminals or victims. Also, the security discourse itself reproduces certain stereotypes and neglects the power of the migrant to de-securitize. This contradicts the acknowledged human rights that should protect refugees and asylum seekers but, thinking back to the enormous number of stateless people before and during World War II, it is tempting to say that human rights reveal their ambivalent character precisely when confronted with yet another tragedy of migration.

To argue this in more detail, I first define what I mean by borders; then, in the second section, I discuss a number of arguments to demonstrate that there are no good moral reasons for closing borders. After that, in the third section, I take you on a brief tour of the empirical world of Europe's external and internal border politics, the growing entanglement between the two, and the inherent power of the securitization of borders. External borders have turned into technically controlled and surveyed border regimes exercising wide power in societies, both internally and externally— a dialectical process of securitization. The Roma, who were defined by the EU as the most prominent European minority shortly after the fall of the

Berlin Wall, are a case in point when it comes to the politics of border securitization. Having been evicted, forced to move, and discriminated against in different ways, the Roma make intra-state and intra-European borders and practices of securitization visible and reveal the coercive power of borders tout court. These practices of securitization transform our societies into securitized societies and offer arguments—too-long neglected—against any right of states to exclude. This is the focus of the fourth part. In the last part, I conclude that human rights, more often than not, appear to be a farce, which has its origins—albeit maybe not exclusively—in the fact that human rights have been turned into the means of claiming to create security.

Borders

The building of borders is booming; even since the fall of the Iron Curtain, which was long considered to be the most insurmountable border. Since 1989, many walls have been built worldwide, allegedly to prevent migration. In Europe alone, there are many examples, with hundreds of kilometres of borders, from the high fences of the Spanish Exclaves of Ceuta and Melilla in North Africa to the 'provisional' security installation on the Hungarian border with Serbia, which is 175 kilometres long. Border crossings are dangerous and cost lives. Data do not describe the dramatically dangerous conditions that migrants and refugees face, but they give some idea of the dimension of the tragedy. In 2015, at least 1,015,078 people crossed the Mediterranean to Europe; 3,771 died in the attempt in 2015. The deadliest year so far was 2016, with at least 5000 deaths. For the journey between Libya and Italy, the likelihood of dying is as high as 1 death for every 47 arrivals. Since 2000, more than 23,000 people have died on their way to Europe (Luft 2016: 47).

This new wall-building may surprise us, as in our post-Westphalian world order, the nation state is by no means sovereign enough anymore to define global political relations and has the overall power to determine or influence other players in the field. A wall by no means convincingly demonstrates national sovereignty. Paradoxically, one could even say that the new phenomena of building walls expresses a weakening of sovereign power and the detachment of sovereignty from the nation state (think about EU border protection) that enforces wall building. The new walls are 'icons of its erosion' (Brown 2010).

Accordingly, borders have changed their function. First, they are no longer just the visible walls that enact the control of a state over its *own territory*. They do not just define physical entry to a country. Second, as borders are a legal and social precondition for fully fledged membership of political and social communities, they also appear to be a form of gaining access to such *membership*, and this function structures the access to membership. Third, there are different kinds of social and cultural boundaries that deny people entry or full access to social and cultural participation in public life, for example, when they are confronted with various types of discrimination. All three of these forms are interconnected, an aspect that is often neglected in political philosophical debates but which becomes prevalent when focusing on security measures aimed at making borders impermeable. There are cases of territorial inclusion, nevertheless, as they do not exclude the occurrence of either political exclusion or cultural disrespect—or even both—with regard to migrants, and, for example, contribute to the framing of immigration as a threat. There are also cases of political inclusion—for instance, in the form of the possession of formal rights of citizenship—but these cases have frequently gone hand in hand with territorial segregation (e.g., through eviction) and cultural discrimination, as in the case of the European Roma. There might also be the rare case of overall cultural acceptance that occurs next to forms of territorial and political exclusion, as in the case of the 'Russian Germans' or of citizens of the former German Democratic Republic (GDR)—although it would be rather rash to say that there was no discrimination against people from the East.

Borders are complex social institutions, characterized by practices of crossing and enforcement mechanisms of all kinds (Mezzadra and Neilson 2013: 3). Nevertheless, borders are never absolutely non-permeable. They remain porous no matter what measures are taken, and migrants not only cross them, but are the ones who make the first move, thereby forcing states to respond to their agency.[1] Even when borders are deployed to facilitate cross-border mobility, migrants remain autonomous subjects with needs, wishes, and rights. On the one hand, borders and border policing constrain the freedom of migrants, while on the other hand, the disciplining effect of these border regimes and their 'correcting force' is limited (De Genova 2017: 30). We see in the following what this means.

The philosophical question here is whether states are entitled to claim this triple combination—that is, legal, political, and cultural exclusion—at all. There are currently a number of predominant arguments as to why states might be morally entitled to enforce their own immigration policies. Most of them are not convincing, as I demonstrate in what follows.

In Favour of Closed Borders

The philosophical debate about the right to close or open borders has become multilayered.[2] I discuss some prominent arguments against open borders to show their flaws and one-sidedness with regard to borders.

One prominent argument against open borders is that states are, to a certain degree, comparable to marriages or private clubs and that, as such, they are in a privileged position to make decisions about the affairs and matters that concern them. Just as a single person has a right to decide whom—if anyone—they will marry, a group of co-nationals has the right to decide whom—if anyone—they will invite to join their political community (Wellman 2008: 110). This argument, however, neglects the fact that there are major differences between the state and a private association. States are not *voluntary* associations; we usually acquire citizenship of a state at birth. Membership of a club can generally be terminated even if there is no other club that will accept you, but citizenship cannot be terminated so easily if no other state is prepared to offer you citizenship. Moreover, Kit Wellman (2008) argues, private associations are allowed to reject or 'blackball' members even if they were born 'in the clubhouse'. A state, in contradistinction, is not allowed to reject the descendants of its fully fledged citizens, and de-naturalization violates international law. A basic idea here is self-determination, and this, it seems, involves sovereignty over entry to the territory, as well as over membership of a political community.

This leads me to another objection against arguments in favour of a right to exclusion. David Miller (2016) argues that we need to bear in mind that freedom of movement is restricted even domestically: one is not allowed to just go anywhere or to enter private property, and public institutions have limited opening hours. Miller (ibid.: 51) concludes that it is sufficient for people to have just an adequate number of options at their disposal when it comes to their 'generic human interests', so that they can make meaningful decisions about their lives with regard to their profession, religion, cultural activities, and so on. However, this assumption is also problematic. Freedom of movement is a substantial freedom; a restriction of this freedom is a major infringement on individual autonomy, as freedom of movement is a precondition of many other freedoms based on physical presence. Just think about the freedom of career choice, of emotional relationships, of housing conditions. The restriction of free movement also infringes a substantial notion of self-determination. To move to places where the economic options seem to be better is a biblical theme; it is probably as old as mankind and independent of any religious roots. It is an important strategy for making decisions about one's life and self, and in that sense it is an important right. Those with an EU passport—which enables them to travel to most of the countries in the world without any visa restrictions—should know.

Another possible objection is that, if self-determination is taken seriously, this would imply rethinking what, exactly, democratic self-determination means. For example, current European immigration regulations have been informed by a *demos* that includes only those who are domestically members (citizens) of a state. If the principle of democracy is taken seriously—that is to say, that any coercive submission to rules requires that one should be the author of these rules—things look different (Abizadeh 2008; Brunkhorst 2014). It means that all those who are coercively prevented from becoming a member—and this also includes immigrants who would like to enter the political community involved—must be included. The inclusion of everybody on the list of those with whom we might create and establish the conditions for democratic norms is aimed at preventing a top-down variety of democracy. A strong notion of democracy, in contradistinction, includes everybody affected by the enforceable rules. Seyla Benhabib's (2011: 124) principle of *juris generativity* may help here. This principle refers to the law's capacity to create a universe of normative meaning that can escape the realm of formal lawmaking. With reference to human rights this can best be explained as follows. Existing Universal Declarations of Human Rights and other international covenants and treaties have enabled actors such as women, and linguistic, ethnic, political, sexual, and religious minorities, to enter the public sphere, and this praxis of inclusion has to be expanded beyond borders (Benhabib 2011: 125). However, rules can only be followed when they are interpreted. Laws, as well as other normative rules, acquire meaning insofar as they are interpreted within the social context of their use. The horizon of interpretation changes any fixed meaning and is open to new points of view. Through the public exercise of the political rules which organize democracy, the implicit inclusive character of democracy may come to the fore. Democracy can thus be interpreted as being based on the normative assumption of including those affected by enforceable rules.

It is exactly this idea of *juris generativity* that could also be applied to refugees and immigrants. Taking the principle of democracy seriously would require taking into account the interests of those waiting in camps as well.

It is still possible to assert that not allowing people to enter a state or a political community is not *coercive*, and so an expansion of the *demos* is not required (Miller 2016: 51). The situation, it could be argued, is comparable to having a neighbour who repeatedly wants to enter your house because, let's say, she does not like hers, or has no hot water, or no water at all (Cassee 2016: 54). You have a right to protect your property, but you might also have a moral obligation to help her with, let's say, hot water. You are not, however, under any obligation to let her in any more than you have the right to use force against her to prevent her from coming in.

Is this kind of argumentation convincing? I do not think so because Miller's argument neglects the structural context, which does not leave qualified life options open. To stay briefly with the earlier example, this would then raise more complex questions: why is there no water? Who is responsible for this shortage or lack? How can the problem of water supply be dealt with in such a way that all parties are satisfied? Who has established the rules for defining the territory? When focusing on this kind of question, the topic becomes multifaceted, and it may turn out that the neighbour has no water not because she has not paid her bill but because the water supply in this part of town has been a low priority and the infrastructure is not well developed. Moreover, it would be important to clarify whether these rules have been imposed on her or whether she was given a say when they were defined.

The issue of migration is somewhat similar to this example. Seen from this angle, the problem can only be solved when the causes are thematized and the existing rules questioned. Neither you nor the neighbour is responsible for the situation, but to tackle the issue, a solution is needed that is acceptable to all parties. Moreover, borders are coercive as long as they hinder people from living a life that allows for qualified options. Qualified options are those—and here we can use Miller's argument against him—which embrace generic interests such as housing, equal access to education, employment, healthcare, the opportunity to find an adequate job that allows one to make a living, and so on. Whereas Miller defines those options more narrowly, claiming that as long of there are, de facto, some of those options available, we cannot speak of a coercive situation, I think this is difficult to argue—especially if we take seriously the principle of democracy—if we don't use the same standards of a qualified option for ourselves. Why shouldn't poor education, lack of healthcare, and career opportunities of a lower standard be seen as a good reason to move (given that people are usually very reluctant to leave their family, friends, and familiar surroundings anyway)? Not to be in the situation of having the choice among equally good options can represent coercion. A choice between Skylla and Charybdis—between being unemployed or working in conditions that do not allow for leaving—is not a qualified option. In this sense, borders do more than hinder people from crossing national or regional boundaries in order to enter new territory and gain political membership. Borders are the *instruments* used to enforce rules on people and constrain their chances in life.

So far, we have seen that it is not acceptable to argue for a right to coercive borders. There is, however, another, often neglected, argument against borders which comes to the fore when existing border policy is examined in more detail. To make this argument more convincing, I now take you on an empirical journey through EU documents, immigration law, and security studies, through which I analyse the relationship between European borders and the creation of threat and securitization practices.

SECURITIZATION OF MIGRATION TO EUROPE

Open borders, refugees, and immigrants, it is said, make our societies less secure, or rather, they make them insecure. Terror attacks, allegedly by asylum seekers, seem to underpin this view. We all know that security issues do not necessarily reflect the objective, material circumstances of the world. Security issues are often the result of efforts by the elite, the media, science, and politics to understand and shape the world. Over the last 20 years or so, a series of studies has tried to understand why and how the issue of 'security' is created and what effects diverse security policy measures have on people's lives. I give only a very rough overview of these literatures here and discuss three profound approaches before offering what I understand as a dialectical approach to securitization, a view that I introduce as an alternative way of understanding Europe's border policies.

The interpretation of securitization from the so-called Copenhagen School has been influential (see, most notably, Waever 1995; Buzan et al. 1998). In the 1990s, the representatives of this group criticized realist and neo-realist theories of international relations and claimed that security was a power balance among nation states with rational and utilitarian agency on the part of states and their elites. According to them, security is not a given prerogative of states but is instead created through the speech acts of political elites, and other actors, for the legitimation of political agency and supremacy. In a process of securitization, speech acts perform security discursively, while invoking a semantic repertoire, the so-called 'grammar of security' (Buzan et al. 1998: 33). A social or political affair is constructed as a 'problem' (e.g., terrorism or migration) through such a securitizing speech act, a process that allows the taking of exceptional (policy) measures by a centralized authority (usually the government). 'Securitization', here, means calling something a security problem and thereby triggering exceptional political measures to deal with it.

This approach has—rightly, I think—been criticized as being too much preoccupied with a mere discursive approach and with the idea that a *pragmatic turn* in security studies would cover most phenomena regarding security. The so-called Paris School, represented by, for example, Didier Bigo (2006) and Thierry Balzacq (2005, 2011), doubts this. They think the speech-act approach to security is too narrow, as it neglects the practices of securitization in a broader sense. What is at stake here are practices that go beyond publicly uttered speech acts, that is, those that include weapons, walls, satellite techniques, and a whole range of administrative practices such as population profiling, risk assessment, and a specific habitus of security professionals (Bigo 2006). At the EU level, this includes data exchange and the activities of Frontex, the European Border, and Coastguard Agency. Thus, this approach not only concentrates on states as securitizing actors but also includes non-state actors, such as companies, professionals, experts, and individuals (Balzacq 2005, 2011; Bigo 2006). Understood along these lines, securitization means discursive and *non-discursive* ways of creating knowledge about security techniques which change the conduct of social, political, economic, cultural, and military affairs.

Plausible as this approach from the Paris School may be, it still undertheorizes at least one aspect and that is *how* exactly, as a result of a securitization policy, security and insecurity are linked. A plausible way of understanding securitizing measures is as follows. Security is not an objective condition but is constructed through intersubjective, shared interpretations within a social context. The public definition of a 'security problem', accepted as such by an audience, is a process that could be called securitization. Paris School scholars would probably agree so far. But these practices of security create insecurity; they are *intrinsically* linked. Even though, also for example, Didier Bigo describes a relationship between security and insecurity, it is better to see them as being inseparably interwoven. These practices come to the fore in a *dialectical relationship* in which the demands of security bring about its opposite, not a *more* secure world but an *in*secure world (Ivasiuc 2018a, Chap. 11, this volume): the one cannot exist without the other. The full range of instruments that the liberal or neo-liberal state can offer—from a stronger administrative executive or the technical control of public spheres to private data resources and the expansion of border control zones—works hand in hand to bring about insecurity for the population. A dialectical approach to security includes not only a reflection on the processes of discursive representation and construction but also a critical interrogation of the techniques and forms of expertise involved in enacting, maintaining, reinforcing, or challenging (e.g., migration related) the processes of securitization (van Baar 2011b, 2015).

What does this approach to securitization imply for the debate about migration and borders as discussed in this chapter? Refugees and migrants are not only unsure of whether they will survive their dangerous trip when they are forced to flee; through the European policy of securitizing immigration, they are also framed as criminals, potential terrorists, and/or non-autonomous victims who need to be helped and who are consequently patronized. To get a better picture of these processes, I take a closer look at how securitization practices are deeply entrenched in European and German migration policies, and how and why this can only be seen as coercive border control.

Immigration became politicized in the mid-1980s through the issue of asylum (Huysmans 2000). As a consequence of the abolition of the EU's internal border control (Schengen) and the interrelated free movement of persons within the EU, its Member States lost their decision-making authority over entry, residence, and exit. This marked the beginning of what was later called Fortress Europe (Mrozek 2017: 84–96). States lost their steering authority as the decisions of a single state in a space without internal frontiers naturally have consequences for all Member States. Nevertheless, the EU, and its Member States in particular, did not want to give up their steering mechanisms for the immigration of citizens from third countries. Two key measures were taken in response: the development of a more effective external border regime and the Europeanization of asylum law. Both, as we will see, have expanded the notion of borders, while at the same time framing migrants.

The EU has also established a policy system of integrated border management through which the Union wants to ensure that it can decide on who can and cannot enter—as in the case of a state—tout court. Many actors are involved, such as the EU institutions (Commission, Council, and even though sometimes not in line with the decisions of the other two institutions, the Parliament), the Member States, and Frontex. Some of the central elements of this system are the increasing use of technology, outsourcing through privatization, and the exterritorialization of parts of the EU's border control and enforcement. The inclusion of third countries in the EU's border management has become possible through the latter in particular. This has happened through cooperation with North African countries (among them Morocco and Libya) which have adopted Euro-style legislation throughout the last 12 years. This has gone hand in hand with the incorporation of a Western national citizenship model, which has created lines of 'inside' and 'outside' and of national citizenship as part of an internal border. This paved the way for the involvement of North African countries in repatriation agreements, through which the countries of origin and transit agree to allow the readmission of immigrants sent back by European countries (Locchi 2014: 13). A similar instrument of exterritorialization is at stake when it comes to 'neighbour politics' with Turkey. Agreements with the EU facilitate the legal immigration of citizens and at the same time hinder refugees from moving further north. It is not that these forms of border exterritorialization have not been criticized, but the critique has so far remained marginal. Amnesty International (Amnesty International 2014) has, for example, accused Turkey of forcing refugees to go back to their countries of origin, which include war-torn Afghanistan, Iraq, and Syria, and the European Court of Justice (EUGH/ECJ/CJEU) and European Court of Human Rights have made it very clear that the norms of international refugee protection are also valid for EU institutions, including Frontex, when they act outside European territory.

What we can see is that there is nothing quite like a border for blocking the way within existing law. Instead, for migrants, blocking the way to Europe entails the options of either trying to flee again after having been deported back to the war-torn or insecure country of origin or becoming an undocumented person in Turkey.

What this shows is that, due to the institutional conflation of migration, terror, transnational (also intra-EU) crime, complex forms of securitizing migration and borders have emerged in Europe. In this system of border control and enforcement, the boundaries between internal and external borders have been blurred. It is through this complex process that 'old-fashioned' techniques of border enforcement—walls and fences at the classic borders of territorialized states—have become just one of the multiple chains in new systems of border control (van Baar 2017a).

Alongside exterritorialization, another link in the chain is border control backed up by scientific knowledge and in cooperation with hi-tech companies. Since the 1980s, asylum has increasingly become connected to illegalized immigration. With the Maastricht Treaty (1992), asylum policies became integrated into the EU's 'third pillar' of cooperation. Next to the first pillar, which handled economic, social, and environmental policies, and the second, which dealt with foreign policy and military matters, this third pillar brought together cooperation in the fight against crime (Huysmans 2000). Asylum law was removed from the sovereignty of individual Member States and submitted to community law in the Stockholm Programme of 2014, and a Europe-wide system of equal protection for asylum seekers emerged. Technology is now used for a Europe-wide system of border controls. It had already started in 1998, with a database of fingerprints from asylum applicants which formed part of an Austrian Presidency work programme on Eurodac, that '[t]he steep rise in the number of illegal immigrants and therefore potential asylum-seekers caught has revealed the increasing need to include their fingerprints in the system' (Statewatch 1998, quoted in Huysmans 2000: 755). Other regulations on migration in Europe soon followed (Kostakopoulou 2000). Eurosur was brought into existence to intensify the information exchange between Schengen states and Frontex through data from satellite control in real time.[3] This functions in cooperation with the European Asylum Support Office (EASO), Europol, the EU Satellite Centre, and the European Maritime Safety Agency, all of which are coordinated through Frontex (Luft 2016: 58).

What we can primarily conclude on the basis of this rough outline of the existing and emerging border policies is that border control has increasingly become an industry in which sciences, technologies, bureaucracies, and politics work closely together. The material and technical ways in which borders are created have led to powerful processes of securitization. This has happened in discursive (as with European legal and political regulations and media coverage) and non-discursive ways (collecting fingerprints, data storage systems, satellite control, and drones) of creating knowledge about security techniques, and through the normalization (surveillance processes in arrival camps, enforced distribution of refugees within an arrival country) of surveillance measures and of data collection (van Baar 2011b, 2015). We see that borders have turned from simple lines to zones and border practices (see also Feldman 2011), so that a mere topological understanding of borders underestimates the ways in which technology, science, and knowledge construct many different kinds of borders, both in and outside Europe. But even this expansion of the notion of borders does not cover all aspects. A more radical blurring of the EU's internal and external borders comes to the fore when we look at the ways in which the EU's internal and external border regimes are inherently connected. For this, I turn the focus from non-European citizens to Roma minorities with a European passport.

SECURITIZATION WITHIN EUROPE

Borders are moving as securitization also takes place *within* Europe. The practices and discourses of securitization have tainted minority policies to the extent that the distinction between immigration and asylum policies, on the one hand, and minority policies as regards indigenous minorities, on the other hand, has become blurred. In particular, the Roma in Europe are affected by a number of different security measures. Shortly after the fall of communism, institutional discrimination and violent attacks by 'ordinary citizens' against the Roma occurred throughout Central and Eastern Europe. Human rights organizations and the EU started to deal with the 'Roma case', framing it as a human emergency (van Baar 2011b). The adequate protection of minorities became one of the Copenhagen Criteria for EU membership, formulated in 1993. It was at this time that the Roma were defined as a European minority in need of human rights protection. From the perspective of EU citizenship, there are at least two types of Romani citizens: those with an EU passport who have migrated from Eastern to Western European countries (mainly to Italy, France, Germany, Spain, and the United Kingdom), exercising their right to free movement, and Romani refugees from the former Yugoslavia who, having fled the war, had already lived in Germany and other European countries for two or three decades.

It was in the context of the problematization of the Roma as a European minority (van Baar 2011a) that the European Commission stated that the Roma were having difficulties in defending their basic human and citizenship rights because of 'their nomadic way of life' (European Commission 1999: 2, quoted in van Baar 2011b: 209). Today—and indeed since the beginning of the twentieth century—no more than 3 per cent of Eastern

European Roma continue to lead a travelling lifestyle. Nevertheless, human rights policies had to be applied, regardless of the fact that these Roma held European passports, and by around 1990, many Italian regions, for example, had already adopted laws aimed at the protection of nomadic cultures. According to these laws, Roma culture needed to be protected through the continued construction and surveillance of segregated camps, the so-called *campi nomadi* or nomad camps. It was, paradoxically, the Italian authorities who nomadized the Roma by evicting them and forcing them to circulate within Italy (Ivasiuc 2018b), entrenching them in a state of 'evictability' (van Baar 2017b). This irregularization of the mobility of the Roma was used to reinforce the widespread prejudice that the Roma do not belong to Italy, even though many of Italy's Roma are Italian or EU citizens (Aradau et al. 2013; van Baar 2011b). What is striking here is that citizenship and human rights are not seen as being unconditional, which is an important criterion of human rights: every human has these rights, regardless of their personal and social circumstances. But here the upshot is that human rights such as the right to live a decent life, with shelter and education, are turned against the rights holder. It is now said that a certain standard of living has to be created before human rights can be exercised. Moreover, and even more problematically, the measures ostensibly taken to achieve this fall short of allowing the Roma to live a decent life. Rather, in the Italian case, the camps produce the condition of evictability par excellence; it is a condition that, by definition, normalizes the presence of the Roma as non-permanent, ephemeral, and transitional, irrespective of the wishes of the camp inhabitants. Human rights have thus turned into an instrument for securitizing the Roma people—regardless of their EU passports (see also Ivasiuc 2018a).

Let me briefly discuss the situation in Germany. The situation of the Romanian Roma in Germany is also grounded in an ambivalence of the existing claim to rights and the de facto exclusion of rights in securitization discourses. Throughout the year, but mainly during the summer, the Roma try to find work; but there is usually no option other than informal work in Berlin, Frankfurt, and some of the other major cities. The media that report on this migration usually avoid mentioning that this group of casual labourers are frequently Roma. Indeed, any mention of this could be seen as discrimination and akin to the outright discrimination historically perpetuated against this group under the Nazi regime. The public debate about the citizenship rights of Roma in Germany, however, has switched from stressing the Roma's right to free movement as EU citizens to the view that they are unwanted foreigners who 'abuse' the hospitality of Germany. Yet again, they have been problematized as a threat to public order and social security (Çağlar and Mehling 2013). At some point, in an emergency situation, some of the Romanian Roma in Berlin were accorded the status of tourists. They were sheltered in a house for asylum seekers—which is not a place for tourists—and were given financial support to enable them to return to Romania at the end of the legally established 90 days that a European citizen without financial means is allowed to stay. What then happened shed glaring light on German and European citizenship rights. The Roma demanded asylum in Germany, and they fulfilled most of the criteria, such as being the subject of permanent and systematic discrimination in their country of origin, being persecuted, evicted and pushed into a status of homelessness, and, as a consequence of this, being traumatized (Çağlar and Mehling 2013). By claiming asylum in Germany although they held EU passports, they blurred the boundaries between European EU and non-European EU citizens. As EU citizens, Roma from Romania are not eligible to enjoy some of the advantages that refugees from third countries have. At the same time, however, they were not able to take advantage of the benefits of European citizenship either. Different 'classes' of EU citizenship obviously exist. Moreover, as I explain shortly, the differing 'quality' of EU passports is ambivalently intertwined with a discourse that constructs the Roma as non-European and thus non-belonging.

Both German and EU citizenship fell short of guaranteeing this minority group their rights, even though they were exercising their citizenship by their mere presence in various places. Having been deported back to Romania, the Romanian Roma from Berlin enacted it by coming back to Germany a few weeks later, exercising their right to free movement (Çağlar and Mehling 2013). The ways in which these Roma articulated their claims to asylum highlighted the limited nature of both EU citizenship and human rights. Basic rights were denied to them in Germany, despite the fact that they held EU passports. The migration of this group is identified as an internal danger, even when they hold EU passports, and as an external danger with regard to the immigration of the Roma from Kosovo, which I am not discussing here (cf. van Baar 2017a). Securitization through, for example, being exposed to techniques of control, normalization and exclusion, is a way of producing forms of non-belonging, and both citizenship and human rights are involved in these exclusion processes.

In all these examples, I have illustrated how the securitization discourse operates in forming and forging external and internal boundaries that exclude 'the other' from citizenship and from becoming a fully fledged member of a political community. The discussion of the cases so far enables us to differentiate three aspects of securitization. First, in the case of access to both residence and citizenship, securitization shapes the outcomes in determining the conditions of access. Second, the securitization discourse contributes to marginalization, both symbolically, as it depicts certain groups as a danger, and socio-economically, as it hinders people from access to a country or from having the chance to get a position. Finally, the case of the Roma in Germany reveals the link between securitization and the denial of the exercise of citizenship rights, even under the condition of being an EU citizen. All these examples enable us to conceptualize at least three aspects of a dialectics of securitization.

First, the Italian and German situations clearly illustrate how measures designed to create security and stability have led to a disputable problematization of the Roma—in the form of nomadism, illegality, and public security threats. The security measures produce insecurity for the Roma. They negate significant options for members of this minority. Second, European regulations governing minorities and migration are neither designed to support inclusion nor to be grounds for normative correction for nationally framed citizenship laws. Rather, these regulations render visible and reinforce external foreclosure, the re-nationalization of human and citizenship rights (in the context of a European dimension), and the problematization of internal border crossing within Europe, in the sense that internal border crossing has been rendered unproblematic in EU discourses, although the case of the Roma highlights the fact that it is still prevalent. Consequently, there are different classes of European citizenship. There is citizenship for those who 'belong', at least for the time being, and for those who should be expelled regardless of their citizenship, as we have seen in the case of the Roma. Citizenship, like human rights, can bring about exclusion instead of more inclusion, and affects even those who have an EU passport. And third, not just the external borders of Europe but also the boundaries within Europe are coercive. I have shown that the establishment of the EU's external borders has led to forms of legal exclusion that may leave migrants with only options (going back to war or poverty) which do not qualify as a decent life (or 'generic interests'). Seen from within Europe, the legal inclusion of EU citizens is also not necessarily followed by political inclusion, nor by a cultural one which is not highly discriminating, as in the case of Italy. The Roma are not just prevented from social participation; instead, harsh living conditions are imposed upon them: they are forced to live in camps, find themselves under the surveillance of vigilantes, and are represented in degrading ways in the media. Freedom of movement, legally guaranteed through human and citizenship rights, can easily be turned into its opposite: into the 'freedom' to be displaced, forced to cross borders, and evicted. The Roma seem not to be eligible for human rights, since they are allegedly nomadic, and therefore pose a security risk. These modes of securitizing people, of excluding and neglecting them, if not infringing upon their rights, are part of a denial of social participation.

The Ambivalence of Human Rights

My analysis of the regimes of the EU's internal and external border politics has revealed aspects that are closely related to what I have called the dialectics of securitization. This aspect deals with the ambivalence of human rights.

In the context of migration, we have seen human rights working as securitizing instruments, identifying Roma migrants as a special group of people who do not belong to the community of human rights bearers and who therefore need first to be brought into a condition in which they become eligible to exercise human rights. Securitization—such as being exposed to control techniques, normalization, and exclusion—is a way of producing forms of non-belonging, and human rights have increasingly become involved in these exclusion mechanisms as part of a process of constructing ambiguous ways of protection. This brings to the fore a more general problem with human rights. I have shown that human rights play an ambivalent role when it comes to processes of securitization. They are—at the same time—conditions of freedom and resistance and instruments of oppression. How can this be the case?

To understand better this dual character of human rights, we briefly need to recall the predominant notion of human rights. According to the liberal tradition, human rights were originally seen in a historical continuity with traditional natural law. They are a reaction to state absolutism and moralizing revolutions. The important characteristic features of the precursors of present-day human rights in natural law, shaped by people like John Locke and Montesquieu, are still important for the understanding of liberal human rights today: they claim to be universally valid; they hold true for every person; and they ask for a political order that protects individual freedom. In this reading, human rights imply that an individual has the right to exercise life, liberty, and property *in security* (Locke 1988). Rights are an institutional guarantee of the *private* enjoyment of various goods and services (see also Menke 2016: 52). Human rights, confronted with the security discourse, face what has been said before: that demands for security always produce insecurity. This is what makes it problematic to speak of the exercise of rights *in security and what*, moreover, plays into the hands of those who demand security—of life, liberty, and property—*against* immigrants.

Aside from this aspect, the list of objections against this liberal notion of human rights has proved to be very long (from Burke, via Bentham and Marx, to post-colonial and feminist critique), which I cannot go into in any length here (but see Kreide 2015). And yet, there is a major pitfall of human rights that was probably signalled for the first time by Karl Marx. That is, freedom does not mean having the externally secured option to act as one likes according to one's will; rather, freedom means the possibility of *social participation*. As long as freedom is understood as the undisturbed *private* realization of one's own will, the real social preconditions remain unnoticed. The normative individualism of liberal human rights that is directed towards protecting individual security—be that the security of personal or economic freedom—is in tension with the idea of being a part of society, being among its respected members. Human beings, Marx argues, do not, first and foremost, want to obtain a fair share of societal resources; rather, they want to be part of a community, to be people *among* others, able to determine their social affairs politically. According to Marx (2008–09), human beings are political animals. Because human rights in their liberal interpretation claim individual security, they do not allow for such a view. They paradoxically deny some groups, inside and outside the territorialized borders of Europe, and migrants and the Roma in particular, the right to be part of the political community.

However, one even needs to go a step further. This tension between human rights and social participation in a community is not just a problem of the *content* of human rights (rights to economic freedom) but also of the *form of liberal rights* (Menke 2016). I think the conception of human rights sets the individual *against* all others (contra mundum) who assert that they are already part of society and belong to it. Hannah Arendt's (1968) often cited phrase that 'one needs to have a right to have rights' means precisely that: that everyone has a legitimate claim to be a member of society, to belong to one rather than simply to have a right to claim something against a state or an official organization. To deny this claim is coercive, as it blocks a qualified option for migrants and migrating European citizens, for which they usually have no or unbearable alternatives. Human rights require something from us as well, to think about who *we* are and what that 'we' actually means.

Conclusion

I have argued that the right to exclude cannot be defended. States are not comparable to private clubs, and since they—liberal democratic states at least—aim to represent universal values such as equality and freedom, they are not morality-free zones and can be criticized for being exclusive. Trust is not necessarily based on national identity, and political self-determination should include everybody, also those outside the territory. On top of this, borders—internal and external, visible and digital—inherently incorporate a force that drastically restricts options, which, as long as they have been established asymmetrically without involving those who are forced to accept them in decision-making, make them coercive. Modern borders establish practices of securitization—both on the outskirts of and within Europe—which make borders not just walls but complex networks of technical, industrial, and administrative control and securitizing power. These practices block not only the entry of immigrants (more or less successfully), they also infiltrate into our daily lives and substantially affect modes of governance for *all* citizens of Europe.

Whereas Georgio Agamben (1998) described the refugee as a symptom of the malaise of the modern state, as an expression of human beings reduced to their bare lives, the public discourses right now tend to identify a permanent threat to public order from those who, following Agamben, have been reduced to bare life. The refugee is no longer the symbol of the excluded, included through their unfortunate position in camps, detention centres, and other sites of exclusion. They have instead become a symbol of the included 'enemy', who is as dangerous as a ticking time bomb, and who must be excluded radically. Human rights do not necessarily embody a system of protection for this group of human beings, as long as there is no strong commitment to making them accepted members of our political community. Instead, as I have shown with regard to migrants and the Roma, human rights can easily be turned against those who are most vulnerable. The power to securitize may be challenged by counter-protests, but de-securitization remains marginal, if not impossible. The Roma sometimes settle around border zones in order to appropriate and subvert them (Piasere 2009: 94; Ivasiuc, Chap. 11, this volume). Border control is coercive, but it cannot be all-encompassing. Yet, securitization measures—and we should be very aware of this—affect us all, not only the immigrants. Who will be the next to be seen as a threat? This is still an open question, but it is one that might be answered sooner than we think.

Notes

1. Many thanks to Ana Ivasiuc who stressed this point.
2. For good overviews, see, for instance, Jansen et al. (2015) and Cassee (2016).
3. Frontex, we should note, is not a European border police force, even though it fulfils police-like duties. It is, rather, a transnational administrative agency and is subordinated to national law. It has an annual budget which has increased from the original 19.2 million euros to 114 million euros in 2015 (Luft 2016: 55). Frontex is responsible for the so-called push-back operations, which are, according to the Geneva Refugee Convention, illegal and which were condemned as being against human dignity by the European Court in 2012. Nevertheless, these operations are still enforced, as Frontex Director Ilkka Laitinen admitted recently. Frontex works—and we should keep this in mind—with the full support of European Interior Ministers, the European Commission, and the majority of the European Parliament. Frontex has several times been criticized by a critical public, and EU Member States tend to blame Frontex, rather than the EU, for abuses of human rights with regard to migration, even though the latter is the contracting authority.

References

Abizadeh, A. 2008. Democratic Theory and Border Coercion. *Political Theory* 36 (1): 37–65.

Agamben, G. 1998. *Homo Sacer*. Stanford: Stanford University Press.

Amnesty International. 2014. Türkei weist Flüchtlinge an der Grenze ab, see: https://www.amnesty.ch/de/laender/europa-zentralasien/tuerkei/dok/2014/syrische-fluechtlinge-an-der-grenze-abgewiesen. Accessed 22 Aug 2017.

Aradau, C., et al. 2013. Mobility Interrogating Free Movement. In *Enacting Citizenship*, ed. E. Isin and M. Sarward, 132–154. Cambridge: Cambridge University Press.
Arendt, H. 1968 [1951]. *The Origins of Totalitarianism*. New York: Harvest.
Balzacq, T. 2005. Three Faces of Securitization. *European Journal of International Relations* 11 (2): 171–201.
———. 2011. A Theory of Securitization. In *Securitization Theory*, ed. T. Balzacq, 1–30. London: Routledge.
Benhabib, S. 2011. *Dignity in Adversary*. Cambridge: Polity.
Bigo, D. 2006. Internal and External Aspects of Security. *European Security* 15 (4): 385–404.
Brown, W. 2010. *Walled States, Waning Sovereignty*. London: Zone Books.
Brunkhorst, H. 2014. *Kritik und kritische Theorie*. Baden Baden: Nomos.
Buzan, B., O. Weaver, and J. de Wilde, eds. 1998. *Security: A New Framework for Analysis*. Boulder, CO: Lynne Rienner.
Çağlar, A., and S. Mehling. 2013. Sites and the Scales of the Law. In *Enacting Citizenship*, ed. E. Isin and M. Sarward, 155–177. Cambridge: Cambridge University Press.
Cassee, A. 2016. *Globale Bewegungsfreiheit*. Berlin: Suhrkamp.
De Genova, N. 2017. The Incorrigible Subject. *Journal of Latin American Geography* 16 (1): 17–42.
Feldman, G. 2011. *The Migration Apparatus*. Stanford, CA: Stanford University Press.
Huysmans, J. 2000. The European Union and the Securitization of Migration. *Journal of Common Market Studies* 38 (5): 751–777.
Ivasiuc, A. 2018a. Reassembling Insecurity. In *The Power Dynamics of Securitization*, ed. R. Kreide and A. Langenohl. Baden Baden: Nomos, in print.
———. 2018b. Social Mobility and the Ambiguous Autonomy of Roma Migration. *Intersections* 4 (2): forthcoming.
Jansen, Y., R. Celikates, and J. de Bloois, eds. 2015. *The Irregularization of Migration in Contemporary Europe*. Lanham, MD: Rowman & Littlefield.
Kostakopoulou, T. 2000. The "Protective Union": Change and Continuity in Migration Law and Policy in Post-Amsterdam Europe. *Journal of Common Market Studies* 38 (3): 497–518.
Kreide, R. 2015. Between Morality and Law. *Journal of International Political Theory* 12 (1): 10–25.
Locchi, M. 2014. The Mediterranean Sea as a European Border. In *Borders, Fences and Walls*, ed. D. Wastl-Walter, 10–29. Farnham: Ashgate.
Locke, J. 1988 [1689]. *The Two Treatise of Government*. Cambridge: Cambridge University Press.
Luft, S. 2016. *Die Flüchlingskrise*. Munich: Beck.

Marx, K. 2008/09 [1844]. 'On the Jewish Question', published Originally in *Deutsch-Französiche Jahrbücher*, see: https://www.marxists.org/archive/marx/works/1844/jewish-question/. Accessed 5 Aug 2017.
Menke, C. 2016. *Kritik der Rechte*. Berlin: Suhrkamp.
Mezzadra, S., and B. Neilson. 2013. *Border as Method*. Durham, NC: Duke University Press.
Miller, D. 2016. *Strangers in Our Midst*. Cambridge, MA: Harvard University Press.
Mrozek, A. 2017. Joint Border Surveillance at the External Borders of "Fortress Europe". In *Der lange Sommer der Migration*, ed. S. Hess et al., 84–97. Berlin: Assoziation A.
Piasere, L. 2009 [2004]. *I Rom d'Europa: una storia moderna* [The Roma of Europe: A Modern History]. Rome: Laterza.
van Baar, H. 2011a. *The European Roma: Minority Representation, Memory and the Limits of Transnational Governmentality*. Amsterdam: F&N.
———. 2011b. Europe's Romaphobia: Problematization, Securitization, Nomadization. *Environment and Planning D: Society and Space* 29 (2): 203–212.
———. 2015. The Perpetual Mobile Machine of Forced Mobility. In *The Irregularization of Migration in Contemporary Europe*, ed. Y. Jansen, R. Celikates, and J. de Bloois, 71–86. Lanham, MD: Rowman & Littlefield.
———. 2017a. Boundary Practices of Citizenship. In *Within and Beyond Citizenship*, ed. R. Gonzales and N. Sigona, 145–158. London: Routledge.
———. 2017b. Evictability and the Biopolitical Bordering of Europe. *Antipode* 49 (1): 212–230.
Waever, O. 1995. Securitization and Desecuritization. In *On Security*, ed. R. Lipschutz, 46–87. New York: Columbia University Press.
Wellman, C. 2008. Immigration and Freedom of Association. *Ethics* 119 (1): 109–141.
Wellman, C., and P. Cole. 2011. *Debating the Ethics of Immigration*. Oxford: Oxford University Press.

CHAPTER 4

Domestic Versus State Reason? How Roma Migrants in France Deal with Their Securitization

Olivier Legros and Marion Lièvre

Thanks to several analytical studies, security policies are currently well documented (Crawford and Hutchinson 2016). However, these studies pay significantly less attention to the effects that these policies have on the everyday lives of the target populations. Didier Bigo (2011) has suggested that this neglect is the result of the post-9/11 trend in security studies to

---

This chapter draws on work funded as part of the French research programme *Marg-In* (2016–2019)—'Marginalization/Inclusion: Medium/long term effects of foreign poverty regulation policies on target populations: the case of "Roma" Migrants in Western European cities (France, Italy, Spain)', supported by the French National Research Council (ANR). We very much thank Ana Ivasiuc, Regina Kreide and Huub van Baar for their critical reading and particularly Ana Ivasiuc for her support in the translation from French to English.

O. Legros (✉)
University of Tours, Tours, France
e-mail: Olivier.legros@univ-tours.fr

M. Lièvre
Paul-Valéry University - Montpellier 3, Montpellier, France
e-mail: marionsli@hotmail.com

© The Author(s) 2019
H. van Baar et al. (eds.), *The Securitization of the Roma in Europe*, Human Rights Interventions, https://doi.org/10.1007/978-3-319-77035-2_4

focus more on political speeches and institutional arrangements than on the practices of social actors. Recent researches on Roma-related policies draw a similar conclusion, hence the interest in, nay, the necessity for a 'bottom-up' approach (van Baar 2011, 2015). In France, this change of approach with regard to policies which target the Roma[1] is all the more relevant given that the authorities seem to be revising their intervention modes in 'illicit camps' precisely as a result of pressures from camp inhabitants themselves.[2] Indeed, rather than complying with the orders of authorities to leave the camps or accept emergency housing following their eviction, the evicted families—in this case from Romania—continue to squat on land or in buildings as close as possible to their former settlements (Mission Campements Illicites 2016). The inability of the public authorities to 'restore order' is all the more surprising since the Roma apparently have limited room for manoeuvre: as foreigners with little or no knowledge of the French language and whose presence in France is constantly illegalized,[3] they also have little insight into the French political culture that affects them.

These two preliminary observations about the impact of repressive policies and the *a priori* weakness of the means of action of Roma migrants[4] invite an interrogation of the practices of the migrants in confrontation with institutions. Are their actions limited to the 'art of the weak', that is to say, to tactics, which Michel de Certeau (1980: 87) regards as different from strategies, and which consist of 'insinuating itself into the other's place… continually turn[ing] to their own ends forces alien to them'? Patently, as we have seen, their practices demonstrate a defiance of injunctions to leave the territory, without, however, engaging in frontal opposition to the institutional actors or the forces of law and order. How can we theorize practices of this kind, which are simultaneously characterized by disobedience and the absence of resistance to authority?

At the end of the 1970s, Michel Foucault (2007: 203) coined the term 'counter-conduct' to designate an array of individual or collective practices which, in various forms, express a refusal to conform with the conduct imposed by society and its institutions, in a 'more diffuse and softer' manner than direct confrontation or revolt. In the case of the Roma migrants, their practices of denial and disobedience do indeed constitute an alternative to the kind of conduct imposed in the two fields affecting their daily existence: free movement and the possibilities of residence—which are heavily constrained by the law and by repressive practices—and access to employment and social benefits. The latter may indeed involve respect for behavioural norms beyond the observance of administrative rules (Duvoux 2009; Chelle 2012).

If the notion of counter-conduct seems pertinent to qualify certain practices of the migrants, can it be extended to the entirety of the practices which we observe in the field? These counter-conducts and practices can only be analysed in relation to the conducts imposed by institutions. Hence, we analyse the conditions and processes of policy-making, the response of the Roma migrants when confronted with these policies and the moral, political or otherwise determined reasons which underlie their everyday dealings with institutions.

Our analysis largely builds on research conducted by Olivier Legros on policies towards the illicit camps and on Marion Lièvre's eight-year long investigation of individuals who have settled in the southern French city of Montpellier. Marion Lièvre has reconstructed the life trajectories of five women: Lenuța, Dorina, Cireașa, Aurelia, and Alba (Lièvre 2016a).[5] These Romanian women originally came from the same town (Brad) in Transylvania, although they used to live in different neighbourhoods. They arrived with their families in Montpellier in the mid-2000s, having passed through other French cities such as Marseille (Lenuța, Aurelia) and Toulouse (Dorina) or through Spain (Alba). Following several years of residential instability, economic precariousness and administrative interventions aimed at improving their circumstances, Alba and Dorina have obtained privately rented studio apartments and employment contracts. Lenuța has managed to get social housing, but her economic integration has remained blocked for administrative reasons. Meanwhile, Aurelia has benefited from support for 'integration through economic activities',[6] which recently allowed her to access social housing after eight years in the slums—or *platz*, if we choose to rather use the name given to them by the inhabitants themselves. Over the past eight years, Marion Lièvre has conducted informal interviews during her visits to the camps or while accompanying subjects to governmental offices in Montpellier. More recently, together with other researchers, we have mainly conducted research in the Paris region and in large towns such as Marseille, Bordeaux and Poitiers; these data complement our observations. These investigations have allowed us to conclude that Roma migrants, motivated mainly by the desire to improve their circumstances and social status, multiply their initiatives in order to reach their aims. Through their practices, they oppose the forms of conduct imposed by institutions only if the latter run counter to family life imperatives or significantly limit their opportunities.

Governing the Roma: The '*dispositif*' and Its History

The policies designed for Roma correspond neither to a pre-established plan nor to a premeditated vision. As these groups began to settle within French cities in the 1990s, and in particular in the 2000s, the public authorities conceived and implemented a set of regulation mechanisms which can be subsumed to a *dispositif*, as defined by Foucault (1994: 299, our translation): that is 'a resolutely heterogeneous set of discourses, institutions, architectural arrangements, regulatory decisions, laws, administrative measures, scientific statements, philosophical, moral, philanthropic propositions… The *dispositif* itself is the network established between these elements'. This *dispositif* is grounded in interpretative models stabilized by institutions, which devalue slums and their inhabitants.

In France, it is the residential practices of these groups rather than their transnational mobility which tend to be constructed as the main problem to be tackled. The slums are sometimes perceived as barriers to urban development, particularly in peripheral urban areas subject to regeneration (Legros 2010; Mireanu, Chap. 6, this volume; van Baar 2017). Furthermore, the reaction among city dwellers who live close to slums oscillates between hostility and empathy. For these reasons, their presence is the equivalent of an ordeal to political actors who, in their turn, want to reduce settling practices which, allegedly, cause a threat to public order and to society more generally.

These 'discursive practices of insecuritization' (Bigo 2011: 10) are sustained by a large array of arguments. For example, politicians such as Nicolas Sarkozy and Manuel Valls readily refer to law and order, pointing to the concentrations of caravans and shacks in French towns as 'zones of lawlessness' or 'illicit camps'. Moreover, they mobilize an ethnic category—in this case, the Roma—recognizing it as one particular and problematic European minority (Vermeersch 2006; van Baar 2011; Lièvre 2013). Finally, political actors frame their discourses on the basis of the official statistics about migratory flows and slum inhabitants provided by the administration.

Permeated with scientific or expert knowledge, as well as with legal and moral considerations, these securitarian discourses depoliticize social and political issues in a similar way to processes of racialization (Fassin and Fassin 2009). By denouncing the allegedly deviant or antisocial behaviour of migrants, those who have the 'power to name' (Varikas 2007) elude, and thus depoliticize, the domination processes at work in the production and reproduction of social inequalities. Moreover, by accusing the Roma of engaging in illegal practices, institutional actors release themselves from any responsibility toward the nationals of Central European or Balkan states with scarce financial means. Yet, by the application of the maximum period of transition measures as stipulated by the EU accession treaties of Romania and Bulgaria (until 31 December 2013), they have, de facto, blocked the access of these migrants to the waged labour market and its related social benefits. In the process, they have significantly contributed to the actualization and dissemination of the image of negative alterity, of which the Roma—inhabiting shantytowns, poor and antisocial—have ended up constituting its salient metaphor in the French context.

Based on a very negative view of the Roma, the dominant interpretative model radically impacts policy formation and transformation. In fact, it promotes and legitimizes the implementation of repressive and integrative policies whose combination ultimately ensures the filtering of these foreigners into a precarious situation. The repressive policies have included two different types: first, expulsion measures, whose main instrument is the 'obligation to leave French territory' (*Obligation à quitter le territoire français*, hereafter referred to as OQTF) and second, the campaign against illicit camps. With the official entry of Romania and Bulgaria into the EU in 2007, French state actors have sought to strengthen their arsenal of repressive measures.

For instance, regarding expulsion measures, in 2006, French law incorporated new conditions under which persons could be expelled from the country. These conditions—such as being considered a 'threat to public order'—were actually provided by European legislation itself.[7] The authorities also—and innovatively—introduced new legal measures which allow the state to remove persons from its territory, such as in cases in which they attempt to abuse the right to free movement, as stipulated by law 2011-672 (of 16 June 2011).[8] More recently, a ban on circulation within French territory has been introduced and added to the OQTF (law 2016-274, 7 March 2016). The fight against illicit camps has similarly resulted in new measures, such as the launch of three ministerial circulars in 2010,[9] and in a law, rejected by the Constitutional Council in 2011, which would have enabled the authorities to circumvent the court and turn the attempt to eliminate these camps into a merely administrative procedure (as has actually happened in Spain; see Vrăbiescu, Chap. 10, this volume).

These repressive policies can be seen as an integral component of the new borders (Fassin 2009) that the French authorities are currently erecting within the European area of free movement. Since the lifting of the transitional measures for Romanians and Bulgarians in 2014, nationals of these countries have been free to enter the labour market, although this change has not solved their problems. Indeed, by means of an economic activity, they must prove to institutional actors their eligibility for the integration trajectory, as well as for social aid and benefits. Moreover, administrative practices are not limited to formalized procedures; they include, in the treatment of the requests, the interpretation of field officers. This interpretation is based not only on a general suspicion of the poor (Duvoux 2012) but also on prejudices against the Roma. In Montpellier, for example, the examination of eligibility for social benefits is particularly meticulous when it comes to Roma migrants, as they are readily suspected of fraud. Last, but not least, we should also take into account the impact of the violence inflicted on migrants during police raids within camps, which usually takes various forms, ranging from expressions of contempt and insulting comments to the violation of privacy by intrusion into households.

Alongside policies of rejection and discrete—and therefore pernicious—discriminatory practices, the public authorities have sometimes set up housing and integration devices. These devices, which, until today, have been the result of local initiatives (Legros 2010; Olivera 2011; Lurbe i Puerto 2015), are now the subject of a national policy in the context of the inter-ministerial circular of 26 August 2012 on anticipating and supporting the eviction of illicit camps.[10] In addition to the provision of special funding for hosting projects, the current trend of interventions in housing entails the multiplication of serviced land temporarily provided to the inhabitants of the evicted slums—integration interventions which commonly involve the mobilization of common law devices (Mission Campements Illicites 2016). In this context, the mediation between the Roma and the institutional actors has become an important aspect of the policy (for the context of mediation, see also Kóczé, Chap. 9, in this volume). This mediation has led to experimentation in several local projects funded by the state and local authorities, such as those in Bordeaux, Montpellier and Poitiers.

In practice, these policies have constituted a *dispositif* in the Foucauldian sense. Those not included in or not fitting into a formal integration path officially have to be evicted. This process of filtering has recently increased, with an unprecedented cooperation between the Border Police (PAF), the

Family Allowances Fund (CAF) and the social services of the General Council. This collaboration effectively controls the right to residence, and, at the same time, the eligibility for social benefits. If Roma migrants wish to stay on French territory, it is consequently very likely that, in the more or less long term, they will be forced to enrol in the integration trajectories determined by institutional actors, which may significantly limit their freedom of choice.

The policies directed at the Roma mobilize a set of 'cognitive and normative frameworks' (Müller 2005: 174–175) which serve to structure and legitimize public action. The policies enacted in Roma camps from the 2000s onwards—in Île-de-France in particular—are grounded in relocation policies that were developed in the 1960s to host slum dwellers (Legros 2010; Costil and Roche 2015; Olivera 2015). Just like the 'transit housing projects', which were implemented to relocate the Algerian families living in slums fifty years ago, the 'Roma integration villages' (*villages d'insertion de Roms*) created by the state and municipalities since the mid-2000s constitute tools of selection and social control.

Other frameworks are more recent, such as the inter-ministerial circular of 26 August 2012 (Interministerial circular 2012) on anticipating and supporting the operations of eviction of illicit camps. This circular encourages institutional actors to opt for common law mechanisms for comprehensive support. Another recent framework is the reform of the social protection system, initiated in the 1990s and still ongoing, which inspired a number of the principles enacted within the policies targeting camps and their inhabitants: performance evaluation and benchmarking with regard to policy-making, or the individualization of integration trajectories and follow-up (Legros 2010; Clavé-Mercier 2014). Similarly, institutional actors tasked with implementing the relocation and integration can use current management techniques. For instance, in 2016, integration structures, together with the General Council of Essonne in the Paris region, organized job interview sessions to select candidates for employment and housing.[11]

These frameworks—whether old or new—certainly have institutional effects not only on professional practice but also on behavioural norms if the subjects wish to access employment and social benefits. For example, in most cases, if those who seek access to employment and social benefits use institutional networks, they must volunteer and then follow the rules set by the authorities and conveyed to them by mediators and civil servants. Enrolling one's children in school, following French language courses, integrating into the labour market and attending all the appointments set by the institutional actors and integration structures become compulsory as steps in the trajectories designed by the institutional actors.

In only a few years, the Roma have thus ended up constituting a policy target, mainly due to economic and residential practices seen as deviant by the host society. Partially unified thanks to circulars—in particular that of 26 August 2012 (Interministerial circular 2012) which is now the main framework for national and local integration measures—these policies remain marked by the heterogeneity of institutional mechanisms—categorizations, judicial procedures, administrative and professional practices, policy mechanisms, official discourses, scientific and expert knowledge—which relates them to the *dispositif*. Moreover, like the Foucauldian *dispositif*, these mechanisms interact, exerting a kind of power, whose effects we now examine on the practices of the population concerned.

Roma Migrants Facing Security Policies

In fact, Roma migrants multiply their initiatives not only to counteract or to try and reduce the most negative effects of security policies but also in order to access social benefits. This might suggest that their action in refusing to conform to the conduct imposed by institutions could be conceptualized as a counter-conduct *and* a tactic, when in fact, on the contrary, they are trying to penetrate the system in order to seize profitable opportunities.

Roma migrants often express their concerns about the threat of eviction in the form of recurring questions about planned operations and their date of execution. These questions undoubtedly express the climate of insecurity that prevails in the slums but they are also part of a form of anticipation, as these are people who usually prepare for their departure carefully. Indeed, they are often 'one squat ahead' (Cousin and Legros 2014: 1277). In some cases, they have even asked the civil constituents who support them to make enquiries with the land registry about the status of the disputed land. A few days before a scheduled expulsion, the families sort out their belongings, pack their bags, and may even seek support from the civil constituents whom they know with storing their belongings during their move. On the day, some of them may even negotiate with the workers who are carrying out the demolition for the preservation of construction materials from their shacks with a view to future reuse. In other cases, adapting to evictions entails revising their style of housing and even their residential strategy. In Montpellier, for example, several families have opted to live in a caravan (mobile home), which minimizes the effect of repeated expulsions: when evicted from one camp, they can simply move a little further. Moreover, there were no 'social orphans' (Ndione 1993) among the people we met, which means that they can always rely on relatives in France or Romania to host them in difficult times. Dorina, a victim of domestic violence, left Toulouse and joined a cousin who lived in Montpellier, while Victor and Traian moved in the opposite direction: sentenced to prison by the judge in Montpellier, they left to settle temporarily with their parents in Toulouse and Avignon. Other migrants may decide to return to Romania for a time, even if it means going back and forth more frequently. This is particularly the case for women and children.

These people seem to get used to the repeated eviction of the camps; they anticipate it and revise their strategies. In turn, they do not oppose resistance to institutional actors or the forces of order who carry out the evictions, but they repeatedly transgress property law and the rules which govern the occupation of land by persisting in the practice of squatting land or buildings. These practices are clearly inscribed within counter-conduct, since they counter not only the law but also the injunction to leave local territory. They are also reminiscent of the 'quiet encroachment of the ordinary' which, according to Asef Bayat, whose work concerns cities in the Middle-East, 'encapsulates the discreet and prolonged ways in which the poor struggle to survive and to better their lives by quietly impinging on the propertied and powerful, and on society at large' (2010: 14). Indeed, just like the popular urban practices that Bayat describes, they are simultaneously transgressive, multiple and recurrent, which probably also explains the persistence of building and land occupations, notwithstanding the intensification of evictions at the start of the 2010s (Cousin and Legros 2014).

If Roma migrants do not have a residence permit, they are constantly running the risk of wasting their efforts in their attempts to access rights and settle down. In particular, due to recent changes in migration policies, expulsion orders can have prejudicial consequences, both in psychological terms and for their administrative efforts. For example, the fact that the OQTFs are now accompanied by a ban on travelling within French territory[12] radically reduces the chances for these migrants to make round trips to Romania. Indeed, those who receive an OQTF run the risk of being denied re-entry to France once they have left the country, or of being detained upon their return. Similarly, the recently established collaboration between the Border Police, the Family Allowance Fund and the services of the General Council may encourage Roma migrants like Lenuţa to take steps towards integration in order to avoid the threat of expulsion.[13] Nevertheless, it is only parenthetically that we learn, for example, that OQTFs have been distributed on a *platz*, or that police controls are very frequent operations at major gathering places such as the Paillade market in the western suburbs of Montpellier. Similarly, it is during an exchange about renting an apartment that Lenuţa mentions the OQTF policy. She wants to rent an apartment for the beginning of the school year in September in order to avoid 'the season of the OQTF which will start again'. The expression that she uses admirably epitomizes this mastered temporality, signifying a kind of domestication and banalization of securitarian policies by the Roma migrants.

This relative self-assuredness can be explained by the fact that, so far, those whom we have met have adapted to the expulsion orders. If they do not purchase travel tickets, they re-mobilize their base by staying with relatives, or even return home to Romania, in order to avoid exceeding the three month period fixed by law.[14] From this point of view, expulsion orders have reinforced the already well-established practices of circular migration rather than promoting the definitive return to the countries of origin. Another counter-move consists of instrumentalizing integration policies in order to neutralize expulsion orders. Lenuţa's life trajectory is particularly illustrative of this practice. On the advice of a *Gadjo*, a non-Roma fellow citizen, Lenuţa sent her children to school, which enabled her to access social benefits. Yet this act was not sufficient to stop the threat of expulsion, and she therefore decided to undertake the necessary approach to administration and integration structures to gain access to employment and social housing. These moves were not so much motivated by material reasons—she is comfortable enough on the serviced land provided by the City of Montpellier where she lives—but in anticipation of a new distribution of OQTFs in the various slums within the urban agglomeration.

Finally, the impact of the internal borders (Fassin 2009: 6; see also van Baar 2017) erected by administrative and bureaucratic procedures should not be underestimated, because their 'practical effectiveness is considerable in terms of access to resources such as education, employment or housing' (Fassin 2009). Roma migrants frequently complain bitterly about these internal borders, because they see them as the cause of contempt and other forms of symbolic violence against them when they visit public administration offices. Most of the time, Roma migrants seek to be accompanied by civil constituents or mediators when they visit administrative offices. The former serve as a kind of moral guarantee for the migrants, setting up genuine communicative performances in order to convince the civil servants of the 'normality' of the migrants. This preponderance of intermediaries in administrative procedures might suggest that it is not the applicants themselves who are taking the initiative, but this is far from being the case. First of all, they are not discouraged, as the example of Cireașa shows. Although exhausted by all the efforts made in vain in the last few years, she has not given up: she carefully preserves all the addresses of the institutions which various people have given her, and, in turn, hands them over to the *Gadjé* (non-Roma) who visit her at home.

Moreover, it is not only the civil constituents or mediators who have to perform during the encounter with the administration. Some of the women, for example, compliment civil servants on their clothing or talk to them like long-standing acquaintances, and, in so doing, succeed in establishing a personal relationship, the aim of which is both to circumvent the rigidity of administrative procedures and to soften their domination (Dubois 2015). Last, but not least, Roma migrants seek to put pressure on the civil constituents and mediators, who are constantly solicited when they visit a *platz*. To this end, they may seek to distinguish themselves from their peers by highlighting the qualities that they assume non-governmental and institutional actors expect from them, in particular their concern for children's schooling and a taste for work and probity, thus devaluing others (Lièvre 2014, 2016b). Similarly, they do not hesitate to pit civil constituents and mediators against each other.

These practices, which undoubtedly require relationship skills as well as perseverance (see the example of Cireașa), relate more to tactics than to counter-conduct, since they are aimed at penetrating the social protection system and the integration structures by adopting what seems to them to be 'the right attitude' in front of their interlocutors, be they activists or institutional actors. Clavé-Mercier and Olivera (2016: 200, our translation) describe this in connection with the MOUS mechanisms set up in Bordeaux and in the Paris region[15]: 'without ever being impermeable to institutional requirements and constraints, the "beneficiaries"… do not, however, become passive recipients of "inclusive pacification' policies"'. In fact, once they are accepted into the integration structures, they can negotiate the established norms—for example, the number and length of visits to Romania—and exploit misunderstandings with social workers in order to maintain some room for manoeuvre (ibid.).

The previous reflections, mainly stemming from research in slums in Montpellier, join recent publications (Clavé-Mercier 2014; Legros and Olivera 2014; Benarrosh-Orsoni 2015; Clavé-Mercier and Olivera 2016) which question the idea that Roma migrants should be considered solely as the victims of security policies. Certainly, we have seen that they are put to the test and often deeply affected by policies and discriminatory practices, but, during their stay in France, they have tested practices amenable either to counter-conduct or to tactics. But these two types of conduct are not mutually exclusive: indeed, the analysis of life trajectories reveals that individuals oscillate between counter-conduct and tactics, adapting their practices to their objectives, as well as to the institutional context.

The Politics of Roma Migrants

Beyond the identification of practices enacted by Roma migrants, it is important to explore their foundations. Foucault (2007: 204–216) establishes a link between, on the one hand, counter-conduct, and, on the other hand, moral or political considerations, even if the enactors of counter-conduct do not explicitly display the latter. What does the observation of daily practices suggest? With what meanings do the Roma migrants infuse their practices when they speak of them?

More often than not, the people we have met do not infuse their action with political meaning. Moreover, in their struggle against the evictions from the camps or for the recognition of fundamental rights, it is rather the civil constituents who find themselves at the forefront, while the people threatened with eviction tend to avoid open confrontation with the institutional actors and the forces of law and order. Yet, the absence of a political project in the usual sense of the term does not exclude political expression or participation.

First of all, Roma migrants are not slow to denounce the administrative practices directed at them during exchanges with civil constituents and mediators. This discontent is expressed in several ways: while some mobilize the register of resignation and complaint, others use that of victimization. Yet others choose the register of injustice, underlining how institutions treat various Roma migrants differently. In any case, they approach intermediaries with virulence. In addition, they constantly ask questions about the steps to be taken or regarding the lawyers to be mobilized.

Mockery is another very common form of political expression which is found particularly in the nicknames that the Roma migrants give to certain civil constituents or mediators. In Montpellier, for example, one is nicknamed Jacques Chirac. In the same vein, humorously, and even with a hint of pride, people sometimes narrate the transgressions in which they engage in everyday life in the frame of their informal activities. For instance, Alba likes to recount how she negotiates everything she can with the drivers whose windscreens she washes at the traffic lights.

Finally, they claim their rights more and more frequently. They know that an employment contract, a pledge to recruit, or the status of entrepreneur can be used to contest an OQTF. This awareness can also lead to unprecedented forms of action. For instance, when the border police go to a *platz*, the inhabitants are less and less hesitant to express their dissatisfaction in front of policemen. In 2010, evicted for the umpteenth time from a squat, Lenuța decided to settle with her family in plain view in an urban car park. She then contacted local civil constituents and emphasized her profile as an integrated Roma to challenge the public authorities (Lièvre 2014). Her strategy of political communication has proved to be successful, because, a while later, she was able to settle on serviced land provided by the City of Montpellier.

The practices that we have described attest to a relationship to politics which, without doubt, can take many forms, not only as 'the infrapolitics of the dominated', which expresses a critique of power under disguise or using irony (Scott 2009 [1992]), but also as acts of speaking out publicly, such as Lenuța claiming her rights, or politicizing squat practices. In any case, Roma migrants are far from being apolitical, even when they are not openly criticizing the system but are first and foremost seeking to pursue the paths that they have traced for themselves.

The Roma migrants we met in Montpellier seemed to be animated by the same obsession: improving their living conditions. The migratory experience is, in essence, leaving your own country in search of better living conditions elsewhere. Our research tends to highlight the insufficiency of wages for poorly qualified or unqualified employment in Romania. Vlad, who was employed as a caretaker in a recycling centre in Brad for ten years, had enjoyed job security. He decided to leave for France in 2011 when his brother-in-law proposed that he join him to 'make scrap' together, for a salary ten times what he was earning in Romania (150 euros).[16] Mărețu, Cireașa's husband, also had a stable job in a public cleaning company, but the wages were 250 euros per month. Dorina had a contract as maintenance agent in a Brad supermarket, but she says that she was 'not being able to make ends meet' earning only 200 euros per month. So, after many trips between Romania and France between 2002 and 2007, she finally decided to settle in Montpellier.

The search for better earnings goes hand in hand with the desire to improve living conditions in their countries of origin. Alba and her partner Ionel lived for two years in Spain. Alba used to beg, while Ionel worked in the construction industry. After two years, the couple were able to set aside enough money to enlarge Alba's house, and even to buy a piece of land in Romania. Liviu, another man from the Brad region, already owned a house before he left Romania for France. Emigrating allowed him to pay for the construction of a gate and buy furniture. Dorina managed to install water and electricity in the family home. The projects seem to be never-ending, giving meaning to the migratory experience (see Benarrosh-Orsoni 2015, with regard to Romanian families who settled in Montreuil, in the Paris region).

Finally, our interlocutors want to take care of their relatives. Stories abound of money transfers to countries of origin.[17] The money sent is used for the subsistence of relatives or to finance costly medical treatment or surgery. The analysis of the life trajectories reveals the importance of their children's future in the eyes of the parents. For instance, schooling is not just a strategy to counter expulsion orders: Cireașa—just like Lenuța, Alba, Dorina et Aurelia—insisted that her children obtain their diplomas. The attachment of children to Montpellier and its region can also encourage their parents to consider permanent settlement in France in order to stay close to their offspring. In such cases, the house in Romania often becomes a second home.

Thanks to migration, the Roma thus seek to upgrade their social status while sustainably improving the living conditions of themselves and their relatives. In terms of their everyday life, a long-term project which involves the purchase, construction or expansion of a home in the region of origin encourages migrants to define three priorities: the accumulation of capital, local anchorage, and overcoming the barriers raised by institutional actors.

The accumulation of capital is achieved through various means. First, people seem always to be looking for opportunities, whether by exploring new territories, or through their choice of economic activities, which is rarely definitive. For instance, for some time now, several people have indicated that they have stopped dealing in scrap metal because 'it doesn't make money'. Montpellier attracted Lenuța and her family as a city because there were not many Roma there to compete with in their economic activities, in this case begging and cleaning windscreens on major roads. The accumulation of capital also implies limiting the costs associated with everyday life. For the Roma migrants in Montpellier, as for those surveyed in the Paris region (Asséo et al. 2015) or in Turin (Manzoni 2015), living in slums or shanty towns allows them to save on rent and other housing costs. All these practices are articulated at a family level. For instance, social benefits provide a regular income for Lenuţa, allowing her husband Andrei to undertake more risky but lucrative activities, such as informal trading in second-hand cars. From this perspective, obtaining an employment contract, even though financially unattractive, is not necessarily experienced as a submission to the conduct imposed by the institutional actors; it is also, and above all, a personal choice that is fully part of their migratory strategy. For instance, by conducting informal and formal activities at the same time, they establish a financial base that allows them to optimize the possibilities of accumulation at the level of the family.

Local anchorage is another priority for Roma migrants. Over the years, they have acquired good knowledge of local territories and their potential, which allows them to access economic resources with more ease (Rosa 2016). In addition, they have gradually become familiar with the institutional environment, and have developed links with the *Gadjé*, enabling them to develop economic activities and to take advantage of support in administrative dealings or to look for housing. However, infiltration of the local social networks does not necessarily entail questioning familial sociality, or pre-existing ties of belonging. In fact, for the people interviewed in Montpellier—as in the Paris region, Marseille or Bordeaux—the extended family remains the first circle of sociality. Events like baptisms or marriages remain privileged occasions to assert social position and to update the link with one's own kind.

Finally, the Roma migrants have to overcome administrative obstacles. The practices analysed in this chapter correspond well to the three major types of behaviour theorized by Albert Hirschman (1970): exit, loyalty and voice. Exit, or defection, is a silent practice (Neveu 2015: 28). It is expressed in the refusal of the poverty wages (*salariu de mizerie*) as they are perceived in Romania, but it can also be observed in the residential choices of certain migrants who, in their host countries, do not hesitate to change city if the administration causes them trouble or appears too finicky. Loyalty, for its part, is reflected in practices of deference or subordination towards civil constituents and mediators, but this apparent submission precludes neither irony nor ruse. Lastly, we emphasize that our interlocutors do not hesitate to raise their voice, especially when they have acquired rights. Roma migrants, therefore, play on several tables at the same time, moving effortlessly from one register to another, a practice which allows them, with varying degrees of success, to adapt their actions and discourse to every situation. More than the possession of knowledge or specialized know-how recognized as political in the host societies, it is ultimately this agility in strategic positioning which, from our point of view, constitutes the main political competence of Roma migrants.

Conclusion: Domestic Versus State Reason

The Roma migrants appear to be like other 'ordinary' migrants; they mainly seek to improve their living conditions and to upgrade their social status within the groups to which they belong. With this aim, they mobilize their kinship networks by preference, in particular those relatives who are able to offer anchoring points in the regions in which they settle, as well as a base to fall back on in case of difficulties. They also, simultaneously, offer newcomers their knowledge of local contexts. In order to regularize their administrative situation and to access financial resources, these migrants may also seek to penetrate the social protection system and various integration structures by resorting to tactics in the sense of De Certeau (1980), as well as by activating networks of intermediation made up of civil constituents, social workers, and mediators. The Roma migrants thus share a set of knowledge and practices, undoubtedly common to many migrants, which could be subsumed under the concept of domestic reason. This knowledge and these practices share three traits: firstly, they are narrowly linked within daily actions; secondly, they rely closely on familiar experience and thought frameworks; and thirdly, they are aimed mainly if not exclusively at the preservation of the family and the household.

However common or banal the domestic reason may appear, it is this reason which encourages Roma migrants to oppose institutions from time to time; yet they do so in particular ways. Confrontations are rare, since the latter privilege milder forms of conflict, such as the persistent practice of squatting, which is reminiscent of the quiet encroachment of the ordinary (Bayat 2010), or practices of circumventing and banalizing administrative obstacles. These practices are also counter-conducts: they express a refusal of the conduct and of the norms which institutions impose. Moreover, it has to be stressed that this counter-conduct is not continuous, but occasional: it takes place only when domestic reason is threatened by reason of the state writ large, understood as a set of means and knowledge mobilized to ensure the day-to-day preservation of the state (Foucault 2007). In fact, from the 2000s onwards, in order to control the mobility and residence of the new European poor and maintain order on French territory, the authorities have progressively set up a wide array of judiciary procedures and techniques, administrative and professional routines, and scientific and expert knowledge. Thus, the domestic reason of the Roma migrants does indeed oppose the reason of the state.

What, ultimately, are the effects of this conflictual interaction on the daily practices of these people? The reflections outlined here suggest a probable normalization of forms of conduct, since the ongoing toughening of migration policies increasingly encourages migrants to engage within integration trajectories following the methods established by institutions. Thus, state reason seems to be winning against domestic reason. However, Lièvre's research on the area of Montpellier shows, as does other recent work (Clavé-Mercier and Olivera 2016; Rosa 2016), that the Roma generally manage to maintain their room for manoeuvre within integration structures. Moreover, her work reveals that not all Roma migrants follow the integration trajectories laid out by institutions. Indeed, policies always affect their target groups, but these effects remain largely unpredictable, even in the case of seemingly limited opportunities.

Notes

1. This policy category designates migrants from Central European or Balkan states with scarce financial means living in precarious housing conditions and rightly or wrongly designated as 'Roma'.
2. We use the category 'illicit camps' as the official expression to designate groups of shacks on land occupied without authorization, and as a policy category. But we prefer to use the expression of 'slums', a category which, in our view, matches the realities we observed on our fieldwork better: housing affected by the precarity of the construction material and the land tenure, but that, unlike camps, is not perceived as ephemeral.
3. We define 'illegalization' as a process of categorization of human activity, which is realized through legal procedures and political speeches (see also, and more extensively, De Genova 2002).
4. By convention with the editors of the book, and considering the Anglo-Saxon language uses, we use the category of 'Roma migrants' to designate the migrants whom we have met during fieldwork; they come from Romania, have scarce financial means and live in precarious housing condi-

tions. Simultaneously, we acknowledge that the term 'Roma migrants' is the result of heterogeneous collective identification processes.
5. The names of the people and towns are anonymized.
6. Insertion through economic activities (IAE) comprises social and professional insertion measures proposed by private companies or specialized organizations to persons considered 'very far from employment'.
7. Art. 27.1 and 2 of the Directive 2004/38/CE of the European Parliament and of the Council of 29 April 2004 on the right of citizens of the Union and their family members to move and reside freely within the territory of the Member States.
8. Indeed, the law introduces a new article defining the different types of abuse of rights: 'renewing residence permits for less than three months with the aim of remaining on the territory, while the conditions required for a residence period above three months are not fulfilled' and 'residence in France essentially with the aim of acceding social benefits' (art L 511-3-1).
9. Ministère de l'Intérieur, 2010, Circulaire IOCK1016329J du 24 juin 2010 relative à la lutte contre les campements illicites, https://www.interieur.gouv.fr/Media/Immigration/Files/Circulaire-IOCK1016329J-du-24-juin-2010-relative-a-la-lutte-contre-les-campements-illicites (accessed 28 August 2017).
10. Circulaire interministerielle NOR INTK1233053C du 26/08/2012 relative à l'anticipation et à l'accompagnement des opérations d'évacuation des campements illicites http://circulaire.legifrance.gouv.fr/pdf/2012/08/cir_35737.pdf (accessed 28 August 2017).
11. See http://www.gouvernement.fr/campements-un-programme-d-insertion-par-l-emploi-dans-l-essonne (accessed 13 July 2017).
12. 'The administrative authority may, by a motivated decision, join to the OQTF... a prohibition to circulate on the French territory of a maximum length of three years' (law 2016-274, art. L. 511-3-2, of 7 March 2016).
13. This cooperation is recent, since before the end of the transitory measures in 2014, few migrants were accessing social benefits.
14. Article 551-1 and 561-2-6, CESEDA (Code for Entry and Residence of Foreigners in France and the Right of Asylum).
15. MOUS (Maîtrise d'oeuvre urbaine et sociale) is a mechanism of housing integration often used in interventions targeting Romanians in precarious housing (squats or camps).
16. 'Making scrap' is a term widely used among migrants and civil constituents to refer to the collection and preparation of recyclable metal products.
17. See, for instance, the ongoing research under the REPIN programme 'Roma migrants: from the processes of urban exclusion to resources for integration', CEE, Sciences Po, Paris, led by Tommaso Vitale, 2014–2017.

References

Asséo, H., et al., eds. 2015. *The Immigration of Romanian Roma to Western Europe*. Paris: Rapport FMSH.

Bayat, A. 2010. *Life as Politics*. Amsterdam: Amsterdam University Press.

Benarrosh-Orsoni, N. 2015. *Des maisonnées transnationales. Une migration rom dans ses routes, lieux et objets entre la Roumanie et la France* [Transnational Households: A Roma Migration in Its Paths, Places and Objects Between Romania and France], Unpublished Ph.D. Thesis. Paris: University of Paris Ouest-Nanterre.

Bigo, D. 2011. Le *"nexus"* sécurité, frontière, immigration: programme et diagramme [The 'Nexus' Security, Border, Immigration: Program and Diagram]. *Cultures & Conflits* 84: 7–12.

Chelle, E. 2012. *Gouverner les pauvres* [Governing the Poor]. Rennes: Presses universitaires de Rennes.

Clavé-Mercier, A. 2014. *Des Etats et des Roms* [On States and Roma], Unpublished Ph.D. Thesis. Bordeaux: University of Bordeaux II.

Clavé-Mercier, A., and M. Olivera. 2016. Une résistance non résistante? [A Non-resisting Resistance?]. *L'Homme* 3 (219–220): 175–207.

Costil, M., and E. Roche. 2015. Traiter les bidonvilles hier et aujourd'hui [Dealing with Shanty Towns, Yesterday and Today]. *Les Annales de la recherche urbaine* 110: 64–73.

Cousin, G., and O. Legros. 2014. Gouverner par l'évacuation? L'exemple des campements illicites en Seine-Saint-Denis [Governing by Eviction]. *Annales de Géographie* 700: 1262–1284.

Crawford, A., and S. Hutchinson. 2016. The Future(s) of Security Studies. *The British Journal of Criminology* 56 (6): 1049–1067.

De Certeau, M. 1980. *L'invention du quotidien*. t. I. *Arts de faire*. Paris: Gallimard.

De Genova, N. 2002. Migrant "Illegality" and Deportability in Everyday Life. *Annual Review of Anthropology* 31 (1): 419–474.

Dubois, V. 2015. *La vie au guichet* [Life at the Counter]. Paris: Editions Points.

Duvoux, N. 2009. *L'autonomie des assistés* [The Autonomy of the Assisted]. Paris: Presses universitaires de France.

———. 2012. *Le nouvel âge de la solidarité* [The New Age of Solidarity]. Paris: Seuil.

Fassin, D., ed. 2009. *Les nouvelles frontières de la société française* [The New Borders of French Society]. Paris: La Découverte.

Fassin, D., and E. Fassin, eds. 2009. *De la question sociale à la question raciale?* [From the Social to the Racial Question]. Paris: La Découverte.

Foucault, M. 1994. *Dits et écrits*. Vol. III. Paris: Gallimard.

———. 2007 [2004]. *Security, Territory, Population: Lectures at the College de France, 1977–1978*. New York: Palgrave Macmillan.

Hirschman, A.O. 1970. *Exit, Voice, and Loyalty. Responses to Decline in Firms, Organizations, and States.* Cambridge, MA: Harvard University Press.

Legros, O. 2010. *Les pouvoirs publics et les grands "bidonvilles roms" au nord de Paris (Aubervilliers, Saint-Denis, Saint-Ouen)* [The Public Authorities and the Large 'Roma Shantytowns']. *EspacesTemps.net.* Available at https://halshs.archives-ouvertes.fr/halshs-01088186/document. Accessed 7 July 2017.

Legros, O., and M. Olivera. 2014. La gouvernance métropolitaine à l'épreuve de la mobilité contrainte des Roms migrants [Metropolitan Governance Facing the Constrained Mobility of Roma Migrants]. *EspacesTemps.net.* Available at http://www.espacestemps.net/articles/les-pouvoirs-publics-et-les-grands-bidonvilles-roms-au-nord-de-paris/. Accessed 7 July 2017.

Lièvre, M. 2013. *Nationalisme ethnoculturel et rapport à la culture des Roms en Roumanie postcommuniste et multiculturaliste* [Ethno-Cultural Nationalism and Its Relation to the Culture of Roma in Post-communist and Multicultural Romania]. Unpublished Ph.D Thesis. Montpellier: University of Montpellier 3.

———. 2014. "Ceux-là sont peu soignés, peu débrouillards" ['Those Are Scruffy, Less Resourceful']. *Migrations Société* 26 (152): 103–118.

———. 2016a. *Trajectoires de vie de Lenuța, Cireașa, Alba, Aurelia, Dorina* [Life Trajectories of Lenuța, Cireașa, Alba, Aurelia, Dorina], Unpublished Research Report Within the Project ANR Marg-In.

———. 2016b. Roms roumanisés, *Ciurari, Ursari*: ethnicité et appartenances sociales [Romanianized Roma, *Ciurari, Ursari*: Ethnicity and Social Belonging]. *Revue Européenne des Migrations Internationales* 31 (4): 36–58.

Lurbe i Puerto, K. 2015. The Insertion of Roma in Sénart Project (2000–2007). *Identities* 22 (6): 653–670.

Manzoni, C. 2015. Between Constraints and Opportunities: Housing Careers of Roma Migrants in Turin. In *Migration: Energy for the Planet, Feeding Cultures*, ed. R. Cortinovis, 87–93. Milan: Fondazione Ismu.

Mission Campements Illicites. 2016. *Stratégie régionale pour les campements illicites en Île-de-France* [Regional Strategy for Illicit Camps in Île-de-France]. Île de France: Préfet de la région Île-de-France.

Müller, P. 2005. Esquisse d'une théorie du changement dans l'action publique [Sketch of a Theory of Change in Public Action]. *Revue Française de Science Politique* 55 (1): 155–187.

Ndione, E.-S. 1993. *Dakar, une société en grappes.* Paris/Dakar: Karthala/Enda.

Neveu, E. 2015. *Sociologie des mouvements sociaux* [Sociology of Social Movements]. Paris: La Découverte.

Olivera, M. 2011. *Roms en (bidon)villes* [Roma in (Shanty)Towns]. Paris: Ed. Rue d'Ulm.

———. 2015. 1850–2015: De la zone aux campements [1850–2015: From the Zone to the Camps]. *Revue Projet* 348: 7–16.

Rosa, E. 2016. Pratiques discrètes de résistance des migrants roms à Turin et à Marseille [Discrete Practices of Resistance of Roma Migrants in Turin and Marseilles]. *Cultures & Conflits* 101 (1): 19–34.

Scott, J. 2009 [1992]. *La Domination et les arts de la résistance* [Domination and the Arts of Resistance]. Paris: Editions Amsterdam.

van Baar, H. 2011. *The European Roma: Minority Representation, Memory and the Limits of Transnational Governmentality.* Amsterdam: F&N.

———. 2015. *Governing the Roma, Bordering Europe: Europeanization, Securitization and Differential Inclusion.* Paper Presented at the Global Governance, Democracy, and Social Justice Conference, Durham (NC), Duke University, April 7.

———. 2017. Evictability and the Biopolitical Bordering of Europe. *Antipode* 49 (1): 212–230.

Varikas, E. 2007. *Les rebuts du monde: figures du paria* [The Waste of the World: Figures of the Pariah]. Paris: Stock.

Vermeersch, P. 2006. *The Romani Movement.* Oxford: Berghahn.

PART II

Marketization

CHAPTER 5

The Invisibilization of Anti-Roma Racisms

Ryan Powell and Huub van Baar

Much academic attention has been paid to anti-Roma racisms and their relationship to processes and mechanisms of exclusion and marginalization, with accounts underscoring the interrelated need to challenge the *ongoing* processes of anti-Roma racism (Agarin 2014; McGarry 2017; Stewart 2012). Significantly less attention has been paid to the ways in which contemporary forms of anti-Roma racism differ from earlier ones, or to the reasons why they are so difficult to challenge.

In this chapter, we argue that the interrelated processes of neoliberalization and securitization have significantly contributed to the de-politicization of the root causes of the societal problems with which many Roma have been confronted since the fall of socialism, and consequently to the trend to 'invisibilize' the racial and racializing dimensions of the precarious conditions under which many Roma live. At the same time, we

---

We would like to thank Ana Ivasiuc and Regina Kreide for their valuable comments.

R. Powell (✉)
University of Sheffield, Sheffield, UK
e-mail: r.s.powell@sheffield.ac.uk

H. van Baar
Justus Liebig University Giessen, Giessen, Germany
e-mail: Huub.van-Baar@sowi.uni-giessen.de

© The Author(s) 2019
H. van Baar et al. (eds.), *The Securitization of the Roma in Europe*, Human Rights Interventions, https://doi.org/10.1007/978-3-319-77035-2_5

explain the ways in which the discourses and practices of racialization and racism have recently changed, leading to the emergence of neoliberal forms of racism which have hampered opportunities to address and challenge novel manifestations of anti-Roma racism.[1] Put differently, when it comes to the current living conditions of many of Europe's Roma—and particularly the poorest and most segregated among them—they have been faced with what David Roberts and Minelle Mahtani (2010: 250) call the simultaneous neoliberalization of 'race' and the 'racing' of neoliberalism.

We bring together two different bodies of literature and two different international case studies to articulate and answer these two key sets of questions. First, we examine critical race theories, and particularly David Theo Goldberg's work, to engage with debates about 'postraciality' (2015), a term used to denote the way in which neoliberal forms of racism tend to invisibilize and deny their own racial and racializing conditions. We use Goldberg's work to explain how racisms themselves have changed under neoliberal conditions and how these changes have affected the position of many Roma in Europe.

Second, we discuss the critical sociology of Loïc Wacquant to address the relevance and scope of what he calls the trend 'to invisibilize problem populations' (2009: 288). We mobilize Wacquant's work to explain the ways in which neoliberalization has significantly contributed to the racial problematization of minoritized groups such as the Roma and how this process and its outcomes vary across space. Wacquant's analytical concepts of the 'hyperghetto' and the 'anti-ghetto' are used to articulate two different but interrelated mechanisms of invisibilizing the conditions under which Roma marginalization and racialization occur in contemporary Europe. We interrogate two case studies, one from Slovakia and another from the United Kingdom (UK) to show how the two complementary dimensions of racial neoliberalism and neoliberal racism have ambiguously come together in the daily realities of many Roma.

POSTRACIALITY AND THE NEOLIBERAL DIMENSIONS OF RACISM

Several scholars of race have discussed how the practices and mechanisms of racialization and racism have shifted significantly under conditions of neoliberalization (Goldberg 2009, 2015; Lentin and Titley 2011).

Building on poststructuralist frameworks of analyses (e.g., Foucault 2004), they have convincingly argued that practices and discourses of racism and racialization have historically functioned differently in different societies and cultures and that these practices and discourses have also successfully adapted the production of their main 'referent object' to the prevailing kinds of racial classification of the time, be they biological, cultural, phenotypical or a mixture of these and other orderings.

Inspired by a typology put forward by Ghassan Hage (2014; see also Goldberg 2015: 29–30), we suggest that the various forms of racism that have been developed throughout history tend to fluctuate between the racisms of exploitation and expulsion.[2] The former is organized when the racialized are considered to be useful and valuable. This racism contributes to the marginalization of the racialized *within* society to guarantee that they have a place in it, even though they frequently have to live in highly precarious conditions that are often also based on forms of exploitation. The racism of expulsion, on the other hand, is deployed when the racialized are considered harmful or more harmful than useful. The racialized are marginalized *from* society, ensuring that they have no social, cultural, political or even physical presence in it. Expulsive racisms usually occur by means of forms of proactive population control, forced removal or complete denial through neglect.

The exploitative and expulsive usually operate interactively and, in their interaction, generate a mechanism of differential inclusion. For example, South Africa's apartheid regime, not to mention the past and current situation of many poor and segregated Roma across Europe. Indeed, the Roma were the target of radical forms of population control—including sterilization, child institutionalization and educational segregation—during state socialism, and have more recently frequently been evicted and deported in several European contexts, while their children continue to be disproportionately isolated in orphanages and 'special' classes or schools. In these examples, the forms of racism involved have overlapped significantly with serious forms of exploitation. While the Roma were exploited during socialism as unskilled labourers, their exploitation today can be related to their precarious status as migrant workers or day labourers in informal economies or to their ambiguous inclusion in workfare programmes (Legros and Lièvre, Chap. 4, this volume; Messing and Bereményi 2017; van Baar 2012; Vrăbiescu, Chap. 10, this volume).

In order to underline the new dimensions of contemporary racisms and the ways in which these are profoundly conditioned by neoliberalization,

Goldberg (2015: 106) suggests that we could add a third kind of racial articulation, which oscillates between the other two and which he relates to his notions of postraciality and 'racial dismissal': 'Postraciality amounts to a general social ecology within which race and racisms are supposedly outmoded but where, in fact, racist expression has gone viral'. Comparable to Wacquant's view of the neoliberal state, Goldberg situates postraciality, or neoliberal racisms, in a sociopolitical context within which a constant interplay between visibilization and invisibilization takes place. Wacquant (2009) conceptualizes the relationship between the unravelling of social protection schemes and the reinforcement and extension of security apparatuses in and beyond the neoliberal state as one in which, due to practices of securitization and penalization, the social problems of racialized populations have largely been invisibilized. Similarly, Goldberg (2016: 2279, our emphasis) argues that 'neoliberalisms have rendered *invisible*... any focus, especially critical, on *structural conditions reproducing inequalities* and the *varieties of violence to keep in place those suffering these conditions*'.

In the neoliberal context, practices of securitization enact specific 'regimes of visuality' (see van Baar et al., Chap. 1, this volume) in which the structural conditions under which marginalization and racialization occur tend to be concealed from sight, while the poor involved are simultaneously made *hyper-visible* through their criminalization and pathologization: 'In expanding its apparatuses of securitization both internally and externally, the [neoliberal] state can simply imply that it is responding to terrorizing violence and criminalization where they occur, inattentive to the racial identification of the perpetrators' (Goldberg 2015: 151; see also Ivasiuc, Chap. 11, this volume; van Baar and Vermeersch 2017).

Goldberg (2015: 108–09) explains that this nexus of racialization, visibilization and invisibilization not only goes hand in hand with the de-politicization of the more complex reasons for the marginalization of the poor but also with a racialized attention paid specifically to the precarious:

> [W]hat in fact has materialized is... a context-bound heightening of the raciality of some groups or subjects while rendering that of others (more) invisible. As the precarious have been made more so, their raciality has been (re-)emphasized... Whiteness, by contrast, has been rendered less racially visible... The less powerful and more marginalized... have had their racial characteristics emphasized, heightened, made a badge of identification. They have been made hyper-visible, even as the conditions producing their precarity have been increasingly ignored by policy-makers and their powerful supporters.

Goldberg (2009: 360–63) qualifies the postracial condition as one of 'racisms without racism', which is an expression used to critique those who suggest that we actually live in a postracial society in which the reference to race and racism is only relevant as something of the past. Therefore, according to Goldberg (2016: 2278, our emphasis), 'post-raciality enacts the *denial* both of the *perpetuation of any legacy of racism* and of *its own amounting to racism as such*'. He qualifies the postracial as 'the racial condition in denial of the structural' because, for the postracial, 'race is (to be) racially erased, racisms are thus rendered illegible, disparate impact is reduced to merely unfortunate happenstance' (2015: 34–35).

Yet, the reduction of structural inequality and the responsibilization of marginalized individuals relate not only to a form of racial dismissal through rendering the structural conditions of racism significantly invisible and illegible but also to a highly ambiguous logic of *reversal*, something that could also be clarified in the case of the Roma. A much-expressed opinion among some citizens and politicians is that their governments pay 'too much attention' to the challenges that are faced by ethnic or religious minorities such as the Roma and Muslims, the implication being that such groups benefit from preferential treatment (e.g., access to municipal housing) relative to the indigenous community. Many even believe that racism against 'whites' is as urgent a problem as is that against minorities or migrants. Populists and nationalists usually go a step further and suggest that preferential treatment for minorities—such as programmes of positive action—should cease, because they discriminate against whites. We have been able to observe several manifestations of this kind of viewpoint in Roma-related contexts, such as during the anti-Roma demonstrations, public actions and riots in a number of Central and Eastern European countries in which the Roma are blamed for all kinds of social problems (Stewart 2012; van Baar 2014).

In these and similar cases, which Huub van Baar (2014) has conceptualized as the emergence of a 'reasonable anti-Gypsyism', we can observe a racial reversibility that 'involves the insinuation that those targeted by racist expression and practice are actually the ones responsible for having perpetrated racial wrongdoing in the first place' (Goldberg 2015: 89–90). In the case of the Roma, this kind of racial reversibility has become quite prominent and follows a logic according to which one would be rightfully entitled to act against the Roma and treat them differently. This reverse logic works alongside the territorialization and culturalization of complex societal problems: it is not the Roma who are confronted with the serious, large-scale violation of their rights, but it is the Roma themselves—their supposed criminal and anti-social behaviour and the bad environment in which they live—who have violated rights and failed in their duties (cf. van Baar 2011a: 243–44).

Characteristic of this line of racial argumentation is that the complex historical, socioeconomic and political conditions which have led to contemporary practices of racial discrimination and marginalization are usually disregarded. When, in the case analysed by Ana Ivasiuc in this volume (Chap. 11), the Roma are accused of polluting the air that 'we' (the members of the majoritarian society) breathe and the water that 'we' drink, the environmental injustice suffered by the Roma themselves is not taken into account at all. In several Central and Eastern European (CEE) countries, impoverished and segregated Roma source wood from the forest to cook with and heat their homes, but when they are accused of theft from state-owned forests or from private property and are fined or even imprisoned for this reason, we are often faced with a similar neglect of the political and economic circumstances under which these practices occur.

More generally, we could state that in these and similar cases, we are dealing with a dual logic:

> Racial dismissal trades on the dual logic of reversal. It charges the historically dispossessed as *the now principal perpetrators of racism*, while *dismissing as inconsequential and trivial the racisms experienced by the historical targets of racism*. In doing so, racial dismissal renders opaque the structures making possible and silently perpetuating racially ordered power and privilege. (Goldberg 2015: 30, our emphasis)

For Goldberg (2009: 21), any serious and effective articulation of antiracism 'requires historical memory, recalling the conditions of racial degradation and relating contemporary to historical and local to global conditions'. Thus, one of the conditions of postraciality is the trend towards forgetting, downplaying or even erasing the histories and memories related to racisms and their legacies.

Ghettoization and the Spatial Dimensions of the 'Racing' of Neoliberalism

While Goldberg's theoretical intervention is particularly useful in underscoring the shifting practices and mechanisms of racism under conditions of neoliberalization at a *general* level, it is less able to account for significant variations in the spatial manifestations of similar processes within different national contexts, and particularly *within* and *across* national territories.³ In the case of the European Roma, while there are general attitudes, sentiments and responses towards them which are seemingly ubiquitous, there are also key differences in terms of the nature, logic and practices of separation, from one state or region to the next, which are shaped and informed by historical relations and societal variations. In this regard, it is useful to complement and synthesize Goldberg's analysis of neoliberal, postracial racisms with Wacquant's relational, theoretical and historicized concept of the 'ghetto'.

We do not seek to classify or develop a typology of Roma separation that is generalizable across Europe here, nor do we argue that all Roma 'settlements' constitute ghettos. Rather, we suggest that Wacquant's empirically and historically informed concepts of the 'ghetto', the 'hyperghetto' and the 'anti-ghetto' are useful analytical devices which can help in understanding the different spatial manifestations of Roma separation and invisibilization discernible across Europe (Powell 2013; Powell and Lever 2017). Wacquant's analysis also draws attention to the role of the state in contributing to the demise, denigration and stigmatization of the ghetto. In this sense, we see the *concept* of the ghetto as 'a powerful [comparative] tool for the social analysis of ethnoracial domination and urban inequality' (Wacquant 2004: 2).

Wacquant (2004: 5) convincingly critiques the conflation of the ghetto with the ethnic cluster or enclave:

> It is fruitful to think of the ghetto and ethnic cluster as two ideal typical configurations situated at opposite ends of a continuum along which different groups can be located or travel over time depending on the intensity with which the forces of stigma, constraint, spatial confinement, and institutional duplication and completeness coalesce with each other and impinge upon them.

When we approach the spatial marginalization of Roma from this standpoint, we not only appreciate the differing contexts of their respective seclusion and separation but are also directed towards the mechanisms and processes which mediate that separation and give rise to it. Wacquant (2012) has suggested that the Roma of CEE represent a European exception due to the fact that there is a discernible trajectory towards segregation and ghettoization, whereas *de*-segregation is the dominant trend for other ethnic minority groups within Europe. But his concept can also be applied to Western Europe and thereby provides a relational framework with which to unpick the variable trajectories of Roma marginalization across the continent, while also highlighting 'common threads and recurrent properties' (Wacquant 2004: 2).

A ghetto is defined in terms of both space and groups and in this regard has two defining characteristics: a single ethnic group forms the entire population of the ghetto area/s, and a significant part of that group resides in such areas (Peach 1996). This basic definition immediately draws attention to the purpose of separation and seclusion: the ghetto prevents its subordinate inhabitants 'from fanning [out] into the city' and is synonymous with stigma, constraint and spatial confinement (Wacquant 2008a: 114). In this sense, the notion of ethnically diverse neighbourhoods—such as the French *banlieues* or inner city areas in the UK—as ghettos is erroneous (Wacquant 2008a, b). Rather, these neighbourhoods can be seen, in Wacquant's terms, as 'anti-ghettos' (2008a: 115); they are characterized by 'ethnic heterogeneity, porous boundaries, decreasing institutional identity and an incapacity to create a shared cultural identity'. Unlike the communal Black ghettos of the 1950s in the US, the *anti*-ghetto is more fragmented, with rapid population change, transience and antagonisms between different ethnicities and religions countering the shared cultural identity often found within a ghetto. As we shall see, this anti-ghetto notion matches the situation of many of the Roma clustered in specific neighbourhoods in the UK, who may well be stigmatized, but who are by no means isolated in 'containers' separated from the wider urban fabric.

In contrast, the current situation of many CEE Roma, in Slovakia for example, has more in common with the scenario detailed in Wacquant's understanding of the 'hyperghetto'. For him, de-industrialization and state withdrawal were key factors in the transition of the Black US communal ghetto of the 1950s into the 'hyperghetto' of the contemporary period. This draws attention to the exploitative nature of the ghetto, as the former functioned separately as a Black space within the white and supplied the factories with a large pool of unskilled labour while also providing the basis for 'parallel institutionalism' in terms of the development of separate minority institutions.

CEE Roma were similarly exploited for their labour under communism, but also suffered economically as a result of post-1989 de-industrialization and de-collectivization in agriculture, which marked a shift towards the mere spatial management of Roma marginality and poverty as opposed to its alleviation. In both cases, the significant loss of economic function was also accompanied by state and institutional withdrawal, resulting in the organizational desertification of the ghetto and in the diminution of opportunities to organize parallel minority institutions, developments which further contribute to territorial stigmatization:

> In cases where its residents cease to be of economic value to the dominant group, ethnoracial encapsulation can escalate to the point where the ghetto serves as an apparatus merely to warehouse the spoiled group or prepare it for the ultimate form of ostracization, i.e., physical annihilation. (Wacquant 2004: 6)

In the examples that follow, we draw upon Wacquant's concepts of the hyperghetto and anti-ghetto alongside Goldberg's notion of racial dismissal in developing a theoretical synthesis. Such an approach can account for the ubiquitous invisibilization of anti-Roma racisms, while also acknowledging the spatial variations in terms of the differential treatment and extent of Roma separation between European Nation States.

'THE PREFERRED MINORITY': THE RACIALIZATION OF ROMA IN CONTEMPORARY SLOVAKIA[4]

In 2015, the mayor of the Slovak town of Medzilaborce proposed that the municipality should subcontract a private security company (PSC) to deal with its 'Roma problem', the town's 'inadaptables', who live in three different segregated localities. The problems with these Roma, he explained, emerged particularly during what is referred to locally as the 'golden week'. This is the week in which the unemployed receive their social benefits, and the Roma among them immediately spend these on alcohol, drugs or gambling, creating problems of public order. The mayor suggested that it would be less costly to hire a PSC than to reinstate a municipal police force to deal with these problems; indeed, the police would have to be paid for the entire month and undertake other duties, whereas a PSC could be subcontracted only for the 'golden week' and would focus exclusively on 'the Roma problem'.[5]

The mayor's proposal is a good example of how, in the context of the neoliberalization of social and penal policies in Slovakia, a form of 'selective "deregulation"' would help to reform the provision of security, the idea being not to 'roll back the state *in general* but to roll back (and restructure) *a particular kind of state*' (Peck and Tickell 2007: 29). In this way, the state's social (welfare) functions could be reduced, its penal functions expanded, and the securitization of 'problem' populations increased:

> [Accordingly] the provision of security has been depoliticized and transformed from a problem to be solved by the welfare interventions of the state into *technical problems* to be *managed* through *security logics*. Social responsibility and direct state intervention have thus been supplemented… by *techniques of crime control* based on *efficiency, surveillance* and *spatial design*. (Abrahamsen and Williams 2011: 69–70, our emphasis)

The mayor of Medzilaborce, who as a member of the ruling populist party (*Smer-SD*) of Slovakia's Prime Minister Fico, claimed that Slovak society has no voice in how to solve the Roma problem: if one really wanted 'to deal with the Roma problem', one was accused of racism and that the 'real problems' were therefore unsolvable. What these 'real problems' were remained somewhat unclear, though one perceived issue was welfare dependency, which manifested as a disincentive to work and caused various public order concerns. Under these circumstances, he suggested, the Roma problem would only worsen, if not escalate catastrophically. He was not able to indicate what such a catastrophe would look like, but he suggested that something similar to what happened in 2004 might happen again, only it would be 'more radical'. In 2004, the Slovak government reformed the system of social benefits and cut several welfare provisions, measures that had a profound impact on the poor and on large Slovak families in particular, including many Roma ones. People began to demonstrate against these measures in what was quickly framed as 'Gypsy unrest'. Shops were looted in some towns, and, for the first time since Slovakia's independence in 1993, the army was mobilized to restore order, a measure that resulted in the heightened surveillance of segregated Roma settlements in particular (van Baar 2012).

During a qualitative analysis of the security situation in several eastern Slovak municipalities, carried out between 2014 and 2017 (see note 4), municipal authorities generally interpreted the question of 'security' as one of public security, crime and Roma-related issues, rather than, for instance, as a question of institutional corruption, social or human security, or of a generally safe situation for all irrespective of their background. Many of these authorities suggested that Roma-related crime mostly involved petty crime. The mayor of Medzilaborce was no exception to this opinion. Nevertheless, he suggested that 'Roma who steal wood from the forest [are] a really serious issue of national importance' which should be dealt with radically through some sort of zero tolerance approach.

The call for this kind of punitive populism, prominent across Slovakia, is a good example of how the *de-politicization* of the provision of security by rendering it technical—that is, suggesting that it is not political, but merely a technical issue—runs concurrently with the trend towards the *politicization* of security and crime through their moralization, and thus also with the one-sided and excessive focus on the behaviour of the Roma in political, public and policy debates about security. This tendency involves 'treating crime as a question of individualized *moral* responsibility rather than as a consequence of social disadvantage or deprivation' (Abrahamsen and Williams 2011: 72), and facilitates the criminalization of poverty and the representation of those who are involved in minor offences 'as wilfully recalcitrant individuals wholly responsible and morally culpable for their own actions and deserving retributive justice and/or requiring removal from society' (ibid.).

In Slovakia, but also more generally, this trend proceeds in tandem with imagined fears and populist demands: calls for the strict application of the law (as distinct from social policy); the exoneration and favouring of the law-abiding (non-Roma), who have become victims of the minor offences (committed by the Roma); the social production of and focus on the fear of becoming a victim; and the related call for more security measures and a larger police presence on the ground. In line with this trend, in the winter of 2016–17, Slovakia's PM Fico announced the end of tolerance and political correctness in dealing with Roma from the segregated and marginalized settlements which could generally be understood as hyperghettos. 'The next [Roma] generation that does not want to work is growing up. Some restrictive measures are required', said Fico, during a party congress dedicated to issues to be addressed in 2017, adding that the 'abuse of the social system' will no longer be tolerated (TASR 2016). When František Tanko, the chair of a Roma political party (*Únia Rómov na Slovensku*), asked for clarification, the Government's Office stated:

> A restrictive and punitive attitude… will be applied to people who reject job offers, abuse the welfare system, and who, by their way of life, disturb peaceful living in towns and villages. The prime minister stands behind this statement and doesn't intend to change his attitude towards this matter. (TASR 2016)

Later, the Minister of the Interior specified that, in some 200 Roma settlements which had been designated as 'problematic', there would be a 'significant increase of police performance', and they would have 'greater presence, and improve the situation regarding the prevention of crime' (Kováč 2017, our translation). Put differently, the radical securitization of the (most segregated) Roma and the criminalization of their poverty results in the territorialization and culturalization of the complex socio-economic and political problems with which many Roma in Slovak society are faced. This leads the government to opt for a form of penalization in which territorial stigmatization and neoliberal racialization are strategically combined. This development is strongly linked to the articulation of what Goldberg (2015: 89–90) qualifies as de-historicized 'postracial reversibility', which 'involves the insinuation that those targeted by racist expression and practice are actually the ones responsible for having perpetrated racial wrongdoing in the first place'. For instance, the director of police of one of the largest eastern Slovak counties stated that the 'real victims' were the immediate (non-Roma) neighbours of the Roma settlements, because 'they suffer the most'.

'The Roma are a nation that will always achieve its aims' the mayor of Medzilaborce stated, in his explanation of the 'real' problems with the Roma. 'They are the preferred minority; their number will grow and they will gradually expel the non-Roma, which is actually already happening. Our citizenry ages and young non-Roma leave Medzilaborce to look for opportunities elsewhere.' In his view, the Roma were responsible for the town's 'decay' and for the changes in its demography and ethnic composition; the Roma were making the town less attractive and less safe, and would even contribute to 'expelling' non-Roma from the municipality.

This last comment is particularly remarkable, because a significant number of the poorest and most segregated Roma currently living in Medzilaborce are still dealing with the consequences of a series of expulsions from villages in the immediate surroundings of Medzilaborce which took place in the 1990s. Contrary to what the mayor and other bureaucrats have reported, Roma activists and the Roma living in Medzilaborce's ghettos generally considered their relationship with the police to be fairly acceptable, even though they had recently been confronted with an aggressive police raid and harassment. Their demonization by the mayor and the long history of the way in which they had been dealt with by local governments were now considered to be the principal problems.

These Roma were originally given permanent residence status in Rokytovce and Nagov, two villages in the then municipality of Krásny Brod immediately adjacent to Medzilaborce, in 1981, after they began working for the local collectivized farm, which also provided them with housing. With the fall of the communist regime, this agricultural cooperative collapsed at the end of 1989, at which point these Roma lost their jobs and were compelled to leave the cooperative in pursuit of jobs elsewhere. Eighteen months later, they returned to Rokytovce and Nagov, but the respective municipal authorities prevented the families from resettling there. In the six years that followed, the Roma concerned moved frequently from one town to another in search of a secure place to live. At the beginning of this period, the Department of Social Affairs of the county of Medzilaborce provided trailers for the families to rent, but none of the villages where the Roma tried to settle permitted them to do so on municipal ground.

In 1997, these Roma started to build small shacks on agricultural land in Čabiny, a village south of Medzilaborce, Rokytovce and Nagov, at which the mayors of several villages met to discuss this 'crisis' situation. The mayor of Čabiny warned of a possible negative response from non-Roma in the village, and in June, the Municipal Council of Rokytovce adopted a resolution prohibiting the Roma from settling there and enabling any transgression to be dealt with by expulsion. In July, the Municipal Council of Nagov adopted a similar resolution. A few days later, on 21 July 1997, self-built Roma dwellings in Čabiny were set fire to, but the perpetrators were never found and the crimes were not properly investigated (ERRC 1997).

The banning of the Roma from these towns and their repeated expulsions, led some regional human rights organizations to bring the case to court. Three of the Roma individuals affected filed an application with the European Court of Human Rights in Strasbourg in March 1999, which led, also under pressure from some national Slovak authorities, to the lifting of the bans in the two villages. Nevertheless, the Roma involved continued to face opposition to their presence, and when the then Slovak government allocated funds to house these homeless Roma in a building in a remote industrial zone of Medzilaborce, the municipal authorities collected a petition of some 2000 signatures in an attempt to block the national government's initiative. Despite the petition, the Roma were eventually tolerated, although they have never been given official residence status in Medzilaborce.

Today, this group of Roma, which has grown to some sixty members, lives in a privately owned, dilapidated building which is considered illegal, and which has no access to electricity, gas or water. There is one water pump for general use, and since there have been regular outbreaks of hepatitis in this housing block, the municipal authorities have recently provided the Roma with some equipment to avoid the spread of this disease. Since they have no possibility of finding better housing in Medzilaborce or elsewhere in the region—even in the country—because of the long history of opposition and violence against them and their presence, they live in a more or less permanent state of evictability (van Baar 2017). Indeed, when the municipality decides that the building in which they live is no longer suitable for habitation (in fact, the municipality has already done so) or when the private owner revokes their status of tolerated, yet, unrecognized inhabitants of Medzilaborce, the story of their rejection and nomadization—being given no shelter and therefore being de facto turned into 'drifting' people—could easily resume (van Baar 2011b; De Genova, Chap. 2, this volume). As the only employed social worker in the town stated in the autumn of 2016, more than 25 years after their history of eviction and denial began, 'nothing substantially can be done for these people'.

Other Roma living in Medzilaborce are also currently faced with the lack of preschool facilities; the municipality sold the centrally located buildings in which preschool facilities used to be organized. Similarly, the Roma complain that the municipality also privatized the building in which they used to be allowed to organize cultural and leisure activities, and the new owner demands such high rents that use of the facility is practically impossible. Currently, the municipality's stated intention is to accommodate both the preschool and cultural activities in a Roma community centre that was recently opened in the isolated industrial zone where many of Medzilaborce's Roma live. But this community centre has recently been left closed due to administrative problems regarding the allocation of funding. Since October 2015, out of the nine social workers and seven community workers who were originally involved, only one social worker is still employed, 'an undoable job'.

The situation in Medzilaborce clarifies two key issues of wider relevance. First, the more recent history of the ways in which the Roma have been confronted with ongoing securitization and racialization is integrally embedded in the complex and influential histories of post-1989 socioeconomic and political transformation and 'backdoor nationalism' (Fox and

Vermeersch 2010), such as the reform of late communist welfarism; sweeping rounds of privatization; the de-centralization of governance and decision-making; the manifestation of institutional and everyday racisms towards the Roma and the mass unemployment and resulting deprivation of many Roma. Second, the neglect and denial of the long history of Roma stigmatization has enabled and conditioned the current irregularization of the status of the Roma and their racial problematization in terms of security threats and their being viewed as aliens who are considered as 'fundamentally different' from their non-Roma neighbours. The radical, racialized segregation of the poorest among the Roma, and the post-1989 combination of their alleged socioeconomic 'worthlessness' and societal 'harmfulness', have turned what are referred to as 'marginalized Roma communities' in Slovak bureaucratic discourse into Wacquantian hyperghettos. The strategic penalization of 'problem' inhabitants, and thus the criminalization of their poverty, has resulted in the explicit denial and reversal of the neoliberal racisms and racializations that affect them.

'SLUMS', EXPULSIONS AND THE MOBILIZATION OF ANTI-ROMA SENTIMENT IN THE UK

The housing situation of Roma in the UK differs markedly from that seen in CEE countries, and from the experiences of marginalized Roma in, for example, Italy, France or Spain (cf. the contributions of Ivasiuc (Chap. 11), Legros and Lièvre (Chap. 4), and Vrăbiescu (Chap. 10), to this volume). In contrast to the processes of spatial segregation and ghettoization in Slovakia for example, migrant Roma in the UK are subsumed within a wider category of urban poor, for whom access to stable housing and the formal labour market has become increasingly constrained in the contemporary period. The global financial crisis of 2007–08 has exacerbated existing trends for households at the lower end of the housing market (i.e., the *least powerful*). Two major changes are important here: the explicit shift from a liberal welfare state to a neoliberal housing policy that denigrates social housing and privileges home ownership, and the relatively recent migration of Roma migrants within a fairly short period, post-EU enlargement, and their perceived concentration in certain urban neighbourhoods.

David Robinson's (2016) notion of 'progressive' and 'retrogressive' housing convergence in Britain is instructive in this regard. He highlights a discernible shift in the housing opportunities, patterns and trends of ethnic minority households in the UK in recent years. From the 1960s to the early 2000s, immigrant households, many of whom had migrated from former British colonies, experienced a relative convergence in housing opportunities and outcomes driven by race relations legislation, ethnic minority activism and advocacy and persistent and hard fought challenges to racism. These trends represented a *relative* 'slow march' towards housing equality and social integration as access to secure housing became more attainable. This produced much more favourable outcomes for migrant households, with the opening up of housing options and upward social mobility paving the way for access to social housing and home ownership. These trends were clearly progressive in the sense of greater housing security, genuine housing choice, improved conditions and the securing of wider citizenship rights. In this regard, many migrant households were able to close the gap in terms of housing inequalities. In the period since the year 2000, however, Robinson argues that this convergence has been flipped for new migrant households, of which those migrating from CEE countries, including the Roma, represent a sizeable proportion.

Since the early 1980s, social housing provision has declined from a peak of 30% of all dwellings in the UK to just 18% in 2014. The private rented sector (PRS), on the other hand, has more than doubled in size over the last 20 years, and now accounts for 19% of all households. The decline in home ownership since 2007 and the entrenched issues of affordability in many parts of the country, particularly for first-time buyers, have resulted in intense competition for PRS properties between those households who, in earlier periods, would have found access to social housing or home ownership far easier. The onset of these trends can be traced back to 1980 and the shift to an explicit neoliberal housing policy, one which involved the privatization of social housing and the privileging of home ownership— for example, the Right to Buy policy whereby municipal housing tenants could purchase their homes at discounted prices—as part of a wider process of housing commodification.

This development has been further accentuated in the current period by the ongoing welfare reforms since 2010, particularly cuts to Housing Benefit (HB), which have resulted in the increasing stigmatization of some households and groups on the part of private landlords, as the cuts to HB have left many households with a significant shortfall in terms of meeting their rental payments (Powell 2015). As a result, households with the least resources—the least powerful—are increasingly channelled to the bottom of the PRS, as many landlords refuse to let properties to tenants who are not in work or to immigrant households. This limits housing options to very poor-quality PRS accommodation, often in denigrated locations marked by 'territorial stigmatization' (Wacquant 2007, 2008b).

Unlike the situation in other European countries, the housing fortunes of the Roma in the UK increasingly resemble those of the marginalized white working-class in de-industrialized spaces, as the processes which serve to exclude apply equally to both, giving rise to housing insecurity and precarity. But while Roma segregation and separation may be less overt and visible than in other EU countries, recent years have seen a more explicit *mobilization of disidentifications*[6] (De Swaan 1997) for Roma linked to EU enlargement, Brexit and the framing of Roma mobility as a security *threat* (Fox et al. 2012; New Keywords Collective 2016). 'Perceived threat fuels fear of loss – of power, of resources, of competitiveness, of life itself – and their attendant antagonisms and aggressivities' (Goldberg 2009: 29). This is evidenced in the transitional arrangements placed on EU migrants from CEE countries, justified on account of fears over corruption and organized crime (i.e. securitization). Citizens of countries which joined the EU in 2004 and 2007 were not afforded full working rights in many older EU Member States and thereby faced a series of citizenship restrictions 'exposing a number of contradictions at the heart of the European citizenship project' (O'Nions 2014: 5). The employment restrictions for Bulgarian and Romanian citizens, for instance, remained in place in the UK until 2014. Since then, the Roma migrants in the UK have been constructed as the perfect 'folk devil' for the xenophobic media and were central to discourses in the 2016 EU referendum campaign in the UK. Familiar stereotypical tropes of criminality and benefit fraud were relentlessly employed by dominant right-wing media sources which served to deny the long history of the persecution of European Roma, with *the Roma themselves framed as the perpetrators*, 'stealing from taxpayers'.

Again, this discourse bears some resemblance to that applied to white working-class benefit claimants, with both imagined groups blamed for their own predicament and invariably contrasted with the 'hard working families' looking to make ends meet in austere times. A newspaper report in the run up to Brexit 'revealed' how Roma families were sending welfare payments received in the UK back to Romania, allowing them to construct £500,000 mansions—'homes millions of hard-working British families can only dream of' (Sheldrick 2016). For example:

We need Brexit to stop Roma gangsters from stealing taxpayers' money (*Daily Express*, 29 March 2016)

REVEALED: How YOU pay for Roma gypsy [sic] palaces – UK benefits funding Romanian mansions (*Daily Express*, 5 April 2016)

Such discourses serve to deny the possibility of upward social mobility for the Roma, of the acquisition of wealth and assets and of a better standard of living. Those Roma families not conforming to the dominant, degraded and inferior perception held of them are automatically categorized as deviant, criminal and conniving. The ghettoized conditions of many Roma communities in CEE countries is not seen as cause for concern, with Roma migration *de*-historicized and articulated primarily in securitizing terms.

The concentration of Roma households within the notoriously under-regulated PRS serves to invisibilize the plight of the Roma; they have less contact with municipal authorities than they might as social housing tenants, and given their persistent experiences of hostility, they tend to engage with authority structures informally and on their own terms. In this sense, the privatization and rationalization of housing provision has served to *privatize the Roma condition*. Dominant discourses focus on specific urban neighbourhoods where there are discernible concentrations of recent Roma settlement, such as Govanhill in Glasgow and Page Hall in Sheffield (Clark 2014; O'Nions 2014). In the absence of a coherent or effective Roma strategy alongside severe austerity, Roma issues and challenges are transposed from a national (state) issue to a local (neighbourhood) one. Local authorities, community groups and the voluntary sector are left with the responsibility for Roma integration within neighbourhoods which correspond to Wacquant's (2008a) concept of anti-ghettos: porous and ethnically diverse areas in which the most marginalized sections of society increasingly concentrate.

This differs markedly from the 'hyperghettoization' experienced by many Roma in Slovakia. This context creates tensions within those neighbourhoods associated with Roma settlement, largely related to the presence of Roma within public space. While Roma and non-Roma antagonisms are more open within some CEE countries, these racisms are invisibilized in the UK through the framing of neighbourhood problems, which appeal to notions of civility and imagined national values of 'Britishness'. Roma cultural differences in intergenerational mixing and the use of neighbourhood space are presented as problems of anti-social behaviour, nuisance, incivility and low level crime: *Roma become the problem* and the non-Roma residents of those neighbourhoods become the 'victims'. For example, the widely reported tensions in Page Hall, Sheffield, in 2013 were largely an over-amplified media creation, but quickly drew comment from prominent politicians eager to point the accusatory finger at the Roma community, which, in turn, perpetuated the perception of that supposed 'problem'. In a recent Government-commissioned review on integration, Page Hall is singled out to illustrate the potential problems caused by the 'sudden growth' in the Roma population there (Casey 2016: 37). Such responses serve to heighten fears and anxieties and, in Page Hall, resulted in informal neighbourhood surveillance. Furthermore, many accounts neglect to acknowledge that Roma families are frequently and involuntarily housed in unhealthy, overcrowded, slum conditions (Searle 2017). So while, on the surface, migrant Roma in the UK may seem fairly well integrated in housing terms, this relative *spatial* integration does not necessarily translate into meaningful neighbourhood interaction. Rather, neighbourhood relations are often characterized by racism, stigmatization and intolerance of Roma cultural practices, with these sentiments equally apparent in the formal educational setting.

The field of education provides a further brief, but particularly clear, example of the trend towards the invisibilization of Roma racism in the UK. In 2015, there were a total of 567 school pupils in Sheffield identified as Gypsy/Roma. In the same year, 148 (or 26%) of these pupils were permanently excluded from school, many for responding to incessant bullying and racism (Searle 2017). These exclusions are justified on the grounds that the conduct of the pupils in question is detrimental to the education or welfare of others, with the majority of the excluded Roma children subsequently placed in special schools *a la* CEE. Once again, it is the *Roma children who are seen as the problem*, with the behavioural reasons justifying their exclusion yet again detached from the wider context of their marginal predicament: their harassment and exclusion.

Conclusion

The vast majority of Roma households resident in the Page Hall area of Sheffield have migrated from Slovakia in a bid to escape the kind of stigmatizing practices and punitive populism that we have described in Medzilaborce. While the historical and political contexts vary enormously, we have drawn on the work of Goldberg and Wacquant in arguing that both are characterized by the invisibilization of Roma racism, with the Roma themselves being represented as the problem and de-coupled from a long history of social disadvantage and deprivation. The two cases are therefore useful in both highlighting the perpetual stigmatization and marginalization experienced by poorer Roma groups as they move through space and cross the borders of Europe, and also in underscoring the differential responses to them in different spatial contexts. In both examples, however, hostility and intolerance are justified with reference to the 'threatening' behaviour and practices of the Roma, which are de-historicized and de-contextualized in constructing the Roma as being at odds with contemporary, normative behavioural expectations: they steal from the forest; they lack self-restraint; they are a public health concern; they are responsible for neighbourhood nuisance and anti-social behaviour; and they disrupt the education of their non-Roma peers. This process of neoliberal racialization goes hand in hand with processes of securitization which transform the *complex and long-term issues* of Roma deprivation, marginalization and exclusion into cultural and group problems requiring penalization and corrective treatment. Non-Roma need protection from Roma.

The latent forms of anti-Roma racism in CEE countries, suppressed, to some extent, under communist rule, have been expressed more freely post-1989 and are shaped by an explicit notion of inferiority. In the UK, however, that history of Roma vilification and subordination is much less apparent, meaning that separation operates more through the dialectics of identification and disidentification than it does through physical containment: 'appealing to national character, patriotism and ethnoracial familiality' (Goldberg 2009: 55) in mobilizing *dis*identifications from those outwith that frame of reference. In this sense, urban encounters with Roma in the UK—be that in the neighbourhood or the classroom—are defined by their perceived *incivility* and the threat that this constitutes, whereas in CEE countries, sites for such encounters are systematically reduced by policies of segregation (Bannister and Flint 2017). Both, however, involve the invisibilization of racism and Roma marginality, while at the same time contributing to the maintenance and reinforcement of ethno-racial divides, with the result that opportunities for meaningful interactions, through which identifications tend to flourish more readily, are severely curtailed (de Swaan 1997).

Notes

1. We do not approach 'neoliberalism' as a new 'grand narrative' or as a set of policies or an ideology that is omnipresent and omnipotent in the sense that it represents everything that is bad. Rather, we understand neoliberalism in terms of complex processes of neoliberalization in which neoliberal rationalities and technologies have significantly intersected and intermingled with other types, ways and styles of governing (see van Baar 2011a: 28–49, 163–74).
2. Hage (2014) distinguishes the racism of 'exploitation' from that of 'extermination', but we believe that the latter could more adequately be qualified as a type of racism of 'expulsion' of which the ultimate and most dramatic consequence could be physical annihilation effected by literally expelling humans from socio-human orders.
3. Despite Goldberg's (2009: 151–98, 370–72) sympathetic call for critical 'racial regionalizations', his theoretical account remains general and often lacks adequate grounding in everyday practices of racism and racialization.
4. The fieldwork material presented here – including interviews, site visits, observations and the study of relevant policy documents and developments – is part of a qualitative analysis of the societal and security situation in several Slovak municipalities carried out by Huub van Baar between 2014 and 2017.
5. Medzilaborce belongs to a minority group of Slovak municipalities that does not have a municipal police force, but relies on the services of Slovakia's state police to deal with issues of public order and security.
6. Identification is 'a cognitive and emotional process in which people increasingly come to experience others as similar to themselves' (de Swaan 1997: 105). Disidentification is the other side of this dialectic whereby people come to experience others as *different* from themselves.

References

Abrahamsen, R., and M. Williams. 2011. *Security Beyond the State*. Cambridge: Cambridge University Press.

Agarin, T., ed. 2014. *When Stereotype Meets Prejudice: Antiziganism in European Societies*. Stuttgart: Ibidem.

Bannister, J., and J. Flint. 2017. Crime and the City. In *Oxford Handbook of Criminology*, ed. A. Liebling, S. Maruna, and L. McAra, 522–540. Oxford: Oxford University Press.

Casey, L. 2016. *The Casey Review: A Review into Opportunity and Integration*. London: DCLG.

Clark, C. 2014. Glasgow's Ellis Island? The Integration and Stigmatisation of Govanhill's Roma Population. *People, Place and Policy* 8 (1): 34–50.
de Swaan, A. 1997. Widening Circles of Disidentification. *Theory, Culture and Society* 14 (2): 105–122.
Editorial. 2016. We Need Brexit to Stop Roma Gangsters from Stealing Taxpayers' Money. *Daily Express*, March 29.
ERRC. 1997. *Two Settlement Bans and a Fire in Northeast Slovakia*. Budapest: European Roma Rights Centre.
Foucault, M. 2004 [1997]. *"Society Must Be Defended": Lectures at the Collège de France 1975–1976*. London: Penguin.
Fox, J., and P. Vermeersch. 2010. Backdoor Nationalism. *European Journal of Sociology* 50 (2): 325–357.
Fox, J., L. Morosanu, and E. Szilassy. 2012. The Racialization of the New European Migration to the UK. *Sociology* 46 (4): 680–695.
Goldberg, D. 2009. *The Threat of Race: Reflections on Racial Neoliberalism*. Oxford: Wiley-Blackwell.
———. 2015. *Are We All Postracial Yet?* Cambridge: Polity.
———. 2016. Vanishing Points. *Ethnic and Racial Studies* 39 (13): 2278–2283.
Hage, G. 2014. Recalling Anti-Racism. *Mail & Guardian*, August 4.
Kováč, P. 2017. Kaliňák ukázal obce, v ktorých chce bojovať s rómskou kriminalitou. *Sme*, January 10.
Lentin, A., and G. Titley. 2011. *The Crises of Multiculturalism*. London: Zed Books.
McGarry, A. 2017. *Romaphobia*. London: Zed Books.
Messing, V., and A. Bereményi. 2017. Is Ethnicity a Meaningful Category of Employment Policies for Roma? *Ethnic and Racial Studies* 40 (10): 1623–1642.
New Keywords Collective. 2016. Europe/Crisis: New Keywords of "the Crisis" in and of "Europe". *Near Futures Online* 1 (1). Available at http://nearfuturesonline.org/europecrisis-new-keywords-of-crisis-in-and-of-europe/. Accessed 20 June 2017.
O'Nions, H. 2014. Some Europeans Are More Equal Than Others. *People, Place and Policy* 8 (1): 4–18.
Peach, C. 1996. Does Britain Have Ghettos? *Transactions of the Institute of British Geographers* 21 (1): 216–235.
Peck, J., and A. Tickell. 2007. Conceptualizing Neoliberalism, Thinking Thatcherism. In *Contesting Neoliberalism*, ed. H. Leitner, J. Peck, and E. Sheppard, 26–50. New York: The Guilford Press.
Powell, R. 2013. Loïc Wacquant's Ghetto and Ethnic Minority Segregation in the UK: The Neglected Case of Gypsy-Travellers. *International Journal of Urban and Regional Research* 37 (1): 115–134.
———. 2015. Housing Benefit Reform and the Private Rented Sector in the UK. *Housing, Theory and Society* 32 (3): 320–345.

Powell, R., and J. Lever. 2017. Europe's Perennial "Outsiders": A Processual Approach to Roma Stigmatization and Ghettoization. *Current Sociology* 65 (5): 680–699.

Roberts, D., and M. Mahtani. 2010. Neoliberalizing Race, Racing Neoliberalism. *Antipode* 42 (2): 248–257.

Robinson, D. 2016. Ethnicity, Housing and Advanced Marginality in England. Paper Presented to the International Conference *Rethinking Urban Inequality with Loïc Wacquant*, Sheffield, UK, June 7.

Searle, C. 2017. Xeno-Racism and the Scourge of School Exclusion. *Institute for Race Relations*. Available at http://www.irr.org.uk/news/xeno-racism-and-the-scourge-of-school-exclusion/. Accessed 20 June 2017.

Sheldrick, G. 2016. REVEALED: How YOU Pay for Roma Gypsy [sic] Palaces – UK Benefits Funding Romanian Mansions. *Daily Express*, April 5.

Stewart, M., ed. 2012. *The Gypsy 'Menace': Populism and the New Anti-Gypsy Politics*. London: Hurst & Company.

TASR. 2016. Fico: Smer to Apply Restrictive Measures to People Who Refuse to Work. *TASR*, December 16.

van Baar, H. 2011a. *The European Roma: Minority Representation, Memory and the Limits of Transnational Governmentality*. Amsterdam: F&N.

———. 2011b. Europe's Romaphobia: Problematization, Securitization, Nomadization. *Environment and Planning D: Society and Space* 29 (2): 203–212.

———. 2012. Socio-Economic Mobility and Neo-Liberal Governmentality in Post-Socialist Europe. *Journal of Ethnic and Migration Studies* 38 (8): 1289–1304.

———. 2014. The Emergence of a Reasonable Anti-Gypsyism. In *When Stereotype Meets Prejudice*, ed. T. Agarin, 27–44. Stuttgart: Ibidem.

———. 2017. Evictability and the Biopolitical Bordering of Europe. *Antipode* 49 (1): 212–230.

van Baar, H., and P. Vermeersch. 2017. The Limits of Operational Representations: "Ways of Seeing Roma" Beyond the Recognition-Redistribution Paradigm. *Intersections* 3 (4): 120–139.

Wacquant, L. 2004. Ghetto. In *International Encyclopedia of the Social and Behavioural Sciences*, ed. N. Smelser and P. Baltes, 129–147. London: Pergamon Press.

———. 2007. Territorial Stigmatization in the Age of Advanced Marginality. *Thesis Eleven* 91: 66–77.

———. 2008a. Ghettos and Anti-Ghettos. *Thesis Eleven* 94: 113–118.

———. 2008b. *Urban Outcasts*. Cambridge: Polity.

———. 2009. *Punishing the Poor*. Durham, NC: Duke University Press.

———. 2012. A Janus-Faced Institution of Ethnoracial Closure: A Sociological Specification of the Ghetto. In *The Ghettos: Contemporary Global Issues and Controversies*, ed. R. Hutchison and B. Haynes, 1–32. Boulder, CO: Westview.

CHAPTER 6

Security at the Nexus of Space and Class: Roma and Gentrification in Cluj, Romania

Manuel Mireanu

In this chapter, I argue that the political economy of urban gentrification is intimately intertwined with security mechanisms of exclusion and control. Using the eviction of the Roma from the Romanian city of Cluj in 2010 as a case study, the chapter contributes to ongoing debates on critical security studies, and particularly to those which, in comparison to more traditional security studies, have expressed more openness to the relevance of social marginality, the role of class, and the construction of urban space. This focus is important because any critical effort to understand how mechanisms of exclusion and exploitation are enacted through security discourses and practices should include a discussion of how categories such as race, class, space, gender, nationality, and political belief

---

I would like to thank Dr. Maria Gkresta, who contributed significantly to the sections on the evictions and the relocation. Earlier drafts of the argument presented here have been written together with her. My special gratitude goes to the three editors of this volume, for their numerous comments and suggestions, as well as for their infinite patience while dealing with the entire process of editing. Not in the last place, I am grateful to Peggy Birch and Chris Engert, the language editors, for clarifying my text and making it more elegant.

M. Mireanu (✉)
Independent Researcher, Timișoara, Romania

© The Author(s) 2019
H. van Baar et al. (eds.), *The Securitization of the Roma in Europe*, Human Rights Interventions, https://doi.org/10.1007/978-3-319-77035-2_6

intersect. Indeed, practices of security do not influence all of us equally, and some of us are, or could be, constructed as more 'dangerous' than others.

I also discuss the 'housing paradox' faced by the Roma. Caught between proliferating gentrification and growing racism, the Roma are neither welcome in their renovated inner-city housing, which is a prime target for property speculation, nor anywhere in any of the more run-down suburban residential areas. Politicians and neighbours reject them, problematizing them as 'criminals' who only make the neighbourhoods more insecure, chaotic, dirty, and less valuable in the property market. The housing paradox stands for the shrinking societal space in which the Roma are allowed to live. The economically induced pressure on the housing market, which dictates the rules for cities, regions, and even states, is not just a free-market endeavour but is tainted by other social factors, such as categorizations along the lines of class, race, and nationality. In Romania, the Roma have historically been the pariahs of society; victims of prejudice and state oppression, while they are, at the same time, problematized as a 'threat' to be wary of.

The case of the evictions of Roma from Cluj is neither exceptional nor singular for Romania. I approach this case study from an academic perspective here, mainly because I want to participate in an ongoing academic debate in security studies. In no way do I consciously desire to be a voice for the Romanian Roma concerned. I am not myself Roma; at most, I might consider myself as an ally. I do not speak for the Roma and I do not consider myself entitled to present their voices here; this is something that they can do very well themselves. For these reasons, the chapter is more technical and theoretical in nature than ethnographical.

I consider the case of the evictions of Roma from Cluj as a good example of the way in which securitization works in practice at its nexus with marketization and gentrification, and how the category of class, in particular, plays a profound role in the process of marginalization. In the case of the Roma, their living and housing standards have always presented a 'problem' for the Romanian state, which has, throughout its pre-modern and modern history, tried to legitimize their misery through various securitization strategies. From slavery in the nineteenth century to their pauperization in the early twentieth century, and from their forced integration during the state-socialist era to their present-day vilification, Romania's Roma have always been part of the state's differential performance of delivering 'security'.

I exercise some caution in using the concept of securitization, since it is, as Thierry Balzacq (2014: 8) has argued, an 'ideal type'. By doing this, I mirror the dissent that exists in the debates within Critical Security Studies. On the one hand, some authors (Buzan et al. 1998; Wæver 1995) define securitization as a concept that denotes a clear-cut process articulated through a speech act by an actor with enough power to 'speak security' (this is usually a state actor in a top decisional position). This process involves emphasizing an existential threat and the emergency measures to be taken against it. On the other hand, other authors (Bigo 2008: 127; Bigo and Tsoukala 2008: 5; C.A.S.E. collective 2006: 457–58; Roe 2008: 620) have subsequently expanded the meaning of securitization to embed it more explicitly in social phenomena, thus highlighting features such as the audience and context of securitizing speech acts.

At the same time, a number of authors have started to move away from the use of the concept of securitization (McDonald 2008: 582) or at least, to highlight its limitations. Jef Huysmans (2004: 307), for instance, has argued for a 'move away from an exclusive focus on the symbolic and discursive process' towards 'powerful technological processes', where security is embedded in everyday routines. He dismisses the main features of the securitizing move, namely, the 'act' and the 'decision', pointing to the difficulty of continuing to use the concept for analytical purposes (Huysmans 2011: 376). Similarly, Holger Stritzel (2011: 348) claims that 'the concept of securitization [has] dramatically [lost] its usefulness', and that it should therefore be avoided. The research on 'risk' that has emerged in the meantime could be considered as a possible alternative to analyses in terms of securitization. Claudia Aradau and Rens van Munster (2007: 98), for example, define their analytical focus on risk as occupying an intermediate space 'between exceptional measures and the immediacy of action on the one hand and the ordinary administrative, police or insurance measures on the other'. Precautionary risk structures the present based on preventing potential catastrophic events (Arias 2011: 369), and in this sense, the focus on risk is much wider and much more embedded in the social realm than the focus on securitization is.

Based on these considerations, in this chapter, I understand security as a *dispositif*, that is, an ensemble of discourses (of the state, the media, and the population), practices, infrastructures, and symbols (Foucault 1980: 194–95). The *dispositif* of security cannot be captured simply by using a clear-cut procedural speech-act of securitization nor is it exhausted by the myriad *practices* of security. Rather, this *dispositif* is embedded in the social, political, and economic realms. The practices and discourses of security are situated among other, different phenomena (ICCM 2010). As Louise Amoore and Marieke de Goede (2008: 178) argue, 'the deviant other' is interpellated 'through an assembly of transactions or associations seen as signifying suspicious activity'.

In line with these reconsiderations, I highlight the numerous other particularities of situations—for example, the evictions of Roma people from Cluj and their relocation to Pata Rât—among which security is but one, and which might be obscured if the focus were solely on securitization.[1] In Cluj, the eviction of the Roma was partly legitimized through numerous complaints from politicians and neighbours. They explicitly demanded that the area inhabited by the Roma should be rendered 'more secure' and 'clean'. The Roma of Cluj were evicted not only because they were racialized as Roma but also because they were classified as 'poor and useful', that is, their labour could be used cheaply, but not in the centre of town where they had been accustomed to living.

This chapter sheds light on how practices of security are enacted in urban space and mobilized against those who, for various reasons, are rejected and displaced. In the first section, I lay out the political and economic context of the security *dispositif*, namely, the processes of gentrification of post-socialist urban space in Romania. These processes have rendered the Roma people 'unfit' to continue living in the spaces in which they had lived before 1990, and have therefore led to a housing paradox—which I analyse in the second section. The treatment of the Romanian Roma is an illustration of the nexus between gentrification and security mechanisms: the Roma people are being pushed out to the margins and also stereotyped because they are seen as dangerous and as criminals. In the third and fourth sections, I exemplify this nexus through the case of the evictions of Roma people from Cluj and their relocation to the slum area of Pata Rât. In the fifth section, I analyse the political economy of the eviction and relocation, and I highlight the economic aspects of the security *dispositif* that has targeted the Roma in Cluj.

Gentrification in Post-socialist Romania

Gentrification describes the process by which poor and derelict urban areas, often occupied by low-income residents, are infused with capital in order to be 'improved' in accordance with the needs of a class with more consumption power. In this process of marketization, buildings and infrastructures are 'modernized', with the result that property values increase rapidly, excluding those who cannot afford the newly increased cost of living there either through 'voluntary' relocation or eviction (Smith 1996, 2002). Under neoliberalism, gentrification has become a complex policy, the chief aim of which is preparing an urban space for the infusion of capital. This may be in the form of investment in property (raising the value of the land in an urban area), in consumption and leisure (building facilities for shopping, artistic endeavours, and leisure pursuits or promoting cultural heritage), and in making the urban space more 'liveable' (improving the 'quality of life', investing in infrastructure and—my main concern in this chapter—raising the perceived level of security in the area).

The peculiarity of urban space and the political economy of housing in Romania are issues that pertain to its state-socialist and totalitarian past. In Romania, as in the other Eastern and Central European countries formerly behind the Iron Curtain, the vast majority of property was either seized or built by the state (Marcuse 1996). During state socialism, the urban infrastructure that existed before 1945 was nationalized, and housing was redistributed by the state according to various criteria. The imposing old buildings erected under a succession of monarchies in the city centres of, for example, Cluj, Timisoara, Bucharest, and Iasi were represented only rarely as an asset in the Communist Party's discourse on the new socialist world belonging to the workers. Instead, the Party chose to finance major urban projects outside the centres, resulting in a high density of blocks of flats that were constructed to house industrial workers. At the same time, the historic centres of these major cities were allowed to deteriorate and were neglected or even destroyed. This process sharpened the dividing lines of property prices and status, which were reinforced by the Communist Party. The old buildings in the centres, despite their imposing character, were left to the 'marginals': to ethnic minorities such as the Hungarians in cities such as Cluj and Timișoara and to unskilled and low-status Roma people in Bucharest, but also elsewhere (Petrovici 2012: 2384).

In the 1990s, after the fall of the Communist regime, this trend was reversed in several ways. First, the state withdrew from almost all social housing projects. The big urban infrastructure projects were terminated and the Romanian state drastically reduced the amount of housing for low-income citizens and other marginalized groups (Zamfirescu 2015: 143). Secondly, after 1990, the Romanian state presided over a massive privatization process. Tenants were encouraged to buy their flats at ridiculously low prices, and many did so, motivated by the desire for private ownership which became acute after almost half a century of a (more or less) Communist regime. The country became 'a republic of homeowners, with more than 95% of the country's housing stock being privately owned' (Chelcea and Pulay 2015: 349). Private ownership inevitably fosters the 'grey' market of student-rentals, especially in big cities like Cluj, where there are also universities. Many properties were rented out, with prices sometimes equalling those in major Central European capitals such as Budapest or Prague. Furthermore, this trend implied that the urban areas closer to the universities—which in socialist Romania were built in the city centres—were more valuable. This process also meant that the state's role in the property market became even smaller, and what was left of the housing stock was insufficient to cope with the demand for social housing.

Thirdly, the former Communist urban projects are now falling into disrepair and disrespect. Seen as a gigantic legacy of the former totalitarian regime, the neighbourhoods consisting of blocks of flats are now regarded as dysfunctional, remote and even dangerous (Pásztor and Péter 2009: 83). Most of these buildings were erected in haste, using cheap materials and unskilled labour. They have thin walls and poor infrastructure; they generally lack the large airy rooms of the pre-1945 buildings and the bourgeois comfort that is once again sought after. Moreover, these blocks were mostly allocated to former peasants who had become factory workers, and who—once the factories were either privatized, closed down, or went bankrupt—entered into a downward spiral of unemployment and precariousness. During the transition to free-market capitalism, the social and economic status of the workers diminished drastically, and they found themselves being pushed not only to the periphery of the new society but also to the symbolic and geographic margins of the city.

This led to a fourth and final way of reversing the urban economy of the Communist era, a process that could be understood as reclaiming the city. Following a slow but steady trend of revaluing the bourgeois past, the Romanians have rediscovered their city centres and have begun to reclaim them. Numerous central historic buildings have been renovated. Having started gradually in the 1990s and 2000s, this trend has dramatically accelerated in recent years, often facilitated by EU funding. The same buildings that were allowed to become derelict during the Communist era, and which had deteriorated further during the transition period, are now being rediscovered in an effort to give them new value. In this way, the workers have sought to compensate for the loss of their symbolic privilege with a pronounced sense of national identity (Petrovici 2012: 2388). Thus, the shared identity originally rooted in class has been replaced by one defined by nation, and also by race, because as Enikő Vincze (2012: 65) argues, since the 2000s, Romania has witnessed a racialization of urban spatial exclusion. In Cluj, the authorities began to evict the Roma from the more integrated urban areas and the centre, redirecting them towards the periphery, and from 2003, to the rubbish dump in Pata Rât. Vincze (2012: 60–61) illustrates how the rationale behind these evictions from the centre oscillated from urban regeneration to a response to 'complaints from the neighbours' and even to 'eliminating poverty' and the 'social integration of the Roma'.

The 'Housing Paradox' of the Romanian Roma

In Romania, Roma and low-income tenants more generally are currently being evicted *en masse* or are being forced out due to the huge rise in rents (Amnesty International 2013b: 4; Ciobanu 2017). The Roma are generally seen as forming a large part of the 'undeserving poor' (Vincze 2012: 66) who are dependent on state benefits. These people were unable to afford the cost of maintaining their buildings over the years, and the general public now consequently considers them to be responsible for the wear and tear suffered by what are now regarded as historic monuments. There is widespread pressure for these 'monuments' to be cleared, renovated, and 'given back' to the city.

The situation of the Roma is similarly dire in terms of social housing. Ideologically, the transition to capitalism signified the transformation of the home into a commodity. This was followed by a shift in the public perception of social housing: 'those who do not have the resources to rent or buy a home in the private housing market do not belong in "our" city' (Vincze and Ciotlăuş 2016). For Romanian Roma, this generally implies a high level of exclusion, as they can no longer afford to live in the big cities due to their general socio-economic precarity. Structurally, this housing inequality has been the main economic cause of the eviction and relocation of the Roma in Romania in recent years.

The Roma in Romania are facing a kind of 'housing paradox'. On the one hand, they are no longer allowed to live in the city centres because the old buildings they used to occupy are now seen to be too precious for them. This attitude is in line with the more general patterns of the stigmatization of the Roma, who are seen as dirty, noisy, and generally as troublemakers. On the other hand, if they live in the suburban housing blocks erected under state socialism, they fall into the category of stereotypes by which these neighbourhoods are usually characterized: filthy, insecure, and disorderly. A good illustration of this dubious dynamic is the situation in Baia Mare in Northern Romania where, in 2011, the mayor erected a wall to separate the neighbourhood occupied by the Roma from the rest of the city (Pop 2015). As a result of this housing paradox, the majority of Roma in Romania now live mostly in either rural areas or in slum-like neighbourhoods on the edges of towns.

In addition to this situation, the Roma in Romania are generally seen as criminals. From the stereotype that 'all Roma steal' to the continuous exposure in the media of 'the gypsy mafia clans', the Romanian Roma are habitually associated with crime, both inside the country and abroad. This representation articulates the Roma as the perfect scapegoat for the poor reputation of Romanians throughout Europe, and elicits nationalistic responses from those Romanians who are in search of a more positive 'true' national identity. In this way, negative stereotypes about the Roma function today—as they have in the past—as an integral part of the process of Romanian nation-building (Poenaru 2016). For this reason, the discrimination against the Roma is so deeply ingrained in Romanian social imaginary that it legitimizes any act of violence against them.

At the level of the state, this violence has primarily been legitimated through security mechanisms. The Romanian Roma have become a 'security problem' at the point at which their economic (class-based) marginalization starts to intersect with their racial marginalization.[2] This security problem usually manifests itself in a number of closely interrelated steps. First, the Roma are collectively criminalized as a group, which means that their behaviour starts to be seen as criminal, dangerous, and anti-social by the state. Similar behaviour—instances of petty crime, for example—is largely left unpunished when perpetrated by non-Roma. Second, their *presence* in certain urban spaces, such as the historic city centres, tends to be seen as detrimental to the safety of those spaces. This is also coupled with the generalized refusal of Romanians, as well as ethnic Hungarians, to move into areas that are predominantly occupied by Roma or to accept Roma as their neighbours.[3] Third, and consequently, the Roma have increasingly found themselves subject to forced eviction from their dwellings in what used to be the derelict areas of the city centres. This is part of a process of an everyday abnormalization of the Roma people. Fourth, following these evictions, many of these evicted Roma have been relocated to slum-like areas on the margins of the city, of which Pata Rât is but one example (Amnesty International 2013b).

In addition, I want to emphasize that actors and agencies that do not have the prerogative to articulate security in the name of the state have also labelled the Roma as a security problem and have thus also played a profound role in the process of the eviction of the Roma. As I have argued more extensively elsewhere (Mireanu 2014), I consider this mechanism of security performed by non-state actors as a 'demand for security'. For example, in Cluj, on Coastei Street, such demands were articulated by the Nokia company, which lamented the presence of the Roma in the vicinity because they allegedly created an 'unsafe' business environment. Moreover, staff at the nearby library (state officials, but without security prerogatives) had also complained about the petty crimes allegedly committed by the Roma. According to one of those evicted, the administrator of the library filed frequent complaints to the police about the various activities of the Coastei Street residents (interview with Ernest Creta, see Dohotaru et al. 2016: 173). The people living in the residential areas around Coastei Street had also complained repeatedly about the 'behaviour of the Roma' who lived there (Dohotaru et al. 2016: 100). Even after the eviction, and based on complaints from those who own land in the vicinity, the police mobilized repeatedly and regularly performed raids on the settlements of Pata Rât to which the Roma were evicted (Dohotaru et al. 2016: 36).

Since the 1990s, Romania has gone through various stages of neoliberal economic and social transformation. Neoliberal interventions have also been presented as the most 'natural' solution to the 2007/2008 financial-economic crisis. Since 2009, the Romanian Presidency has promoted such interventions, and all subsequent governments have tried to legitimize their implementation (Vincze 2015). As Neil Brenner and Nik Theodore (2005: 102) have argued, 'neoliberalism' does not mean 'state withdrawal' and 'deregulation' but rather, a complex mechanism of the reconstitution of state/economy relations in which a process of *re-*regulation takes place whereby state institutions and actors 'are actively mobilized to promote market-based regulatory arrangements'. Thus, a neoliberal state is one which *enables* and *actively* facilitates marketization and the gentrification of urban space according to a logic of profitability (also *for* the state in material and immaterial ways, e.g., with regard to symbolic nation-building through the beautification of historic city centres).

As I show in the case of the Roma people from Cluj, the role of the Romanian state has shifted from the unconditional provision of social welfare and assistance to the Roma and other marginalized groups, to encouraging private capital, withdrawing itself from market regulation, and criminalizing the poor. The Romanian state now provides only conditional access to benefits. The Roma people of Romania have fallen prey to this shift, as their precarity and marginality have become an obstacle to urban economic development. Instead of being a problem that the state could resolve through policies of assistance, the precarity of the Roma becomes another layer in their exclusion, and, as I show later, it renders them a security problem for the city.

Neoliberalism is a spatially specific political and social strategy, which tends to favour the urban scale over other geo-economical spaces, such as regions or nations. Indeed, 'cities have become central to the reproduction, mutation, and continual reconstitution of neoliberalism' (Brenner and Theodore 2002: 375). I take inspiration from Brenner and Theodore's (2002) argument that we are consequently witnessing an 'urbanization of neoliberalism'. Security—particularly in the context of urban spaces—plays a crucial role in this overall process (Becker and Müller 2013). Cities are not only arenas of financial and trade flows but also 'central agents in the many forms of violence brought about by capitalist imperialism' (Graham 2010: 11). Many scholars (Coaffee and Wood 2006; Coward 2009) have analysed the intersection of violence and war in urban spaces. Due to their strategic role and their concentration of capital, critical infrastructure, and large populations, cities have become extremely vulnerable to violent conflicts, war, and even utter destruction (Coward 2009: 401). Various practices of security have increasingly been articulated in urban contexts because the identification of possible threats and their solutions have increasingly been connected to urban spaces.

The Cluj Evictions

On 17 December 2010, nearly 300 people—mostly Roma—were forcibly evicted from their social housing in Coastei Street (European Roma Rights Centre 2012). This street is in the centre of Cluj-Napoca, in northeast Romania. Some of the evicted families had been living there for more than 20 years. The eviction was preceded by a visit from municipal representatives of Cluj-Napoca two days prior to the event, during which the Roma who lived in the apartments in Coastei Street were informed that they would have to submit a request at the local mayor's office by noon of the following day in order to be allocated social housing. The following evening, the police and other law-enforcement officers told the residents that they should pack their belongings, because they would be moved the next morning. Early on the morning of the 17th, while the temperature outside was about minus 10° Celsius, the authorities mobilized massively for the eviction. Their representatives, together with bulldozers, removal lorries, and a huge number of enforcement officers (military and local police) announced to the residents that the demolition of their houses was going to happen whether or not they agreed to their relocation. The residents succumbed to the pressure from the authorities and accepted the housing that they were offered without knowing the exact conditions and location.

Prior to 2010, the area cleared—Coastei Street and its surroundings—had been seen as a dangerous place in the heart of the city. In 2009, one journalist lamented that the shanties were built in a 'privileged position… in Nokia's backyard', behind the County Library and the NATO information point (Boncuțiu 2009). The city administration had issued several complaints about the 'vandalism' and 'precarious hygiene' of the Roma living in the Coastei Street area. Moreover, the authorities were also concerned about the 'visual' aspect of these people, the sight of them having allegedly caused the uneasiness of various international guests. A few days prior to the eviction, the then mayor of Cluj declared that the administration had received several 'complaints from the library and from Nokia' and that the area was known to be insecure and full of 'illegal' people (Giurgiu 2010).

Until 2009, several of the families in Coastei Street had tenancy agreements with the municipal authorities. During the socialist era, these families had initially received their accommodation as part of their employment contracts. Since 1990, however, they had been repeatedly threatened with eviction due to the privatization of the area in which they were living. For 20 years, this threat had not led to any action (Criticatac 2011). They continued to pay rent normally and the municipality assured them that they could continue living there. However, because of existing urban regeneration plans, their contracts had not been renewed. The municipality had tolerated the construction of informal, makeshift dwellings adjacent to the social housing in Coastei Street, and although the occupants of these had no contracts, they had been living there for years. For example, some of the children of official tenants now occupied these informal dwellings with their families. Romanian law only guaranteed the security of tenure and protection against forced evictions for those tenants with formal tenure.[4]

The houses in Coastei Street were destroyed in the days following the eviction. A few months later, in April 2011, a parcel of 5000 square metres of the Coastei Street area was donated to the Christian Orthodox Archbishop of Cluj. The Archbishop had previously requested this land in exchange for another piece of land, also received free by the Church in 2003 but which had since been given back to the municipality (Cluj City Hall 2011). The Church built a church and a multi-functional building to house the Faculty of Orthodox Theology, with dormitories for students and a centre for palliative healing, on the newly acquired land. With unintended sarcasm, the *mitropolit*—the regional leader of the Orthodox Church—declared that the multiple charitable and educational benefits of the new religious complex would 'surely' fulfil a number of 'social functions' that would compensate for the eviction of the Roma (Raț 2011). The municipality subsequently built a children's playground and a recreational park on the remainder of the evicted terrain. At the time of writing, nothing in the area stands to remind passers-by of the tragedy of the evicted Roma people. Even the street name has changed; it now bears the name of an orthodox bishop.

In November 2011, the National Council for Combating Discrimination fined the municipality approximately 2000 euros (Amnesty International 2013a). However, the evicted of Coastei Street were never compensated for their losses. In 2014, the judicial authorities of Cluj decided to reject a court ruling that those evicted should each receive 2000 euros in compensation (Romitan 2014). In April 2017, there was a final ruling in the compensation trial, with the court deciding 'irrevocably' that those evicted would not receive any money (Bacalu 2017).

The eviction of the Roma from Coastei Street can be understood as a measure forming part of a larger array of security assemblages directed against these people by the state authorities and a number of other social actors. The eviction was the scene of a number of security practices and discourses: the deployment of police, the forced containment and removal of the tenants, and their criminalization through the narrative of the 'dangerous area' that needed to be reintegrated in the fabric of the city.

The Relocation to Pata Rât

The new social housing provided by the municipal authorities is on the outskirts of the city, on a hill in the Pata Rât area, next to the city's rubbish dump, which is situated some eight kilometres from the city centre. The land on which the social houses were built used to belong to the Brantner Veres public sanitation company. In 2010, prior to the evictions, the company offered this land to the municipality in exchange for 300 square metres in a 'more adequate location in Cluj' (Vincze 2012: 64; Ziua de Cluj 2010). The municipality built ten houses on the newly acquired land in Pata Rât, each with four rooms. These were insufficient to house all the evicted families. The 40 families that were allocated this social housing were forced to sign tenancy contracts without ever having the chance to read them.

The other 30 families with no contracts were effectively made homeless. These people neither received substantial help from the authorities nor any legal documents that would ensure their right to construct new houses (Creta and Fekete 2012). The families that did manage to build, and who invested money into doing so, thus live in a constant state of 'evictability' (van Baar 2017) and precarity: not only could they be evicted at any time, but the absence of official safeguards prevents them from installing basic utilities such as electricity and water.

The new social houses were substandard as a result of deficiencies and haste in their construction. Together with the evicted from Coastei Street, about 1500 (mostly) Roma people currently live in the area. Other residents of Pata Rât make ends meet by collecting refuse from the dump, plastic and metal which they then sell. Living in various communities, the city landfill is both their home and their place of work; in fact, some people—the most traditional of the four communities of Pata Rât—actually live on the landfill itself.

The residents report experiencing a number of health problems. They can still go to hospital, but the closest medical facility is five kilometres away. If they are caught travelling without a bus ticket, they will not only fined but will also lose their welfare benefits and as a result their access to free public healthcare. In the Romanian public health system, a person is assigned to a family doctor according to the address on their ID card. Faced with discrimination because of where they live, many people are reluctant to put their new address on their ID. Since their mobility has been significantly curtailed, their access to doctors is limited, resulting in an increased number of emergency calls. The residents report that ambulances have refused to respond to their calls and that the average waiting time is much higher than before the eviction (European Roma Rights Centre 2012: 6). They also report increased health problems.

In addition to the very limited access to transport services in Pata Rât, some of the inhabitants have reported that they have been rejected for employment because of living at the landfill area. The children's access to education has also been restricted since the relocation. Children can still attend school but have to use the only two available buses at 7:00 and 14:00. This timetable prevents them from attending evening classes or any extra-curricular activities (Amnesty International 2013b: 14). Some of them have dropped out, others were forced to leave their schools in the city centre because other parents complained about children from Pata Rât being registered there (European Roma Rights Centre 2012: 12). Other children were placed in schools for children with mental disabilities, although this had not been the case before the relocation (European Roma Rights Centre 2012: 12).

On the other hand, a few months prior to the eviction, the authorities built a new police station in the Pata Rât area (Păcurar 2010). This decision was motivated by the large number of complaints from the people living close to Pata Rât about the 'violence and aggression caused by alcohol consumption'—in the words of the Chief of Police in Cluj. Since then, the police have had an active presence in the area, with frequent raids and arrests. In March 2016, 50 members of the police intervened in Pata Rât and arrested 20 people for 'anti-social behaviour' (Clujust 2016), as well as handing out numerous fines to people living there. Pata Rât is considered to be the most dangerous area of Cluj, with the number of crimes committed there exceeding the total of crimes for the rest of the city (Stiri de Cluj 2011a).

The relocation of the Roma from the centre of Cluj to Pata Rât is part of a *dispositif* of security that constructs these people as a dangerous category and leads to their constant harassment by the police (Vincze 2012b: 12). Security was one of the main drivers of the eviction and continued to be an important part of the 'renewal' process once the unwanted people had been removed. Moreover, in the slum area of Pata Rât, security is one of the only public services available. Yet this focus on security does not exhaust the analysis of these situations of eviction and relocation.

The Political Economy of Eviction and Relocation

The practices and discourses of security articulated towards the Roma in the case of the Cluj evictions and relocations to Pata Rât have a fundamental economic component. This political economy of the Cluj evictions and relocations has two different dimensions. On the one hand, the area that was cleared—around Coastei Street—has been at the forefront of gentrification since the eviction. The area cleared of the improvised shelters and homes of the Roma has now, through closely interrelated processes of securitization, racialization, and gentrification, been integrated into the urban fabric of the city centre of Cluj. This area includes a newly constructed park with facilities for children and fitness. The total investment in the park has been estimated at around 250,000 RON or approximately 55,000 euros (Stiri de Cluj 2011b). The local administration not only offered substantial funding to the Orthodox Church for the site of the newly built Faculty of Theology, but an area of 7000 square metres of the area on which the Roma had previously built their homes was also donated. An imposing office building has also been erected on the spot since the evictions. In 2012, and more recently in 2016, there were discussions about building an IKEA store in Coastei Street. More importantly, it has finally become a 'safe' space in which the County Library and the NATO Infopoint can function and attract visitors. Thus, by reclaiming it, the authorities of Cluj have also managed to achieve economic heterogeneity for the eastern part of the city centre. Having a Roma slum in the midst of an area that houses thriving businesses, a shopping mall, and sports centres—all for the leisure and consumption of the new Romanian middle class—was seen as unacceptable. Tourists who strayed from the monuments and clubs of the centre would not have felt very comfortable amid the 'dangerous shanties' of Coastei Street. With the clearances, the neoliberal urban policies of the Romanian state have rendered the urban poor invisible and harmless (Wacquant 2008: 203; Powell and van Baar, Chap. 5, this volume).

But the relocation of the Roma from Coastei Street to Pata Rât, next to the landfill site, was not in any way contingent on the city's lack of housing space nor was it contingent on the concentration of other Roma communities in this area. The Roma from Pata Rât perform a very specific economic function in the area. Most of them work on the landfill site. They gather, select, and sort the refuse, which they then sell for very little money to the company that owns the dump. The director of Brantner Veres, the public sanitation company that manages the Pata Rât rubbish dump, was quoted as saying that the Roma people living there are extremely 'useful', because they reduce the quantity of waste his company has to deal with by taking the waste and reselling it in Cluj (Stiri de Cluj 2012). The Roma of Pata Rât are also exploited as a cheap labour force, able and willing to operate at the margins of legality and social protection. One report

(Dohotaru et al. 2016: 66) states that the Roma who work on the Pata Rât landfill have very precarious work contracts at best, and most of the time their work is informal. This means that they lack any protection as regards health and safety, not to mention the lack of any pension arrangements.

This exploitation happens in the context of a number of profitable arrangements between private capital and the municipality, similar to those discussed by Ryan Powell and Huub van Baar (Chap. 5, this volume) at the nexus of exploitative and expulsive racisms. The authorities of Cluj facilitate the interests of capital. For the general purposes of minimizing waste and pollution, companies responsible for producing waste are forced by law to become members of associations which then sort and recycle their waste. These associations have certain quotas, agreed with the local authorities. However, these quotas are often not respected and are avoided by signing fake contracts with the refuse companies operating the landfills. The refuse trucks are not checked when they enter and leave the landfill, which makes any estimation of the amount of waste recycled impossible (Dohotaru et al. 2016: 322). Thus, the informal work of the Roma in Pata Rât has a direct and crucial role in the local economy. Their cheap and precarious labour force brings inestimable profits to the refuse company, the recycling associations, and the local authorities. At the same time, the costs— in social, economic, and environmental terms—are significantly reduced for these actors. By relocating and maintaining a pauperized workforce in the area, the local authorities have solved both the problem of having undesirable groups of people in the city centre and the problem of waste management. As I have already mentioned, this cheap labour force is kept in check by numerous police interventions, and by turning a blind eye to the other forms of abuse against Roma people, such as their exploitation and their forced participation in the informal economies present in the Pata Rât communities (see also Vincze 2012b).

The nexus of gentrification and security underlines the importance and relevance of economic processes for security practices. The containment, exclusion, control, and oppression of Roma people have an indisputable economic aspect. This argument helps to show that, alongside racialization, the role of class and space are prominent in how the security *dispositif* has been enacted against the Roma. The gentrification of urban space brought about by neoliberalism in Romania means that security has become a public good for some and a mechanism of exclusion for others.

The spaces of the city become stakes in the political and economic processes enacted by various actors. This aspect shapes practices of security along a differential continuum of inclusion/exclusion, one that is affected by the position of the social actors within the economic hierarchy. Security articulations become successful and are legitimized when the authorities respond to the security demands articulated by the public. These demands are directed as a plea to rid the urban space of unwanted elements—not only of the Roma but also migrants, the homeless, the poor, drug dealers and users, and sex workers.

Conclusion

I have argued that the eviction and relocation of the Roma from the centre of Cluj to the landfill area of Pata Rât were the result of the articulation of a security *dispositif* in which racialization, classification, and gentrification have become intermingled, and which led to the exclusion of the poorest among the Roma in particular. The Roma of Pata Rât live in some of the harshest, most precarious, and most miserable conditions to be found in the EU. Their daily existence is fraught not only with the poverty and exclusion that are constructed as being inherent and inescapable for them but also with constant harassment by the police. Their precarity is enforced by the place they have been assigned in the local informal economy—that of a cheap labour force that can and must survive without, or with only a minimum of, social, human, and public security. To make matters worse, in recent years, the municipality of Cluj has conducted a process of normalizing the situation of these people by enforcing the permanent status of Pata Rât as a marginal space that does not belong to the city, and that should therefore function independently of its help, or perhaps with the occasional help of civil society organizations.

At the same time, the people of Pata Rât have not remained silent throughout these years. Starting with their eviction, and continuing with their relocation to poorly built houses and the city's attempts to normalize their continued residence at the landfill, the people have expressed their opposition and resistance on numerous occasions. In protest after protest, petition after petition, and one court case after another, the people from all the communities in Pata Rât have spoken up against their marginalization, exclusion, constant harassment and surveillance, against the life that is being imposed on them by a cynical and disinterested system.[5]

NOTES

1. This Foucauldian approach is used, in the case that I present in this chapter, to highlight the limits to circulation imposed on the Roma on the one hand, and the intersection between the different mechanisms aimed at the Roma people—expulsion, coercion, containment, and control—on the other hand. These mechanisms come to complement a purely process-based approach to security, which is only concerned with how the Roma have been constructed discursively as a threat. The concept of a security *dispositif* illustrates the plethora of mechanisms through which the Roma are managed as a problematic population which poses a security problem.
2. Here, my point of view differs from that of Enikő Vincze (2012a: 65) who, in the general Romanian discourse, understands the racialization of the Roma as an explanation of their economic precarity and as a technology through which they are 'de-proletarized'. While I agree with the importance of race, I argue for the continued relevance of class. The Roma are also considered to be a security problem because they are poor, not only because they are racialized.
3. A survey published in 2013 showed that more than 50% of Romanians would prefer not to have Roma as neighbours. The same poll showed that 68% of the respondents believed that the Roma are more likely to be criminals than other Romanians (Agerpres 2013).
4. Law 202/2010, paragraph 38, article 578,1, published in Monitorul Oficial, Part I, Nr. 714, 26 October 2010, available at http://www.dreptonline.ro/legislatie/legea_202_2010_masuri_pentru_accelerarea_solutionarii_proceselor_mica_reforma_a_justitiei.php (accessed 4 September 2017).
5. For instances of these acts of resistance, see Desire Foundation (2014).

REFERENCES

Agerpres. 2013. *Sondaj de opinie: 65% dintre români cred că în țara noastră există o problemă cu romii.* February 7. Available at https://www.agerpres.ro/social/2013/02/07/sondaj-de-opinie-65-dintre-romani-cred-ca-in-tara-noastra-exista-o-problema-cu-romii-16-25-32. Accessed 4 Sept 2017.

Amnesty International. 2013a. *Romania: Equality Body Decision on Discrimination of Roma by Cluj-Napoca Municipality Now Final.* May 31. Available at https://www.amnesty.org/en/documents/eur39/007/2013/en/. Accessed 4 Sept 2017.

———. 2013b. *Pushed to the Margins: Five Stories of Roma Forced Evictions in Romania.* June 18. Available at https://www.amnesty.org/en/documents/EUR39/003/2013/en/. Accessed 4 Sept 2017.

Amoore, L., and M. de Goede. 2008. Transactions After 9/11: The Banal Face of the Preemptive Strike. *Transactions of the Institute of British Geographers* 33 (2): 173–185.
Aradau, C., and R. van Munster. 2007. Governing Terrorism Through Risk. *European Journal of International Relations* 13 (1): 89–115.
Arias, G. 2011. The Normalisation of Exception in the Biopolitical Security Dispositive. *International Social Science Journal* 62 (205–6): 363–375.
Bacalu, M. 2017. Pretenţiile persoanelor evacuate de primăria Cuj de pe strada Coastei în colonia Pata Rât au fost respinse irevocabil. *Ora de Stiri Cluj*, April 14. Available at http://oradecluj.oradestiri.ro/pretentiile-persoanelor-evacuate-de-primaria-cuj-de-pe-strada-coastei-in-colonia-pata-rat-au-fost-respinse-irevocabil. Accessed 4 Sept 2017.
Balzacq, T. 2014. The "Essence" of Securitization: Theory, Ideal Type, and a Sociological Science of Security. *International Relations* 29 (1): 1–41.
Becker, A., and M. Müller. 2013. The Securitization of Urban Space and the "Rescue" of Downtown Mexico City. *Latin American Perspectives* 40 (2): 77–94.
Bigo, D. 2008. International Political Sociology. In *Security Studies. An Introduction*, ed. P. Williams, 116–130. London: Routledge.
Bigo, D., and A. Tsoukala. 2008. Understanding (In)security. In *Terror, Insecurity and Liberty*, ed. D. Bigo and A. Tsoukala, 1–9. London: Routledge.
Boncuţiu, S. 2009. Maghernite in Curtea Nokia. *Gazeta de Cluj*, June 14. Available at http://gazetadecluj.ro/maghernite-in-curtea-nokia/. Accessed 4 Sept 2017.
Brenner, N., and N. Theodore. 2002. Cities and the Geographies of "Actually Existing Neoliberalism". *Antipode* 34 (3): 349–379.
———. 2005. Neoliberalism and the Urban Condition. *City* 9 (1): 101–107.
Buzan, B., O. Waever, and J. de Wilde. 1998. *Security: A New Framework of Analysis*. Boulder, CO: Lynne Rienner.
C.A.S.E. Collective. 2006. Critical Approaches to Security in Europe: A Networked Manifesto. *Security Dialogue* 37 (4): 443–487.
Chelcea, L., and G. Pulay. 2015. Networked Infrastructures and the "Local". *City* 19 (2–3): 344–355.
Ciobanu, Claudia. 2017. Roma Fear There Is No Place for Them as Romania's Cities Modernize. *Reuters*, March 22. Available at http://www.reuters.com/article/us-romania-roma-property-feature-idUSKBN16T043. Accessed 4 Sept 2017.
Cluj City Hall. 2011. *Documents Regarding the Donation of Land in Coastei Street*. Available (as Pdf File in Romanian) at http://www.primariaclujnapoca.ro/userfiles/files/PH%20Mapa%2010.05.2011/PH1_10.05.2011.PDF. Accessed 4 Sept 2017.

Clujust. 2016. *Polițiștii au făcut razie la PataRât*. March 24. Available at http://www.clujust.ro/politistii-au-facut-razie-la-pata-rat-au-fost-ridicate-20-de-persoane-si-6-caini-comunitari-video/. Accessed 4 Sept 2017.
Coaffee, J., and D. Wood. 2006. Security Is Coming Home. *International Relations* 20 (4): 503–517.
Coward, M. 2009. Network-Centric Violence, Critical Infrastructure and the Urbanization of Security. *Security Dialogue* 40 (4–5): 399–418.
Creta, E., and P. Fekete. 2012. Roma Community Forcibly Evicted from Coastei Street Share Their Story. *Amnesty International*, April 4. Available at https://www.amnesty.org/en/latest/campaigns/2012/04/roma-community-forcibly-evicted-from-coastei-street-share-their-story/. Accessed 4 Sept 2017.
Criticatac. 2011. Apel pentru solidaritate și acțiune împotriva proiectului primăriei clujene: "locuințe sociale" în Pata Rât. *Criticatac*. Available at http://www.criticatac.ro/4392/apel-pentru-solidaritate-si-actiune-impotriva-proiectul-primariei-clujene-%E2%80%9Elocuinte-sociale%E2%80%9D-in-pata-rat/. Accessed 4 Sept 2017.
Desire Foundation. 2014. *Roma Socio-Territorial Segregation and Ghettoization. Local Activist Perspectives, 2010–2014.* Desire Foundation. Available at https://www.desire-ro.eu/?p=671. Accessed 4 Sept 2017.
Dohotaru, A., H. Harbula, and E. Vincze. 2016. *Pata*. Cluj: Editura Fundatiei pentru Studii Europene.
European Roma Rights Centre. 2012. *Romania: Bring Roma Back to the City of Cluj-Napoca!* December 14. Available at http://www.errc.org/article/romania-bring-roma-back-to-the-city-of-cluj-napoca/4078. Accessed 4 Sept 2017.
Foucault, M. 1980. The Confession of the Flesh. In *Power/Knowledge*, ed. C. Gordon, 194–228. New York: Pantheon.
Giurgiu, A. 2010. Primăria evacuează romii de pe strada Coastei și Cantonului luna aceasta. *Cotidianul Transilvan*, December 14. Available at http://www.cotidiantr.ro/primaria-evacueaza-romii-de-pe-strada-coastei-si-cantonului-luna-aceasta-46061.php#.V0iRnVIh2AZ. Accessed 4 Sept 2017.
Graham, S. 2010. *Cities Under Siege*. London: Verso.
Huysmans, J. 2004. A Foucaultian View on Spill-Over: Freedom and Security in the EU. *Journal of International Relations and Development* 7 (3): 294–318.
———. 2011. What's in an Act? On Security Speech Acts and Little Security Nothings. *Security Dialogue* 42 (4–5): 371–383.
ICCM. 2010. International Collaboratory on Critical Methods in Security: Method 4 "Situated Knowledge". Blog. Available at http://www.open.ac.uk/researchprojects/iccm/methods/method-4/description.html. Accessed 4 Sept 2017.
Marcuse, P. 1996. Privatization and Its Discontents. In *Cities After Socialism*, ed. G. Andrusz, M. Harloe, and I. Szelényi, 119–191. Oxford: Wiley-Blackwell.

McDonald, M. 2008. Securitization and the Construction of Security. *European Journal of International Relations* 14 (4): 563–587.
Mireanu, M. 2014. *Vigilantism and Security: State, Violence and Politics in Italy and Hungary*, Unpublished Ph.D. Thesis. Budapest: Central European University.
Păcurar, A. 2010. Locuitorii din Pata Rât au capela si birou de politie. *City News*, April 22. Available at http://citynews.ro/din-oras-10/locuitorii-din-pata-rat-au-capela-si-birou-de-politie-79590. Accessed 4 Sept 2017.
Pásztor, G., and L. Péter. 2009. Romanian Housing Problems. *Studia Universitatis Babes Bolyay Sociologia* LIV (1): 79–100.
Petrovici, N. 2012. Workers and the City. *Urban Studies* 49 (11): 2377–2397.
Poenaru, F. 2016. The Roma Business 160 Years Since the End of Roma Slavery in Romania. *LeftEast*, February 26. Available at http://www.criticatac.ro/lefteast/the-roma-business-160-years-since-the-end-of-roma-slavery-in-romania/. Accessed 4 Sept 2017.
Pop, V. 2015. The Art of Exclusion. *The Economist*, February 20.
Raț, C. 2011. Și țiganul este aproapele meu? *Criticatac*. Available at http://www.criticatac.ro/7533/si-tiganul-este-aproapele-meu/. Accessed 4 Sept 2017.
Roe, P. 2008. Actor, Audience(s) and Emergency Measures. *Security Dialogue* 39 (6): 615–635.
Romitan, C. 2014. Romii mutați de pe Coastei nu vor primi despăgubiri. *Transilvania Reporter*, October 7. Available at http://transilvaniareporter.ro/actualitate/romii-mutati-de-pe-coastei-nu-vor-primi-despagubiri/. Accessed 4 Sept 2017.
Smith, N. 1996. *The New Urban Frontier*. London: Routledge.
———. 2002. New Globalism, New Urbanism. *Antipode* 34 (3): 427–450.
Stiri de Cluj. 2011a. *Pata Rât, cea mai periculoasa zona din Cluj*. May 10. Available at http://www.stiridecluj.ro/social/pata-rat-cea-mai-periculoasa-zona-din-cluj-in-zona-au-loc-mai-mult-de-jumatate-din-infractiunile-inregistrate-in-oras. Accessed 4 Sept 2017.
———. 2011b. *Parc de joaca in locul locuintelor de tigani de pe strada Coastei*. August 16. Available at http://www.stiridecluj.ro/social/parc-de-joaca-in-locul-locuintelor-de-tigani-de-pe-strada-coastei-video-si-foto. Accessed 4 Sept 2017.
———. 2012. *Experiment la Pata Rat! Tiganii care locuiesc pe rampa sunt ca termitele*. March 29. Available at http://www.stiridecluj.ro/social/experiment-la-pata-rat-tiganii-care-locuiesc-pe-rampa-sunt-ca-termitele-video. Accessed 4 Sept 2017.
Stritzel, H. 2011. Security, the Translation. *Security Dialogue* 42 (4–5): 343–355.
van Baar, H. 2017. Evictability and the Biopolitical Bordering of Europe. *Antipode* 49 (1): 212–230.

Vincze, E. 2012a. Rampa de gunoi: spațiul marginalității urbane avansate rasializate în România de azi. In *Antologia Criticatac*, 53–67. Bucuresti: Tact.

———. 2012b. Landfill: Space of Advanced and Racialized Urban Marginality in Today's Romania. *SPAREX*. Available at http://sparex-ro.eu/?p=487. Accessed 4 Sept 2017.

———. 2015. Glocalization of Neoliberalism in Romania Through the Reform of the State and Entrepreneurial Development. *Studia UBB Europaea* LX (1): 125–151.

Vincze, E., and S. Ciotlăuș. 2016. Housing and Class (Trans)formation in Romania. *LeftEast*, September 3. Available at http://www.criticatac.ro/lefteast/housing-and-class-transformation-in-romania/. Accessed 4 Sept 2017.

Wæver, O. 1995. Securitisation and Desecuritisation. In *On Security*, ed. R.D. Lipschutz, 46–86. New York: Columbia University Press.

Wacquant, L. 2008. Relocating Gentrification. *International Journal of Urban and Regional Research* 32 (1): 198–205.

Zamfirescu, I. 2015. Housing Eviction, Displacement and the Missing Social Housing of Bucharest. *Calitatea Vietii* XXVI (2): 140–154.

Ziua de Cluj. 2010. *"Cartier" de romi la PataRât*. May 10. Available at http://ziuadecj.realitatea.net/administratie/cartier-de-romi-la-pata-rat--5384.html. Accessed 4 Sept 2017.

CHAPTER 7

The Entertaining Enemy: 'Gypsy' in Popular Culture in an Age of Securitization

Annabel Tremlett

'There is no reality show I'm aware of', says reality TV producer Troy DeVolld 'that's comprised of a straight-up, uncut piece of source footage. Someone's there, pulling strings behind the scenes to at least some extent' (DeVolld 2016: 1). The amount of control that producers and editors have on 'reality' television has evolved. In early productions of *Big Brother*, a degree of editorial control was sacrificed, as programmes had to be edited according to the developments of that day and were therefore done very quickly without a known outcome. This 'promise of demystification' became part of the marketing strategy (Andrejevic 2004: 5). However, producers (wanting to be sure of high viewing figures) started to instigate 'dramatic interactions' among the participants of these shows to ensure certain outcomes which they thought would attract the most viewers (Andrejevic 2004: 159). At first, such interventions were commented on

---

I am grateful to the editors of this volume for their useful comments on this chapter. Many thanks to organizer Huub van Baar for the invitation to the University of Giessen, and to all the attendees for the days of lively discussions.

A. Tremlett (✉)
University of Portsmouth, Portsmouth, UK
e-mail: Annabel.tremlett@port.ac.uk

© The Author(s) 2019
H. van Baar et al. (eds.), *The Securitization of the Roma in Europe*, Human Rights Interventions, https://doi.org/10.1007/978-3-319-77035-2_7

by viewers, but have since become a normal part of reality TV. The ways the 'strings are pulled'—in DeVolld's words—are now barely noted. These types of programme now work to give the appearance of live television in a documentary style, even though they might have been filmed months before and are highly controlled and edited during production (e.g., see Blanchet 2016).

'Gypsy' people started to be included in reality formats from the early 2000s. The very favorable ratings for these TV shows have meant that Gypsy stories have become highly popular, and therefore profitable, with broadcasting companies—such as Channel 4 in the UK—actively producing such stories and facilitating their large-scale consumption. This chapter examines the ways in which 'the Gypsy' has been edited and produced for this market as both a fetishized celebrity and an 'enemy' of the nation state, exploring the changing relationship between popular culture and discourses of securitization. The profitable logic of this television programming means the continued and reinforced circulation of specific, securitizing ideas of 'the Gypsies'.

From the late 1990s, the early stage of this modern form was the 'Gypsy celebrity', with Gypsy rap artists and pop singers of Roma origin gaining a popular fan base. For example, Hungary's *Fekete Vonat* ('Black Train') addressed the broader political and social conditions of the Roma in Hungary, as well as more everyday issues of relationships, jobs and discrimination (Simeziane 2010). More mainstream vocalists of Roma origin then began to win prizes on prominent TV music talent shows such as *The X-Factor* (UK), *American Idol* (USA) or *Megasztár* and *Superstar* (Hungary, Romania and the Czech Republic).[1] At this time, the cultural landscape for the public representation of Roma seemed to be shifting, with these celebrities offered follow-up reality shows or prominent public appearances, for example, in advertisements, on chat shows or in support of charities. Such appearances—while still positioning Roma celebrities as 'Roma' and 'other'—did at least offer an alternative to the continually circulating negative public image of the Roma, which had previously only been mired in notions of difference, underclass and criminality.

Reality TV shows focusing on Roma, Traveller or Gypsy people became popular from around 2005—for example, see *Győzike* (RTL Klub in Hungary, from 2005), *Adventurile familiei Vijelie* (Prima TV in Romania from 2005), *Big Fat Gypsy Weddings* (Channel 4 in the UK from 2010) and *My Big Fat American Gypsy Wedding* (TCL in the USA from 2012). Such reality formats have proved controversial: on the one hand, there is an argument that these shows have normalized previously abnormalized/

marginalized groups by bringing them into the sphere of popular culture. On the other hand, much of this attention has been vitriolic, with reports of an increase in racism directly attributed to the broadcasting of these shows (Imre and Tremlett 2011).[2] These reality formats have been produced at an increasingly tumultuous time for the Roma in Europe, with widening inequality occurring in a more precarious economic and political climate. The wider political shift to an era of securitization has also altered the landscape, and in this environment, the initial signs which suggested that 'the Gypsy celebrity' might challenge common stereotypes have also changed. This chapter argues that the most recent shifts in reality TV formats have moved away from the flamboyant 'other' denoted by the Gypsy celebrity to the Gypsy as a threat, an 'enemy' to the nation state or national culture.

This chapter focuses on UK popular culture, where there has been a move from the type of Gypsy celebrity that emerged from the series focused on UK Travellers, *Big Fat Gypsy Weddings*, to the stigmatization of migrant Roma as benefit cheats and criminals apparent in programming such as *Benefits Street* (2014, Channel 4), *Gypsies On Benefits & Proud* (2014, Channel 5) and *Keeping up with the Khans* (2016, Channel 4). The most watched of these programmes were the *Big Fat Gypsy Weddings* (which regularly attracted an audience of over 8 million viewers and gained some of the highest ratings ever achieved on Channel 4, see Deans 2011) and *Benefits Street* (with over four million viewers, it was one of the most watched shows on Channel 4 in 2013, see Collier 2014). Such programmes, this chapter argues, used editorial control to utilize and marketize certain images of the Gypsy, from fetishized celebrity to a threat to the welfare system and the security of the nation state. The chapter explores how such shifts in popular culture turn the 'other' into an 'entertaining enemy', as Roma are shifted out of the realm of ordinary popular culture (and politics) and into the realm of exceptional measures.

Theorizing 'the Other': Securitization and Cultural Studies

Cultural studies, with its very focus on 'culture' as a practice—as Street (1993: 25) said, 'culture is a verb'—has links to the strand of critical security studies that focuses on securitization as a practice rather than a state of being:

> Security [is] a practice of making 'enemy' and 'fear' the integrative, energetic principle of politics displacing the democratic principles of freedom and justice… [S]ecurity can thus be understood as a political force. It is not simply a policy responding to threats and dangers. Neither is it a public good or value. It is a practice with a political content. It enacts our world as if it is a dangerous world, a world saturated by insecurities. It invests fear and enmity in relations between humans and polities. (Huysmans 2014: 3)

Here, Jef Huysmans writes about how the making of the 'enemy' is fundamental to the process of securitization. In cultural studies, the notion of the 'other', stemming from Edward Said's (1979) conceptualization, has been the basis for understanding the power of language and exclusion in the way minorities are depicted in Western cultures. As Stuart Hall (1992: 189) says, it is the discourse of 'the West/the rest' that draws 'crude and simplistic distinctions and constructs in an over-simplified conception of difference'. Securitization discourses on 'the enemy' moves cultural studies' discourses of 'the other' into a particular framework of 'existential threats' (Balzacq 2011) and 'suspect communities' (Bigo 2002). Thierry Balzacq, Didier Bigo and Jef Huysmans' ideas of 'making an enemy' are useful touchstones for this chapter, as we see how the stories of Roma told by reality TV shows work this culture of securitization into their storylines.

In terms of Roma minorities, 'the other' is a recognizable trope in expressions of public representations (Tremlett 2009, 2013, 2017). However, the characterization of Roma as 'the enemy' has taken a contemporary turn, one that Huub van Baar has shown is prevalent in a much more widespread form of a 'reasonable anti-Gypsyism' that legitimizes the violence of 'unreasonable anti-Gypsyism' (2014: 28, 38). Van Baar examines various racist incidents or police/state actions across Europe, showing how Roma are targeted and blamed for crimes when it is in fact they who are the victims. Roma thus become a 'security problem':

> More often, and almost self-evidently, politicians, the police, and citizens consider the Roma to be a 'security problem' – a menace to public order requiring unorthodox and in part drastic measures. (van Baar 2014: 29)

Such discourses mean that anti-Gypsyism becomes normalized, 'the framing of the Roma as a security issue is part of a political problem and of the legitimization of anti-Gypsyism' (2014: 30). Van Baar uses Foucault's work on 'truth regimes' to look at the practices of this kind of anti-Gypsyism:

Interrogating the history of different kinds of truth regimes, Foucault suggested, is 'a matter of analyzing, not behaviors, or ideas, nor societies and their 'ideologies', but the *problematizations* through which being offers itself to be, necessarily, though – and the *practices* on the basis of which these problematizations are formed'. (van Baar 2011: 206)

Looking at problematizations, continues van Baar, does not focus on solutions and answers but rather on why and how certain things become a problem. By deconstructing the ideologies and problematizations produced by the output of popular culture, we can explore the ways in which this political economy of securitization is used in the production and marketing of 'entertainment'.

The Essentialized Other: Materialism, Gender and Threats in *Big Fat Gypsy Weddings*

The rise of the Gypsy celebrity in European popular culture was an exciting, albeit rather curious, phenomenon of the early 2000s. At a time when Gypsy communities were appearing across Europe in news and human rights reports as increasingly suffering from poverty and discrimination, the concept of a Gypsy celebrity seemed incongruous. *Big Fat Gypsy Weddings*, a UK Channel 4 production (2010–2015), followed an increasing trend in the Gypsy celebrity already established in Central and Eastern Europe. Certain figures from *Big Fat Gypsy Weddings* went on to gain celebrity status or were sometimes referred to as 'TV personalities.' Irish Traveller Patrick 'Paddy' Doherty, for example, went on to star in *Danny Dyer's Deadliest Men* (Bravo, 2009) and *When Paddy Met Sally* (Channel 5, 2012). Paddy became a regular guest on chat shows and won *Celebrity Big Brother 8* (Channel 5, 2011). Despite instigating a new wave of Gypsy celebrities, *Big Fat Gypsy Weddings* was widely criticized for its sensationalist and frequently sexist focus on the bodies of young women, with reports of an increase in the bullying and harassment of Traveller communities directly linked to the show's broadcast (see endnote 2). This section of the chapter examines how this reality format—originally about the inclusion of the ordinary person (what Turner (2006) called the 'demotic turn' in broadcasting)—started to create an extreme type of 'other'.

First, a note about the television format itself. Channel 4 listed *Big Fat Gypsy Weddings* under the category of documentaries,[3] which included other programmes purporting to reveal the otherwise hidden lives of others, such as *Living with the Amish* (2011) and *The Undateables* (about people with various disabilities trying to find romance) (2012—). Channel 4 pitched the series as fulfilling the channel's remit of 'shining a light on marginal communities' (David Abraham, Channel 4's chief executive, quoted in *The Independent* 2012). However, *Big Fat Gypsy Weddings* has been widely described in the media as a reality TV format—online stores such as hmv.com and amazon.co.uk both place DVDs of the series in the reality TV section—whilst Channel 4 actually commissioned the series under the heading 'Factual Entertainment'. This not-quite-documentary but not-quite-reality format is important, as it brings together the style of serious documentary making and popular entertainment. Channel 4 calls this 'Constructed Factual', described on its website as follows:

> We strive to say something new about the world and reinterpret PSB [Public Service Broadcasting] for a young generation, making shows about broad issues that are contemporary, popular, carry public service values and are also mischievous and counterintuitive in approach.[4]

From this, we can see that the approach is both serious—'striving' to say something new about broad issues—and attractive—'mischievous and counterintuitive'. This sets the tone for *Big Fat Gypsy Weddings*, which includes serious topics such as domestic violence, eviction and discrimination, among 'funny' shots of young women, with their huge wedding dresses and over-the-top ceremonies. Such reality shows, as Tyler argues, draw on the formal techniques of serious, socially committed documentaries (e.g., 'fly-on-the-wall' camera angles) in order to create some kind of authenticity that will serve to 'justify the exploitation and voyeurism involved in such programmes through an implied association with "documentary realism"' (2013: 144–145).

In a previous article (Tremlett 2014), I analysed how the original 'demotic' approach of reality television (Turner 2006) is made 'demonic' through the techniques in *Big Fat Gypsy Weddings* that depict Travellers as racialized, inferior and other. Here, I want to extend this analysis to look at how the series also portrays Travellers as a threat by developing threads of unease in the programmes, which point to what Huysmans calls a 'general context of social insecurities' (2014: 85; see also Bigo 2002; Huysmans and Buonofino 2008, both quoted in Huysmans 2014: 85). There are two main ways in which this unease is achieved. First, through gender divisions: Traveller women are portrayed as 'for show', while male Travellers are depicted as shadowy, violent and dangerous. Second, in the construction of the participants as extremely different; essentializing their 'otherness' so that anything they do—choosing a dress, getting married, buying furniture, visiting a hairdresser, buying a home—becomes something that proves their difference from an imagined mainstream societal norm. Both these constructions are emphasized over and over again as the following examples reveal.

First, let us discuss the emphasis on stark gender divisions. While Traveller women are predominantly shown as obsessed by cleaning, sparkly dresses and weddings, reducing them to 'sluts' or 'doormats' (Jensen and Ringrose 2014), Traveller men are depicted as threatening and the perpetrators of illegal activities. In the first instance, this is very visual—many of the men shown in the series have had their faces pixelated so they cannot be recognized, creating an unsettling image of the community. The practical answer as to why this might be is that they had refused to sign consent forms, and so, ethically, the editors were obliged to blur their faces. However, as Berg and Schwenken (2010: 112) point out, this technique is culturally associated with 'the representation of criminals and persons who shamefully hide themselves'.[5] Pixelated faces give a very visual impression that the men are 'undercover'—shadowy characters who do not want to be identified because they have something to hide.

Furthermore, extreme masculinity is emphasized as being key to Gypsy culture, and this adds to a sense of unease about their volatility, shown most vividly in an incident in which the camera operators themselves appear to be in danger. In the episode entitled, 'Boys will be Boys' (Season 1, Episode 4), bare knuckle fighting, which takes place in secret places, is described as a vital part of 'their' culture. The voice-over informs us that the film crew even needed special permission from a 'Gypsy elder' to film it. The overt masculinity and tribal connotations are clear. Despite this hype, the actual fight comes to nothing; it is stopped before it has properly started and the dispute is settled without violence. However, the parting shot is the voice-over saying, 'Our film crew, however, has outstayed its welcome', with the camera focusing on a young, half-naked man saying as he walks away: 'Point the camera out of my face now. Otherwise I'll send round a couple of boys to beat you up'. Despite there being no fight to film, the editors still manage to convey a dangerous, threatening, volatile type of masculinity. Tracey Jensen and Jessica Ringrose (2014: 11) point out how a similar hyper-masculine representation has also been used against Muslims, 'where "backward" Muslim culture is positioned as inherently sexist and repressive to women as a way to justify racialized hatred'. Hyper-masculinity is also typical in securitization discourses and serves to destabilize trust with certain groups and to legitimate interventions for the protection of vulnerable women and children (Cudworth 2013). In the constructions of male Gypsies as secretive and hyper-masculine, they are portrayed as an essentialized 'other' who exist outside or beyond the norms of the nation state (McGarry 2017: 10–29).

The second way in which unease is conveyed is less overt than the previous examples of male violence, and this is where the securitization discourse becomes more nuanced, an example of 'the multiple circulations of multiple insecurities' (Huysmans 2014). In this second construction, a focus on 'Gypsy difference' is not only directed at violent, half-naked men with their faces pixelated but also at 'nice' 'ordinary' Travellers whose 'difference' is marked by a subtle process of provocation and editing. In *Big Fat Gypsy Weddings*, the interviewers/researchers are always out of shot and are barely audible, yet the glimpses we get reveal the mechanisms of the narration and the otherwise hidden agenda setting. Such a silent agenda setting is manifest of the claim to truthfulness put forward by the series makers, noted by Nichols (1991: 109) as enabled through the 'heightened realism' of the documentary format.

Here, I take one example in detail to show how the editing process works in a subtle way to produce an impression of the 'other' as 'enemy'. In the episode entitled, 'No Place Like Home' (Season 2, Episode 2), the focus is on the wedding of a non-Traveller woman (Sam) to a Traveller man (Pat). This couple is always shown in a positive way as childhood sweethearts, with Pat depicted as a caring, sensible man with a job and stable family background. However, when the camera follows Pat's fiancée Sam as she looks around potential caravans for their future married home, it is difference that is evoked and imposed on Sam by the out-of-shot interviewer, even as she tries to resist it:

Interviewer:	'What do you say to people who are watching who think, "she's crazy, she's gonna move into a trailer!"?'
Sam:	'Well they're crazy 'cos they've never tried it! I don't really think it's, like, a big deal really, it's just like going looking at houses, it's not...'
Interviewer:	'But it's not a house, it's a caravan!'
Sam:	'I know but it's just the same innit [isn't it]... it's just where we're gonna live.'
Interviewer:	'No! It's different! It's a caravan!'

Sam's attempt to compare her caravan to any other home is refuted by the interviewer, who wants to make his point that Sam's chosen life is ultimately 'other'. In another example, Pat tells the (out-of-shot) interviewer that the relentless focus on difference between Travellers and non-Travellers is unacceptable. 'I think it's very unfair to point out differences', he says to the interviewer, 'what's that going to do for anyone? It's unacceptable if you ask me. We ain't different'. Immediately after Pat's protest, the camera zooms in on his non-Traveller bride's dress, as the narrator tells us how non-Travellers are 'expected to discard their own culture and adopt Gypsy ways'. By choosing a dress 'to end all wedding dresses', Sam will prove her Gypsy girl credentials. Patrick's protest that 'we ain't different' is lost as the visual attention is transferred to the incredible mechanical fluttering butterflies being attached to Sam's wedding dress. 'She looks more of a Traveller than a Traveller' comments the only visible narrator, the non-Traveller dressmaker Thelma. It's no surprise that when Sam protests, 'I don't see it as a Gypsy marrying a non-Gypsy. He's just my partner and I'm marrying him', we don't really hear it, as our visual senses are assailed by Sam's glittering transformation.

At this point, the programme uses 'humour', as Sam's small, tanned frame is engulfed in a pink glittery monster of a dress. We learn that at 20 stone (127 kilos) the dress is twice the weight of its owner, while the inbuilt fairy lights mean that a fire extinguisher must be constantly on hand. We can laugh at the tackiness of her Cinderella-style pumpkin carriage into which she must squeeze herself in a rather ungainly way. We are told that it is the very same carriage that the (in)famous (working-class) UK celebrity Jordan (aka Katie Price) ordered for her wedding to Australian pop star Peter Andre. We are now in familiar territory for British viewers' class-based stereotypes of trailer trash and chavs focused on working-class female stereotypes (inappropriate bodies, ridiculous dresses), while the reference to Jordan—glamour model, reality TV star and celebrity chav—situates the participants firmly in derogatory class discourses (see Jones 2011; Skeggs et al. 2008; Tyler and Bennett 2010; Wood and Skeggs 2011). The degrading humour serves to make us, the viewers, feel smug in our middle-class worlds (Skeggs and Wood 2008) and echoes Mark Neocleous' remarks (2007: 354) on the politics of securitization: 'security is the supreme concept of bourgeois society'. Humour, mixed with the potency of essentialized difference, represents Travellers as outside the norm. The dark undertones that make up their (albeit at times entertaining) position are situated outside of the normative (bourgeois) parameters of mainstream life. In terms of securitization discourses, 'the Gypsies' are on their way to becoming "abnormalized", transformed into "legitimate" objects of suspicion' (Bigo 2014: 219).

In *Big Fat Gypsy Weddings,* the marketing of the show played on both the Gypsy as different and a potential celebrity, and the Gypsy as different and a potential threat. However, in more recent reality TV output, the focus has shifted to portraying Gypsies as impoverished migrants and a burden to the welfare state. The next section moves on to look at this more recent television output, which has been labelled 'austerity porn' (Allen et al. 2014). In this output, the concept of a Gypsy celebrity is mostly lost as the focus turns to the migrant Roma as the 'abject figure' (Tyler 2013), the ultimate enemy threatening the safety of our homes and livelihoods.

THE ENTERTAINING ENEMY IN 'AUSTERITY PORN'

Post *Big Fat Gypsy Weddings,* there were a number of 'one off' specials. However, amid protests from the Traveller community and complaints to the Advertising Standards Authority that were upheld (ASA Report 2012), the then Channel 4 creative officer Jay Hunt stated (without mentioning any accusations of poor quality broadcasting): 'Entirely for creative reasons, we have reached the end of the line'.[6] The next 'line' in popular programming in the UK then shifted to a mass interest in programming focusing on people on benefits. In 2013, the BBC broadcast *We Pay Your Benefits,* in which four taxpayers scrutinized the lifestyle and spending habits of four people on benefits to assess whether the financial support they received was too high. A spate of other programming then focused on the benefits system, including *On Benefits and Proud* (Channel 5, 2013) followed by a special focus on Roma in *Gypsies on Benefits and Proud* (Channel 5, 2014). Dubbed 'poverty porn' in media commentaries, the most popular of these shows was *Benefits Street* (Channel 4, 2014), which tapped into the explosion of public debate about the welfare state in the UK (Jensen 2014). The opening of each episode of *Benefits Street* followed a woman walking down a terraced street and pointing at each door, shouting 'Unemployed! Unemployed!', with heaps of rubbish on the street visible in the background. Watching the series was only a part of the experience. The associated sideshow of lavish media coverage, booming twitter feeds and the perception that everybody was watching and talking about the programme is a now recognizable factor in the highly constructed yet 'authentic' format of documentary-as-diversion (Corner 2002; Hill 2008).

In *Benefits Street*, while the focus was on the unemployed, there was a rapid demarcation of characters, as white and Black British-born residents were seen to be in opposition to migrants. In Episode Two, this became focused on Roma migrants in particular. This episode showed a number of residents calling out racist comments to a Romanian Roma family as they walked down the street. The residents accuse the family of splitting open the bin bags put out for collection in their search for scrap metal, leaving a mess of spilled rubbish across the street which the council refuses to pick up. But when we see the Romanian Roma family at work, they are picking up big pieces of scrap metal and hauling them onto a large truck. These do not look like people who would waste time splitting open and rummaging through bin bags. Despite learning about the family's struggles—to get paperwork, their refusal to claim benefits (in direct contrast to the stated purpose of the series to look at people on benefits) and problems with their rented accommodation—it is the accusation of uncleanliness and parasitical behaviour which hangs in the air as the voice-over repeats that the family 'live off other people's rubbish'.

When the Romanian Roma family suddenly leaves, no one tells us why or where they have gone, leaving viewers with a sense of unease at the transience of migrant lives. We learn, shockingly, that the next residents to move in—a group of 14 Romanian men—are working very long hours for very little money. These men are eventually forced out of their new home by the intimidating behaviour of their boss and his associates, who are shown circling the house in a car after the men's complaint to the police of slave labour fails to prompt any action. The Romanian men leave, and the street goes back to 'normal'. Despite the clear evidence of migrants working rather than relying on benefits, and in fact being the victims of bad (local) landlords and exploitative (local) labour practices, the programme ends with the feeling that with the migrants gone, the threat is gone. It is thus the migrants here who epitomize the ultimate threat—the transient insecurity of migration, which 'aggregate(s) the various insecurities into one particular threat that connects them all: migration' (Huysmans 2014: 84).

There is a similar framing of Roma migrants in the 2016 series *Keeping up with the Khans* (Channel 4). This series 'explores the lives and aspirations of new migrants in Britain, and the impact that immigration has on one community: Page Hall in Sheffield' (Channel 4 website).[7] Page Hall became notorious in 2013, when the media reported on the anti-social behaviour following a recent influx of Slovakian Roma. It was reported that between 1500 and 3000 Roma had migrated to Sheffield since Slovakia joined the EU in 2004, with 500 of these estimated to be living in the suburb of Page Hall.[8] The media reported tensions between local residents—made up of British-born working-class people of both white and Pakistani heritage—and Slovakian Roma, who were said to come, in particular, from Bystrany, Žehra and Letanovce in Eastern Slovakia. The media reports told of building tensions:

- 'Slovakian Roma in Sheffield: This is a boiling pot ready to explode' (*The Guardian* 15 November 2013);
- 'Fears of civil unrest in Sheffield as locals take action against new arrivals' (*The Daily Mail*, 12 November 2013)
- 'Roma migrants cause terror for South Yorkshire residents' (*The Express*, 14 June 2014).

Such headlines highlight the hysteria surrounding Roma migrants as a security threat. We have seen the UK use a similar approach in public discourses with other migrant, Muslim and white working-class communities in the UK, which have led directly to the idea that 'something must be done' (Brown 2008: 483; Tyler 2013: 17). The Page Hall example did indeed evoke political commentary: former Home Secretary and the then MP for Sheffield David Blunkett gave an interview in which he warned that tensions in Page Hall could lead to rioting, saying 'We have got to change the behaviour and the culture of the incoming community, the Roma community, because there's going to be an explosion otherwise. We all know that'.[9] Similarly, the then Deputy Prime Minister Nick Clegg, a Liberal Democrat, criticized Roma migrants for behaving in a 'sometimes intimidating, sometimes offensive way', and saying that Roma migrants needed to be more 'sensitive' to the British 'way of life'.[10]

It was against this political backdrop that Channel 4 launched its 2016 series *Keeping up with the Khans*, a title mimicking the US show about a wealthy celebrity family, *Keeping up with the Kardashians* (E! cable network 2007) with an implicit mockery of opposing ends of the socio-economic scale occupied by the characters. The second episode focused on migrant Roma and suggested from the start that members of the Roma community were criminals. Similar to *Big Fat Gypsy Weddings*, the crowds shown in the street mostly had their faces pixelated, immediately suggesting criminal activity. This approach was also very similar to the way in which images were shown in the news media, with individuality subsumed by the faceless collective. This gives the impression of a faceless gang or mob, a dehumanized group (Messing and Bernáth 2017). A white British couple, retired and in their sixties, was interviewed outside their home. They recurred throughout the episode as the 'normative' voices of those who had been brought up in the area. The couple said that they had been monitoring the area and had installed a camera in their car so that when they drove around they could gather 'evidence' which they sent to the police. They admitted that they had never stopped to talk to any of the Roma residents, and the man said he had nicknamed Sheffield 'Shefflavia' because of the number of Slovakian Roma living there. 'We feel really pissed off', he complains. Surveillance and reporting (rather than dialogue) are the ways shown to deal with this situation. This is further emphasized by the police meeting with local residents, including the Pakistani Advice and Community Association, a meeting to which the Roma were not invited (as the voice-over tells us). While the police commissioner is discussing problems with the local residents, someone points out a group of Roma boys playing football in the street. Their faces are blurred in the footage. Someone says they should not be there, but no one goes to talk to them. The Roma boys do not appear to be either dangerous or offensive but are yet again shown as a faceless collective—as if they are a 'mob'—not to be spoken to but just 'dealt with'—even though they are just children playing football.

When the programme moves from the collective 'faceless' Roma threat to the individual, it reverts to the technique of the 'entertaining Gypsy'. Erik, a Slovakian Roma, has managed to get a job in a local Pakistani restaurant. The owner of the restaurant, Wahid, has already been filmed saying he will give anyone a chance. Erik is singing loudly and rather out of tune in the kitchen, and Wahid says, he will mentor Erik and try to help him fulfil his dream of becoming a singer. The relationship between Erik and Wahid is touching—Wahid and the other workers say they love Erik. Erik calls them his Uncles and Aunties just as Asian people would do. He is generous, and gives money to poor people in the community. Wahid tries to give Erik some advice about his singing, as Erik wants to audition for the popular TV show *Britain's Got Talent* (ITV 2007—). Wahid takes Erik to a clothes shop to get him a 'look' for his audition and tries to dissuade Erik from choosing a tacky, glittery top to wear. The relationship is both touching and humorous; although similar in style to *Big Fat Gypsy Weddings*, it points to a bourgeois type of humour in which the audience is invited to laugh at the characters' expense. Such 'affective textual encounters' in television viewing (as defined by Skeggs et al. 2008: 17) allow viewers a certain 'moral authority': viewers are treated like duplicitous witnesses; viewers have taste. They will understand that Erik has a terrible singing voice and that, as a chubby middle-aged man with no particular style who runs an Asian restaurant in a dilapidated suburb, Wahid cannot be much of a mentor. The 'charming Gypsy' thus serves as a means to tell the 'rest of the story' from a classed perspective: that is, some of these poor people are trying, but it's hopeless; Erik is lovely, but his destiny is to work in a takeaway and grocery shop in a tatty suburb. Erik is indeed lovely but also an exception. The programme shows his peers failing to turn up for work, hanging about in crowds on the street and living among piles of litter.

In fact, litter has a central role in the construction of the Gypsies who are not Erik. In the same episode, various residents are shown complaining about the litter, which is shown in close-up camera shots. 'It's obligatory here, the mattress on the street', says a local resident. The programme then cuts to a rubbish tip in Slovakia, and the voice-over informs us that this is where the Roma migrants in Page Hall come from. Roma people are shown getting onto a bus, expressing their hopes for a better future in the UK. The symbolism is clear—the Roma themselves *are* the 'litter problem'. This echoes Zygmunt Bauman's arguments about 'wasted humans': that refugees, asylum seekers and immigrants are all, in effect, 'the waste products of globalization':

> The images of 'economic migrants' and of 'asylum seekers' both stand for 'wasted humans', and whichever of the two is used to arouse resentment and anger, the object of the resentment and the target on which the anger is to be unloaded remains much the same. (Bauman 2004: 66)

It is true that, due to poverty and housing crises, some impoverished Roma communities have been forced to live on or near rubbish tips (Ivasiuc, Chap. 11, this volume; Mireanu, Chap. 6, this volume; Timmer 2010), but the way the camera cuts from litter on the street in Page Hall to the rubbish tip in Slovakia here sends out a strong message—this community is embedded and embodied in the litter which surrounds them, and this is what they bring to the UK. This encourages the 'equation between poverty and delinquency' that increases the fear of Gypsies and which has led to 'the precarious situation of the Roma, the police and citizens alike have unanimously perceived various Roma groups as violent and backward' (Pasqualino

2008: 337). Gypsies are equated with waste and are to be feared *and* repulsed—they become the ultimate 'revolting subject' (Tyler 2013).

Conclusion

The 'othering' of Roma minorities in reality television programming is not only about obvious security issues such as Gypsies living beyond the law or threatening neighbours, but is also about fixing their difference in racialized terms as an oddly different, a bad 'other', an enemy. This relates to securitization discourses about the 'abnormalized', that is, when people are 'transformed into "legitimate" objects of suspicion' (Bigo 2014: 219). At the same time, these shows do also depict stories of struggling people trying to make their way in life, and certain characters or activities are shown with humour or charm. Nonetheless, as we have seen, this humour is aimed at enabling the bourgeois viewer's idea of their status as compared to that of the Travellers or migrant Roma who are beneath them, not only in terms of economic status but also in terms of taste, morals and proper behaviour. Roma, Travellers or Gypsies (no matter what their nationality, ethnicity or migrant status) are seen as either dangerous or as something to be laughed at and looked down upon. The way in which these communities are shown as hyper-materialistic, vain or with over-the-top tastelessness does not seem to fit with the security issues raised in other parts of the programming, and can be confusing, unless we see it all as a way of abnormalizing this community so that they remain beyond the parameters of ordinary, respectable law-abiding life in the UK. As the term securitization infers, this is a process, not a static set of practices or products:

> Securitization does not necessarily mean that the word 'security' is used, but that an imminent danger is constructed, that a threatening future is invoked, which demands urgent attention. Securitization is about dramatizing and bringing urgency to a certain matter, because it threatens the world as we know it. (Malmvig 2005: 335, cited in Brown 2008: 476)

By framing security in these broad terms, this chapter has shown how popular culture can produce and market Roma and Travellers as a type of enemy—an entertaining enemy—using a powerful affective dynamic of threat *and* charm as a potent way to justify denunciation and even venomous hatred of the community, which is produced as the 'other' to British communities and the welfare state, and ultimately, the enemy of an imagined British way of life.

Notes

1. For example, Roma singer Vlastimil Horvath won the 2005 season of *SuperStar* in the Czech Republic, in the same year as Caramel, aka Ferenc Molnár, won *Megasztár* in Hungary. Shane Ward and Cher Lloyd, contestants of the UK's *X-Factor* (2005 and 2010) revealed, respectively, Irish Traveller and Welsh Romany roots. The *Eurovision* song contests of recent years have also provided a 'European playing field' for the performance of 'non-normative ethnic and sexual identities' (Imre 2009: 125), with Hungary's Roma singer Ibolya Oláh performing in the 2005 contest (one of her popular songs starts 'I can hear my father's voice. You may not like this, but this is my country'); Bulgaria entered singer 'Azis', a gay Roma 'superstar' drag queen in 2006; 'Gipsy.cz', a Roma rap group from the Czech Republic performed in 2009.
2. For example, see: reports from Traveller Education Support Services staff in the report 'Bigger Fatter Gypsier' by Brian Foster (available at: http://acert.org.uk/wp-content/uploads/2012/10/Report_of_Brian_Foster_7.6.pdf [accessed 21 November 2016]; Harper v Housing 21, in which the Employment Tribunal upheld all of Irish Traveller Ms Harper's claims of race discrimination and harassment when her employer likened her to a character from *Big Fat Gypsy Weddings* (details available at http://www.redmans.co.uk/blog/employment-law-posts/harper-v-housing-21-banter-about-protected-characteristics-will-normally-constitute-discrimination [accessed 21 November 2016]; the open letter written to Channel 4 by Pip Borev 'My Big Fat Gypsy Wedding Ruined My Life' (18 February 2012, available on his blog, http://pipopotamus.blogspot.co.uk/2012/02/open-letter-to-chanel-4.html (accessed 21 November 2016).
3. See Channel 4's 'Features and Factual Entertainment' section of their website, available at http://www.channel4.com/info/commissioning/4producers/features (accessed 21 November 2016).
4. Available at: http://www.channel4.com/info/commissioning/4producers/factualentertainment (accessed 21 November 2016).
5. The fact that so many men have their faces blurred does also suggest that consent was not straightforward. As film scholar Bill Nichols (2001: 9) said 'Ethics becomes a measure of the ways in which negotiations about the nature of the relationship between filmmakers and subject has consequences for subjects and viewers alike'. Anecdotally, reports on the way consent was garnered by the production company, Firecracker films, suggest that younger Traveller women and men were targeted, as they would give their consent more easily. See the report in the *Travellers' Times*, 'Big fat film crew descends on Traveller Christmas party,' published 4 January

2014, available at: http://travellerstimes.org.uk/News/Big-fat-film-crew-descends-on-Traveller-Party.aspx (accessed 20 May 2016).
6. Available at: http://www.theguardian.com/media/video/2012/aug/24/jay-hunt-channel-4-audiences-video (accessed 21 November 2016).
7. Available at: http://www.channel4.com/programmes/keeping-up-with-the-khans/episode-guide (accessed 21 November 2016).
8. These figures were reported as estimates from the local council in *The Guardian* newspaper, 15 November 2013, available at: http://www.theguardian.com/uk-news/2013/nov/15/sheffield-page-hall-roma-slovakia-immigration (accessed 21 November 2016) and also in *The Observer*, which gave the higher figure of 3000, available at: http://www.theguardian.com/uk-news/2013/nov/17/roma-page-hall-sheffield (accessed 21 November 2016). There are no reliable figures of Roma minorities in the UK. In October 2013, Migration Yorkshire in partnership with the University of Salford estimated that about 200,000 Roma were living in Britain, see their report available at: http://www.salford.ac.uk/__data/assets/pdf_file/0004/363118/Migrant_Roma_in_the_UK_final_report_October_2013.pdf (accessed 21 November 2016). This caused a huge controversy in the media and academic circles. The media used the figures to comment on problems on integration and the increasing numbers of EU migrants, while academics defended and refuted the figures (see Brown et al. 2014; Matras et al. 2015).
9. Available at: http://www.theguardian.com/uk-news/2013/nov/15/sheffield-page-hall-roma-slovakia-immigration (accessed 21 November 2016).
10. 11. Available at: http://www.bbc.co.uk/news/uk-politics-24949349 (accessed 21 November 2016).

References

Allen, K., I. Tyler, and S. De Benedicts. 2014. Thinking with "White Dee": The Gender Politics of "Austerity Porn". *Sociological Research Online* 19 (3): 1–7.
Andrejevic, M. 2004. *Reality TV: The Work of Being Watched*. Lanham, MD: Rowman & Littlefield.
ASA Report. 2012. *ASA Adjudication on Channel Four Television Corporation*. October 3. Available at: http://www.asa.org.uk/Rulings/Adjudications/2012/10/Channel-Four-Television-Corporation/SHP_ADJ_197451.aspx. Accessed 12 Jan 2013.
Balzacq, T., ed. 2011. *Securitisation Theory*. London: Routledge.
Bauman, Z. 2004. *Wasted Lives*. Cambridge: Polity Press.

Berg, O., and H. Schwenken. 2010. Masking, Blurring, Replacing. In *Images of Illegalized Immigration*, ed. C. Bischoff, F. Falk, and S. Kafehsy, 111–127. Bielefeld: transcript.

Bigo, D. 2002. Security and Immigration: Toward a Critique of the Governmentality of Unease. *Alternatives: Global, Local, Political* 27 (1): 63–92.

———. 2014. The (In) Securitization Practices of the Three Universes of EU Border Control. *Security Dialogue* 45 (3): 209–225.

Blanchet, E. 2016. Bigger, Fatter, Staged and Manipulated. *The Travellers' Times*, April 22. Available at: http://travellerstimes.org.uk/Blogs--Features/Bigger-fatter-staged-and-manipulated.aspx. Accessed 21 Nov 2016.

Brown, K. 2008. The Promise and Perils of Women's Participation in UK Mosques. *British Journal of Politics & International Relations* 10 (3): 472–491.

Brown, P., P. Martin, and L. Scullion. 2014. Migrant Roma in the United Kingdom and the Need to Estimate Population Size. *People, Place and Policy* 8 (1): 19–33.

Collier, H. 2014. *Channel 4's Benefits Street Claims 4.3 Million Viewers*. January 6. Available at: http://www.theguardian.com/media/2014/jan/07/tvratings-channel4. Accessed 21 Nov 2016.

Corner, J. 2002. Performing the Real: Documentary Diversions. *Television & New Media* 3 (3): 255–269.

Cudworth, E. 2013. Armed Conflict, Insecurity and Gender: The Resilience of Patriarchy? *Resilience: International Policies, Practices and Discourses* 1 (1): 69–75.

Deans, J. 2011. Big Fat Gypsy Weddings Invites 5.6m Viewers. *The Guardian*, January 20. Available at: http://www.guardian.co.uk/media/2011/jan/20/ratings-big-fat-gypsy-weddings Accessed 21 Nov 2016.

DeVolld, T. 2016. *Reality TV. An Insider's Guide to TV's Hottest Market*. Studio City, CA: Michael Wises Productions.

Hall, S. 1992. The West and the Rest: Discourse and Power. In (2006) *The Indigenous Experience*, ed. R. Maaka and C. Andersen, 165–173. Toronto, ON: Canadian Scholars' Press.

Hill, A. 2008. *Reality TV: Audiences and Popular Factual Television*. London: Routledge.

Huysmans, J. 2014. *Security Unbound*. London: Routledge.

Huysmans, J., and A. Buonofino. 2008. Politics of Exception and Unease. *Political Studies* 56 (4): 766–788.

Imre, A. 2009. *Identity Games*. Cambridge, MA: MIT Press.

Imre, A., and A. Tremlett. 2011. Reality TV Without Class: The Post-Socialist Anti-celebrity Docusoap. In *Reality Television and Class*, ed. H. Wood and B. Skeggs, 88–103. London: Palgrave Macmillan.

Jensen, T. 2014. Welfare Commonsense, Poverty Porn and Doxosophy. *Sociological Research Online* 19 (3), 3. Available at: http://www.socresonline.org.uk/19/3/3.html. Accessed 26 July 2017.

Jensen, T., and J. Ringrose. 2014. Sluts that Choose vs Doormat Gypsies. Exploring Affect in the Postfeminist, Visual Moral Economy of *My Big Fat Gypsy Wedding*. *Feminist Media Studies* 14 (3): 369–387.

Jones, O. 2011. *Chavs. The Demonization of the Working Class*. London: Verso.

Malmvig, H. 2005. Security Through Intercultural Dialogue? *Mediterranean Politics* 10 (3): 349–364.

Matras, Y., D.V. Leggio, and M. Steel. 2015. "Roma Education" as a Lucrative Niche. *ZEP: Zeitschrift für Internationale Bildungsforschung und Entwicklungspädagogik* 38 (1): 11–17.

McGarry, A. 2017. *Romaphobia*. London: Zed Books.

Messing, V., and G. Bernáth. 2017. Disempowered by the Media: Causes and Consequences of the Lack of Media Voice of Roma Communities. *Identities* 24 (6): 650–667.

Neocleous, M. 2007. Security, Commodity, Fetishism. *Critique* 35 (3): 339–355.

Nichols, B. 1991. *Representing Reality*. Bloomington, IN: Indiana University Press.

———. 2001. *Introduction to Documentary*. Bloomington, IN: Indiana University Press.

Pasqualino, C. 2008. The Gypsies, Poor But Happy. A Cinematic Myth. *Third Text* 22 (3): 337–345.

Said, E. 1979. *Orientalism*. New York: Vintage.

Simeziane, S. 2010. Roma Rap and the Black Train: Minority Voices in Hungarian Hip Hop. In *Languages of Global Hip Hop*, ed. M. Terkourafi, 96–119. London: Continuum.

Skeggs, B., and H. Wood. 2008. The Labour of Transformation and Circuits of Value 'Around' Reality Television. *Continuum: Journal of Media & Cultural Studies* 22 (4): 559–572.

Skeggs, B., N. Thumin, and H. Wood. 2008. "Oh Goodness, I *Am* Watching Reality TV" How Methods Make Class in Audience Research. *European Journal of Cultural Studies* 11 (1): 5–24.

Street, B. 1993. Culture Is a Verb. In *Language and Culture*, ed. D. Graddol, L. Thompson, and M. Byram, 23–43. Clevedon: British Association of Applied Linguistics.

The Independent. 2012. Channel 4 Apologises Over Big Fat Gypsy Weddings Photo Requests. October 16. Available at http://www.independent.co.uk/news/media/tv-radio/channel-4-apologises-over-big-fat-gypsy-weddings-photo-requests-8213687.html. Accessed 21 Nov 2016.

Timmer, A. 2010. Constructing the "Needy Subject": NGO Discourses of Roma Need. *Political and Legal Anthropology Review* 33 (2): 264–281.

Tremlett, A. 2009. Bringing Hybridity to Heterogeneity: Roma and the Question of "Difference". *Romani Studies* 19 (2): 147–168.
———. 2013. "Here are the Gypsies!" The Importance of Self-Representations & How to Question Prominent Images of Roma Minorities. *Ethnic and Racial Studies* 36 (11): 1706–1725.
———. 2014. Demotic or Demonic? Race, Class and Gender in "Gypsy" Reality TV. *The Sociological Review* 62 (2): 316–334.
———. 2017. Visualising Everyday Ethnicity: Moving Beyond Stereotypes of Roma Minorities. *Identities* 24 (6): 720–740.
Turner, G. 2006. The Mass Production of Celebrity. "Celetoids", Reality TV and the "Demotic Turn". *International Journal of Cultural Studies* 9 (2): 153–165.
Tyler, I. 2013. *Revolting Subjects*. London: Zed Books.
Tyler, I., and B. Bennett. 2010. Celebrity chav: Fame, Femininity and Social Class. *European Journal of Cultural Studies* 13 (3): 375–393.
van Baar, H. 2011. Europe's Romaphobia: Problematization, Securitization, Nomadization. *Environment and Planning D: Society and Space* 29 (2): 203–212.
———. 2014. The Emergence of a Reasonable Anti-Gypsyism in Europe. In *When Stereotype Meets Prejudice. Antiziganism in European Societies*, ed. T. Agarin, 27–44. Stuttgart: Ibidem Verlag.
Wood, H., and B. Skeggs, eds. 2011. *Reality Television and Class*. London: Palgrave Macmillan.

PART III

Development

CHAPTER 8

From 'Lagging Behind' to 'Being Beneath'? The De-developmentalization of Time and Social Order in Contemporary Europe

Huub van Baar

Since 1989, it has been possible to observe what I have called the 'Europeanization of the representation of the Roma' (van Baar 2011). This Europeanization designates, firstly, the problematization of the Roma in terms of their 'Europeanness'; secondly, the classification of heterogeneous groups scattered throughout Europe under the largely homogenizing umbrella term 'Roma'; and, thirdly, the devising and implementation of large-scale and Europe-wide programmes dedicated to, most notably, their inclusion, development, empowerment, rights, community building, cultural memory, and societal participation. This third dimension of the Europeanization of Roma representation has gone hand in hand with the institutionalized promise to include the Roma in European states, societies and cultures, and with the assurance of their European citizenship.

I would like to thank Ulderico Daniele, Ana Ivasiuc, and Regina Kreide for their helpful comments on earlier drafts of this chapter.

H. van Baar (✉)
Justus Liebig University Giessen, Giessen, Germany
e-mail: Huub.van-Baar@sowi.uni-giessen.de

These promises represent what I call 'institutional developmentalism' (van Baar 2017b). Institutional developmentalism represents a neo-modernist narrative according to which, by means of various development rationales and initiatives dedicated to inclusion, participation, empowerment, human and minority rights, and community building, the 'underdeveloped' Roma will gradually join with Europe's 'developed' majorities. I have argued recently (van Baar 2017a) that this developmentalism tends to 'fail',[1] partly because, at the current security-development nexus, the dominant biopolitics of development has largely departed from the diagram of a *gradual scale* between 'us' and 'them'—that is, 'the Roma'—and introduced that of a *fault line* between 'their' lives and 'ours'. Hence, we are facing a clear, but non-linear, trend towards the racialization of poverty in contemporary Europe; a process in which, for the poorest among the Roma, it has become acutely difficult to escape poverty and societal isolation, not least because of the trend towards 'containing' their migrant and socio-economic mobilities (van Baar 2017a).

In this chapter, I continue my reflection on this institutional developmentalism towards Europe's Roma and the correlated ambiguous commitments to improve their situation. First, I discuss the racialization of poverty from the perspective of the ways in which anti-Roma racism has been analysed in scholarship. I explain that, in the field of enquiry associated with research regarding 'Romaphobia' or 'antigypsyism', a specific kind of analysis has been underrepresented. I argue that anti-Roma racism has rarely been examined from the perspective of its intersection with those policies officially dedicated to the improvement of the situation of the Roma, or of the development of the more general milieu in which they live. I show that an analysis of anti-Roma racism from this angle sheds new light on the intersection of development and security in Europe's ambiguous commitment to the Roma.

In the second half of the chapter, I further elaborate on the security-development nexus and analyse the consequences of institutional developmentalism from the historicizing perspective of what James Ferguson (2006: 188) has called the 'de-developmentalized notion of history' in narratives and practices of development, race, and modernity. I argue that the de-developmentalization of historical time—that is, the departure from the idea that the 'underdeveloped' Roma in Europe will undergo a 'progressive passage' through several stages of development—occurs in conjunction with a de-temporalization and racialization of societal status according to which the lagging behind of the allegedly underdeveloped

Roma has ambiguously been translated into their 'being beneath'. These general shifts have been accompanied by concerns that are not so much about the time-based conditions of development and gradual inclusion, but rather about edges, walls, and borders—spatial articulations which have all gained new prominence, both within and outside Europe.

ANTI-POLICIES AND THE PECULIARITY OF ROMA-RELATED ANTI-RACISM PROGRAMMES

A worrying trend is apparent within Europe in which poverty tends to be racialized (van Baar 2017a). This racialization is a generally neglected issue in public, political, and, to some extent, also academic debate. Poverty among Europeans more generally is an issue that tends to be overlooked as something which has no widespread occurrence in Europe or which is comparatively less structural than elsewhere in the world. Poverty among the Roma, more specifically, tends to be overlooked even more fundamentally. I do not suggest that it is not an issue at all; it certainly is to a considerable extent, but the question is whether it has been effectively addressed. Nor am I suggesting that all the Roma in Europe are poor. What I do contend, however, is that, among the poor in Europe, the Roma are over-represented and that it seems that a fundamental debate about their precarious status has yet to begin.

In this section, I explore how we can understand Roma-related racialization in Europe *vis-à-vis* the ways in which antigypsyism has prevailingly been addressed in scholarship. Antigypsyism —either under this label or under that of Romaphobia or antiziganism —has usually been discussed in relation to questions that discuss the *what*, the *who*, the *where*, the *when*, the *why*, and the *how* of antigypsyism. These questions generally focus on the following kinds of issues.

Firstly, some of the analyses (End 2013; Nicolae 2007) focus on the *epistemological* question: what is antigypsyism? The pivotal questions to answer then become, for instance, the extent to which antigypsyism represents a particular form and practice of racism that can be described by its characteristics or emergences; how we should define or demarcate antigypsyism and how it relates to, for instance, anti-Jewish, anti-Black, and anti-Muslim racisms. This set of questions also involves the fundamental question of why, and, if so, how, we should distinguish anti-Roma racisms from other types of racism.

Other sets of questions are more *actor*-focused, and concentrate on the question of who and what have been involved in antigypsyism, or on issues that deal with the *situational* question of *where* antigypsyism has become manifest, for instance, in on- and off-line practices of hate speech, in cultural, visual, and discursive Roma representations and their histories, in academia, in media discourses, and in educational, or other institutional settings (Agarin 2014; Bartels et al. 2013; Kyuchukov 2012; Stewart 2012). These questions, in their turn, are closely related to *when* questions, which concentrate on the *historicizing* question of how antigypsyism has evolved in the course of history and to what extent contemporary practices of antigypsyism are different from or historically re-articulate earlier practices (Bogdal 2011; Hancock 1997).

To some extent, all these questions relate to *why* and *how* questions, which are primarily concerned with the complex question of why, and under what conditions, antigypsyism has occurred and with the question of what mechanisms and discourses are involved in antigypsyist manifestations, as well as in challenging them (Bancroft 2005; McGarry 2017; Selling et al. 2015).

What has been investigated less frequently, and what has therefore been insufficiently studied, are the ways in which the discourses, mechanisms, and practices of antigypsyism have intersected with a variety of programmes and policies officially or indirectly dedicated to the development and improvement of the situation of the Roma, or which have been introduced to deal actively with supposedly Roma-related phenomena. This dimension of antigypsyism remains somewhat different from what is called 'institutional racism', even though it has both institutional elements and affects institutional realms.

The dimension that I want to articulate also differs from intersectional analyses (Selling et al. 2015: 138–191) which focus on the intersections of, for instance, race, gender, and class, even though these kinds of intersections undoubtedly matter in what I consider to be the intersection of antigypsyism with programmes intended to improve the situation of the Roma and which I have brought together under the label of 'development programmes' (van Baar 2011), intended, in a broad sense, to include more or less institutionalized programmes dedicated to issues such as empowerment, participation, community building, human and minority rights, social inclusion, and human security. The complex ways in which this dimension of antigypsyism relates to its institutional and intersectional dimensions implies that we cannot easily suggest that antigypsyism begins to play a role only *after* the devising or implementing of these programmes dedicated to the improvement of the Roma's societal position. Rather, in the *intersection* of antigypsyism and such programmes *at the moment of their articulation*, the programmes themselves often become ambiguous.

I particularly want to investigate the relationship between antigypsyism and what William Walters (2008) calls 'anti-policies'. These are policies that are officially introduced to combat or prevent 'bad things', such as policies dedicated to the combatting of corruption (anti-corruption), racism (anti-racism), and radicalization (de-radicalization), but also in policies introduced in the context of the 'wars' on crime, drugs, poverty, and terror. Walters (2008: 269) does not consider these anti-policies to be 'a particular kind of policy'; nor does he see them as referring 'to a new political logic' transforming political culture. Rather, he suggests that the focus on anti-policies allows us to trace some 'family resemblances' between different policy formations and thus to 'express certain features and aspects that are shared across a set of things which otherwise might differ in all sorts of other ways' (ibid.).

What interests me in Walters' analysis of anti-policy is the way in which it allows us to interrogate how, and to what extent, the emergence of anti-policies has happened together with the interrelated processes of de-politicization and securitization that have legitimized Roma-related manifestations of racialization and racism, and which also tend to make it harder, but certainly not impossible, to challenge these manifestations. I return to this issue later, but first I try to convey a better sense of how an analysis of anti-policies could help to develop a new methodological viewpoint from which we could interrogate practices of anti-Roma racialization and racism.

Translated to the Roma case, anti-policies have been launched on a number of institutional levels to combat 'bad things' such as poverty, underdevelopment, insecurity, inequality, discrimination, urban or social deterioration, segregation, and other mechanisms of marginalization and exclusion, whether or not under the label of 'anti-policy', such as in anti-discrimination and anti-racist policies that are meant to combat antigypsyism and to encourage social inclusion more generally. But there is, additionally, an entire umbrella under which newly devised anti-policies which do not relate directly to the Roma have nevertheless been associated with them in a strong way. Here, I am thinking of programmes dedicated to anti-trafficking (Jovanović 2015), anti-social behaviour (Clark and Taylor 2014), anti-crime (van Baar 2014), zero tolerance (Ort et al.

2016), and anti-'illegal' migration (van Baar 2017b). As Walters (2008: 281) states: 'it is hard to overlook the operation of a powerful moral coding and valuation that lies embedded in the very language, the very design of anti-policy'. Indeed, who would be in favour of human trafficking? Who could possibly have any objection to policies designed to combat discrimination, crime, or poverty? This moral coding becomes even more prominent when these anti-policies are embedded in the discourses and practices of developmentalism, humanitarianism, and 'humanrightsism', for example, when anti-trafficking or anti-crime programmes are combined with culturalized narratives of assistance for the Romani women and children who have become victims of the human trafficking supposedly organized *inside* Romani communities (Jovanović 2015; van Baar 2014; Vrăbiescu, Chap. 10, this volume).

Two critical issues have to be addressed if we are to understand the intersections of antigypsyism and anti-policies and their impact on how we analyse processes of racialization and racism. The first relates to Walters' suggestion that 'policies and programmes that claim to repress bad things should be regarded as programmes of government in their own right' (2008: 271). The second concerns the ambiguous ways in which, at the intersection between antigypsyism and programmes meant to improve the situation of the Roma, we have been able to observe a more general flowing together of problematizing the Roma in terms of development, and in those of security, a merging that is the central theme of the second half of this chapter. I first discuss these two issues, after which I position them within the broader horizon of the ambiguities at the security-development nexus.

INTERROGATING ANTI-POLICIES AS PROGRAMMES IN THEIR OWN RIGHT

What does it mean to interrogate anti-policies as programmes *in their own right*? Analyses of policies that have been prefixed by 'anti', 'de', or 'counter'—such as in anti-discrimination, de-segregation, or counter-terrorism programmes—frequently suggest that we can explain them by the thing to which they are opposed, as merely the inverse of the thing to be combatted. Interrogating these anti-policies as programmes in their own right implies a more critical look at how the measures proposed and conducted in the name of these anti-policies (such as education, raising awareness, surveillance, targeted financing, expulsion, etc.) are devised and legitimized and how these counter-measures demonstrate the way in which the phenomenon to be countered should be understood. The phenomena which are the target of these anti-policies contribute to the construction and maintenance of a discourse on the phenomena to be countered, and thus it is this discourse and the way in which the particular phenomenon to be counter is problematized that must be interrogated.

Alana Lentin (2004), for example, has argued that anti-racism programmes do not deal with a uniform notion of anti-racism. Rather, partially dependent on the kinds of actors involved in the development and articulation of such programmes, we are dealing with a dynamic in which we can distinguish 'a variety of anti-racisms, often competitive or even conflictual' (Lentin 2004: 4). This dynamic might lead to public debate, and thus to a *politicization* of how we should understand and challenge racism, but it could also lead to relatively strong forms of *de-politicization*, in particular, when we are dealing with an 'externalization effect' (Walters 2008: 280). For instance, when a national government adopts a particular kind of anti-policy, it is possible that state actors may territorially externalize the causes or emergence of the 'bad thing' which they believe should be combatted. We have frequently seen this occurring in the War on Terror and also in the 'migrant'/'refugee' 'crisis' in Europe (New Keywords Collective 2016). By means of imagining the 'threatening' actors and the reasons for their actions as coming *from outside* their territorial borders, states can present themselves as agents that will guarantee security and protection rather than as actors that are themselves involved in the complex historical, socio-economic, and political causes of the 'bad thing' that needs to be challenged.

A similar kind of externalization can also take place with regard to a state's institutional realm, for example, when the institutional and more structural dimensions of racism are not adequately addressed by anti-racism programmes. Lentin (2008: 101, my emphasis) argues that, according to the mainstream version of anti-racism policies articulated in Western states:

> Racism is a *perversion* of the logical course of modern politics that comes to affect western political culture *from beyond the pale*. In mainstream thought, the origins of racism are rarely considered to be political. It is thought of as *a pathology, that may infect politics*… but which does not emerge from political processes inherent to the state… Moreover, state discourses of anti-racism rest on a general presumption that the Western, democratic state is *de facto anti-racist*.

The ways in which racism has been represented in such views make it harder to challenge institutional racism, even while non-state actors may try to contest the de-politicization involved in how anti-policies are articulated through externalization and pathologization.

In the Roma-related context, EU actions against discrimination, and against antigypsyism more specifically, serve as an example of a similar trend at both national and European institutional levels. In April 2015, for example, the European Parliament (2015) adopted a resolution under the title 'International Roma Day – anti-Gypsyism in Europe and EU recognition of the memorial day of the Roma genocide during WW II'. In this resolution, the primary focus on generic programmes of anti-discrimination which, among other programmes, has characterized European Roma-related policies—at least since the launch of the Race Equality Directive in 2000—has shifted towards the combatting of antigypsyism. According to the resolution, the rise of antigypsyism has become manifest:

> … through anti-Roma rhetoric and violent attacks against Roma in Europe, including murders, which are incompatible with the norms and values of the European Union and constitute a major obstacle to the successful social integration of Roma and to ensuring full respect for their human rights. (European Parliament 2015: §1)

At the same time, antigypsyism is defined as:

> … the special kind of racism that is directed towards Roma [and as] an ideology founded on racial superiority, a form of dehumanization and institutional racism nurtured by historical discrimination, which is expressed by, among other things, violence, hate speech, exploitation, stigmatization and the most blatant kind of discrimination. (European Parliament 2015: §C)

These quotations reveal that antigypsyism is primarily connected to anti-Roma rhetoric, violent attacks against the Roma, dehumanization, and 'violence, hate speech, exploitation, stigmatization and the most blatant kind of discrimination'. While the issue of institutional racism is mentioned, it is primarily related—and not even that clearly—to its occurrence at the level of the state, because, in the text of the resolution, the phenomenon of antigypsyism is unmistakably identified as being 'incompatible with the *norms and values* of the European Union'. Thus, antigypsyism tends to be represented as a kind of aberration which occurs outside the

European institutional sphere, rather than as an embedded and more structural aspect of the current climate in Europe, in which institutions at various levels also play an ambiguous role.[2]

Furthermore, if antigypsyism is predominantly understood in the context of 'the most blatant kind of discrimination', resulting in violent attacks, hate speech, and exploitation, it becomes much harder to challenge and combat what I have called manifestations of 'reasonable antigypsyism' (van Baar 2014). These include the sort of antigypsyism according to which one could be seen as being 'rightfully' entitled to act against the Roma and treat them differently because they are inconvenient, indulge in criminal activity, and can generally be expected to be disruptive. According to this allegedly reasonable argument, it is not 'we', the non-Roma but rather 'they', the Roma, who violate rights and fail in their duties. Consequently, unorthodox measures such as the expulsion of the Roma and the confiscation or destruction of their property, not to mention the harsh treatment and policing of Roma in cases of minor or even alleged or fabricated confrontations, have been tolerated and *normalized* throughout politics and wider society within Europe, with their *legitimization* largely grounded in 'reasonable antigypsyism'. Thus, the sweeping articulation of reasonable antigypsyism has turned out to be a *condition of possibility* for the justification of the rigid forms of anti-Roma racism that are inextricably related to practices which are now institutionalized at subnational, national, *and* European levels.

The Merging of Security and Development Through the Lens of Anti-policies

It is particularly important that the phenomenon of reasonable antigypsyism, as well as its normalization and legitimization in present-day Europe, is addressed in order to enable an adequate interrogation of the ways in and the extent to which—in the name of morally encoded anti-policies—programmes of security and development tend to flow together. Indeed, the proclaimed objective of any anti-policy to repress 'bad things' largely depends on how, within dominant regimes of visuality, the 'bad' qualities of the things to be combatted are perceived, constructed, and reproduced. This dimension of anti-policies becomes clearer when the repression of 'bad things' is related to risk assessments, alleged threats, and societal mechanisms which are seen as being dangerous in the sense of destabilizing neighbourhoods, towns, or even states, nations, and cultures. For example, in those cases in which risk assessments are related to the spatial concentration of what are often understood as societal problems, proactive forms of policing poor or 'coloured' neighbourhoods (*banlieues*, suburbs, ghettos, or slums) and their inhabitants are usually legitimized to combat these perceived problems. They include, for example, pre-emptive practices of profiling, the trans-local, or international exchange of information gathered by security experts and stop and search policies (Bigo 2008; Fassin 2013).

Relatedly, when Roma, Muslim, and other minorities, or migrants and refugees, are looked at through the lens of security, they are habitually considered to be a threat to public, social, or even national order and to social security systems at home or abroad. Anti-crime, anti-trafficking, anti-social behaviour, anti-terror, anti-'illegal' migration programmes, as well as tools such as police raids and patrols, enforced border control, expulsions, and other 'crisis' measures, have been legitimized and ambiguously enacted to target, in particular, those minority and migrant groups which have been racialized as a security problem. Last, but not least, in the case in which underdevelopment, for example, is seen as something dangerous—in the sense of the societal or socio-economic cost of poverty or of the deterioration of 'inter-ethnic relations'—anti-discrimination, anti-racism, de-segregation, and anti-poverty policies have been introduced and legitimized to encourage development, human security, social inclusion, recognition of minorities, empowerment, and social, economic, and political participation.

But this is also where the problem starts. Indeed, securitarian and developmental anti-policies intermingle constantly, and in the case of the Roma, policies that focus on 'people at risk' and those targeting 'risky people' have frequently been articulated at one and the same time or even at one and the same place. Thus, the repression of 'bad things' can ambiguously be translated into the repression of 'dangerous' people or 'risky' societal processes. Consequently, concerns about development and improvement have started to overlap with those about security and vice versa. Here, the difference between those 'at risk', who are usually the targets of development programmes, and those 'risky' persons, who are normally among the targets of security policies, may no longer be clear, particularly at the moment of their articulation. This is what I describe as the Roma-related 'security-development nexus' (van Baar 2017a).

Anti-policies can consequently be understood as *contact points* between what, in Roma-related scholarship, have often been considered to be two *different* dimensions of intervention regarding development on the more positive side and security on the negative. A focus on examining anti-policies underscores the ambiguities of the politics of protection when it comes to current European commitments to the Roma. On the one hand, according to a juridical-political reading of protection—as in the EU's Copenhagen Criteria for the 'protection of minorities' and its development and human rights regimes—'protection' refers to something that has primarily been encoded as morally good. Yet, at the same time, according to a biopolitical reading, protection refers to an ambiguous hierarchization of life that needs to contribute to the 'well-being' and 'security' of a population. This double meaning, and the ways in which the boundaries between these two readings have been blurred, has become manifest, for instance, in the context of the creation of 'humanitarian zones' or 'zones of protection' for refugees, in the activities of the neighbourhood watch schemes (Ivasiuc 2015) or security guards that organize the protection of citizens from below, and in the practices of policing mobilized in Central and Eastern European towns during anti-Roma protests, and in which Roma neighbourhoods and counter-protesters have been 'quarantined' to avoid further escalation.

In these and similar cases, the key questions have become: who can legitimately claim a need for protection? Against which dangers can they legitimately make these claims? And who is going to do the protecting? (Huysmans et al. 2006: 2). In this respect, 'anti-policy draws lines' (Walters 2008: 281); its moral encoding, in particular, tends to engender an 'us-and-them' rhetoric that is also typical of 'reasonable antigypsyism'. Even while some may strenuously protest and try to challenge the politics of protection in which the reinforcement of symbolic, social, or material borders continues to draw very tangible lines between 'us' and 'them', the powerful modality of de-politicization that seems to be involved here looks very much like what Slavoj Žižek (1998: 992) has called 'ultrapolitics': 'the attempt to depoliticize the conflict by way of bringing it to extremes, via the direct militarization of politics' and via the reformulating of political conflict 'as a war between us and them', as in Schmittean decisionism and its central 'friend-enemy' dialectics.

More generally, the ways in which, in the course of post-1989 European commitment to the Roma, development and security have been merged can explain how the idea that, through development, the Roma might gradually join in with their fellow citizens increasingly tends to be challenged and changed into that of the Roma as 'the naturally poor' who do not so much 'lag behind' but are rather 'beneath'. While this racialized perception of who the Roma actually are has always dominated the popular non-Roma view of the Roma, it is only more recently and more gradually that this perception has become an ambiguous aspect of Roma-related policy formation at a national, sub-national, and supra-national level in Europe. It is in order to explain this gradual, non-linear transition to the racialization of poverty in Europe that I want to explain more extensively why the post-1989 institutional developmentalism directed towards the Roma has ambiguously begun to support the racialization and very fragile status quo regarding the Roma in Europe.

Post-Socialist Institutional Developmentalism Revisited

In *Global Shadows: Africa in the Neoliberal World Order* (2006: 178), James Ferguson included a graph, entitled 'The Time of Modernization', in which we see a line that gradually rises. The horizontal axis of the graph represents time, while the vertical represents status. The rise of the line over the course of time represents a simultaneous improvement in social status. Ferguson uses this 'painfully simple' (ibid.) graph to tell the familiar story of modernization in the context of twentieth-century postcolonial developmentalism: the traditionally poor and underdeveloped populations of developing countries in the Third World undergo a 'progressive passage' through several stages of socio-economic development in order to become connected to the modern, developed First World and to enjoy a gradual, simultaneous, increase in their social status.[3]

Like many who have reflected on this contested yet powerful narrative of development and modernization more generally, and on its related historical sequence from tradition to modernity—and, accordingly from a backward to a modern social status—Ferguson (2006: 183) claims that developmentalist models have lost much of their credibility and that this 'developmental narrative is increasingly visible as a failure not only in the domain of academic theory but also in practical economic terms'. Whereas the main idea of post-colonial developmentalism was that of the gradual socio-economic convergence of the Third and First Worlds, this story is no longer heard. Many people in Africa, and elsewhere in what is now dubbed 'the Global South', Ferguson states, no longer buy into this narrative of modernization and teleological progress in which, through developmental investment in their nation states, economies, societies, and communities, their status will gradually improve and their distance from the modern world of prosperity, welfare, and well-being will increasingly shrink. 'What is most striking in the recent history of Africa', Ferguson maintains (2006: 166), 'is not the breakdown of boundaries, but a process in which economic decline and political violence have produced new political and economic exclusions that distance Africa from the rest of the world'. Consequently, 'in a world where developmentalist patience has little to recommend it, the promise of modernization increasingly appears as a broken promise, and the mapped-out pathways leading from the Third World to the First turn out to have been bricked up' (ibid.: 186).

To some extent, the first part of this story—which, in the visual narrative of the graph, corresponds to the interruption of its horizontal axis—may still be assessed positively. The doing away with the mythical, teleological unfolding of time implies that the evolving of history cannot easily be understood as something logical, necessary, and uniform but has to been seen as a contingent, plural, and non-teleological process in which, as some post-colonial scholars have suggested, we are able to trace 'alternative modernities' that could or should be analysed both as and through a radical 'provincialization' of Eurocentric conceptions of history and historiography (Chakrabarty 2000; Escobar 1995; Pollock et al. 2000).

But this is only one part of the story, which becomes much more ambiguous when we take into account the impact of the interruption of the horizontal axis on that of the vertical, which represents the axis of hierarchy:

> … with the idea of temporal sequence removed, location in the hierarchy no longer indexes a 'stage of advancement.' Instead, it marks simply a rank in a global political economic order. Insofar as such ranks have lost any necessary relation to developmental time, they become not stages to be passed through but non-serialized statuses that are separated from each other by exclusionary walls, not developmental stairways. Modernity in this sense comes to appear as a standard of living, as *a status*, not a *telos*. The global hierarchy is thereby de-developmentalized and appears as static, without the promise of serialization. (Ferguson 2006: 188–189, emphasis original)

Ferguson argues that the consequence of the disruption of continuity at both the horizontal axis of time and the vertical of hierarchy is twofold. Firstly, this disruption has increasingly resulted in a change in the self-perceptions of those who live in the Global South. They consider themselves, or at least the countries that they inhabit, to be 'less' as opposed to 'less-developed'. 'Rather than the poorest countries being understood as *behind* "the West" – playing catch-up, developing, emerging – they are increasingly understood as naturally, perhaps even racially, *beneath* it' (Ferguson 2006: 189–190). These self-perceptions and the view of the living conditions in the countries in which they live do not necessarily result in a kind of paralysis, for, secondly, the de-developmentalization of status has increasingly resulted in the view that a change in their circumstances can only be achieved by leaving the place where they live. Indeed, if the developmental promise has been broken, the only way to achieve the preferred status is to migrate to those countries where the standard of living is higher.

This story of the increasingly challenged promise of modernization is also similar to that of the Roma-related institutionalized promises of social inclusion and European citizenship; a story that has also been disputed in the Roma-related academic debate and, increasingly, in European Roma-related policy circles, even while the story still strongly dominates in the latter. In the aftermath of 1989 and the two decades which followed, the arrangement of nationally and internationally organized non-governmental and governmental attention to the Roma had led to a historically novel type of 'institutional developmentalism' within Europe's contested borders (van Baar 2017a). The Roma would become the focus of a socio-political endeavour in which the generic development of various institutions and infrastructures—from parliamentary democracy, rule of law, human rights, and 'minority protection' to accessible public services and a market economy with the capacity 'to cope with competitive pressure and market forces within the Union' (European Council 1993: 13)—would inevitably lead to the 'protection' of the Roma's rights and to their progressive 'inclusion' in Europe's majority societies and cultures.

The central narrative of this institutional developmentalism was—and, in many respects, still is—that by means of large-scale and Europe-wide programmes dedicated to human and minority rights, development, empowerment, participation, and inclusion, the Roma would gradually merge with their fellow European citizens. Much like the post-colonial developmentalism that Ferguson discusses, the post-socialist developmentalism which has been dedicated to Europe's Roma in the last two decades is based on the logic of gradual progress and on that of a developmental continuum, according to which the Roma are on the same trajectory as 'we', the 'developed' Europeans, are. 'They' are 'only lagging behind', but this can and will be solved because 'they' will undergo a passage through several stages of socio-economic and human development that will ultimately connect them to 'our' modern, competitive, multicultural, and unified Europe. While they were once the externalized outsiders of Europe, against whom Europe defined itself, they have now become the 'internalized outsiders' who will slowly but surely become included as true Europeans.

The reasons why this developmentalism has, from the mid-1990s onwards, tended to turn these institutionalized promises into broken ones are many and complex, and I will summarize here the main line of argumentation, which I have developed elsewhere (van Baar 2017a). First, this trend has to do with what I consider to be the 'biopoliticization' of Roma-related development, according to which development programmes are focused on attempts to improve biopolitical qualities at an individual and communal level. Globally, a 'biopolitical turn' (Duffield 2007) has taken place in the ways in which development is articulated, and we have been able to trace a similar turn in Roma-related development contexts. Increasingly, Roma-related policy discourses and programmes primarily conceive and perceive development 'in terms of how life is to be supported and maintained, and how people are expected to live, rather than according to economic and state-based models' (Duffield 2010: 53). Consequently, development-related governmentalities *vis-à-vis* the Roma strongly tend to isolate them socially (particularly, the poorest among them) and contribute more to governing their poverty than to structurally improving their living conditions or guaranteeing their 'inclusion'.

Here, biopolitics does not imply a kind of trans-historical regulation of populations and their socio-economic and migrant mobilities on the basis of their health, wealth, and productivity; rather, it involves a historically specific modality of biopolitics that has strongly resonated with processes which, as David Roberts and Minelle Mahtani (2010: 250) state, have neoliberalized 'race' and 'raced' neoliberalism (van Baar and Powell, Chap. 5, this volume). Processes and policies of neoliberalization and their profound impact on the erosion and transformation of public services have both reinforced 'the racial structure of society' and re-articulated processes of racialization, most notably through culturalizing the problems of the target groups of these policies and through securitizing the representation of these groups while simultaneously de-politicizing the complex socio-economic, political, and historical causes behind these problems (van Baar 2011, 2017b). Consequently, the neoliberalization of development is closely related to its biopoliticization. Consistent with the biopolitical dimensions of development, a people-centred, human-development approach to the situation of the Roma concentrates, most notably, on material, as well as spiritual, self-reliance at an individual and communal level; local community-based forms of development; 'active' citizenship; 'community' and 'capacity building'; raising awareness; formation of human and social capital; stimulating 'desired' ways of living; and guaranteeing 'basic needs'. Notwithstanding their diversity, these programmes centre on the *bio*political, rather than on the socio-economic conditions that would have to be fulfilled in order to improve the Roma's circumstances and increase their capacities.

The biopoliticization of development has substantially gone together with the merging of the latter with security. This merging is largely grounded in the neoliberal idea that (European) 'society must be defended' (Foucault 2004; van Baar 2017b) and that, accordingly, 'dangerous underdevelopment', based on what is often framed as 'inter-ethnic', 'inter-cultural', or 'inter-religious' group conflict, must be combatted. To a great extent, the qualification of underdevelopment as dangerous for the prosperous evolution of mainstream society explains the emergence of 'liberal interventionism' (Duffield 2010), that is, the legitimization of intervention in areas and populations qualified as 'underdeveloped' on the basis of the alleged necessity to improve life and circumstances and to reduce the risk that poverty will result in destabilizing conflict and migration. Here, the humanitarian and securitarian logic of a Roma-related 'politics of protection' are clearly mingled (Vrăbiescu, Chap. 10, this volume).

But there is more at stake. To a significant extent, Roma-related biopolitical development focuses on improving the local and adaptive self-reliance of the poorest among the Roma in particular. Indeed, one of the central elements of the present-day, neoliberal way of organizing development is 'the privileging of notions of sustainability based upon adaptive patterns of household and communal self-reliance' (Duffield 2010: 55). While the post-Cold War advent of people-centred forms and practices of development—usually under the guise of 'human security' and 'human development' (as in the programmes of the World Bank or the UNDP)—has often, and naively, been seen as the consequence of a blossoming humanism within international relations and organizations, this emergence has gone together—much more ambiguously—with both the biopoliticization of development and its neoliberalization by means of significant outsourcing to non-state actors—civil society organizations (CSO) in particular (van Baar 2011, 2017a). Yet, at the same time, these actors do not usually have the financial and logistic means to do much more than promote self-reliance and resilience. In the case of the poorest, and often the most segregated, among the Roma, local and adaptive self-reliance are primarily articulated through NGO-led projects, frequently supported by formal or informal private-public partnerships with local actors, such as municipal offices, social and community workers, the police, landlords, privatized housing companies, or charitable foundations.

However, since the self-reliance promoted by these programmes primarily tends to result in various types of delicate, temporary repair networks which largely take place in relative isolation from more sustainable socio-economic conditions, these programmes constantly need to be revitalized *and* legitimized as such, something that Mark Duffield (2010: 66–67) has characterized as the 'permanent emergency of self-reliance'. Indeed, one of the ambiguous consequences of the way in which neoliberal development has been organized through delivering 'basic needs' and stimulating self-reliance and resilience is that, at the site of their local articulation, development programmes maintain, more often than not, a fragile *status quo*. Ultimately, therefore, they primarily tend to function 'to *reproduce* and *maintain* the generic biopolitical divide between development and underdevelopment' (Duffield 2010: 66). As I have argued here and elsewhere (van Baar 2017a), the biopoliticization of development in this particular constellation at the security-development nexus has largely departed from the diagram of a *gradual scale* between 'us' and 'them'—the Roma—and has introduced a *fault line* between 'their' lives and 'ours'.

Egress and Narratives of 'Coming Catastrophes'

In many cases, the fragile *status quo* achieved through the biopolitical articulation of development is actually more a kind of *status aparte,* in which the poorest among the Roma are segregated from the rest of society, and in which, not infrequently, the tangible borders between 'them' and their neighbours have been governed and reproduced institutionally through securitarian anti-policies. This transition has been a process that has been gradual and non-linear, for example, as the consequence of historically changing living conditions—often deteriorating since late socialism—and of the increase of the frequently almost irreversible processes of urban or rural segregation. But, in many instances, this transformation has also occurred much more suddenly, for instance, in the case of involuntary, and thus forced, mobility through eviction, deportation, or other, often discriminatory, practices of housing allocation involving both public and private actors.

But the racialization of poverty, the increasing division of life-chances between the poorest among the Roma and their fellow citizens (the more affluent Roma among them) and other manifestations of the re-articulated colour line in post-1989 Europe are processes that the Roma involved have not undergone passively and unresponsively. Many of them have started to realize that the 'gap between Roma and non-Roma' (European Commission 2014) cannot be bridged, the 'dependency trap' (UNDP 2002) not avoided, and the 'poverty circle' (World Bank 2005) not be broken by means of a developmental promise that is largely based on the idea of a *temporal* dynamics of societal progress and gradually upward socio-economic mobility. Several of those who have lost patience—or who never were patient enough to wait and see whether institutionalized promises would really materialize in their part of the world—replaced the temporal strategy with a *spatial* one of mobility and moved elsewhere. 'Not progress, but egress', as Ferguson (2006: 192) puts it, with the proviso that, in the case of Europe's Roma, the ambiguous promise of 'free mobility' is an integral part of the institutionalized promises of inclusion and European citizenship.

This resort to migration, which had already begun in the early 1990s and which can be viewed from the angle of the Roma's autonomy of migration and their 'right to escape' (Mezzadra 2004; van Baar, Ivasiuc and Kreide, Chap. 1, this volume), is not simply the traditional migrant story of pull and push factors, as Jan Grill (2012) has convincingly argued. It has much more to do with the experience of social status and the lived and experienced quality of the place where one is used to living. In the knowledge that status is related to a better standard of living which can only be achieved elsewhere, egress has to be seen as a strategy of leaving the home village where 'there is nothing to do' and where one feels trapped with 'no chance [of] a better life' (Grill 2012: 1282). Knowingly or not, Grill suggests, they take for granted the risk that, particularly if one fails to be successful abroad and is forced to return, one will be confronted with new forms of socio-psychic isolation and disillusion that could contribute to the feeling of 'being beneath' in even more ways.

Relatedly, due to the ongoing irregularization of the Roma's status as European citizens, primarily through the persistent processes of securitization, orientalization, and nomadization (van Baar 2015), the Roma are faced with the need to develop strategies for coping with the everyday manifestations of discrimination and racism. These include mostly covert and mundane survival strategies, including those of hiding their identity, but also attempts to publicly challenge the ways in which they are commonly treated (cf. Legros and Lièvre, Chap. 4, this volume).

As well as the resort to migration, we have been able to observe at least two other responses to the (broken) promises of social inclusion and European citizenship, and to the de-developmentalization of time and social order that has led to novel forms of racialization and a highly problematic emphasis on the Roma's allegedly inferior social, or even racial, status. Both responses can be understood as answers to marginalization, segregation, and securitization, even though they may ultimately lead to the strengthening, rather than to the challenging, of the latter three processes. While the first response is primarily a minoritarian and the second mainly a majoritarian one, both responses could be considered as *re*-temporalizations, even while they are what Ferguson (2006: 190) qualifies as '*non-progressive* temporalizations' of socio-economic distress, although both responses also have certain apocalyptic dimensions in different ways.

The first response, to which various scholars and studies have paid extensive attention, relates to the development of new eschatologies in the context of neo-religious movements, and neo-Protestant movements in particular (Gog and Roth 2012; Thurfjell and Marsh 2014). Most notably, the rapid post-1989 rise of the popularity of Pentecostalism among the Roma not only in Central and Eastern Europe, but also in countries such as Spain, has facilitated not only 'a religious community that strives for other-worldly salvation', but also, and most importantly in the context of development, 'an explicit social project that aims at generating a shared ethnic identity and social de-marginalization' (Gog and Roth 2012: 398). This response involves a *re*-temporalization that is multiple, being personal, social, and eschatological at the same time. This re-temporalization is based on a radical rupture through what Birgit Meyer (1998) has called a 'complete break with the past'. Only through a radical break with the individual past of sins and troubles, as well as with a social past formed by social and historical relationships that have disenchanted the entire community, could a new start be made, in the sense of becoming 'born again', and through which a relationship with God could be established. This relation could progressively be established through the ritualized public confession of sins. This embodied and actively performed worldview enables a solution to poverty, exclusion, and suffering in terms of personal and individual transformation, and emphasizes a shift of focus from that of the worldly 'war against poverty' led by NGOs, international organizations, and other mundane actors to one of the personal and personified 'war against the demons' (Freeman 2012: 2) responsible for poverty and misery. This complex Pentecostal ethic transforms poverty, underdevelopment, misery, violence, and exploitation into almost apocalyptic signs of redemption which offer a future and a horizon of promises of salvation that some have dubbed a 'new heavenly citizenship' (Gog and Roth 2012: 398). Thus, the temporalization involved in this neo-religious response is also eschatological: in order to prepare for the End Days, in which born-again Christians will go to heaven to enjoy their heavenly citizenship, they anticipate how their Roma background, in mundane circumstances, can be seen as a gift from God which will help them to achieve a higher form of spirituality and collectively overcome their social marginalization and feelings of inferiority. Last, but not least, from the anthropo-sociological viewpoint of religious practices, this response to poverty and the racialization of poverty can serve both to isolate them further from their non-Roma neighbours through self-chosen separation, and cause conflict within and among Roma groups through the practice of a morally charged distinction between converted and non-converted Roma.

The second response to the perceived gap between Roma and non-Roma is primarily a majoritarian one, even though better-off Roma might also be involved to some degree. This response is informed by the perception that, in general, the situation will only get worse. The 'temporal dynamic is one not of progress but of decline, decay and disintegration' (Ferguson 2006: 190). Consequently, the temporalization involved in this view is based on the idea of degeneration and a downward movement towards deeper poverty and more tensions, chaos, or even clashes. In Western Europe, this response is particularly related to the idea, deeply rooted in historical stereotypes, that as soon as migrating Roma arrive and start to live in a neighbourhood, or in the vicinity, the situation is going to go downhill: houses prices will decrease, insecurity and criminality will increase, tourism (if there is any) will be affected, and the behaviour of the Roma will lead to decay (Ivasiuc 2015, Chap. 11, this volume). We have seen similar trends in Central and Eastern Europe, but these have often been more dramatic in terms of both discourse and practice, even though the local differences may be significant. In the context of migration and mobility in Europe, we have also seen what I have called the emergence of the discourse about 'the return of the *Zigeuner* (Gypsy)' (van Baar 2014), according to which the stereotypes are no longer seen as stereotypes, but simply as truths or facts that should not be hidden, but openly discussed. I have argued that the emergence of this problematic discourse that the Gypsy has returned, which has sometimes been supported by criminologists, is closely related to the rise of reasonable antigypsyism.

Finally, the idea of degeneration central to this second kind of response brings me back to where I started this chapter: at the intersection of anti-Roma racism and the introduction of anti-policies. One of the delicate factors is that the ineffectiveness and insufficiency of development interventions, which were themselves partially legitimized on the grounds of the riskiness of underdevelopment, have led to the further intensification of diverse practices of securitization. A good example is the Czech Republic, where, in various towns with substantial Roma populations and increasing segregation, the local governments have introduced zero-tolerance policies to deal with the so-called 'inadaptables' (for which read the Roma). The suggestion that the situation will deteriorate and could easily lead to violent clashes has been mobilized to articulate new kinds of securitarian anti-policies under the name of zero-tolerance programmes (Ort et al. 2016). The (contested) philosophy behind this zero tolerance is that the severe punishment of petty crime will prevent the development of more serious criminal behaviour. Even though statistics from several of the Czech towns involved show a decline in crime, the perception and imagination of an almost catastrophic future, in which the situation will deteriorate drastically as a result of crime, further decay and urban degeneration has legitimized the introduction of anti-policies which serve primarily to maintain the status quo and to the reinforcement of the racialization of poverty.

Notes

1. We should discuss Roma-related programmes beyond the well-established binaries of plan vs. implementation, intention vs. achievement or success vs. failure (van Baar 2011: 5–6, 252–53, 258–60). I have therefore put 'fail' in inverted commas here. In the end, 'because "failed" development projects

can so successfully help to accomplish important strategic tasks behind the back of the most sincere participants, it does become less mysterious why "failed" development projects should end up being replicated again and again' (Ferguson 1990: 256).
2. This representation is not imposed on the Roma in a top-down manner, for Roma and pro-Roma activist networks have also mobilized and upscaled (through lobbying at the EU level) discourses of antigypsyism against EU Member States in order to strategically articulate where their governments have 'failed' (cf. van Baar 2011: 267).
3. The idea of developmentalism inherent in post-colonial thinking was not entirely new historically, but had clear predecessors in anti-imperial thinking in the Enlightenment (van Baar 2011: 92–99, 140–46), as well as in 19th century schemes of social evolution (Ferguson 2006: 179). Yet, Ferguson (ibid. 180–81) emphasizes that, with the emergence of racial thinking in its modern form in the 18th century, racial difference had started to be seen as *a result of history,* and the correlated thinking in terms of different 'races' reflected a reified hierarchy in which 'inferior' races were seen as degenerative.

References

Agarin, T., ed. 2014. *When Stereotype Meets Prejudice: Antiziganism in European Societies.* Stuttgart: Ibidem.
Bancroft, A. 2005. *Roma and Gypsy-Travellers in Europe.* Aldershot: Ashgate.
Bartels, A., et al., eds. 2013. *Antiziganistische Zustände 2.* Münster: Unrast.
Bigo, D. 2008. Globalized (in)security. In *Terror, Insecurity and Liberty,* ed. D. Bigo and A. Tsoukala, 10–48. London: Routledge.
Bogdal, K.-M. 2011. *Europa erfindet die Zigeuner.* Frankfurt am Main: Suhrkamp.
Chakrabarty, D. 2000. *Provincializing Europe.* Princeton, NJ: Princeton University Press.
Clark, C., and B. Taylor. 2014. Is Nomadism the "Problem"? In *Anti-Social Behaviour in Britain,* ed. S. Pickard, 166–178. Basingstoke: Palgrave Macmillan.
Duffield, M. 2007. *Development, Security and Unending War.* Cambridge: Polity.
———. 2010. The Liberal Way of Development and the Development-Security Impasse. *Security Dialogue* 41 (1): 53–76.
End, M. 2013. Antiziganismus: Zur Verteidigung eines wissenschaftlichen Begriffs in kritischer Absicht. In *Antiziganistische Zustände 2,* ed. A. Bartels et al., 39–72. Münster: Unrast.
Escobar, A. 1995. *Encountering Development.* Princeton, NJ: Princeton University Press.
European Commission. 2014. *Report on the Implementation of the EU Framework for National Roma Integration Strategies.* Brussels: European Commission.

European Council. 1993. *European Council in Copenhagen*. Brussels: European Council.
European Parliament. 2015. *International Roma Day – Anti-Gypsyism in Europe and EU Recognition of the Memorial Day of the Roma Genocide During WW II. Resolution P8-TA(2015)0095*. Brussels: European Parliament.
Fassin, D. 2013. *Enforcing Order*. Cambridge: Polity.
Ferguson, J. 1990. *The Anti-Politics Machine*. Minneapolis, MN: University of Minnesota Press.
———. 2006. *Global Shadows*. Durham, NC: Duke University Press.
Foucault, M. 2004. *"Society Must Be Defended"*. *Lectures at the Collège de France 1975–1976*. London: Penguin.
Freeman, D. 2012. The Pentecostal Ethic and the Spirit of Development. In *Pentecostalism and Development*, ed. D. Freeman, 1–38. New York: Palgrave Macmillan.
Gog, S., and M. Roth. 2012. The Roma People of Romania. In *The Wiley-Blackwell Companion to Religion and Social Justice*, ed. M. Palmer and S. Burgess, 388–401. Oxford: Blackwell.
Grill, J. 2012. "Going up to England": Exploring Mobilities Among Roma from Eastern Slovakia. *Journal of Ethnic and Migration Studies* 38 (8): 1269–1287.
Hancock, I. 1997. The Roots of Antigypsyism. In *Confronting the Holocaust*, ed. J. Colijn and M. Sachs Littell, 19–49. Lanham, MD: University Press of America.
Huysmans, J., A. Dobson, and R. Prokhovnik, eds. 2006. *The Politics of Protection*. London: Routledge.
Ivasiuc, A. 2015. Watching Over the Neighbourhood. *Etnofoor* 27 (2): 53–72.
Jovanović, J. 2015. *'Vulnerability of Roma' in Policy Discourse on Combatting Trafficking in Human Beings in Serbia*. Budapest: Center for Policy Studies, CEU.
Kyuchukov, H., ed. 2012. *New Faces of Antigypsyism in Modern Europe*. Prague: Slovo 21.
Lentin, A. 2004. *Racism and Anti-Racism in Europe*. London: Pluto Press.
———. 2008. Racism, Anti-racism and the Western State. In *Identity, Belonging and Migration*, ed. G. Delanty, R. Wodak, and P. Jones, 101–119. Liverpool: Liverpool University Press.
McGarry, A. 2017. *Romaphobia*. London: Zed Books.
Meyer, B. 1998. "Make a Complete Break with the Past": Memory and Postcolonial Modernity in Ghanaian Pentecostalist Discourse. *Journal of Religion in Africa* 28 (3): 316–349.
Mezzadra, S. 2004. The Right to Escape. *Ephemera* 4 (3): 267–275.
New Keywords Collective. 2016. Europe/Crisis: New Keywords to the "Crisis" in and of "Europe", *Near Futures Online* 1 (1). Available at http://nearfuturesonline.org/europecrisis-new-keywords-of-crisis-in-and-of-europe/. Accessed 20 June 2016.

Nicolae, V. 2007. Towards a Definition of Anti-Gypsyism. In *Roma Diplomacy*, ed. V. Nicolae and H. Slavik, 21–30. New York: Idebate Press.
Ort, J., F. Pospíšil, and Š. Ripka. 2016. *Bezpečnost a sekuritizace Romů v České Republice*. Prague: Open Society Foundation.
Pollock, S., et al. 2000. Cosmopolitanisms. *Public Culture* 12 (3): 577–590.
Roberts, D., and M. Mahtani. 2010. Neoliberalizing Race, Racing Neoliberalism. *Antipode* 42 (2): 248–257.
Selling, J., et al., eds. 2015. *Antiziganism*. Cambridge: Cambridge Scholars Publishing.
Stewart, M., ed. 2012. *The Gypsy 'Menace': Populism and the New Anti-Roma Politics*. London: Hurst & Co.
Thurfjell, D., and A. Marsh, eds. 2014. *Romani Pentecostalism*. Frankfurt am Main: Peter Lang.
UNDP. 2002. *Avoiding the Dependency Trap*. Bratislava: United Nations Development Programme.
van Baar, H. 2011. *The European Roma: Minority Representation, Memory and the Limits of Transnational Governmentality*. Amsterdam: F&N.
———. 2014. The Emergence of a Reasonable Anti-Gypsyism in Europe. In *When Stereotype Meets Prejudice*, ed. T. Agarin, 27–44. Stuttgart: Ibidem.
———. 2015. The Perpetual Mobile Machine of Forced Mobility. In *The Irregularization of Migration in Contemporary Europe*, ed. Y. Jansen, R. Celikates, and J. de Bloois, 71–86. Lanham, MD: Rowman & Littlefield.
———. 2017a. Contained Mobility and the Racialization of Poverty in Europe: The Roma at the Development-Security Nexus. *Social Identities*. https://doi.org/10.1080/13504630.2017.1335826.
———. 2017b. Evictability and the Biopolitical Bordering of Europe. *Antipode* 49 (1): 212–230.
Walters, W. 2008. Anti-Policy and Anti-Politics. *European Journal of Cultural Studies* 11 (3): 267–288.
World Bank. 2005. *Roma in an Expanding Europe: Breaking the Poverty Circle*. Washington, DC: The World Bank.
Žižek, S. 1998. A leftist plea for "Eurocentrism". *Critical Inquiry* 24 (4): 988–1009.

CHAPTER 9

Illusionary Inclusion of Roma Through Intercultural Mediation

Angéla Kóczé

For more than two decades, various scholars, experts, activists, and international development agencies have variously qualified Europe's Roma as an 'underdeveloped' population (Barany 1994; Gheorghe 1991; Simionca 2013), a 'prominent poverty risk group' (Ringold et al. 2005), 'welfare dependent' (United Nations Development Programme 2002), and 'victims of human rights violations' (Human Rights Watch 1996). These discourses have become particularly widespread in post-socialist countries, where the protection, development, and integration of the Roma have been advocated, or where they are expected to at least become self-reliant citizens, productive workers, and active job seekers.

Since 1990, the increasing interest of the academic and political class in targeting the Roma has led to a proliferation of various policy-oriented studies (Surdu 2016) and transnational developmental interventions zealously aimed at integrating the Roma and improving their social inclusion.

The writing of this chapter would not have been possible without the generous patience and constructive criticism of the Editorial Team.

A. Kóczé (✉)
Central European University, Budapest, Hungary
e-mail: koczea@wfu.edu; koczea@ceu.edu

Moreover, the interest in Roma-targeted research and policy has coincided with the changing nature of, and interest in, global development and security (Stiglitz 1998). After the Cold War, these developments, inextricably linked to the history of capitalism and (neo)colonialism, remained interconnected with security, but their target and focus have changed (Gardner and Lewis 2015).

This chapter elaborates on the inspirational work of several scholars who have drawn attention to the hegemony of Euro centrism and to particular forms of discourse, representation, and knowledge which have produced the notion of so-called 'underdeveloped' countries (Escobar 1995). I also build on the work of those scholars who have discussed the paradigmatic shift towards neoliberal development which, for them, has been fundamentally linked with issues such as neoliberal governmentality, biopolitics, securitization, de-politicization, and the management of various 'crises' (Duffield 2001, 2005; Ferguson 1994; Li 2007; Mezzadra et al. 2013; Sharma 2008). Finally, I discuss the work of scholars who have made a connection between these broader global developments and the social inclusion of the Roma in Europe (van Baar 2011, 2017; Voiculescu 2017).

In dialogue with Huub van Baar's theorization of 'institutional developmentalism' (Chap. 8, this volume), which is part of what he calls 'the Europeanization of the Roma representation', I seek to understand the problematization, framing, and rationale that inspired the Council of Europe and the European Commission Directorate General for Education and Culture (DG EAC) to design and implement the multi-country, joint 'intercultural' mediation programme ROMED.[1] Without dismissing the efforts and goodwill to improve the inclusion of the Roma, I take a critical stance towards ROMED and interrogate its strategic function as a development programme. This chapter is particularly interested in the way in which developmental programmes have changed context and have also started to focus on the Global North, rather than primarily on the Global South. What is the relevance of this shift towards 'institutional developmentalism' *within* Europe and how exactly does it relate to a Europe-wide 'intercultural mediation programme' dedicated to improving the social inclusion of the Roma?

Based on a ROMED document, on contextual analysis and on several interviews, my aim is to focus on the design and content of the programme, as well as on its unintended effects, rather than on the practical policy dimensions and results; the latter would require a thorough empirical examination of outcome and in-depth ethnographic research among those who have directly experienced its outcomes. Some recent scholarship (Clark 2018) has focused more extensively on the successes and failures of the Roma mediation programme. I want to reflect instead on the ideology, rationale, framing and strategic function of mediation, which remains a primary developmental technique used by the Council of Europe to improve the social inclusion of the Roma. My intention is to go beyond the critical perspective on the practice of developmental policies and approach them instead as discursive interventions comprising political objectives such as governing, controlling, policing, and securitizing allegedly underdeveloped populations (see also Duffield 2001; Escobar 1995; Ferguson 1994). This chapter focuses mainly on the critique of institutional developmentalism targeting Roma, based on the articulation of a Foucauldian biopolitical regime. Although such policies and programmes may entail a subversive potential to create the so-called 'counter-publics' (Fraser 1990) among those on the receiving end, and to instigate forms of public deliberation to promote a more just and inclusive society, the scope and length of the chapter does not allow for an examination of this dimension.

In this chapter, I argue that the social inclusion of the Roma, through what the Council of Europe considers as 'intercultural mediation', is deeply ambiguous. First, the Council's mediation programmes focus strongly on the *intercultural* and thus tend implicitly to omit the broader socio-economic, political, and historical contexts that have contributed to the marginalization of Roma. Second, these programmes focus on the mediation of both Roma and non-Roma mediators and thus emphasize the 'change of attitudes and behaviour at individual level' (Ivanova et al. 2017: 51), with the consequence that a culturalist and behavioural gloss is laid over more structural issues. Third, in some cases, the institutionalization of Roma mediation has taken place in relative isolation from larger political and policy infrastructures, such as the relevant ministries or local bodies (Council of Europe 2016; Kolev et al. 2006; Open Society Foundations 2011). Due to this development, the programmes run the serious risk that the Roma mediators are perceived, received, and awarded (e.g., salaried) differently to government officials, who are fully and more adequately incorporated in state bureaucracies (Council of Europe 2016, 2017). Hristo Kyuchukov (2012: 375) also emphasizes that Roma mediators are challenged by issues such as low status, precarious employment conditions, and institutional dependency or can even be expected to work on issues that are not included in their job description. Thus, although the institutionalization of Roma mediation might suggest that 'something has been done for the Roma', mediation programmes also risk becoming little more than token measures or even leading to new forms of societal and institutional marginalization.

To examine the ambiguous rationale of the ROMED programmes, I will mobilize a conceptual framework that is linked to the *securitization of development* and the deployment of a Foucauldian *biopolitical* regime. Through institutional developmentalism, the Roma have become a culturally distinct, racialized group, who need to avoid the 'poverty trap' and are often 'symbolized through the metaphor of bridges and the institutionalization of bridging "mediators" in the domains of healthcare, schooling, policing and community or labour-market interventions' (van Baar 2017: 7). I would like to follow van Baar's arguments by exploring the securitization and biopoliticization involved in Roma-related institutional developmentalism through the case of the Council of Europe and European Union (EU) co-funded ROMED joint initiative consisting of two consecutive parts, known as ROMED1 and ROMED2.

The Council of Europe's ROMED Programmes: A Genealogy of 'Roma Mediation'

In the early 1990s, shortly after the collapse of state socialism in Central and Eastern Europe, the Council of Europe was one of the first intergovernmental institutions to Europeanize the Roma by defining them as a 'true European minority' (van Baar 2011: 156–157, see also Kovats 2001; McGarry 2014). The Council of Europe has a long legacy going back to the 1960s of dealing with Roma-related issues. In 1983, the Council proposed that the Roma should be recognized as an ethnic group within Europe, and, later on, the Council periodically discussed the situation of 'nomads', 'populations of nomadic origin', and 'Gypsies and other travellers in Europe' (Council of Europe 1969, 1975, 1981, see van Baar 2011). In 1993, the Parliamentary Assembly of the Council of Europe adopted the report *Gypsies in Europe*, prepared by the Dutch socialist Josephine Verspaget. This document subsequently led to Recommendation 1203 (Council of Europe 1993). This important document declared that 'the Gypsies' are 'a true European minority', and, in 1995, the Council prepared an updated and extended version of Verspaget's report—*The*

Situation of Gypsies (Roma and Sinti in Europe)—for its European Committee on Migration (CDMG). Martin Kovats (2001) has extensively critiqued this report for its narrow, essentialist, and culturalist understanding of the situation of the Roma in Europe. He argues that the report simplifies both the diversity amongst Europe's Roma and the complexity of their situation. Kovats (2001: 100–101) offers an example:

> The issue of Roma asylum seekers. Instead of this phenomenon being perceived as a symptom of significant structural problems that need to be addressed, the 1995 report argues that 'the increase in mobility since 1990 must not conjure up pictures of a "tidal wave" of Gypsies sweeping over the West, it is merely a return to the normal mobility of Gypsies' (1995: 13). Perceiving the asylum issue as essentially one of (Roma) culture undermines understanding of the actual causes of this ongoing movement of people, as well as the chances of developing effective and necessary policies in response.

Kovats critiques the culturally driven framing of the migration of the Roma in the early 1990s which undercut the structural discrimination and racism against Roma in Europe, and, in particular, omitted to mention the war situation in the former Yugoslavia as a major reason for their migration. The reports adopted by the Council of Europe in 1993 and 1995 can be seen as part of the complex and significantly changing genealogy of how the Council has articulated the idea of 'mediation' since the early 1990s. In Recommendation 1203 of 1993, a specific measure is recommended:

> *a mediator for Gypsies should be appointed* by the Council of Europe, after consultation with representative organisations of Gypsies, with the following tasks at least:
>
> a. *to review the progress* made in the implementation of measures taken or recommended by the Council of Europe concerning Gypsies;
> b. *to maintain regular contact* with representatives of Gypsies;
> c. *to advise governments of member states* in matters concerning Gypsies;
> d. *to advise the different bodies of the Council of Europe* in matters concerning Gypsies;
> e. to investigate government policy and the human rights situation related to Gypsies in member states;
> f. *to investigate the position of stateless Gypsies* or Gypsies with undetermined nationality;

g. *to receive replies to questions addressed to governments* or government representatives of member states;
h. *to enjoy full access to relevant government archives* and other material;
i. *to question citizens of member states* of the Council of Europe. (Council of Europe 1993, emphasis added)

The 1995 report calls on the Council's Committee of Ministers to a give a reaction to the proposed 'mediators for Gypsies' in the 1993 Recommendation, a measure regarded as still relevant, which it was felt should be taken by the Council of Europe. The report states:

> A more far-reaching proposal, to which the Committee of Ministers has not yet given its final reaction, is that contained in Assembly Recommendation 1203 (1993) to the effect that a *mediator for Gypsies* should be appointed by the Council of Europe… The CDMG does not feel able to take up a position on this proposal, which requires a political decision. It can only point out that this is a matter to which Gypsy organizations attach a lot of importance but it clearly has many implications, which need to be considered in depth by a specialist in Gypsy affairs. (Council of Europe 1995: 28, emphasis added)

In contrast to the later ROMED mediation programmes, these early documents envisaged the position of mediator at a transnational or national level. No rationale is given in these documents to explain why mediation in particular would be the most appropriate way of improving the 'inclusion of the Roma'. The mediator seems to have been envisaged, first and foremost, as a non-Roma person or even a 'Gypsy (policy) expert' who should be consulted in all kinds of cases, such as those listed in Recommendation 1203 quoted above. In these early 1990s documents, the mediator was primarily conceptualized as a kind of 'rapporteur' who would investigate the situation of the Roma and the violation of their human rights locally and nationally. Accordingly, the mediator would update the Council on any kind of policy, or organizational, or leadership change in the community, as well as advising Council bodies and Members States on matters concerning the Roma.

At more or less the same time in the 1990s, Romani CRISS, a local Roma NGO in Romania, developed and implemented its own model of Roma mediation on the ground. This initiative could be considered—certainly in hindsight—as an important grassroots development which challenged the 'authorized', and, in many respects, top-down, conceptualization of the 'mediator for Gypsies' introduced by the Council of Europe in the early 1990s. Romani CRISS first used mediation as a 'form of social action' in various local 'inter-ethnic conflicts' (see WHO 2013: 6). Later on, 'these mediators were trained to become liaisons among Roma communities, non-Roma and local authorities and to facilitate the identification of peaceful solutions to local problems' (ibid.). There was a change in defining mediation *vis-à-vis* the Council of Europe and local policies and practices, from 'conflict resolution' to the 'improvement of social condition of Roma'. Liégeois (2012: 2) also explains that mediation was often conceptualized as 'the art of conflict management'; the trend has changed, however, and mediation can now be a more 'proactive' facilitation to create social cohesion. In 1996, Romani CRISS initiated a pilot project on health mediation, which the Romanian Ministry of Health institutionalized in 2000–2002. In this way, the role of Roma Health Mediator has become an official profession in Romania. Most of the appointed mediators were Romani women 'living in the communities where they worked' (WHO 2013: 6). Their responsibilities included 'raising the health literacy of Roma, with a focus on preventive health care, raising awareness among the health care providers of the situation of Roma and addressing the social determinants of access to health, such as absence of identity documents' (ibid.).

Thanks to the political lobbying of prominent Romani activists, such as Nicolae Gheorghe (who founded Romani CRISS in 1993), these 'local' Romanian practices of mediation also played an important role in reshaping the concept of Roma mediation at a European, as well as a local, level (interview with DG, Roma mediator from Romania). We have been able to observe the impact of these changes in the way in which the Council of Europe began to change its notion of Roma mediation from the beginning of the new millennium onwards. In a Council Recommendation of 2000 on the education of Roma children in Europe, for instance, there is a proposal to use a more grassroots-based concept of mediation. In the context of school mediation, the Recommendation mentions that 'mediators [should come] from within the Roma/Gypsy community, in particular, to ease the contacts between Roma/Gypsies, the majority population and schools, and to avoid conflicts at school; this should apply to all levels of schooling' (Council of Europe 2000).

When we compare the status of the mediator in this document with that in the documents of the mid-1990s, we can observe that its original status at a transnational and national level was changed to a more local, community level. This trend reflects the Council of Europe's policies towards the Roma, particularly with regard to its ROMED programme, which envisions and advocates for the implementation of Roma mediation at community level throughout Europe.

The Securitization and Biopoliticization of Development

The so-called Strasbourg Declaration on Roma, adopted by the Council of Europe in 2010, is an explicit reaffirmation of the commitment to the protection of human rights and the promotion of the social inclusion of the Roma by the Council's Member States. A Council employee whom I interviewed referred to the Strasbourg Declaration as a political reaction to the disturbing 'repatriation' of Roma migrants from France back to Romania and Bulgaria in 2009 and 2010. On 29 July 2010, the French President Nicolas Sarkozy announced an action plan against 'illegal migrants' which legitimized the demolition of their camps, described by him as a 'source of illegal trafficking and exploitation of children for the purpose of begging, prostitution or crime' (quoted in McGarry and Drake 2013: 82). The Strasbourg Declaration was issued during this political turbulence and refers indirectly to the discriminatory French repatriation in very cautious terms. The Declaration (2010) states, for example, that '[w]hile the primary responsibility for promoting inclusion lies with the Member States of which Roma are nationals or long-term legal residents, recent developments concerning Roma in Europe have demonstrated that some of the challenges we face have cross-border implications and therefore require a pan-European response'.

There is a striking parallel political context between the Council of Europe reports of the mid-1990s and this 2000 Declaration. In the 1990s, the Council was among the first inter-governmental organizations to raise concerns about the migration of the Roma from the post-socialist countries, for instance, the 1995 report stresses:

> In the face of this dramatic increase in the number of asylum-seekers in major Western European countries (in 1993 Germany received 322,599 asylum applications, 23% of which concerned Romanian citizens), certain governments have decided to step up the repatriation of unsuccessful applicants... (Council of Europe 1995: 19)

While this report explicitly discusses the challenge posed by the migration of the Roma from Eastern to Western European countries, the 2010 Declaration uses only an implicit reference to the 'migration crisis', without naming those countries which deported and evicted the Roma. It states that the 'challenges we face have cross-border implications and therefore require a pan-European response' (2010). The final ROMED evaluation report also confirms that the Strasbourg Declaration was of 'critical importance for the birth of ROMED as a *systemic pan-European effort in the area of effective mediation*' (Ivanova et al. 2017: 46, emphasis added).

The emergence of ROMED is in line with the global trend to securitize and biopoliticize development (Duffield 2005). The Roma population, according to several Hungarian Roma activists,[2] has always been conceptualized as an 'ethnic threat' on the national security agenda; but it was only after 1989, and with the emerging migration of Eastern European Roma, that 'Roma issues' became explicitly securitized on the international and mostly European level (Kovats 2001). Van Baar (2017: 4–8) persuasively explains the rationale of the 'developmentalities' towards Central and Eastern European Roma, partially based on the logic of migration prevention. He also exposes the 'institutionalized nexus of freedom and security' in EU policy that brings together 'its approach to migration with the combating of transnational crime, shadow economies, trafficking and terrorism' (2017: 7). The Strasbourg Declaration is strongly linked to this logic of the 'institutionalized nexus of freedom and security', which differentiates the politically preferred movement of the various goods and services attached to highly skilled migration (business, tourism, student exchanges) from the movement of those who are 'unwanted' and perceived as a 'threat' and 'destabilizing danger' to the EU and its precious 'freedom of movement' (van Baar 2017; see also New Keywords Collective 2016). This political differentiation, which is based on separating 'valuable' migrants from those who were unwanted, poor, and racialized (from the Global South and including the EU's 'internalized outsiders' such as the Roma) has transformed the mobility of the latter into what has euphemistically been called 'irregular' or 'illegal' migration. However, in point of fact, this differentiation is fully and integrally part of the mechanism and practice of securitization. Similarly, various scholars have discussed the 2010 expulsion of Bulgarian and Romanian Romani migrants from France as a case which involves the intertwined securitization, irregularization, and racialization of the Roma (Kóczé

2017; McGarry and Drake 2013). As a developmental programme, ROMED was launched in the context of these events and in that of the significant securitization of Roma mobility and their differential treatment as EU citizens and migrants (see Part I, this volume).

Closely related to its security concerns, as a mediation programme, ROMED has become part of the significantly biopolitical governance of the Roma (van Baar 2011, 2017, Chap. 8, this volume). Michel Foucault (1990, 2003) introduced the term biopolitics in the mid-1970s, defining it as the set of discourses, institutions, and policies that had emerged from the redefinition of political life at the end of the eighteenth century. In Foucault's understanding, biopolitics coalesces biology and politics in the conceptualization of power. Consequently, race, racialization, and racism have also become central governing concepts in his notion of biopolitics:

> What in fact is racism? It is primarily a way of introducing a break into the domain of life that is under power's control: the break between what must live and what must die. The appearance within the biological continuum of the human race of races, the distinction among races, the hierarchy of races, the fact that certain races are described as good and that others, in contrast, are described as inferior: all this is a way of fragmenting the field of the biological that power controls. (Foucault 2003: 254–255)

Biopolitics is a technique of governing aimed at managing populations differentially and according to their contribution to productivity, fertility, security, longevity, and the like. The population regulated through bio power is divided into various human groups. Biopolitics tainted by racism controls a racialized population—perceived as inferior—through the use of ambiguous development programmes; programmes to improve the 'social inclusion' of an allegedly underdeveloped, unproductive, passive or dependent population such as the Roma, for example, as classified in development discourses. McWhorter (2004: 39) argues that the modern concept of race and racialized practices has been developed 'within the same networks of disciplinary normalization and bio power that gave us the modern concept of sex'. He points out that biopolitics deploys strategies of population management, based on the same assumptions of intersectionally categorized (gender, sexuality, race, class, etc.) human life and governmental responsibility.

Historically, development discourse has always been linked to the anthropological knowledge of 'underdeveloped', 'savage', and racialized populations (Gardner and Lewis 2015). Thomas Acton (2016) critiques and exemplifies scientific racism via the knowledge production of the Gypsy Lore Society, a leading and primarily scholarly organization founded in 1888 and involved in the development of the more contemporary Romani Studies. The Gypsy Lore Society is still active, but, according to Acton, it did not go through the self-reflexive and self-critical stage that took place in the 1980s in Western anthropology regarding the representation of the Third World and its supposedly underdeveloped or developing populations. Acton (2016: 2) dissects the various structures of knowledge that fostered scientific racism, emphasizing that 'the failure to acknowledge [the] effects [of scientific racism] has a continuing effect in naturalizing the acts of oppression, discrimination, murder and state violence against Gypsies, Roma and Travellers in the twenty-first century'. Ian Hancock has argued that such 'scientific' discourses are intimately connected with the historical roots of antigypsyism. He mentions several historical and sociological factors that have contributed to the 'institutionalized prejudice against Romani people' (Hancock 1997: 20), which includes the following: over the centuries, the Roma have been associated with Asiatic invaders, Islamic and non-White, non-Christian outsiders, and Romani culture has been treated as an exclusivist and separatist culture.

Following the pioneering work of several scholars in development studies (Escobar 1995; Ferguson 1994), the tradition of conceptualizing development has often been based on uni-linear, Eurocentric social progression. Arturo Escobar (1995) is one of those who has critiqued this approach. He considers development as a post-colonial, Eurocentric construction in which 'the West' is labelled as 'developed', whereas the rest of the world is perceived as 'underdeveloped' and on a trajectory towards the more developed Western world. In this way, development discourses constitute 'First World' societies as the norm and those of the 'Third World' as deviations from that norm. Accordingly, these discourses neglect numerous other possible conceptions and indicators for a 'good life' or a 'good society'; indeed, these other ways of perceiving development are assessed on the basis of a primarily European or Western experience and idea of progress. Several post-colonial critics reject development because they consider it to be 'a postcolonial form of orientalism transformed into a de-politicized "neutral" science for action in the contemporary world' (van Baar 2011: 70).

Just as the traditional target groups—the 'underdeveloped' Third World populations of Africa, Asia, and Latin America—Europe's Roma are similarly considered as the underdeveloped in the heart of Europe (Mirga and Gheorghe 1997; Simionca 2013; van Baar 2017). The late involvement of development agencies in improving the situation of the Roma can be explained by the geographical location of the vast majority of the Roma who are living in 'developed' European countries. Their social and economic dispossession has only been recognized by international development agencies since the mid-1990s, with the transition of post-communist regimes to market capitalism (Abrahamson 2010). Mark Duffield characterizes this era as a 'universalistic commitment to poverty reduction and human rights that gained ground during the 1990s [which] has now stalled' (2005: 143). He cross-examines the interdependency of development and security, which has become even stronger since the mid-1990s. He emphasizes that 'geopolitical' development became more focused on the 'biopolitical' after the Cold War (ibid.). International development agencies, he argues, have mobilized their resources to change the power relations between social groups (defined in biopolitical terms), to integrate the excluded population in order to create global stability in developed countries (Duffield 2005).

In Europe, a significant reframing of Roma issues took place during the same period, something which van Baar (2011) has characterized as the 'Europeanization of Roma representation'. Notions of Roma integration, social inclusion, representation, empowerment, and participation emerged as a key vocabulary associated with the Roma in Europe. This terminology had also become prominent with the declaration in 2003 of the Decade of Roma Inclusion 2005–2015 and became even more firmly established in 2011 with the EU Framework for National Roma Integration Strategies by 2020.[3]

Some scholars (Li 2007; Sharma 2008) have suggested that this new kind of development vocabulary has emerged to transform the discourse on welfare. In line with neoliberalization and the radical transformation of the redistributive welfare system, there is a trend, manifested in transnational development projects, to target marginalized populations such as the Roma. The structural transformation of state redistribution via the privatization of social, educational, and health institutions, and the withdrawal of funds from local welfare institutions, have disproportionately disadvantaged poor and racialized Roma families (Kóczé 2018).

Intercultural Mediation for the Roma

As I have discussed, ROMED has to be seen in the context of earlier policy recommendations by the Council of Europe (1993, 1995) and in that of the experiences of intercultural mediation programmes devised and implemented at local and national level by other organizations like Romani CRISS in Romania (Council of Europe 2009; WHO 2013). The Strasbourg Declaration on Roma fostered the need to develop 'European training on intercultural mediation for Roma communities', which led to the emergence of the Council of Europe's ROMED programme (Council of Europe 2010). The work and lessons that emerged from the ROMED programme contributed to the adoption of the Recommendation of the Committee of Ministers to Member States on Mediation as an Effective Tool for Promoting Respect for Human Rights and Social Inclusion of Roma (Council of Europe 2012). Furthermore, the Recommendation of the Council of the European Union (2013) on effective Roma integration measures in the Member States reiterates the importance of the 'training and employment of qualified mediators dedicated to Roma and [of using] mediation as one of the measures to tackle the inequalities'.

The ROMED programme consists of two separate, but interconnected, phases: ROMED1 or the so-called 'European training programme on intercultural mediation for Roma communities' and ROMED2 or 'Democratic governance and community participation through mediation'. The concept of ROMED was designed in 2010–2011 with the involvement of leading experts in Roma inclusion and intercultural mediation, supported by the training and capacity-building materials of the Council of Europe's Youth Centre. They developed the ROMED Curriculum, which provided a conceptual and practical tool for mediators. One of the most important materials is the *ROMED1 Trainer's Handbook* (Rus et al. 2016), which consists of a comprehensive framework elaborating on key concepts and the vision of the programme. The handbook is built around the core principles of the ROMED1 mediation approach, namely: cooperation, intercultural mediation, human rights, and participatory planning. Training for mediators began in 2011.

ROMED1 aimed to 'improve the quality and effectiveness of the work of school, health, employment and community mediators, with a view to supporting better communication and co-operation between Roma and public institutions (school, healthcare providers, employment offices, local authorities, etc.)' (Ivanova et al. 2017: 46). To achieve this aim, the programme focused on the following objectives:

To promote effective *intercultural mediation* to improve the communication and co-operation between Roma and public institutions;

To ensure the integration of a *rights-based approach* in the mediation between Roma communities and public institutions;

To support the work of mediators by providing tools for planning and implementation of their activities, which *encourage democratic participation* while generating *empowerment of Roma communities* and increased accountability of public institutions. (Ivanova et al. 2017: 46, emphasis added)

The term 'intercultural mediation' is not defined in either of the main documents of the programme: *Experiencing ROMED: A Legacy for Improved Participation of Roma Communities* (Gillard 2017) and the *Trainers Handbook* (Rus et al. 2016). It remains an ambiguous culturally coded concept, which assumes some common understanding. Anthony Liddicoat (2016) distinguishes two ways of understanding 'intercultural mediation'. The first way is as a 'problem-solving activity that deals with the communication breakdown caused by cultural difference' (2016: 355). This approach signifies culture as static and conceptualizes mediation as a technique that resolves communication problems based on cultural differences. The second way to approach intercultural mediation is to see it as a 'relational and interpretative activity' (ibid.). This second approach is more complex, for it deals not only with resolving communication problems, but is also involved in a complex meaning-making process of 'understanding, explaining, commenting, interpreting and negotiating' social phenomena (ibid.). So, in the case of ROMED, the intercultural mediator engages in a complex translation and interpretation of language and culture, as well as in a meaning-making process between the Roma community and the respective local authority. Based on this explanation, the intercultural mediator is in a position to have knowledge of, and participate in, two cultures, as well as having the capacity to interpret and comprehend the complex relationship between the two parties.

ROMED1 was a training programme that ran during the period 2011–2013 to prepare mediators to facilitate communication between (mainly racially segregated) Roma communities and public institutions, as well as to professionalize and institutionalize the role of mediator as a specific occupation. As a result of the training programme, there are now 1479 mediators working in over 500 municipalities in 22 countries; 90%

of the trained mentors are Roma, and over 50% of the trained and certified mediators are women (Ivanova et al. 2017: 60–61).

While ROMED1 focused on developing the capacity of individual mediators, ROMED2 (2013–2016) shifted the focus; it recognized the limitation of one person (the mediator) and was initiated to set up and facilitate the so-called 'Community Action Groups' (CAGs) within Roma communities. These groups are 'voluntary Roma citizens from the community, who agree to function in an open, democratic and transparent way in order to contribute to the improvement of the situation of the Roma community, based on a constructive dialogue with local authorities and other institutions' (Ivanova et al. 2017: 48). ROMED2 started in April 2013 and was active in 54 municipalities in 11 countries. Mediators who were trained in the first phase of the programme remained active as 'local facilitators, to provide needed information and assist the emerging civic groups in their communication with institutions' (Ivanova et al. 2017: 77). ROMED2 was a response to the 'need for a more systematic approach to stimulate processes of community change and the engagement of local stakeholders with each other in a constructive dialogue' (Ivanova et al. 2017: 77). ROMED2 aimed to contribute to the changing attitude towards and the discourse about Roma communities by using the language of human rights, participation, and democracy; a new vocabulary which has been seen as marking a departure from the earlier ROMED1 framing (Clark 2018).[4]

Ambiguous Design and Framing

Given the scope and importance of the programme in Europe, I concentrate on the less obvious, yet ambiguous design and framing of the programme within the discussed security-development context in Europe. My approach entails three critical points. The first involves the diagnosis of the problem that relates to *intercultural* mediation. My second critical point concerns the framing of the programme in terms of *individual* communication and behavioural matters. In this framing, structurally unequal power relations and the structural changes required are largely ignored. My third critical point discusses the way in which the ROMED programme tends to *institutionalize Roma mediation* in a *detached* way.

The first key point of ROMED is *intercultural* mediation. As I see it, this framing occludes the broader socio-economic, political, and historical contexts which have contributed to the marginalization of the Roma. The

ROMED1 Handbook states that the 'real' intercultural mediator 'has a good knowledge of the "cultural codes" of the community and of the institution, is impartial and focused on improving communication and cooperation and on stimulating both parties to take responsibilities and to be actively involved in a change process' (Rus et al. 2016: 11). The reference to 'cultural codes' implies that the mediator in ROMED1—or the 'Community Action Group' in ROMED2—needs to 'understand' the Roma community and to have a good knowledge of it, as well as of related local institutions. This model suggests that, in order to improve the 'social inclusion' of the Roma in segregated communities, we need intermediaries—such as the envisioned members of CAGs—'trustees' who are open, democratic, transparent, and cooperative, with the aim of conducting a 'constructive dialogue' with local authorities based on an understanding of the alleged 'cultural codes'. Elsewhere it is suggested that 'one of the main assets of mediators is that they come from the Roma community and *know its culture*. They are therefore more sensitive to people's needs and can generate more trust within communities' (Ivanova et al. 2017: 22, emphasis added). Another cultural trope typically identified with Romani people is that they are 'welfare dependent', inactive, and more likely live on social benefits than look for a job or be employed. Liégeois (2012: 6, emphasis added) justifies the importance of Roma mediation by strengthening these specific stereotypes about Roma: 'inaction is the expensive option. It is cheaper to do something positive rather than to perpetuate a situation which makes people *dependent on the social services* and prevents them from contributing to the economic life of the countries they live in. Money spent on training and employing mediators is money well spent'. He perceives the 'inaction' and unemployment of the Roma as deviant characteristics which he tends to isolate from the neoliberal socio-economic restructuring in Europe—particularly since the 2008 financial crisis—that has further intensified wealth disparities across class, gender, and racial lines (Walby 2009).

The second point central to ROMED which I want to critique revolves around *individual changes*. The programme envisages that mediation would work by making the Roma involved responsible for solving conflicts within the community, as well as by improving local cooperation and securing better services in the community. Thus, the development of self-management, self-reliance, and responsible community members, achieved by altering the relationship between them and state and other social actors, envisages development projects as self-regulatory forms of racialized community government, under the regime of neoliberal governmentality (Voiculescu 2017). Indeed, cooperation between authorities and mediators in ROMED1 (and CAGs in ROMED2) starts from the idea that trustees whose behaviour is accepted by the local authorities and who are familiar with the alleged 'cultural codes' in and of the community should be employed. Indirectly, this approach promotes a de-politicized and racialized discourse about mediation, which, on the basis of their technical competences, emphasizes the individual responsibility of Roma community members for their self-management. Accordingly, ROMED tends to focus by design on the individual level and to de-politicize the larger structural injustices and institutional exclusionary mechanisms. ROMED documents, even while they acknowledge the 'syndrome of social exclusion', nevertheless speak of an 'interaction of individual exclusion risks' augmented by other factors, such as 'exclusion drivers', and 'the specifics of the local context in which the Roma live' (Ivanova et al. 2017: 44). Instead of considering the collective racialized social and spatial exclusion of the Roma as a condition that the mediator should attempt to challenge, the status of marginalization tends to be treated as an individual matter and a 'natural' foundation of the work of mediators. This indicates that mediation is supposed to improve 'the quality and effectiveness of the work of school, health, [and] employment' (Ivanova et al. 2017: 57) through communication, interpretation, and negotiation. This approach relies on how and what the Roma community members should do in order create better communication and cooperation with local institutions. In 2012, the recommendation of the Committee of Ministers, which is one of the foundational documents of ROMED, explicitly recalled the previous recommendation, which had 'advocated the use of Roma mediators to improve *communication and relations between Roma and public institutions*, which in turn *can help overcome barriers to social inclusion* and effective access of human rights, as well as improve access of Roma to public services' (Council of Europe 2012, emphasis added). Using intercultural mediation as a central framework, and focusing primarily on *individual* changes instead of racialized structural conditions, risks understanding the social and spatial exclusion of the Roma as a 'cultural specificity'.

My third critique revolves around the contradiction in ROMED which means that, instead of providing a mainstream and inclusive social, educational, health, and employment service, the programme tends to create a *detached institutionalization of Roma mediation* which legitimizes, sustains, and reproduces the socio-spatial exclusion of the Roma. Giovanni

Picker (2017) has eloquently discussed the various spatial segregating mechanisms, such as displacement, containment, omission, and cohesion, from both a historical and a contemporary point of view. Picker maintains that spatial segregation can be served, sustained, and reproduced by various projects and policies supposed to establish 'social cohesion'. Liégeois persuasively explains the function of mediation as 'restoring social cohesion' (2012: 2). Although one of ROMED's general aims was to promote the social inclusion of the Roma, in practice, instead of socio-spatial integration and inclusion, it has provided a 'mediation between Roma communities and public institutions' (Rus et al. 2016: 12). Similarly, and in line with Picker's observations (2017: 107–21), a programme that aims at social cohesion without changing the racially structured socio-spatial conditions may, in practice, function in such a way as to induce and *legitimize* socio-spatial segregation.

ROMED and other mediation programmes have played an important role in the institutionalization of mediators as employees of local institutions. The mediators, or local facilitators, are 'Roma person[s] preferably employed to work on Roma issues, with good connections within the Roma community and with good knowledge of the local institutions' (Ivanova et al. 2017: 48, see also Open Society Foundations 2011). The design of this model shows some striking similarities with—and some important differences to—the so-called 'Native Administration' that Frederick Lugard described in his book *The Dual Mandate In British Tropical Africa*, first published in 1922 and used as a guide for all British administrators in tropical Africa (cited by Duffield 2005). Duffield (2005) has pointed to an illuminating similarity between Native Administration and what he considers a biopolitical development regime. To some extent, I consider the design, logic, and structure of this colonial model as an analogue to ROMED, in which Native Administration is now represented by the position of the mediator—who plays the extended hand of the local institution—or by the CAG, which represents the Roma and needs to improve their 'social inclusion' in local public institutions. The ROMED programme suggests that the mediator has a 'neutral and impartial role' and that this clearly differs from understanding the mediator as either a Trojan horse—an instrument in the hands of the authorities with the purpose of changing the attitudes and behaviours of the community—or as a community activist, fighting against local institutions and representing only the interests of the community (Ivanova et al. 2017: 57; Rus et al. 2016: 11). I want to question the 'neutral and impartial role' of the mediator, for, in reality, their role is much more ambiguous. In countries such as Romania, Bulgaria, Macedonia, and Slovakia, the professionalization and institutionalization of the mediators and their employment by local authorities are considered to be a great achievement (Council of Europe 2016; Liégeois 2012; Rus et al. 2016; WHO 2013), but if local institutions employ them, they are inevitably no longer neutral. Alexandra Raykova, a member of the ROMED International Pedagogical Team and a ROMED Trainer from Bulgaria, underlines the essential need for mediators who fill the vacuum left by shrinking social services. She suggests that 'the work of *mediators is often the only service provider* in Roma communities which is appreciated and needed by Roma in accessing social rights' (Council of Europe 2017: 12, emphasis added).

Native Administration was based on transferring various administrative responsibilities, such as public works, tax collection, rural courts, local police, and primary education, to indigenous tribal or feudal authorities. Though ROMED mediators are not tasked with some of the duties that were performed by Native Administration, they nevertheless 'need to support better communication and co-operation between Roma and public institutions (school, healthcare providers, employment offices, local authorities, etc.)' (Ivanova et al. 2017: 57). Kyuchukov (2012: 375) succinctly points out that mediators can 'be used [by local authorities] as an excuse to avoid direct contact with the community, or they are expected to shoulder full responsibility for solving problems'. The presence of the mediator is not just an assurance of representation for the interests of the local authorities but also exempts them from providing services to the Roma community.

The aim of Native Administration was the scale of the self-determination achieved. To secure this aim, the 'backward races' were not to have an alien model imposed on them, rather they had to be empowered through 'their own efforts in their own way, to raise themselves to a higher plane of social organization' (Lugard 1965: 215). Duffield poignantly argues that Native Administration shows some surprising similarities with contemporary technology and development formation, interconnected with security. Moreover, he states that 'the biopolitics of Native Administration aimed to initiate a process of controlled social change through incremental self-management that maintained social cohesion' (Duffield 2005: 150). In the context of ROMED, by focusing on 'intercultural mediation' and maintaining the racially structured boundaries between the Roma and the local majority (institutions and populations), it eventually defends and preserves the security of majority communities from interaction with the 'culturally other' Roma via the institution of mediation.

In an interview, Deyan Kolev, chair of the Bulgarian Roma organization Amalipe, critiqued the ways in which Roma mediation functions. It creates a specific institutional layer that is not part of the relevant local institutions and mainstream ministries (of education, healthcare, social affairs, etc.). He emphasized that 'instead of health, employment and school mediators, we need highly educated Roma professionals (doctors, nurses, teachers, social workers, etc.) who are working in mainstream local institutions'.

Roma mediators employed by local institutions are perceived similarly to Native Administration, where the colonizing power delegated a native administrator to represent its interests and maintain a questionable social order by governing at a distance. Through this separate institutionalization of the position of the mediator, ROMED tends to create a new structure of dependency, and, indirectly, second-rank employees (in some places where the position of the mediators has been institutionalized in local public institutions). In the interviews I conducted with several mediators and administrators of the programme, they said that they are given less recognition and are often paid less than official social workers. Thus, in practice, the apparently positive, 'empowering' action towards the Roma through 'intercultural mediation' tends to turn into a new neoliberal racialized institution.

From a critical point of view, ROMED's mediators could be seen as democratic and enlightened versions of a number of old forms of traditional Romani leadership. From this perspective, Roma mediators have become the guardians of the community, and the neoliberal version of Native Administration, tasked with regulating social order in Roma communities.

Concluding Remarks

In this chapter, I have critically examined ROMED in the context of developmentalism and securitization in Europe. The ROMED mediation programme aimed to empower Roma community members and create inclusive public institutions, while ignoring deep structural socio-racial and spatial inequalities. The programme's design, ideology, and rationale are based on prevalent discourses about the Roma as 'underdeveloped' and culturally 'other'. Devised as an 'intercultural mediation' programme, ROMED has incorporated several prominent discourses on the Roma, such as those on cultural and human rights, participatory and democratic governance, and self-managed and self-responsibilized citizens. But instead of challenging the foundations of the structural violence against and racial oppression of the Roma, ROMED tends to entrench the securitization of the Roma and, unintentionally, to contribute to the depoliticization of wider structures of marginalization and racialization.

Notes

1. Available at: http://coe-romed.org/ (accessed 28 April 2017).
2. Interviews with Agnes Daroczi, Aladar Horvath and Jeno Zsigo in the research project on 'Institutionalization of Roma politics in Hungary after 1989' supported by The Hungarian Scientific Research Fund (OTKA). The research was carried out during the period 2012–2016 and coordinated by Angéla Kóczé.
3. In 2011, the European Commission adopted a communication advocating for the development of national strategies for Roma integration and detailing the concrete policies and measures to be taken (Communication on an EU Framework for National Roma Integration Strategies by 2020).
4. 'ROMED2 – Democratic Governance and Community Participation through Mediation', leaflet, available at: http://coe-romact.org/sites/default/files/leaflets/ROMED2%20-%20ENGLISH.pdf (accessed 20 September 2017).

References

Abrahamson, P. 2010. European Welfare States Beyond Neoliberalism. *Development and Society* 39 (1): 61–95.

Acton, T. 2016. Scientific Racism, Popular Racism and the Discourse of the Gypsy Lore Society. *Ethnic and Racial Studies* 39 (7): 1187–1204.

Barany, Z. 1994. Living on the Edge: The East European Roma in Post Communist Politics and Societies. *Slavic Review* 53 (2): 321–344.

Clark, C. 2018. Romani Activism and Community Development: Are Mediators the Way Forward? In *Community Organising Against Racism*, ed. C. Craig, 185–198. Bristol: Policy Press.

Council of Europe. 1969. *Situation of Gypsies and Other Travellers in Europe*, Recommendations 563. Strasbourg: Council of Europe.

———. 1975. *Social Situation of Nomads in Europe*, Resolution No (75)13, 22 May. Strasbourg: Council of Europe.

———. 1981. *Report on the Role and Responsibility of Local and Regional Authorities in Regard to the Cultural and Social Problems of Populations of Nomadic Origin.* Strasbourg: Council of Europe.
———. 1993. *Gypsies in Europe*, Recommendation 1203. Strasbourg: Council of Europe.
———. 1995. *The Situation of Gypsies (Roma and Sinti) in Europe.* Strasbourg: Council of Europe.
———. 2000. Recommendation No. R (2000) 4 of the Committee of Ministers to Member States on the Education of Roma/Gypsy children in Europe, 3 February 2000. Strasbourg: Council of Europe.
———. 2009. Recommendation CM/Rec (2009) 4 of the Committee of Ministers to member states on the education of Roma and Travellers in Europe. Strasbourg: Council of Europe.
———. 2010. *The Strasbourg Declaration on Roma.* Strasbourg: Council of Europe.
———. 2012. Recommendation of the Committee of Ministers to Member States on Mediation as an Effective Tool for Promoting Respect for Human Rights and Social Inclusion of Roma. Strasbourg: Council of Europe.
———. 2016. Thematic Report of the Group of Experts on Roma Health Mediators, CAHROM (2016)7. Strasbourg: Council of Europe.
———. 2017. *Taking Stock and Looking Forward*, High level Stakeholder Seminar, 28 March 2017, European Commission, Brussels. ROMED Programme. Available at http://coe-romed.org/sites/default/files/documentation/Conference%20Report%20web.pdf. Accessed 23 Oct. 2017.
Council of the European Union. 2013. Recommendation of 9 December 2013 on effective Roma integration measures in the Member States (2013/C 378/01). Brussels: Council of the European Union.
Duffield, M. 2001. *Global Governance and the New Wars.* London: Zed Books.
———. 2005. Getting Savages to Fight Barbarians: Development, Security and the Colonial Present. *Conflict, Security & Development* 5 (2): 141–159.
Escobar, A. 1995. *Encountering Development.* Princeton, NJ: Princeton University Press.
Ferguson, J. 1994 [1990]. *The Anti-Politics Machine.* Minneapolis, MN: University of Minnesota Press.
Foucault, M. 1990 [1976]. *The History of Sexuality, Volume 1.* London: Penguin.
———. 2003. *"Society Must Be Defended": Lectures at the Collège de France, 1975–1976.* New York: Picador.
Fraser, N. 1990. Rethinking the Public Sphere. *Social Text* 25–26: 56–80.
Gardner, K., and D. Lewis. 2015. *Anthropology and Development.* London: Pluto Press.
Gheorghe, N. 1991. Roma-Gypsy Ethnicity in Eastern Europe. *Social Research* 58 (4): 829–844.

Gillard, O. 2017. *Experiencing ROMED: A Legacy for Improved Participation of Roma Communities*. Strasbourg: Council of Europe.
Hancock, I. 1997. The Roots of Antigypsyism. In *Confronting the Holocaust*, ed. G. Colijn and M. Littell, 19–49. Lanham, MD: University Press of America.
Human Rights Watch. 1996. *Rights Denied*. New York: Human Rights Watch.
Ivanova, A., et al. 2017. Evaluation of the Council of Europe and European Union Joint Programme "ROMED". In *Experiencing ROMED: A Legacy for Improved Participation of Roma Communities*, ed. O. Gillard. Strasbourg: Council of Europe.
Kóczé, A. 2017. Race, Migration and Neoliberalism: Distorted Notions of Romani Migration in European Public Discourses. *Social Identities*. https://doi.org/10.1080/13504630.2017.1335827.
———. 2018. *Gender, Race, and Class: Romani Women's Political Activism and Social Struggles in the Post-Socialist Countries in Europe*. Budapest: CEU Press, forthcoming.
Kolev, D., T. Krumova, and B. Zahariev. 2006. *Evaluation Report for the Implementation of PHARE BG 0104.01 "Roma Population Integration"*. Veliko Turnovo: Center for Interethnic Dialogue and Tolerance "Amalipe".
Kovats, M. 2001. The Emergence of European Roma Policy. In *Between Past and Future*, ed. W. Guy, 93–116. Hatfield: University of Hertfordshire Press.
Kyuchukov, H. 2012. Roma Mediators in Europe: A New Council of Europe Program. *Intercultural Education* 23 (4): 375–378.
Li, T.M. 2007. *The Will to Improve*. Durham, NC: Duke University Press.
Liddicoat, A. 2016. Intercultural Mediation, Intercultural Communication and Translation. *Perspectives* 24 (3): 354–364.
Liégeois, J.-P. 2012. *Developments in Mediation, Current Challenges and the Role of ROMED*. Strasbourg: Council of Europe Publishing. Available at http://coe-romed.org/sites/default/files/documentation/Developments%20and%20challenges%20in%20Mediation%20ENG.pdf. Accessed 15 Oct 2017.
Lugard, F. 1965. *The Dual Mandate in British Tropical Africa Mandate in British Tropical Africa British Tropical Africa*. London: Frank Cass.
McGarry, A. 2014. Roma as a Political Identity. *Ethnicities* 14 (6): 756–774.
McGarry, A., and H. Drake. 2013. The Politicization of Roma as an Ethnic "Other". In *The Discourses and Politics of Migration in Europe*, ed. U. Korkut et al., 73–91. New York: Palgrave Macmillan.
McWhorter, L. 2004. Sex, Race, and Biopower. *Hypatia* 19 (3): 38–62.
Mezzadra, S., J. Reid, and R. Samaddar. 2013. *The Biopolitics of Development*. New Delhi: Springer.
Mirga, A., and N. Gheorghe. 1997. *The Roma in the Twenty-First Century*. Princeton, NJ: Project on Ethnic Relations.
New Keywords Collective. 2016. Europe/Crisis: New Keywords of the "Crisis" in and of "Europe". *Near Futures Online* 1 (1). Available at http://nearfuturesonline.org/europecrisis-new-keywords-of-crisisin-and-of-europe/. Accessed 23 Aug 2017.

Open Society Foundations. 2011. *Roma Health Mediators: Successes and Challenges*. Available at: https://www.opensocietyfoundations.org/reports/roma-health-mediators-successes-and-challenges. Accessed 21 Feb 2017.

Picker, G. 2017. *Racial Cities*. London: Routledge.

Ringold, D., M. Orenstein, and E. Wilkens, eds. 2005. *Roma in an Expanding Europe*. Washington, DC: The World Bank.

Rus, C., A. Raykova, and C. Leucht. 2016. *ROMED1 Trainers Handbook: European Training Programme on Intercultural Mediation for Roma Communities*. Strasbourg: Council of Europe.

Sharma, A. 2008. *Logics of Empowerment*. Minneapolis, MN: University of Minnesota Press.

Simionca, A. 2013. Development, Underdevelopment and Impoverished Roma Communities. *Studia Universitatis Babes-Bolyai* 58 (2): 55–75.

Stiglitz, J. 1998. *Towards a New Paradigm for Development*, Prebisch Lecture. Geneva: UNCTAD.

Surdu, M. 2016. *Those Who Count*. Budapest: CEU Press.

United Nations Development Programme. 2002. *The Roma in Central and Eastern Europe*. Bratislava: UNDP.

van Baar, H. 2011. *The European Roma: Minority Representation, Memory, and the Limits of Transnational Governmentality*. Amsterdam: F&N.

———. 2017. Contained Mobility and the Racialization of Poverty in Europe: The Roma at the Development-Security Nexus. *Social Identities*. https://doi.org/10.1080/13504630.2017.1335826.

Voiculescu, C. 2017. *European Social Integration and the Roma*. London: Routledge.

Walby, S. 2009. *Globalization and Inequalities*. London: Sage.

WHO. 2013. *Roma Health Mediation in Romania*. Copenhagen: WHO Regional Office for Europe.

CHAPTER 10

Voluntary Return as Forced Mobility: Humanitarianism and the Securitization of Romani Migrants in Spain

Ioana Vrăbiescu

This chapter analyses the practices of 'voluntary return'[1] directed at EU migrants and implemented by state social services and private actors in Madrid and Barcelona. These practices are officially presented as 'services' offered to immigrants from Romania, and they are instrumented as benevolent forms of state bureaucracy. Emphasizing the constant state pressure and surveillance enforced on vulnerable Romani migrants, I argue that these voluntary returns do not, as state officials and non-state agents suggest, represent a socially inclusive policy, rather that they are problematic practices of exclusion. Within the logic of humanitarianism, the condition of possibility for these state practices is created by the securitization of

---

This work was supported by the European Research Council under Starting Grant [number 336319]. I take this opportunity to express my gratitude to Ana Ivasiuc and Huub van Baar for their rich and insightful comments on previous versions of this chapter.

I. Vrăbiescu (✉)
University of Amsterdam, Amsterdam, Netherlands
e-mail: i.vrabiescu@uva.nl

Romani migrants and by the ways in which they are discursively and recurrently denounced as a threat to both society and to themselves.

In the broader context of the criminalization of Romani ethnics (Feischmidt et al. 2013; van Baar 2015) and the increasing over-surveillance of urban spaces, the investigation of the Spanish 'pay-to-go' schemes, or voluntary return programmes, reveals that Romani migrants have been targeted unevenly. Nevertheless, the Spanish authorities do not per se devote return policies to Romanian Roma; rather, they implement social projects to encourage and assist the 'repatriation' of Romanian citizens in marginal situations. In doing so, the social services design and implement several initiatives for inclusion that concern Romani migrants.

Approached by social workers, marginalized Romani migrants are, by default, suspected of having 'failed' to integrate as subjects. Distrustful of the ability of these people to integrate, those who work for social services adopt benevolent attitudes, implementing projects ranging from measuring their aptitudes for inclusion to evaluating failure. Operating within the social services, the allegedly voluntary return programmes can, I will argue, more accurately be conceived and described as acts of 'soft-deportation' (Kalir 2017). For example, Barak Kalir explains that state-led policies of voluntary return should be deemed problematic because they deflect welfare engagement while assuming a warm welcome for returnees in their country of origin, which is often the opposite of what happens in real life. Following other studies which have tracked down and exposed the potentially harmful and marginalizing effects of current practices of voluntary return, I challenge the mainstream understanding of the term, questioning the allegedly voluntary character of these returns (Webber 2011). I will argue that in Spain, the practices of voluntary return are exercised within the security-development nexus: they are practices depicted as benevolent acts towards those Romani migrants deemed to have failed social integration programmes and who consequently have become a social threat to the host country.

Based on research conducted in Barcelona and Madrid between 2013 and 2015, I will describe the implementation of the voluntary return programmes made available to some European citizens by investigating the commitment of civil servants and NGO workers to facilitating the return of Romani migrants to Romania. The case studies expose the state's modalities of using social support services, whilst aiming to execute forced (im)mobility and expatriation. Firstly, assessed as being 'at risk' by the local authorities, the children of poor Romani migrants are taken into state custody in order to persuade the entire family to return to Romania. Secondly, instead of being provided with social housing, Romani families are admitted to socio-educational projects which oblige them to live in camps, or they are encouraged to opt for voluntary return.

Aimed at documenting the voluntary return practices which target Romanian Romani migrants in Spain, the chapter focuses specifically on the attitudes and actions of public servants and social activists. The prominent role played by civil servants and NGO workers in the processes of repatriation points to their enhanced involvement in practices of soft deportation. Recalling that most agents not only act according to what is considered to be their duty but also behave in accordance with their moral values (Lipsky 1980), the chapter outlines how the decisions of street-level bureaucrats maintain and reproduce the humanitarian logic at the nexus of security and development.

Unravelling the multi-faceted security-development nexus, I critically reflect on the ability of the state to present voluntary return programmes as a benevolent act facilitated by social services. While 'deportability' (De Genova 2002) and 'evictability' (van Baar 2017a) can help to explain the situation of Romani migrants under the conditions of their securitized mobility in Europe, I argue that it is the humanitarian logic (Fassin 2012) which reveals the potential for the normalization of violence. The voluntary return apparatus underpins the humanitarian logic and its correlated instruments of governance. By analysing the discourses and practices of humanitarianism, I want to engage with the ethical and *emo*-political notions underpinning our society: benevolence, voluntariness, and threat. In doing so, I explore and interpret the security-development nexus behind Spain's benevolent politics which manifests itself in the practices of those services providing protection and provision to poor and racialized migrants. The institutionalized and exclusionist 'integration' system promotes voluntary returns among Romani migrants coming from Romania.

Alongside the official politics of repatriation, decisions are taken on the spot and on the ground by way of bureaucratic attempts to 'help' Romani migrants return to their country of origin. It is primarily civil servants who decide whether a case fits the requirements for voluntary return or not. Then, through direct interaction with Romani migrants, they decide upon the exact level and type of NGO action in the process of voluntary return.

I develop my argument in three sections. Firstly, I describe case studies researched in Barcelona and Madrid and elaborate on the ways in which bureaucratic practices work against those whom they claim to help.

Secondly, I analyse the process of securitization of Romani migrants under the regimes of deportability and evictability. Thereafter, I discuss the debate on humanitarianism and the resulting 'benevolent' politics in their relationship to the security-development nexus and to the actual practices of voluntary return more specifically. The chapter concludes with a discussion of how humanitarianism could be understood as the ethical grounds for the exercise of security-development techniques of governance which maintain and reinforce the exclusion of Romani migrants. My goal in this chapter is to reveal the ways in which both state and private actors endorse practices of eviction and soft deportation for Romani migrants.

Failed Integration Subjects and Voluntary Return

EU models of the governance of mobility are based on assessing and educating their subjects while enacting a civilizing mission implemented through a politics of integration (Powell 2013; Vrăbiescu 2016a). Disciplining methods are introduced and worked out through the retributive system of allotting provisions and benefits in exchange for the completion of various tasks: attendance at training programmes or language courses and participation in mediation and educational programmes aimed at internalizing socio-cultural norms. When the disciplining tools prove insufficient and the subject 'fails' to integrate, a punishment system is activated (Vrăbiescu and Kalir 2017). This mechanism designates the option of repatriation, a sort of benevolent self-expulsion. The discourse on and public perception of voluntary return programmes nevertheless remain circumscribed to moral benevolence.

This section contextualizes the specific regional and local policies which hamper rather than facilitate the integration of marginalized EU migrants into Spanish society. The overlapping and contradictory laws on migration and mobility allow for the possibility of the social services applying different sets of rules.[2] For example, Romanian citizens in Spain are protected by European laws governing the rights of freedom of movement, and have, since 2014, benefited from the right to work and reside in the country. However, local and regional regulations can and do limit these rights, imposing conditions upon the granting of residency and/or social protection.

The complexity of legal documentation makes policies for the social and labour inclusion of poor EU migrants particularly difficult. The situation has the greatest impact on migrants in marginal conditions who have to rely on social support in order to maintain minimum requirements for daily living. In the context of a challenging economic reality, this legal framework has led to the exclusion of migrants from basic social provisions such as education, health insurance, training, and facilities to integrate or reintegrate into the labour market. In fact, without the support of a professional team of civil servants and social workers, excluded people would have no access to basic social services. The condition for receiving protection and provision is strict surveillance and control of their lives and living circumstances: income justification, transparent and justifiable spending, performance of parental duties, and so on. Offering different services, civil servants and social workers enter into and intervene in the lives of Romani migrants in various ways, which I discuss later. Contrary to the declared objective of social services, which is inclusion, the end game for Romani migrants is often, as we will see, forced mobility: evictions, expulsions, and voluntary returns.

Further, I discuss in greater detail the multi-layered control and decision-making processes to emphasize the connection between public services and those provided by NGOs. According to the principles of subsidiarity and of decentralized institutional responsibility for the integration of migrants, the regional and municipal authorities are charged with creating and implementing relevant social policies. Nonetheless, the third sector takes an active part in the process of integration by coordinating programmes and providing services.

Ethnicized Mediation Programmes: Between Protection and Securitization

In Catalonia, there are two different sources of funding for social projects under public-private collaboration. When the local authority enters into a contract, professional social workers act as civil servants employed by the local or regional administration. The social services budget—and therefore the employment of social workers—is guaranteed for the entire project. But the regional/local authority does not oversee the implementation of the entire project; instead, it analyses the reports received from the NGOs/companies, maintaining a clear internal hierarchy among the employees of state and non-state structures.

The other modality of contracting social services is through public subvention. For this type of public-private collaboration to be binding, an NGO or company which specializes in delivering social services must identify a social problem and propose a specific framework of intervention. It should be remarked that the public subvention may only supplement an already existing project, which implies that the main financial contribution is made by a private funding body. Moreover, this public support usually covers only a small part (one fifth) of the total amount necessary, whereas the NGO or private company is accountable for the entire project. Regardless of the alleged autonomy of the NGO/company to decide the implementation process, the risk of discontinuation of funding weakens its position.

There are two parallel sets of programmes focusing on the Roma within the metropolitan area of Barcelona. This distinction has political and ideological roots. On the one hand, since 2002, the regional government of Catalonia has assumed responsibility for the inclusion of autochthonous Gitanos by designing a strategy to address Gitano culture and social integration, thus elaborating the Comprehensive Plan for the *Gitano* People in Catalonia.[3] On the other hand, the local administration in Barcelona has been sensitive to the presence of Romani migrants from Eastern Europe, initiating specific actions which have resulted in programmes targeting Romani families, as I will detail further.

The first set of programmes was based on the Comprehensive Plan for the *Gitano* People in Catalonia (hereafter referred to as the Comprehensive Plan) alongside the implementation of the National Roma Integration Strategy and the Roma Action Plan at regional level.[4] The Comprehensive Plan has been widely criticized for its 'lower-than-expected perceived leverage on the target population, and because of other organizational, conceptual and management weaknesses' (Bereményi and Mirga 2012: 16) by Gitano organizations in particular, which have questioned its general impact and outcomes for the local Gitano population. One of the main criticisms was the failure to incorporate local resources, instead supporting the existing NGOs as strategic partners, which led to a lack of transparency and accountability. Even more importantly for my argument is the exclusion of immigrant Roma without Spanish citizenship from the target group. The failure to include Romani migrants in the target group for Catalan government policies for the Gitano minority resulted in conflicting dynamics at an administrative level with parallel projects led by the municipal administration and their private partners. The process reflects the securitization of Romani migrants, who benefit from a supplementary 'othering' in which the state sees them as different from the local vulnerable category of Gitano. They become the preferred target of benevolent actions, precisely at the security-humanitarianism nexus.

The second set of programmes reveals the decision of the local administration in the Metropolitan Area of Barcelona to address the presence of Romani migrants from Eastern Europe.[5] Successive interviews with local representatives have shed light on a certain pattern of public-private collaboration, which gathered NGOs and state representatives in regular meetings, roundtables, conferences, and exhibitions.[6] The authorities contracted private for-profit or non-profit companies to implement the mediation programmes,[7] such as *SISFA Rom*[8] or *Roma minors at risk*,[9] with a dual goal: to respond to public complaints about the presence of Romani migrants, and to approach the Romani migrants considered to be vulnerable, or incapable of demanding their rights from the social services, or both. The mediation programmes work with the idea that the social services should make the first step in approaching Romani migrants, otherwise, they will not demand their rights. Emma,[10] a social worker with an NGO, explained to me the importance and challenges of mediating between the institutions—which are not easily accessible—and Romani migrants, who allegedly lack the interest in schooling for their children and do not know that health insurance should be a priority in their life: 'I am aware that, for many families, the health insurance, the schooling system… are impossible without the help of professional [social workers]. And we are talking about families for whom these are not priority issues'.

In practice, the framework of mediation programmes reveals the securitization of Romani migrants: they are seen as a threat to society and to themselves. For instance, a project for cultural mediation directed at Romani migrants was sub-contracted by the mayor of Santa Coloma and handed over to a private company. The mediation team contained no professional social workers, but consisted of people trained in controlling social conflict. Their task was mainly the surveillance of the Romani migrants, who had supposedly not managed to integrate and who had allegedly created problems at community level. One of the mediators put the social project into context, explaining that many cultural and social conflicts start when the proportion of immigrants is very high. When asked about the details of the mediation programmes, Enrique insisted that the prevention methods were 'less bureaucratic and much more face-to-face and on-the-spot dialogues' which were necessary to manage the 'discomfort of the autochthonous citizenry'. Specifically, Enrique told me, in the case of Romani migrants, the mediation team had identified 'not more than 7–8 families, but these are *extremely* [emphasis through his tone of voice] extended families. There are 20 people in each family'. He then explained the reasons for starting the project addressing Romani migrants:

> We started to work with the 'Romanian *Gitanos*'[11] six to eight years ago when they arrived in the city. Before that, we had not registered the presence of Roma in the city. The arrival of these citizens had an impact on the citizenry. Why? Because there were many who arrived, and their clothes and their way of living with the children… the children being on the street, etc., that was what raised the alarm. That created a particular social alarm. Because there were situations never seen before. Indeed there were, historically, autochthonous *Gitanos Calé* in the city, and when these Romanian *Gitanos* arrived, they looked a lot like the *Gitanos* from here, but like [the way they were] 20 years ago: they lived with the children underdressed, without shoes, in the streets, dirty… It was because of problems like this that we started to intervene.

Enrique supported the idea that 'the lack of knowledge of the local social services and of the mediation team about their reality' legitimized and initiated the mediation programme to approach Romani migrants. In practice, the mediation team collaborated with the local police in order to force the mobility of those migrants who had not registered their children at school or did not have legal residency: they worked to evict Romani migrants from informal dwellings or pressured them to leave the administrative area.

A similar mediation project started by focusing on children 'at risk' and on controlling the contact of Romani families with the social services. Since 2009, the Vincle association has implemented a self-designed programme, conceived in 2004–2006 (Vincle 2006). Dora, a social worker at Vincle, explains the difficulties of working with Romani families from Romania. The living conditions of Romani families justify the social intervention, she suggests, and the so-called 'cultural' challenges that the social workers have to face legitimize a special type of intervention, especially when 'anything else had no results':

> Romanian families started to come to the DGAIA.[12] At the cultural level, nobody could understand them. Proposals offered by the services for social intervention had no results. They were in the utmost precarious situation; they did not have any legal connection with the health system; they did not have any link with the local [institutions]; they were not literate; and these families were very poor and [had] no housing.

Although Dora was aware of the complete social exclusion of Romani migrants, she paradoxically concludes that the social intervention of the state with this group had no effect on their integration. In practice, within this project, Vincle had to deliver annual reports about the Romani children, separating them into 'imputable' and 'non-imputable' categories according to their age—below or above 14 years of age. The securitization of migrant children follows their profiling as Romani and their control by the state apparatus in the form of the direct action of the association. The reports detail the positive outcomes of taking children identified as potentially 'at risk' into state custody, while constructing new scenarios for securitized intervention (Vincle 2013: 10):

> It can be seen that there is almost twice the number of female minors compared to male without a legal tutor in the territory. The answer lies in the fact that girls travel from Romania leaving their parents there, and come to live with the family of their husband here, marrying within the Roma ritual. It is a custom that leads to another issue, that when a girl who has no legal guardian is found participating in offenses such as begging, she is taken to the OAM[13] for reasons of protection. In almost all cases, complying with the protocol of protecting minors, we have realized that the relatives of people who are responsible for them have travelled from Romania or from another country.

In Barcelona, the local authorities design mediation programmes for Romani migrants without engaging the support, expertise, and knowledge of those involved in developing and implementing the Comprehensive Plan. Rather, these programmes have been designed from a securitization perspective, addressing Romani migrants in terms of a threat to society or of themselves being 'at risk'. These programmes were supposed to cover an institutional gap between the problems identified by the municipal administrations—Romani migrants living on the Catalan territory—and the set of government measures—programmes supposedly directed at all Gitano. In the absence of a coherent and participatory strategy for Romani migrants not included in the government programme, local authorities disguised this securitization as the benevolent practice of so-called voluntary return. The manager of the Immigration Department of Catalonia has repeatedly stated that the authorities do not aim to expel the migrants but to apply sanctions in full agreement with the legal system:

> In any case, here, we don't want to expel anyone. [It does not even] cross our minds. We work hard to include them [Romani migrants] in this society… We approach everybody not from the viewpoint of equality, but of justice.[14]

The voluntary returns are a bureaucratic practice that can be found in several social services. Under certain circumstances, some Catalan institutions[15] will directly book the flights or bus tickets for entire families, for example, when the children taken into state custody are released back to the families (Vrăbiescu 2016b). After the violent state intervention which enabled the social services to take the children from their parents and keep them in care for long periods in order to assess the living conditions of Romani families, the same state social services finally offer the parents the possibility of being reunited with their children only if they agree to voluntary return to Romania.

Another institution, part of the local authority of Barcelona (*Servicio de Inserción Social*), provides social services in emergency situations. In addition to offering food to homeless people, the service has a generous budget for the organization of the voluntary return of marginalized Romani migrants to their country of origin. Working together with associations specializing in running projects for the integration of Romani migrants, this public service has provided these 'last resort' solutions for 'failed' subjects at the request of social workers and, allegedly, of the Romani migrants themselves.

Thus, at the intersection of the absence of a strategy for the inclusion of Romani migrants and their securitization, regional and local authorities have created voluntary return deals. Instead of defining these services as expulsions, such programmes are given the aura of just and benevolent acts.

Socio-educational Programmes: Life Between Camp and Shanty Town

In the Madrid region, the migration from Romania, and, in particular, the necessity of eliminating the informal dwelling places of 'nomadic Romanian gypsies', as they are commonly called, has been the subject of lively debate for years. In his analysis of long-term political debates about disadvantaged Romanian migrants in Madrid, McMahon (2016) shows how political discourse has been shaped around these informal dwelling places and their inhabitants, identified as Roma. Initially, the local authorities justified the existence of shanty towns and their subsequent eviction using the language of social inclusion and human rights protection. In the media, these poor and marginalized residents were subject to the politics of 'camp clearance as a charitable resolution to modernize and improve their standards of living' (McMahon 2016: 9), which has led to the Romani migrants' hyper visible presence as shanty town dwellers. At the same time, other Roma either pass undetected by the local authorities or remain completely invisible to the state. They are not identified on the basis of their ethnic background and are thus to some extent 'integrated' into mainstream society.

In comparison to the general migrant population stemming from Romania in Spain, the number of hyper visible Romani migrants is relatively insignificant. According to recent data,[16] Romani migrants in the Madrid region total about 70–80 families, living in informal dwellings—mostly in the shanty towns of El Gallinero, Cañada Real, and Delicias. They live in extreme poverty, either in segregated neighbourhoods or are continuously forced to move from one place to another. On the one hand, the forced movement of Romani migrants happens as a result of the evictions that take place within the perimeter of the city. Those evicted need to remain in the same area to maintain their connection with the social services if they are to follow the integration process which is their only way of accessing minimum social protection or even social housing. On the other hand, the civil servants tasked with relocating people in social housing[17] identify and contact people living in informal dwellings and offer them a socio-educational programme in the camps.

At the end of the 1990s, two NGOs started socio-educational programmes implemented by *Asociación Comisión Católica Española de Migraciones* (ACCEM)[18] and The International Red Cross with the aim of providing Romani families with social housing. In fact, in order to access social housing, Romani migrants—either homeless or living in shacks (*chabolas*)—are first required to spend a period of up to one year in the camp, at the end of which they are expected to be 'fully' integrated. This rule is part of the initial project design, implemented by these NGOs and supported and financed by the regional authorities of Madrid. Designed initially as a socio-educational programme, the two identical camps, one in Valdelatas and the other in San Roque, are still open to 'ethnic migrants from the East'.

Without insisting on the precariousness of the dwelling space—eight square metres in a container for each family—it is worth detailing the conditions which must be met to access the housing service provided within the camp. To enter the camp, a family must have a recommendation from the local social services, another NGO, or a private company working in the field of charity and specializing in delivering social services. Once a family has been accepted to live in the camp, the members have to sign a social contract and start working through their one-year period to improve their situation, which entails finding a job and becoming financially capable of renting a house. Aside from a list of regulations[19] imposed by the camp management, control and surveillance is extended from the compulsory activities which must be accomplished to life strategies or parental duties being closely watched by the personnel. Even if there is some margin for negotiating the aims of the initial contract, the animosity between the managers and the inhabitants, as well as the consumption of alcoholic beverages—which breaks one of the camp rules—are the two most frequent causes of conflicts (fieldwork notes 2015). The socio-educational project's time limit of one year and the strict conditions imposed on the families have resulted in a very low success rate, with only one Romani migrant family approved to access social housing since the beginning of the project.

During my interview with a Romanian woman who has worked as the manager of the ACCEM camp in Valdelatas, I noticed that she expressed an ostensible contradiction several times: that the 'families are receiving [NGO's] help' when they agree to enter the camp, but at the same time, that 'the project is not to help people, but to educate them'. Emphasizing the importance of her work as mediator, the manager expressed the biggest fear of the neoliberal bureaucracy: the prospect of creating the dependency of their clients on the welfare state. She further underlined the educational dimension of the project, saying: 'our task is to eradicate their [the Roma's] dependency and prepare them for the outside world'. In fact, by racializing the education programme, the state is enacting a disciplinary apparatus against a determined group, for example, through expulsions. These expulsions may be temporary—one day, three days, one week—or permanent and occur when the manager is not satisfied that the clients have accomplished their duties as set out in the social contract. Besides, there is always the offer of voluntary return on the part of the NGO management, a service which those who acknowledge their failure within the programme can apply for.

It is important to note that the first camp managed by the Red Cross was set up in another location, in Valdecarros, but its proximity to the about-to-be inaugurated highway to Valencia was given as the reason for its closure and dismantling in 2002. Next to the original site of this camp, Romani families who had been 'clients' of the socio-educational programme, or whose relatives were still involved in the programme, had settled in a deserted farm called El Gallinero, where they had access to a source of water and electricity. Since then, they have gone through the cycle of being welcomed, helped, registered, punished, and evicted many times by different organizations and institutions. Currently, at El Gallinero, which is some four kilometres outside the city centre of Madrid and about 20 minutes away by bus, a community of around 400 Romanian Roma can still be found living in informal dwellings. However, the story of El Gallinero, as told by one of the social workers, who explains the entanglements between the camp socio-educational project—called APOI and run by the Red Cross—and the creation of the shanty town, is rather different:

> El Gallinero was an old farm. [The shantytown] was formed in 2001–2002 while we were managing a camp in Valdecarros together with ACCEM, right next to El Gallinero. Actually, if you go up the bridge you can see the place that we had. The APOI camp was designed for families from Eastern Europe. Families who had been excluded because they did not accept the rules... started to settle outside the camp... because there was water and electricity. Initially there were a few families who stayed there because their relatives were inside the APOI camp. The families who left the camp went to settle together in El Gallinero. The majority of the families were originally clients of APOI. That is why they do not want to return [to the programme].

State and third sector interventions in El Gallinero are prodigious, while the material presence of charity work is almost imperceptible. Although the goal of social intervention is to get the migrants into houses, the conditions on offer to people living in El Gallinero is that they re-enter the socio-educational programme in the camps; only after this, following evaluation, might the families be allocated social housing. As a matter of fact, the new type of social intervention performed at El Gallinero, which includes programmes for adults (Spanish language, hygiene classes for women, etc.) and accompanying children to school and football training, represents allegedly positive services delivered in parallel with another type of state intervention. Three or four times a year, the authorities enter the neighbourhood of El Gallinero with eviction orders and demolish a few of the improvised shacks. The legal basis for these interventions is court decisions to evict people from the land on which the shanty town has developed. The decisions are usually taken after a complaint from the private owner of the land, but the demolition orders have never been applied to the whole site.

The goal of integration into society is manifestly delusional and unsustainable under present conditions of employability, documentation, and opportunities for social housing. Most of the marginal migrants or impoverished citizens cannot afford a market rent, given the fact that they have no secure employment. If, in the course of one year, the Romani migrants have been unable to find a job, they are deemed to have failed the socio-educational programme, and having failed, the families are also excluded from social housing. Their only option is to remain homeless and live in informal dwellings. Moreover, the social workers who manage the camps offer these families, who have been confirmed as 'failed integrated subjects', the alternative of voluntary return. Those who are deemed incapable of receiving help, and hence of integration, are relegated to the punishment mechanism of the state. It is only after failing the socio-educational programme or the re-integration projects that the Romani migrants are eligible for voluntary return.

The Securitization of Romani Migrants and Their Subsequent 'Soft Deportation'

These administrative mechanisms work against the unwanted/misfit Romani migrants by creating conditions of 'deportability' (De Genova 2002) or 'evictability' (van Baar 2017a). Forced removal and voluntary return reveal themselves as instruments of statecraft, explicated through these paradigms, which respond to a securitization issue (see Kreide, Chap. 3, this volume). Explaining the concept of deportability as 'a defining and enduring feature of the "legality" of those non-citizens who have been "authorized"', De Genova (2013: 1188) reveals the process of inclusion through exclusion by which migrants and other non-citizens are conditionally admitted to the society. These inclusions 'almost universally impose a susceptibility for deportation as a defining horizon' (ibid.). Evictability explains even further the situation of internal migrants and the racialized poor, who are recurrently subjected to state violence. As van Baar (2017b) argues, evictability premises the condition of 'nomadization' and allows the enactment of mechanisms of exclusion (see also De Genova, Chap. 2, this volume). The term 'nomad' suggests the cultural or innate voluntary mobility of Romani migrants, exploited and subsequently augmented through programmes of voluntary return.

In the specific case of the Roma in Europe, securitization theory has been used (Hepworth 2012; van Baar 2011) to point to the discourses in which Romani migrants are connected to social and health-security issues (Bărbulescu 2012; Alunni 2015) and are exposed to housing and space-related strategies of exclusion (Vincze and Raț 2013). As Parker (2012: 477) puts it:

> [I]ndividuals and groups, such as the Roma, that are designated or produced as delinquent citizens become subject to a combination of a political realist logic of security, which seeks to eliminate existential threat to community or citizenry, and a liberal logic, which seeks to manage risks to the internal market as a space of mobility and economic freedoms.

In Spain, Romani migrants have regularly been presented as a social security issue, associated most notably with extreme poverty, bad parenting, lack of housing, health-threatening living conditions, non-integration, and crime. The social securitization of Romani migrants, who are discursively portrayed as a threat to Spanish society and different to Gitano citizens, allows the state to intervene in people's lives and to suspend its moral responsibility regarding both the justification and the effects of the intervention. In analysing the securitization process of Romani migrants in Spain, my focus on the practices of the social services unveils and explains the workings of the security-development nexus. Under the guise of social inclusion, social services provide socio-educational programmes for Romani migrants but are also involved in recurrent administrative orders for eviction and other joint police actions, such as the taking of children into state care or raids on shanty towns. It is this merging of different types of actor, contributing to ambiguous inclusive and repressive actions, which indicates the articulation of the security-development nexus.

The voluntary return of Romani migrants has become a hotly debated political issue (Carrera 2013; Castañeda 2015; Vrăbiescu 2016a), in which the principle of freedom of movement has been contrasted with the politics of securitization (Balzacq 2010). Yet, as I have argued earlier, voluntary return is a set of practices implemented by local or regional authorities against Romani migrants, who are EU citizens. The fact that voluntary return is operated at sub-state level has two direct consequences. Firstly, local or regional decisions alleviate the political responsibility of the host state for its failing integration policies. Secondly, state authorities disregard the way in which voluntary returns actually punish and stigmatize Romani migrants.

The resorting of the state to voluntary return practices is inscribed within both securitization strategies and humanitarian logic. The inclusion of voluntary return practices in the range of services provided through social welfare suggests a humanitarian moral ground. At the same time, voluntary return is the outcome of the social securitization enacted against marginalized EU migrants. Local authorities make use of a strategy of combining a civilizing mission with securitization acts.

For state agents, the subjects of integration have to conform to a standard of vulnerability in order to obtain benefits and support. Sometimes, Romani migrants 'do not look poor enough' or are considered culturally different, allegedly because 'they want to live like that', sentiments which a few social workers have expressed in explaining their work. The pre-designed programmes for social integration exert pressure on the Roma who, by virtue of their migrant condition, are seen as potential returnees. Romani migrants exposed to voluntary return programmes, or those who are the beneficiaries of bureaucratic and NGO benevolence, face the double standard of state institutions. On the one hand, social workers adopt the humanitarian attitudes of assisting the poor, who are struggling through the integration process. On the other hand, however, the same institutions, under threat of punishment, provide an exit solution for failing subjects, namely, their voluntary return.

In Barcelona and Madrid, authorities have adopted similar programmes directed at migrants, the Roma in particular. The objective of these local authorities is to enact a special system of surveillance and control in order to force Romani migrants to leave their administrative area (López Catalán 2012). These humanitarian programmes, ostensibly designed to assist and accommodate the inclusion of migrants, have been supported by practices which demonstrate that the administration does not see Romani migrants as integrated into society. Instead of eliminating 'undesirable' migrants, the local authority has built a system for measuring 'deservingness' and imposed thresholds for accessing social benefits. As I have shown in the case studies, social services measure inclusion aptitudes and assess inadequate integration in order to exclude the Roma from state protection and provisions.

Challenging Humanitarianism as the Moral Grounds for Migrant Governance

Humanitarianism reveals itself as a model of governance which supports development and security interventions, as well as—in its universalistic approach—the grounding morality of the dominant world. Beyond the illusion of ensuring the same treatment for all, humanitarianism simultaneously defines people as underdeveloped and a danger to mainstream society (van Baar, Chap. 8, this volume). Humanitarian ideology, preaching compulsory aid for the poor and racialized, opens the door to the control and containment of destitute migrants.

In a similar way, Didier Fassin (2012: 2) explains the two dimensions of humanitarian morality, constituted as a dynamic between the universalist claim to rights and the obligation to assist others, 'a language that inextricably links values and affects, and serves both to define and to justify discourses and practices of the government of human beings'. Detractors of humanitarian ideology unambiguously criticize the aim of providing protection and provision to populations 'at risk', as well as the practices of NGOs and humanitarian agents, actions, and programmes which create and maintain a 'needy subject' (Timmer 2010).

Various authors have explained the security-development nexus (Duffield 2010; Stern and Öjendal 2010), pointing to the shift of focus from the state to the people. Reflecting upon the nexus at domestic or sub-state level, others have outlined the growing eagerness of our current in-securitized 'risk society' to implement exclusionary political strategies towards marginalized and destitute people (Howell 2014; Mead 2015). Two distinct layers can be observed by problematizing this dynamic in governance. On the one hand, the security-development nexus has emerged as a biopolitical tool of governance where development entails the tactic of separating bodies and lives worth living from those perceived as 'disposable' or 'dangerous'. Maria Stern and Joakim Öjendal (2010: 20) have described the concept of security as the 'techniques of biopower through which subjectivity, imagination and ultimately life are governed'. Thus, the notion of security implies the surveillance and control of life itself.

On the other hand, when the practices subsumed under the security-development nexus are rendered as a technical issue, the moral responsibility for governing people and the democratic accountability of doing so tend to be suppressed, while life is simultaneously depoliticized (Li 2010). Considering the technical aspect of political practice, the state makes possible the control and disciplining of populations to be secured and of those portrayed as a threat. However, both the rich and the poor—those belonging and those excluded—take up distinct roles: people affected by poverty, disease, or lacking education become a danger to society; hence, they should be aided, educated, disciplined. The problematization of underdevelopment in terms of danger reveals how, in the cases that I have analysed, this is the key to the merging of security and development, of control and humanitarianism.

The state employs a range of conceptual tools and institutional frameworks to implement development projects in spaces, places, and for people characterized as underdeveloped, and to enact securitization in social areas, for example, when combating poverty and exclusion. To legitimize and facilitate humanitarian intervention, the state works together with non-state actors to construct and endorse social securitization issues. It then intervenes to combat the defined threats, enacting emergency measures aimed at saving lives. Using mediation practices and problematic education programmes, social securitization has become part of the daily work of bureaucrats, shifting from a role of protection to the regulation of human lives, which continues to entail the violence which state agents might legitimately use (see also Kóczé, Chap. 9, this volume). Through securitization, the state identifies, defines, and mitigates the potential dangers for a society or specific community. These threats must be contained and kept at a safe distance from the mainstream community (see also van Baar 2017b, Chap. 8, this volume). At the same time, development becomes the tool for eradicating these threats, which include poverty, precarious health, and lack of education. To educate and regulate the destitute and marginalized people and maintain a legitimate position, the state must control and discipline.

Conclusion

In this chapter, I have explained the ways in which voluntary return practices contribute to the framework of the security-development nexus, in which humanitarianism vindicates the approach of bureaucracy to marginalized and racialized migrants with a Romani background. My case studies have revealed the ways in which voluntary return practices are inscribed in the logic of humanitarianism and social securitization. Romani migrants, as outsiders, have become a threat to the autochthonous community, supposedly challenging its values and norms. This bureaucratic mechanism is aimed at the exclusion and expulsion of vulnerable migrants by means of soft deportation. In order to exclude *some* people from the social protection system, social services act as benevolent do-gooders, implementing projects to evaluate the risk of migrants who do not integrate according to a strict set of measures and contradictory assessments. Social workers often advise Romani migrants who are in a socio-economically marginal situation to engage in return migration. The initial aim of integration and access to social benefits thus remains largely out of reach. While the capacity of Romani migrants to integrate is measured, evaluated, and recorded, their lives are under permanent surveillance and control. The files and protocols are filled; the unwanted people are made to disappear.

The authorities in the regions of Barcelona and Madrid have attended to Romani migrants from Romania only when they have become visible by virtue of their precarious living conditions. The interventions thus triggered are situated at the security-development nexus, while, in each case, the eventual voluntary return confirms the normalization of violence underpinned by the humanitarian ideology.

This chapter has interrogated and documented the practices of voluntary return targeted at Romanian Roma migrants in Spain. Following several years of extensive practice, voluntary return has entered the common language of social services all over the country. Governing by techniques of differential inclusion, institutions and private organizations have contributed to the marginalization of vulnerable migrants. Roma are simultaneously the most visible 'clients' of the programmes of repatriation and the most invisible subjects of the state once they have become the subjects of such policies. In this chapter, I have presented the imbalanced situation whereby vulnerable migrants are constrained to accept return following various forms of threat to their well-being.

Building upon theorizing on the humanitarian logic, as well as on the security-development nexus, I have brought into the debate the allegedly voluntary consent of the recipients of such state services. As I have demonstrated, in the case of Romani migrants, social workers act in response to an alleged voluntary action, the presumed agreement of destitute citizens to subject themselves to state intervention. Charity evokes the uncontested power structure where those at the bottom of the hierarchy are continuously obliged to receive the defined aid or 'good', with their consent taken for granted. The consent of the migrants—even that wrested from them by means of coercion—is presented as ultimate proof of the benefit and legitimacy of political action. Charity has thus been translated into benevolent politics, whereas the acceptance of the recipient is translated into the 'voluntary' nature of the action, obscuring forceful state practices of removal. These *emo*-political notions of benevolence, consent, and 'voluntary' subjection to state power are produced at the intersection of humanitarian intervention and emergency measures in response to catastrophe, harsh social exclusion, and extreme poverty, while in practice simultaneously forcing the mobility of Romani migrants.

Notes

1. I use scare quotations here to question the 'voluntary' character of these practices, but for readability purposes, I avoid the use of scare quotations for the remainder of the text.
2. The European directive on freedom of movement (2004/38/EC).
3. *Plan integral del pueblo gitano de Cataluña 2014–2016*.
4. In Spain, the outcome of the EU Framework of National Roma Integration Strategy is a decentralized politics that pushes the autonomous regions to take responsibility for designing, budgeting for, and implementing policies for the integration of Spanish Gitanos.
5. *Gitanos del Este*.
6. For example, different events organized by ROMEST (2014) network.
7. During my research in Barcelona, the two programmes discussed were financed by the local budget, whereas Madrid has benefited from ministerial funds for its social projects in El Gallinero. However, I could not find evidence that the allocated funds were initially from programmes such as ROMED (see Kóczé, Chap. 9, this volume).
8. Service for Social Inclusion for non-Autochthonous Roma Families with Dependent Children. See URL: https://w30.bcn.cat/APPS/portaltramits/portal/channel/default.html?&stpid=20100000368&style=ciudadano&language=es. Until recently, the social service was called *SASPI* (social service for attending to the itinerant population), then changed its name in 2016, making the ethnic profiling of the target group even more transparent.
9. Social Service for Minors of Roma Origin at Social Risk programme run by Vincle association since 2009.
10. In order to protect the anonymity of my informants, all the names from field notes and interviews have been changed to fictional ones matching the gender of the person.
11. While I problematize the distinction between Romani (migrants from Eastern Europe) and Gitanos (Spanish citizens), I place the exact words in quotations, to reveal the internalized racialization and the institutional exclusion of Romani migrants.
12. *Direcció General d'Atenció a la Infancia i l'Adolescencia* is the General Direction for Child Protection authority in the Catalan region.
13. Office for the Minors (*Oficina a l'Atencio de Menor*), Mossos d'Esquadra, Catalonia. The department is part of the regional police force.
14. The interviews were recorded in Spanish and translated into English by the author. The translation from Spanish of written text is also by the author.
15. Like DGAIA.

16. The European Roma and Travellers Forum (2016: 3) estimates the entire Spanish Gitano population to be about 750,000 (or 1.57% of the Spanish population). In the Madrid region, the data circulating about Romanian Roma migrants stem from one source, namely, the Fundación Secretariado Gitano, which estimates the Romani migrants to be a few hundred.
17. The Institute for Relocation and Social Reinsertion of the Madrid regional authority has the task of relocating people to social housing. The civil servants work in coordination with the Red Cross and ACCEM (*Asociación Comisión Católica Española de Migraciones*) within the project APOI.
18. ACCEM is an NGO which offers services for vulnerable groups, migrants, and refugees in the regional area of Madrid. Available at www.accem.es (accessed: 20 June 2016).
19. The socio-educational programme for integration has three dimensions: (1) offering basic necessities in a camp for individuals/families, in exchange for full transparency of their incomes and expenditures; (2) reimbursing the transport costs for people who go to find work or accompany their children to school; (3) compulsory good behaviour in the camp (alcoholic beverages are completely forbidden).

References

Alunni, L. 2015. Securitarian Healing. *Medical Anthropology* 34 (2): 139–149.
Balzacq, T., ed. 2010. *Securitization Theory*. London: Routledge.
Bărbulescu, H. 2012. Constructing the Roma People as a Societal Threat. *European Journal of Science and Theology* 8 (1): 279–289.
Bereményi, B.Á., and A. Mirga. 2012. *Lost in Action?* Barcelona: The FAGIC and the EMIGRA Group, Universitat Autònoma de Barcelona.
Carrera, S. 2013. *Shifting Responsibilities for EU Roma Citizens*. Available at https://www.ceps.eu. Accessed 12 June 2015.
Castañeda, H. 2015. European Mobilities or Poverty Migration? *International Migration* 53 (3): 87–99.
De Genova, N. 2002. Migrant "Illegality" and Deportability in Everyday Life. *Annual Review of Anthropology* 31 (1): 419–447.
———. 2013. Spectacles of Migrant "Illegality". *Ethnic and Racial Studies* 36 (7): 1180–1198.
Duffield, M. 2010. The Liberal Way of Development and the Development-Security Impasse. *Security Dialogue* 41 (1): 53–76.
European Roma and Travellers Forum. 2016. *Fact Sheet on the Situation of Roma in Spain*. Available at https://www.ertf.org/images/Reports/The_situation_of_Roma_in_Spain_06012016_FIN.pdf. Accessed 15 June 2016.
Fassin, D. 2012. *Humanitarian Reason*. Los Angeles, CA: University of California Press.

Feischmidt, M., K. Szombati, and P. Szuhay. 2013. Collective Criminalization of the Roma in Central and Eastern Europe. In *The Routledge Handbook of European Criminology*, ed. S. Body-Gendrot et al., 168–187. Abingdon: Routledge.
Hepworth, K. 2012. Abject Citizens. *Citizenship Studies* 16 (3–4): 431–449.
Howell, J. 2014. The Securitisation of NGOs Post-9/11. *Conflict, Security & Development* 14 (2): 151–179.
Kalir, B. 2017. Between "Voluntary" Return Programmes and Soft Deportation. In *Return Migration and Psychosocial Wellbeing*, ed. R. King and Z. Vathi, 56–71. London: Routledge.
Li, T.M. 2010. To Make Live or Let Die? *Antipode* 41 (s1): 66–93.
Lipsky, M. 1980. *Street-level Bureaucracy*. New York: Russel Sage Foundation.
López Catalán, Ó. 2012. The Genesis of a "Romanian Roma Issue" in the Metropolitan Area of Barcelona. *Revista de Estudios Urbanos y Ciencias Sociales* 2 (1): 95–117.
McMahon, S. 2016. A Magnificent Atmosphere? *Ethnic and Racial Studies* 39 (11): 2022–2040.
Mead, T. 2015. *Between Care and Control*. Unpublished M.A. Thesis. Vancouver, BC: University of British Columbia.
Parker, O. 2012. Roma and the Politics of EU Citizenship in France. *Journal of Common Market Studies* 50 (3): 475–491.
Powell, R. 2013. The Theoretical Concept of the 'Civilising Offensive' (beschavingsoffensief). *Human Figurations* 2 (2). Available at http://hdl.handle.net/2027/spo.11217607.0002.203. Accessed 30 Aug 2016.
ROMEST. 2014. L'observatori de la població gitana procedent de l'est d'Europa a Catalunya. Available at www.romest.cat. Accessed 13 July 2014.
Stern, M., and J. Öjendal. 2010. Mapping the Security-Development Nexus? *Security Dialogue* 41 (1): 5–29.
Timmer, A.D. 2010. Constructing the "Needy Subject". *PoLAR: Political and Legal Anthropology Review* 33 (2): 264–281.
van Baar, H. 2011. Europe's Romaphobia. *Environment and Planning D: Society and Space* 29 (2): 203–212.
———. 2015. The Perpetual Mobile Machine of Forced Mobility. In *The Irregularization of Migration in Contemporary Europe*, ed. Y. Jansen, R. Celikates, and J. de Bloois, 71–86. Lanham, MD: Rowman & Littlefield.
———. 2017a. Evictability and the Biopolitical Bordering of Europe. *Antipode* 49 (1): 212–230.
———. 2017b. Contained Mobility and the Racialization of Poverty in Europe: The Roma at the Development-Security Nexus. *Social Identities*. https://doi.org/10.1080/13504630.2017.1335826.
Vincle. 2006. *Gitanos procedents de l'Europa de l'Est a Catalunya*. Barcelona: Generalitat de Catalunya, Departament de Benestar i Família.

———. 2013. *Memoria annual 2012. Servei d'atencio a menors d'origen romanès en situació de risc social.* Unpublished Report 2012.

Vincze, E., and C. Raț. 2013. Spatialization and Racialization of Social Exclusion. *Studia Universitatis Babes-Bolyai-Sociologia* 2: 5–21.

Vrăbiescu, I. 2016a. Eviction and Voluntary Returns of the Roma in Barcelona and Bucharest. *Intersections* 2 (1): 199–218.

———. 2016b. Roma Migrant Children in Catalonia. *Ethnic and Racial Studies* 40 (10): 1663–1680.

Vrăbiescu, I., and B. Kalir. 2017. Care-full Failure: How Auxiliary Assistance to Poor Roma Migrant Women in Spain Compounds Marginalization. *Social Identities.* https://doi.org/10.1080/13504630.2017.1335833.

Webber, F. 2011. How Voluntary Are Voluntary Returns? *Race & Class* 52 (4): 98–107.

PART IV

Visuality

CHAPTER 11

Sharing the Insecure Sensible: The Circulation of Images of Roma on Social Media

Ana Ivasiuc

As I write these lines, a protest march is scheduled to take place in the centre of Rome. Its aim is to prompt the Roman administration to close down what are generally referred to in popular parlance as the *campi nomadi*, camps where part of the Roma population of large Italian cities has been concentrated, segregated, and controlled since the beginning of the 1990s. The protest has been organized by a group of inhabitants of the Eastern Roman district of (Nuova) Ponte di Nona, who, since 2013 have mobilized themselves to carry out the surveillance of their neighbourhood. To this aim, they enact 'voluntary surveillance' (*vigilanza*),

---

I am grateful to Huub van Baar, Regina Kreide, Václav Walach, and the participants of the conference 'The Politics of Security: Understanding and Challenging the Securitization of Europe's Roma', held in Giessen, Germany, in June 2016, for very helpful comments on an earlier version. The research which has made this work possible took place within the project 'Dynamics of Security: Forms of Securitization in Historical Perspective' (SFB/TRR 138), financed by the German Research Foundation (DFG).

A. Ivasiuc (✉)
Justus Liebig University Giessen, Giessen, Germany

© The Author(s) 2019
H. van Baar et al. (eds.), *The Securitization of the Roma in Europe*, Human Rights Interventions, https://doi.org/10.1007/978-3-319-77035-2_11

organizing nocturnal car patrols in the neighbourhood with the stated aim of deterring property-related crimes; when they witness suspicious activities, they alert the forces of law and order. They post several times daily on a network of Facebook pages, the most popular of them reaching an audience of over 2000 and dating back to the beginnings of the group's activity. The topics of their posts concern their own surveillance activity (with short 'reports', photographs, and sometimes videos produced mostly during their nightly patrols, as well as updates regarding their organization), their security-related lobby undertakings, and various conservative commentaries on political topics (immigration, Islam, national and local politics). A fierce nativism and nationalism emerges from the posted content; praise for 'real' and strong authority (embodied by the military in particular and profusely represented visually), the law, and the forces of order in general. They often share content from the right-wing nationalist newspaper *Il Tempo*, as well as press releases issued by the police headquarters and other state institutions, and articles from the online press.

Today's protest is neither unique nor unusual: it has become something of a tradition for the group to organize a protest march demanding the closure of the camps every year since 2013. While the poster announcing the first protest displayed a single image from the camp situated 3.5 km from Ponte di Nona on Via di Salone, this year's—the fourth protest—has been announced by two posters. The most widely circulated of them displays no less than four photographs of various views of the camp, which occupy half of the poster's area; the images, from the top right to the bottom of the poster, move progressively from internal views of the muddy pathways between the rows of containers within the camp to the image of a dense, black cloud of smoke rising from the camp, and photographed from one of the blocks of flats in Ponte di Nona. Whereas the first image, displayed in 2013, was taken from a good few hundred metres away from the entrance of the camp and was surrounded by copious amounts of text, on subsequent posters the space taken up by text has progressively diminished to a minimum, while the images have multiplied and diversified, showing views of the interior of the camp as well. The evolution of the visual economy of the posters not only hints at the proliferation of images of Roma circulated by the group on social media but is also characteristic of a more intrusive gaze and a more articulated anti-Roma discourse. Regarded as the 'ultimate enemy territory' (Pusca 2010), the camp is constructed as a space of squalor and insecurity on multiple levels, and is the main stated reason for the mobilization of these voluntary security 'entrepreneurs', who conduct what have been called 'anti-Roma patrols' for this reason.

The digital ethnographic analysis performed on the visual content shared by the group on Facebook follows the principle of non-digital-centric-ness (Pink et al. 2015; see also Andersen et al. 2015), posing, as point of departure, the idea that digital media and the ways in which it is used are part of larger worlds, intersecting social, sensory, and material practices, and constitutive of ample relations. In fact, the use of social media is not the group's core activity; I have provided an observation-based, in-depth analysis of the rationale behind the mobilization of the group, as well as of their discourses and practices elsewhere (Ivasiuc 2015), and I consistently link the current digital ethnography to the already observed broader material and spatial practices. As a consequence, my approach is only partly representational: the question of how the Roma are represented in the social media content shared by the vigilantes is secondary to the *effects* of the circulation of these visual representations. Thus, I focus on a non-representational approach to visuality, examining the underlying social relationships signified by the 'spectacle' of Facebook posting; the spectacle, Debord (1992) claims, 'is not a collection of images; rather, it is a social relationship between people that is mediated by images'.

I show how the practice of sharing Roma-related visual content dovetails with the articulation of Mirzoeff's complex of visuality in the security register. My reflection is intended to expand upon Mirzoeff's (2011) 'post-panoptic' complex, analysing locally based forms of visuality. I argue that these simultaneously localized and de-localized (because virtual) mechanisms of visuality form what could be called 'the complex of securitarian visuality'. As a complex, it has the functions posed by Mirzoeff: it is classifying and separating the undesirables while aestheticizing respect for the *status quo*; I expand on this in the first section of the chapter. But, at the same time, this complex is locally embedded, amid the familiar landscapes of the neighbourhood where these images work to produce the neighbourhood anew through 'vigilant visualities' (Amoore 2007), together with a sense of community based on subjectivities of fear and hate; this will be the focus of the second part. In the last part, I interrogate the implications of these vernacular forms of securitarian visuality for Mirzoeff's theorization of a 'post-panoptic' visuality and argue that the contemporary complex of visuality is organized around 'security' as a social structuring principle of the classification and segregation of subjects, and as the fundament for the aestheticization of authority.

The Insecure Sensible[1]

In this section, I describe some of the categories of the visual content shared by the group on their Facebook profile, analysing its imbrications with their material and discursive practices, and the operations constructing particular visions of danger through the classification of people in sources of security or insecurity. My discussion oscillates between a representational scrutiny of images through an intertextual approach (Hansen 2011), focusing on what the images suggest about the subjects and their practices, in close relation to texts accompanying the photographs or the context of their production, and the non-representational analysis of the pictorial power of images as a truth-constituting mode (Andersen et al. 2015) about security, insecurity, and the dominating order.

The first 'genre' consists of images of men in movement; generally young, walking either alone or in pairs, mostly in the dark (Fig. 11.1).[2] The shots are taken from the inside of a car lurking behind the men, at a distance of about 10 to 12 metres. The photographs are displayed without any accompanying text, yet their affordance is not polysemantic or ambiguous: they depict the iconic stranger, whose image 'comes first in the form of stereotypes, search templates, tables of classification, and patterns of recognition' (Mitchell 2012: 127). Strangers are anticipatedly identified as 'not belonging' through ways of reading their bodies (Ahmed 2000: 21): the darker colour of the skin, the hoodie, the act of walking in a largely post-pedestrian suburb, the bulky bags carried by some of the men, their mobility in the dark, all portend an out-of-placeness, an illegitimate presence, a transgression suggested as threatening. The semantic strength of the image and its power to securitize lies in the contextual cues of its production, in its synchroneity with the explicit pursuit of security enacted during patrols; these images speak of security as the absence of the transgression they illustrate. But the fetishization of transgression through such visualizations eliminates the very promise of security, making the need for security insatiable, while contemporaneously legitimizing the neighbourhood patrol practices through which the transgression is made visible. Through the repetition of images substantiating transgression, the group reinforces the legitimacy of its practice of policing the borders of the

Fig. 11.1 The iconic stranger. (Source: Facebook)

neighbourhood: the border, perceived to have already been violated and always insecure (De Genova 2015) is actualized through the very act of transgression (Ahmed 2004), pointing to the need to attend to it. In practice, they do: periodically, during the night, the men stop their cars at crossroads demarcating the territory of the neighbourhood, calling these moments *presidio*: 'guard', 'defence', or 'garrison'. It is the very ineffectuality of their border policing, displayed through the image of the strangers' presence, which, in fact, allows them to pursue the quest for more security, as 'a thankless and relentless task, a job that can never be completed' (De Genova 2015) and legitimizes their expansion into neighbouring territories, thus pushing the border which needs to be attended to further away.[3]

These transgressions are sometimes spectacularized in a sort of neighbourhood-based, digitally shared 'border spectacle' (De Genova 2013), rendering the presence of putative strangers in the neighbourhood indisputably illegitimate and strengthening the border's symbolism as that

Fig. 11.2 'Bad people walking up and down'. (Source: Facebook)

which protects against polluting matter out of place (Heyman 2014). In the text accompanying one such photograph (Fig. 11.2), the audience is explicitly told that the depicted men are 'Gypsies', and the entire episode of their expulsion from the neighbourhood is narrated in detail:

> *Intercepted at 2.40 last night three gypsies* (sic) *who were wandering suspiciously near* Via *Mosca. Given the time, it was unavoidable to keep them under control. Bad people who were walking up and down on* Via *Ponte di Nona. Obviously, a guard* (presidio) *organized immediately at the intersection between* Via *Mosca and* Via *Ponte di Nona has 'dissuaded' them from approaching the area of the condominiums. One of our volunteers, you can imagine who, got out of the car and shouted clearly 'GO AWAY!!' Then, when another of our cars arrived in support, they vanished towards Prenestina. Followed at a distance, they got into the abandoned farmhouse, now occupied by other Gypsies (…). Apart from that, a quiet night.* (Facebook page, 2.11.2013)

Fig. 11.3 Rooting through containers. (Source: Facebook)

The presumed criminal intent is carefully constructed by the narration of the details: the men were 'walking up and down' at an unusual time, with the aim of approaching the area of the condominiums; the actions of the group 'dissuaded' them, and their 'vanishing' into a house presumably 'occupied by other Gypsies' fabricates undeniable proof of the solid grounds for suspicion, confirming the rightfulness of the act of expulsion. This instance of how security entails exclusion (Neocleous 2009) requires an examination of the conditions which allow the fabrication of *excludendi* to take place, discursively and visually, for the action of separation presupposes a pre-existing classification.

Depictions of Roma as a danger in the register of presumed criminal intent like the earlier example are fairly scarce. Another genre, the second to be examined here, abounds on the group's Facebook profile and represents women and children, in particular, rooting through rubbish containers (Fig. 11.3). Their rendition is highly ambiguous, blending the registers of civility/civilization, victimhood, and abjection: Roma women, and particularly children, would be prone to exploitation by a barbaric culture constructed as inferior to the 'culture of civility which is ours': instead of opting for a 'normal' job, they choose, by culture, to live parasitically and disgustingly off 'our' garbage, making themselves worthy of abjection. In the discourse of the group, there are evident slippages towards criminalization: mention of child exploitation is recurrent and often associated with the suggestion of removing children from their families. In an interview on an online news platform emphasizing the group's fight 'against the exploitation of minors', the leader explains that, against the backdrop of the increasing presence of Roma women and children rooting through containers, they have filed an official complaint with the closest *Carabinieri* station, denouncing the exploitation of these children and urging the authorities to take action.[4]

However, this discourse on the exploitation of minors as heartfelt humanitarian concern is hypocritical rather than genuine: under one of these photographs, which depicts a child rummaging through a container (Fig. 11.4), a commentator suggests that the photographer should have given the child a push into the container; within minutes, the leader replied that the temptation had been great and that they had resisted it with difficulty. The cruelty of such suggestions, the obscene whimsicality of the exchange and the objectification of the child's half-visible body, fantasized about as disposable and at the mercy of the watchers, produce a voyeuristic experience of abjection and longed-for violence which betrays the real intent behind any humanitarian concerns expressed, offsetting the otherwise efficacious agglutination of 'risk' and 'pity' (Aradau 2004).

In April 2015, the leader announced, at the end of a night patrol report, that, in light of the increasing presence of 'coloured immigrants' rooting through containers, as well as the 'usual neighbours' from the Salone camp, they had lobbied for the application of a law criminalizing the act of searching through rubbish and introducing a sentence of a maximum of three years of prison and a fine of over €500 for the perpetrator. Such lobbying actions are not new on the Roman scene (Ivasiuc 2015), but while other actors have constructed their arguments around the theme of crime (refuse is the property of the municipality, hence rooting through it amounts to theft) and security threat (sensitive data may have been carelessly disposed of in the containers and could be misused for forgery), the justification in the case of the group is rather visual in nature: the practice of rooting through containers would lead to an intolerable 'deterioration of the

Fig. 11.4 Disposable body. (Source: Facebook)

image' of the neighbourhood (*degrado di immagine per il nostro Territorio*). The care for an urban aesthetic of order, indeed, the 'obsessed politics of neighbourhood civility-and-security' (Comaroff and Comaroff 2016) is concerned both with the physical separateness of things—keeping the impure rubbish contained and intangible—and with a racialized social order in which the Roma and other 'coloured immigrants', contaminated by their contact with the impure, become dangerous (Douglas 2001) while simultaneously defiling the image of the 'Territory'. The haptic dimension, implicit, but obvious in the narrative of rooting through refuse containers because of the impurity of rubbish, is fused with the visual.

What the members of the group call 'Gypsy vans' (*i furgoni degli zingari*) are depicted in the third category of visualizations. They are usually photographed at night as men load them up with bulky objects collected from the side of the road or from containers (Fig. 11.5): parts or entire pieces of furniture and domestic appliances, discarded construction material or other domestic objects. The image selected is accompanied by

Fig. 11.5 'Gypsy vans'. (Source: Facebook)

a lengthy text in which the vans are described as 'a constant danger': disregarding regulations regarding maximum loads and automobile safety norms (worn-out tyres, defective brakes) and disrespecting traffic rules, the vans and their drivers are 'a danger to whoever drives legally'. Derelict to the point of being an eyesore, and smellier than a garbage truck, they are 'third degree encounters' which recur almost every night during patrols:

> *The problem of the gypsies* (sic) *and of the decay they produce on our Roads*[5] *during their search through refuse takes place 24h a day, but at night, especially in the small hours, the ones who drive around are certainly not the most commendable, and it's becoming almost impossible for us to keep them under observation on all our Territory. While we keep one of their vans under control in one of the side streets, at the other side of the Territory, there are other vans driving up and down. What we see every night only happens in Italy. The Forces of Law and Order do everything they can with the means they have, considering that just one car, either of the* Carabinieri *or the State or Local Police,*

Fig. 11.6 'Abusive market'. (Source: Facebook)

has to cover ample zones. And then, when they stop these vans, They also know that it's useless to issue fines, because they never get paid, and if they confiscate the Van, after a few days they find it driving again, and so on and so forth. (Facebook page, 23.12.2013)

The fourth depiction relates to the informal markets where some of the Roma sell various objects (Fig. 11.6). The texts accompanying these images emphasize the illegality of the commerce, rhetorically constructed as contrary to the presumed correctness of native taxpaying businesses, as well as the visual disorder produced by the display of the merchandise, usually on the pavement:

We wonder if the owner of the M. car rental company deserves, given the taxes he pays for his activity, to live next to so much disgust and shame. An illegal market of the gypsies (sic), *as you can see in plain view. Soon, they will even take the middle of the road for themselves!* (Facebook page, 7.06.2013)

Finally, a recurring pictorial theme on the Facebook profile of the group is one of dark smoke, of varying density, often photographed from a distance curling up against the background of the neighbourhood's condominium buildings (Fig. 11.7). Linked to the existence of camps in Rome, the practice around which most anti-Roma discourse is nowadays structured is the burning of such remnants of refuse which the Roma cannot recycle for economic purposes and which the public sanitation services will only collect rarely, on demand, and using extraordinary means.[6] This practice occurs particularly in Rome[7]; a recent journalistic investigation (Belli et al. 2015) has revealed its place as part of a larger chain of shady, mafia-related practices of refuse management in which bulky detritus from construction sites is ultimately dumped near camps or given to the Roma instead of being transported to special sites. Also, large furniture or domestic appliances are disposed of to the Roma by private individuals or small firms for a considerably smaller sum than the one charged for removal to special facilities—the so-called ecologic islands, where labyrinthine rules

Fig. 11.7 Smoke. (Source: Facebook)

and regulations make the process complicated, tiresome, and expensive. This cost-cutting strategy of private firms or individuals results in a practice which facilitates the scapegoating of the Roma, while effectively obfuscating a much more widespread profit-making machinery. The refuse pyres have come to lie at the heart of securitarian discourses on the *campi nomadi* in Rome, taking precedence over discourses securitizing the Roma on the grounds of concerns about petty crime. The discourses woven around this practice enact a different narrative of securitization, referring predominantly to health-related concerns about the inhalation of dioxin, or the environment, and cast the Roma as perpetrators of environmental crime. The narrative claims that the Roma are poisoning the inhabitants of the Roman peripheries and their children, together with the air that they breathe and the water that they drink. The inhabitants of Ponte di Nona and Tor Sapienza[8] complain on social media that they have to barricade themselves inside their homes because of the foul-smelling toxic smoke. The criminalization of the Roma on the grounds of this practice participates in the production of a 'reasonable anti-Gypsyism' (van Baar 2014), casting the Roma as life threatening and, as I discuss in the next section, legitimizing their extermination. At present, no other narrative generates more social alarm and discontent than that which revolves around the smoke produced in or near the camps. It is this particular moral panic which, following on from lobbying by neighbourhood committees, has forced the authorities to organize police patrols around some of the camps specifically to control the fires.

With the exception of the category depicting the iconic stranger, the visualizations of the Roma displayed on social media substantiate moments from the informal economy in which most of the Roma living in camps engage. While the search for reusable items in refuse containers is predominantly a task fulfilled by women and children—who, by virtue of their size, play an essential role in accessing the contents of the locked containers for second-hand clothing—scrap-metal collection is mostly performed by the men. In second-hand markets, women predominantly act as the vendors, selling either re-purposed items found in containers on the streets or donated objects which they themselves do not need. This entire informal sector of the disposed-of and disposable at the margins of the formal labour economy is central to and perfectly well integrated into the wider economic processes dictated by dominant capitalist modes of production.[9] The economic marginality of the Roma camouflages the very centrality of their labour to the functioning of the capitalist economy, the production logic of which is structured around planned obsolescence, inevitably leading to the rampant replacement of goods which must then be disposed of. This practice substantiates the ghettoization of the Roma as 'an organic part of the waste-disposal mechanism set in motion in times when the poor are no longer of use... and have become instead flawed, and for that reason also useless, consumers' (Bauman 2001: 120). The camp has thus become, quite literally, a 'dumping ground' for both the people and the objects for which society no longer has economic or political use (Wacquant 2007).

Rejoining Piasere in his observation that the Roma are particularly able to exploit (and thus reveal) the incongruities of 'Gadjé' modes of functioning (Piasere 2009), Martin Olivera recently advanced that 'those who, like the Roma, live in and off waste, are not so much the cause of disorder as the most visible products of the paradoxes and other constitutive contradictions of liberal urban life' (2015: 507, my translation). The 'insecure sensible' is thus a form of spectacle, the language of which 'is composed of signs of the dominant organization of production – signs which are at the same time the ultimate end-products of that organization' (Debord 1992): material waste fabricating disposable humans.

The casting of these economic practices as a safety and security issue and the emphasis on their illicit nature is reminiscent of what Nicholas De Genova (2013: 6) called the 'obscene inclusion' of 'illegal' immigrants as precarious labour, contemporaneous to the spectacularization of their 'illegality'. Here, while the spectacularization of the illegality of these economic practices allows a quick glimpse into the obscene inclusion of the Roma, their securitarian framing, and the border spectacle performed by the neighbourhood patrol, warrants greater concealment of their centrality to capitalist modes of production, and the naturalization of existing hierarchies, and exclusionary ideologies structured around notions of security and insecurity.

Sharing the Sensible: *'Whoever Truly Loves the Territory like We Do'*

Exclusion is not the sole dynamic upon which securitarian discourses are constructed. The subtitle of this section takes Jacques Rancière's (2000) 'distribution of the sensible' as the definition and apportionment, alongside power lines, of what is visible and what is not in any given, shared space, back to its original French wording, where '*partage (du sensible)*' has a connotation of 'sharing', and thus of community-making, as well as the more mundane recent meaning of sharing content on the social media. By superimposing all these meanings and analysing them under one lens, I thus examine how the practice of sharing specific types of visual content on social media constructs an insecure community around the security discourse. The social production of proximity and distance commanding indifference or outright violence towards certain groups (Basaran 2015) presupposes the fabrication of communities of 'we', a process pertinently grasped when the Roma are described as a 'threatening internal other against which non-Roma society builds community identities, unity and a sense of security' (Clough Marinaro and Sigona 2011: 583). As I show in the following, the practice of neighbourhood patrolling and the sharing of visual content on the social media contribute to the creation of an acute sense of insecurity and an insatiable demand for more security.

Practices of surveillance may take various forms along a spectrum ranging from protective care to coercive control (Lyon 2001). As a corollary, a given practice may entail both care and inclusion, on the one hand, and control and exclusion, on the other hand, for different groups: where an enemy is to be contained, a friend is to be protected. This Manicheistic worldview requires the continuous de-humanization, sub-humanization, and abjectification (Heckenberger 2012; Hepworth 2012; Maneri 2010) of the Gypsy or the immigrant, often referred to as *letame* (muck or manure), and the glorification of 'true Italians', 'decent people' (*gente per bene*), taxpaying entrepreneurs and—repeatedly and pompously—the military and the forces of law and order. Within the neighbourhood, friends are all those who 'truly [love] the Territory' and are thus called, every year, to take part in the protest marches against the Roma camps, the presence of which 'is imagined as a threat to the object of love' (Ahmed 2004: 117). 'Friends' commend the group's vigilance on- and offline and express gratitude for their protection (Ivasiuc 2015).

Correspondingly, the group refers to the space of the neighbourhood as the 'Territory'—systematically capitalized and thus fetishized—the object of protection and geographical theatre of its patrols, guards, and surveillance. In contrast to the *Territorio*, '*vicinato*', etymologically derived from the notion of nearness (*vicino*) and always used between scare quotes, refers ironically and metonymically to the inhabitants of the camp of Via di Salone, constructed as socially and culturally very distant, notwithstanding their geographical proximity. In the face of this depicted and deplored 'invasion by alterity' (Feldman 2015: 5) the intent of the neighbourhood patrol is to render the territory an unassailable fortress. The 'peacetime war discourse' (Maneri 2010) deployed to construct a legitimate presence on the 'Territory' of a collective 'we' to combat an invading uncivilized 'them' conceals the fact that neither the 'Territory' nor its inhabitants are 'protected' in homogenous ways, and the neighbourhood patrol bestows security discriminately, according to hierarchizations of people and the spaces they inhabit. Their priority, as can be seen in the recurrence of photographs taken during the night-time patrols, is the protection of the condominiums and the shops of Nuova Ponte di Nona, while the social housing areas of the neighbourhood, with their poorer residents, and the entirety of the old Ponte di Nona neighbourhood, are demonstrably omitted (Ivasiuc 2015). The plethora of photographs of shops and condominium parking lots, entrances and gates made secure depict an apparently homogenous, neat, civilized middle-class neighbourhood worthy of protection (Figs. 11.8 and 11.9). This focus on the condominiums and commercial areas visually and

Fig. 11.8 The protected 'Territory': condominiums. (Source: Facebook)

Fig. 11.9 The protected 'Territory': shops. (Source: Facebook)

politically reshapes the neighbourhood, redefining what is seen as valuable and worthy of defence in the urban landscape, and what has the right to the neighbourhood patrol's protection and hence to security. This operation thus isolates those who are entitled to 'cohere as a political subject' (Mirzoeff 2011: 3), posing security as their central claim and legitimizing the mobilization of the group. The grassroots 'politics of protection' (Huysmans et al. 2006) enacted here is, in fact, a politics of protecting the dominant order and its social hierarchies.

Claiming to protect the security of this particular community effectively silences the insecurity that is produced by this very process, and is legitimized and naturalized through the construction of the Roma as threat. On the Facebook profile of the group, references to physical violence, lynching, and the downright extermination of the Roma are not only uncensored but are 'liked' in the digital space of the Facebook community where people do not have to worry about reprimands, or being rejected for hate speech or incitement to violence. On the contrary, it seems that such comments engage their authors in a relationship of complicity: members 'like' each other's suggestions of violence against a common enemy, weaving a shared subjectivity of fear and hate and enacting a digital necropolitics of sorts (Mbembe 2003).

These economies of fear and hate are deployed through signs whose affective value seems to increase the more they are circulated, agglutinating meanings through what Sara Ahmed calls 'the rippling effect of emotions':

> [T]hey move sideways (through 'sticky' associations between signs, figures, and objects) as well as backward (repression always leaves its trace in the present – hence 'what sticks' is also bound up with the 'absent presence' of historicity)... [H]ate 'slides' sideways between figures, as well as backward, by reopening past associations that allow some bodies to be read as the cause of 'our hate', or as 'being hateful'. (Ahmed 2004: 120)

This double movement is cogently illustrated in the following vignette. In November 2013, 'for the protection (*tutela*) of the citizens', the group

Fig. 11.10 'Suspicious van'. (Source: Facebook)

posted the photograph of the back of a 'suspicious' van, with its visible foreign licence plate, asking people to report any suspicious movements of this van that they might observe around the condominiums (Fig. 11.10); a dialogue then unravelled between followers, in which they suggested that the van—fabricated by the securitarian discourse of the neighbourhood patrol as a new object to be feared—was associated with the leitmotif of child kidnappings, an enduring trope often associated in the past, but also today, with Roma women (Tosi Cambini 2008):

GD: *We can't even walk safely in our neighbourhood anymore!!! I'm terrorized by kidnappings, especially of children. And these vans give me such anxieties!!!*
LT: *The kidnapping of children is the fear of every parent... the problem is ever more serious, this neighbourhood is becoming bad and we're the only ones who must avoid its total decay!*
CR: *Stop them and burn them*[10]

This vignette—the rich significance of which cannot be fully rendered here for reasons of space—provides a glimpse into the perverse politics of security, the pursuit of which is not only *not* a zero-sum game (meaning that one person's security necessarily entails someone else's insecurity, as discussed earlier), but multiplies insecurities through the rippling effect of fear.

The recurrent exhortations to residents to remain alert to suspicious presences around the condominiums, as well as the exhibition of photographs and videos taken during the night patrols, effectively transform the audience of those 'who love the Territory' into an army of surveillants, producing what Louise Amoore (2007) has described as 'vigilant visuality': a permanently watchful mode of seeing which produces 'a ubiquitous border' between the self and the 'other'. It is this invitation to what the neighbourhood patrol group perceives as a form of 'civic participation' that lays down the premise for what I propose to call the complex of securitarian visuality.

The Complex of Securitarian Visuality

In *The Right to Look: A Counterhistory of Visuality*, Mirzoeff (2011: 5) defines the 'complex of visuality' as the 'imbrication of mentality and organization produc[ing] a visualized deployment of bodies and training of minds, organized so as to sustain both physical segregation between rulers and ruled, and mental compliance with those arrangements'. For Mirzoeff, visuality stands for the supplement needed by authority to legitimize itself and become self-evident in a naturalizing move (ibid. 7). Visuality does not simply entail visual perception: rather, it is spanned by a set of relations in which imagination, information, and insight participate in rendering space in particular ways, so as to classify and separate those who possess the right to constitute a collective political subjectivity and those who do not, while imposing the evidence of the authority's legitimacy (ibid. 3). Visuality operates through three interrelated processes. First, in a move that Mirzoeff borrows from Foucault as 'the nomination of the visible', it classifies by defining and naming categories, thus bringing into existence categories of subjects. Second, visuality effectuates the social organization of these subjects by separating them and segregating those to whom it denies the right to cohere politically. The third and final effect of visuality is to render the social organization thus accomplished as a self-evident given, seemingly right and thus aesthetic.

Together, Mirzoeff takes these three processes to constitute a 'complex of visuality', which he then historicizes. For Mirzoeff, the history of visuality starts from the second part of the seventeenth century with the plantation complex, whose metonymic figure was the overseer, then continues with the imperial complex of the nineteenth and twentieth centuries, and reaches the present day in the form of what he calls the 'military-industrial complex', the contemporary traits of which are global counter-insurgency and post-panoptic visuality. In each of these complexes, the operations of classification and separation of the ruling from the ruled have produced corresponding social orders; through the aestheticization of these orders—their rendition as rightful—visuality has legitimized authority, coalescing it to power and rendering this association natural (ibid. 6). As for the 'right to look', it is the opposite of visuality: the claim to an autonomous subjectivity in the constitution of the sayable and the visible through which the social order is rendered unnatural and authority stops being authorized. It is the attempt to reconfigure the distribution of the sensible.

In Mirzoeff's theorizing of the current military-industrial complex, post-panoptic visuality is inscribed not in disciplinary surveillance, as with the Panopticon, but in a necropolitics of expulsion, exclusion, and the extermination of the undesirables, who are no longer seen as disciplinable (ibid. 278–79). He connects post-panoptic visuality with the military-industrial complex and focuses his scrutiny on the global, US-led, counter-insurgency practices, 'whose goal is nothing less than the active consent of the "host" culture to neoliberal globalization' (ibid. 19). Mirzoeff's rich and convincing insights refer mostly to the global scale and to international relations in a regime of military interventions; his account accommodates few and relatively vague references to domestic dynamics, and, in general, these mentions refer to dramatic events such as the military response to the disaster caused by Hurricane Katrina in 2005 in New Orleans (ibid. 281).

By using Mirzoeff's theory of visuality, I intend to render his conceptual framework fruitful as a means of accounting for the kind of everyday, small-scale dynamics reflected by the ethnographic material discussed. The surveillance practices deployed by the group, together with the photographs they share on the social media and the texts which accompany them, betray visual, discursive, and material practices which can be read as a complex of visuality: they classify subjects, attempt to segregate, expel, if not exterminate, the undesirables, and generate a discourse which aestheticizes the social order thus produced, legitimizing the authority from which it emanates. While Mirzoeff deplores a state in which 'the body-politic of our own society [has become] so enmired in "security" as to have lost a sense of purpose' (ibid. 283), I contend, on the contrary, that Western societies fabricate a sense of purpose—and of community—precisely around security, which has become a central principle of social ordering and the core of what could be called 'the complex of securitarian visuality'.

I conceptualize the complex of securitarian visuality as the social and mental ordering of the experienced world, structured around conceptions of security/insecurity as a central ordering principle of 'social sorting' (Lyon 2003): classifications and separations effectuated between those who are seen to cause, to various degrees, various types of insecurity, and those who, in contrast, present themselves as uniquely capable of producing and imparting security, and those in need of protection. The utility of such a conceptualization is that it can account for what plays out between people in local settings rather than on the macro scene of global politics, in what Deleuze (1992) has sketched as 'societies of control': the form of rule in which power and control are exercised through the capillaries of society in the 'brains and bodies of the citizens' (Hardt and Negri 2000: 23), through flexible networks and the use of technology, well beyond the institutions traditionally entrusted with control.

The proliferation of private and hybrid forms of crime fighting in which citizens are imbricated suggests that community is increasingly a technology of government pursuing security (Cruikshank 1999; Gressgård 2016; Johnston 1992). The increased popularity and dissemination of neighbourhood-watch schemes is potentiated by digital technologies enabling the representation and dissemination of visuals and messages, which multiply such vigilant visualities, producing skilled visions (Grasseni 2009), able to anticipate and pre-judge danger. The constitutive embeddedness of this visuality of prejudice as a pre-judgement of what is suspicious and needs to be watched (Amoore 2007) is what moulds the complex of securitarian visuality into a particularly powerful mode for categorizing subjects and aestheticizing the dominant order. The use of technologies of representation and dissemination such as social media enables an unsettling function which may be performed by the spectacle of surveillance: the collective transformation of residents into neighbourhood overseers who pre-judge danger and thus preserve the dominant order. Fault lines such as those of race, class, and citizenship are institutionalized and exacerbated through surveillance (Coaffee et al. 2009).

Taking a clue from Shapiro, who notes that the 'techno-geography of security' has evolved from physical barriers to communication nodes (2009: 448), we can grasp how, alongside the barriers protecting the condominiums' parking lots and the iron gates defending the entrance, the photographs posted suggest that these spaces can only be made truly safe by the work of watchful visuality, not only on the part of the neighbourhood patrol but—with the mediation of digital technologies—of all those 'who love the Territory'.

Conclusion

The visuals circulated on the social media by the neighbourhood patrol display unmistakable 'complicities with prevailing power and authority' (Shapiro 1988: 131), participating in operations of classification, separation, and aestheticization through which the dominant order becomes naturalized. This chapter has set out to examine the mechanisms through which the visuals circulated on the social media by the neighbourhood patrol perform these operations in the wider context of the relations in which they are embedded.

We have seen how the circulation of images of the 'iconic stranger' suggests inevitable transgressions, legitimating the vigilant mobilization of the group and laying the groundwork for the subsequent construction of the friend/enemy dichotomy. The spectacularization of transgression through the depiction of episodes of expulsion stages a neighbourhood 'border spectacle' naturalizing the group's actions as rightful. Through the depiction of various abject and dangerous figures performing reviled practices, but also iconic objects participating in multiple securitizations, the Roma are constructed as a source of insecurity even as they enact economic practices which betray their 'obscene inclusion'. Framing their economic practices as issues of security contributes to the obfuscation of their imbrications in capitalist modes of production and naturalizes their domination as disposable.

While these mechanisms of categorization and separation operate via exclusionary dynamics, affect circulates through images so as to produce a digital, collective subjectivity built on fear and hate, but whose aggregation is coagulated through a purported 'love for the Territory'. The production of the community entails the exclusion of the poorer segments of the neighbourhood, ultimately revealing the order worthy of protection, embodied in the recurrent icons of the condominium and the shop. The claim to the security of this collective political subjectivity unleashes fantasies of violence towards the Roma and unmasks 'security' as a producer of insecurities, feeding economies of fear. While the group calls upon the residents to report suspicious activities and share their very watching of the neighbourhood on the social media, they produce 'vigilant visualities', participating in the capillarization of power and control through the workings of security itself.

These vernacular deployments of visually mediated (in)security reveal how 'social sorting', centred on security/insecurity, becomes the central mechanism of a post-panoptic complex of securitarian visuality in which vigilant visualities, mediated through digital technologies and engaging the minds and bodies of individuals, divide the world into sources of security and insecurity, on the one hand, and subjects worthy of protection or, to the contrary, of extermination, on the other hand. Methodologically and theoretically, the affordances of the ethnographic material discussed here point to the productivity of an approach which traces the fabrication of insecurities through networks in which objects are nodes no less prolific than human agents (Walters 2014). The van, the condominium, the rubbish container, the scrap-iron, the disposable objects, the smoke rising from the camp—but also the technologies of representation and its dissemination—become just so many mediators (Latour 2005) in the multiplication of insecurity around the Roma in Rome.

Anyone who visits the camp of Via di Salone is likely to find, whatever the time, a local police car parked opposite the entrance gate, almost invariably on the same spot. The police wait watchfully at the entrance while the Roma go about their daily business, moving in and out of the camp, in and out of their vans, in and out of their conversations with each other. The police and the Roma glance at each other from their respective roles of observer and observed as they pass. Until recently, moreover, one of the NGOs entrusted with the administration of the camp has employed guards (*vigili*) to keep an eye on the Roma and alert the organization in the event of any issues, thus increasing the number of watchers in the camp. Yet, near the entrance, on a piece of fabric tied on the iron fence surrounding the camp, a *graffito* marks the 'guard post' (*posto per i vigili*), hinting facetiously at the possibility of a role-reversal between the watchers and the watched, in which the latter assign the former a particular place from which to watch and warn them that they themselves are being watched in turn. This apparently inconsequential piece of *graffiti* is perhaps the discrete sign of the presence, alongside the securitarian visuality, of a counter-visuality whose grasping is just as momentous as the agency of the watched (Monahan 2011: 498). As Mirzoeff puts it,

> [t]he authorizing of authority requires permanent renewal in order to win consent as the 'normal', or everyday, because it is always already contested. The autonomy claimed by the right to look is thus opposed by the authority of visuality. But the right to look came first, and we should not forget it. (Mirzoeff 2011: 2)

Notes

1. Although, for reasons of space, I limit my analysis to visual representations, it is important to understand the 'sensible' in relation to all senses. Taking a clue from W. J. T. Mitchell (2005), who reminds us of the illusion of purely visual media, I emphasize the pertinence of scrutinizing multi-sensorial constructions of insecurity beyond the 'sovereign sense' of seeing. In the case of the Roma, Piasere (2005) has shown the way in which they are constructed as a nuisance on all sensory dimensions; the examples discussed here show that security concerns fuse with 'anti-gypsy senses' to construct the Roma as dangerous on the visual, haptic, and olfactory dimensions.

2. All photographs have been taken from the public Facebook page of the group. The copyright belongs to Facebook and the images are used under the fair use legislation. The images presented are only a selection from those available; the main criterion for selecting certain images is their quality.
3. In May 2015, the group had already managed to mobilize the inhabitants of two neighbouring territories who now patrol their neighbourhoods, tripling the number of cars engaged in night patrols (Ivasiuc 2015).
4. The *Carabinieri* are the Italian military police.
5. My translation reproduces the capitalization of various words in original.
6. This generally entails subcontracting the activity to private firms.
7. Fires related to camps are completely absent, for instance, in Milan, but have also been reported, although less frequently, south of Rome.
8. Tor Sapienza, in the eastern part of Rome, is the neighbourhood where the 'tolerated' camp of Via Salviati is indented into the urban fabric, relatively close to residential areas. The neighbourhood committee of Tor Sapienza is one of the most active on the Roman stage when it comes to camp-related issues, with a considerable on- and off-line presence; also, it has more than once supported the neighbourhood patrol group in their protests against the camps.
9. The economic processes in which the Roma are involved are not only local and national but global: the fluctuation of the price of metals on the international market encourages the Roma to stockpile scrap-metal and wait for the best moment to sell. What look to others like heaps of refuse are in fact part of a commercial logic dictated by capitalist modes of production.
10. I have retained the punctuation of the original Facebook posts in the translations, even where it was missing or incorrectly used.

References

Ahmed, S. 2000. *Strange Encounters*. London: Routledge.
———. 2004. Affective Economies. *Social Text* 22 (2): 117–139.
Amoore, L. 2007. Vigilant Visualities. *Security Dialogue* 38 (2): 215–232.
Andersen, R., J. Vuori, and C. Mutlu. 2015. Visuality. In *Critical Security Methods*, ed. C. Aradau et al., 85–117. London: Routledge.
Aradau, C. 2004. The Perverse Politics of Four-Letter Words. *Millennium: Journal of International Studies* 33 (2): 251–277.
Basaran, T. 2015. The Saved and the Drowned. *Security Dialogue* 46 (3): 205–220.
Bauman, Z. 2001. *Community: Seeking Safety in an Insecure World*. Cambridge: Polity.
Belli, E. et al. 2015. *A Ferro e Fuoco: Fumi tossici nella 'città eterna'* [To Fire and Sword: Toxic Smoke in the 'Eternal City'], Rome: Kogoi.

Clough Marinaro, I., and N. Sigona. 2011. Introduction: Anti-Gypsyism and the Politics of Exclusion. *Journal of Modern Italian Studies* 16 (5): 583–589.
Coaffee, J., P. O'Hare, and M. Hawkesworth. 2009. The Visibility of (In)security. *Security Dialogue* 40 (4–5): 489–511.
Comaroff, J., and J. Comaroff. 2016. *The Truth About Crime*. Chicago, IL: University of Chicago Press.
Cruikshank, B. 1999. *The Will to Empower*. Ithaca, NY: Cornell University Press.
Debord, G. 1992 [1967]. *The Society of the Spectacle*. London: Zone Books.
De Genova, N. 2013. Spectacles of Migrant "Illegality". *Ethnic and Racial Studies* 36 (7): 1180–1198.
———. 2015. Extremities and Regularities. In *The Irregularization of Migration in Contemporary Europe*, ed. Y. Jansen, R. Celikates, and J. de Bloois, 3–14. Lanham, MD: Rowman & Littlefield.
Deleuze, G. 1992. Postscript on the Societies of Control. *October* 59: 3–7.
Douglas, M. 2001 [1966]. *Purity and Danger*. London: Routledge.
Feldman, A. 2015. *Archives of the Insensible*. Chicago, IL: University of Chicago Press.
Grasseni, C., ed. 2009. *Skilled Visions*. Oxford: Berghahn Books.
Gressgård, R. 2016. Welfare Policing and the Safety-Security Nexus in Urban Governance. *Nordic Journal of Migration Research* 6 (1): 9–17.
Hansen, L. 2011. Theorizing the Image for Security Studies. *European Journal of International Relations* 17 (1): 51–74.
Hardt, M., and A. Negri. 2000. *Empire*. Cambridge, MA: Harvard University Press.
Heckenberger, M. 2012. Marginal Bodies, Altered States, and Subhumans. In *Human No More*, ed. N. Whitehead and M. Wesch, 199–216. Boulder, CO: University Press of Colorado.
Hepworth, K. 2012. Abject Citizens. *Citizenship Studies* 16 (3–4): 431–449.
Heyman, J. 2014. "Illegality" and the US-Mexico Border. In *Constructing Illegality in America*, ed. C. Menjívar and D. Kanstroom, 111–135. Cambridge: Cambridge University Press.
Huysmans, J., A. Dobson, and R. Prokhovnik, eds. 2006. *The Politics of Protection*. London: Routledge.
Ivasiuc, A. 2015. Watching over the Neighbourhood: Vigilante Discourses and Practices in the Suburbs of Rome. *Etnofoor* 27 (2): 53–72.
Johnston, L. 1992. *The Rebirth of Private Policing*. London: Routledge.
Latour, B. 2005. *Reassembling the Social*. Oxford: Oxford University Press.
Lyon, D. 2001. *Surveillance Society*. Buckingham: Open University Press.
———., ed. 2003. *Surveillance as Social Sorting*. London: Routledge.
Maneri, M. 2010. Peacetime War Discourse. In *Conflict, Security and the Reshaping of Society*, ed. A. Dal Lago and S. Palidda, 153–170. London: Routledge.
Mbembe, A. 2003. Necropolitics. *Public Culture* 15 (1): 11–40.

Mirzoeff, N. 2011. *The Right to Look: A Counterhistory of Visuality*. Durham, NC: Duke University Press.
Mitchell, W.J.T. 2005. There Are No Visual Media. *Journal of Visual Culture* 4 (2): 257–266.
———. 2012. *Seeing Through Race*. Cambridge, MA: Harvard University Press.
Monahan, T. 2011. Surveillance as Cultural Practice. *The Sociological Quarterly* 52 (4): 495–508.
Neocleous, M. 2009. The Fascist Moment. *Studies in Social Justice* 3 (1): 23–37.
Olivera, M. 2015. Insupportables pollueurs ou recycleurs de génie? *Ethnologie Française* 45 (3): 499–509.
Piasere, L. 2005 [1991]. *Popoli delle discariche* [Peoples of Landfills], Rome: CISU.
———. 2009 [2004]. *I Rom d'Europa* [The Roma of Europe], Roma and Bari: Laterza.
Pink, S., et al. 2015. *Digital Ethnography*. London: Sage.
Pusca, A. 2010. The "Roma Problem" in the EU. *Borderlands* 9 (2): 1–17.
Rancière, J. 2000. *Le partage du sensible*. Paris: La Fabrique éditions.
Shapiro, M.J. 1988. *The Politics of Representation*. Wisconsin, WI: University of Wisconsin Press.
———. 2009. Managing Urban Security. *Security Dialogue* 40 (4–5): 443–461.
Tosi Cambini, S. 2008. *La zingara rapitrice* [The Kidnapping Gypsy Woman], Rome: CISU.
van Baar, H. 2014. The Emergence of a Reasonable Anti-Gypsyism in Europe. In *When Stereotype Meets Prejudice*, ed. T. Agarin, 27–44. Stuttgart: Ibidem.
Wacquant, L. 2007. *Urban outcasts*. Cambridge: Polity.
Walters, W. 2014. Drone Strikes, *dingpolitik* and Beyond. *Security Dialogue* 45 (2): 101–118.

CHAPTER 12

The "gypsy Threat": Modes of Racialization and Visual Representation Underlying German Police Practices

Markus End

The perception of a specific threat, supposed to originate from "the gypsies",[1] has been a core element of antigypsyist discourses[2] since their emergence in Western Europe in the fifteenth century. These discourses have to be understood as a major driving force behind scientific attempts at thoroughly understanding the "gypsies", as well as being behind major antigypsyist policies targeting Roma, Sinti, Yeniche, and other groups and individuals perceived as "gypsies" by religious and state authorities.

State institutions have contributed to these discourses throughout history, but people stigmatized as "gypsies" have become a specific focus of police and other security institutions only since the eighteenth and mainly since the nineteenth centuries (Lucassen 1996). At that time, scientific and police discourses to some extent functioned autonomously of each other. While scientific discourse started to focus on the true "nature" of a perceived essential "gypsiness", the police discourse began to focus on a

---

This chapter is widely based on the research I did for the *Dokumentations- und Kulturzentrum Deutscher Sinti und Roma*, published in End (2014).

M. End (✉)
Indepedent Scholar, Berlin, Germany

specific form of behaviour, perceived as deviant and described as the "gypsy way" (Patrut 2014: 276–77, 317–20).[3]

To a great extent, these two discourses represent the two key elements of racist ideology, which I understand as the racialization of the social (Rommelspacher 2009: 25). At the end of the nineteenth century and with the emergence and increased integration of racializing concepts into criminology, those discourses merged once more, with "gypsies" being described as "born criminals", thus recombining fixed notions of social deviancy with mechanisms of racialization. In this chapter, I build on an argument that I have explained elsewhere (End 2015) and according to which these two key strands of racist definition, though distinguishable from an analytical perspective, have become inseparable in racist ideology. First, I analyse contemporary police discourses in Germany. Second, I examine police press statements (PPSs) and public information delivered by the German police in order to understand the ways in which the police create, apply, and disseminate the construction and perception of a "gypsy threat" (End 2014: 236–74). I argue that these police practices have to be understood as an integral part of the way in which the securitization of the Roma in Europe has been articulated and reinforced.

In post-war Germany, the police have a century-long history of discriminating against and persecuting Sinti and Roma. The German police were much influenced by practices and discourses established both before and during National Socialism, and these continued at least until well into the 1970s. Some German states even maintained specialized 'Traveller Divisions' (*'Landfahrerzentralen'*), which often employed the same officers who had been involved in the systematic persecution and extermination of Sinti and Roma during the Roma Holocaust (Rose 2008: 125–42). There is historical research into police approaches to the perceived "gypsy threat" in the late nineteenth and early twentieth centuries (Bonillo 2001; Lucassen 1996) and also about the approach of the National-Socialist police (Fings 2008; Wagner 2007; Zimmermann 1996), but, until now, there has been no research specifically directed at the work, history, and methods of—most importantly—the Bavarian police unit which became the 'Central Reich Office for Combating the Gypsy Nuisance' (*'Reichszentrale zur Bekämpfung des Zigeunerunwesens'*) in Berlin in 1938, whose officers actively participated in the organization of the mass extermination of the European Sinti and Roma. These officers continued their work after the war, functioning as "gypsy experts" and setting the standard for future generations of police officers (Rose 1987: 31–46). In the

1950s and 1960s, they also played a crucial role in frustrating the process of recognition of the Roma Holocaust, as well as in minimizing the chances for victims to claim compensation. Police institutions worked with Nazi documents until well into the 1970s, something which felt like a form of 'second persecution' (Greußing 1979) for many survivors and their families.

Police attitudes towards the Sinti and Roma changed to some extent in the 1970s, in particular because of pressure from the civil rights movement of the German Sinti and Roma. But the general perception that "gypsies" were a security problem largely remained in place (Feuerhelm 1987): when an officer who had worked for the German Federal Criminal Police (*Bundeskriminalamt* or *BKA*) retired in 2001, he revealed a set of about 50 folders, and other materials, containing information about 'various groups of "mobile ethnic minorities"' (Stephan 2011: 281–84).

It is difficult to collect information about whether today's police force still upholds mechanisms, processes, and forms of expertise that relate to the construct of a "gypsy threat". One main source involves media coverage which relies explicitly or implicitly on information given by police officers (End 2014: 265–71). There is a wide variety of media coverage of crimes supposedly committed by the Roma or the Sinti and Roma, based on interviews with police officers, representatives of police unions, or state prosecutors (End 2017).

The most important sources are PPSs, which are published by specialist police press officers (End 2014: 236–37). PPSs are one of a few police sources that are publicly available (for a thorough research into PPSs and their effects on local media coverage, see Bohn et al. 1993). Because they are written for publication, they represent a very specific type of source, as one can safely assume that those who compose them keep their public nature in mind.

The PPSs published online on the news portal *News Aktuell* (2014) in 2011, as well as the PPS from Bavaria (Polizei Bayern 2014) and Baden-Württemberg (Polizei Baden-Württemberg 2012), form the main empirical basis of my analysis. However, these sources do not include all German states, so the results cannot be understood as statements about differences in PPSs issued by different police institutions. It is not my primary aim to provide a comparative analysis of these police communications but rather to understand whether, and, if so, to what extent the institution of the police reproduces the narrative of a specific "gypsy threat".

I then analyse how this discursive frame creates, maintains, and reinforces a visual regime of a "Roma threat" within the broader visual antigypsyist regime of "the Roma" (see Busch 2011). I use the latter term to describe the 'current mode of representing the Roma', extensively analysed by Frank Reuter (2014: 472) in his groundbreaking study of the 'photographical construction of the gypsy' (2014). As I understand it, this regime enables 'a quick fixing of the reference by visual means' (Surdu 2016: 225). Like Reuter, Mihai Surdu has analysed images of the "Roma"—in his case, in policy literature—and concluded that: 'The image ensued from the amalgamation of descriptions of Roma as a (target) group in policy literature creates a uniform appearance that continuously fuels and refuels the (mostly negative) social representation of Roma' (2016: 227). This representation can be understood as 'a complex of textual and visual depiction' (Reuter 2014: 472) and, accordingly, such a visual regime is in part created without actual images.

Within the sub-regime of the "Roma threat", suspects and fugitives are described through their visible features and actions, which are qualified as being characteristic of "the Roma". I explain how and to what extent police institutions have responded to the much expressed critique that they attempt to conceal this racialization through supposedly neutral coding. Finally, I show how this visual regime supports the spreading of the narrative of a "gypsy threat".

THE NARRATIVE OF A "GYPSY THREAT"

The narrative of a specific "gypsy threat" forms the ideological basis for the visual regime that I propose to analyse. As many studies have shown, it is widely accepted in mainstream society. According to Elmar Brähler, Oliver Decker, and Johannes Kiess (2016: 50), close to 60% of the German population admit to thinking that the 'Sinti and Roma tend to be criminal'. The police version of this narrative is no different. A good illustration of this can be found in a press release from December 2011 (PPS 2011a).[4] The extensive statement reports the successful investigation of an internationally active group of pickpockets. The last paragraph of the statement begins with the words: 'The Roma families…' This formulation reveals the underlying racialization of the group, as up to this point there has been no explicit mention of a "Roma" belonging. The statement continues to claim that, 'according to experts', the 'commission of crimes of theft of any kind' is perceived as a 'natural and valuable form of work' among the

'Kalderash'—who are described as 'a small group of Roma living in Bulgaria' who would originally have been rooted in the 'Indian caste system'—and that 'young children' will already have been trained to engage in theft 'by their parents and grandparents'. The press release thereby suggests that the tendency to engage in theft is essentially part of Kalderash culture. Although the press release reveals some attempt to avoid homogenization and essentialization, it is nevertheless openly racist. Indeed, theft is ascribed to an entire group—the Kalderash—and indirectly expanded to "Roma" in general. The Kalderash are imagined as a homogenous group, and conceptualized as having essential characteristics by, for example, describing them as being 'rooted in the [Indian] caste system'.

A press release from July 2013 provides another example of such open racialization (PPS 2013). It reports a specific type of theft by trickery which the police refer to as the 'Budscho phenomenon'. After a description of the suspects and the progression of events in the case, under the sub-heading 'Background Information', the press release states that '"Budscho" means "bag", "handbag", or "bundle" in the Roma language' 'and denotes a modus operandi that nearly all traditional Romani women have mastered as an operating procedure' (PPS 2013). This press statement attributes a particular form of socially deviant behaviour—theft by trickery—to 'nearly all traditional Romani women' and thus generalizes this supposed behaviour. Such an explicit explanation of crime on the basis of supposed "Roma culture" is not common, but, because of the homogenizing and generalizing nature of the statements, these two PPSs represent classic expressions of the narrative of a "gypsy threat". This narrative has to be analysed in the context of the history of the German police's surveillance and control of people stigmatized as "gypsies", as discussed. Accordingly, one important way to question the present-day police discourse consists of regarding the continuities among the personnel involved—along with the archives, knowledge, practices and teaching materials which conjointly constitute the resources that the police has at its disposal to fight the supposed "gypsy threat".

From my analysis, we can also observe that the "gypsy threat" discourse is connected to a more general process of securitization which encourages those police and surveillance activities dedicated to combating the supposed increase in crime that would result from migration more generally.

For example, in what became one of the bestselling non-fiction books in Germany in 2015, police officer Tania Kambouri wrote about the problems encountered by the German police with a variety of supposedly "foreign" groups, which included "Sinti and Roma". In a chapter entitled 'Sinti and Roma – everywhere and nowhere', she claims that, in the case of crimes committed by these groups, it is possible to 'draw conclusions on the basis of their cultural characteristics' (Kambouri 2015: 146).[5] We can observe another prominent example of this essentialist way of thinking in a speech delivered by Elke Bartels, the chief of the Duisburg police, at the annual BKA conference in 2016. At the beginning of her speech, she mentioned three groups of migrants who 'play a role' in police work (Bartels 2016: 2), one of which was 'the Roma'. They were described as forming 'a homogeneous group of migrants who live in family structures with many children' (2016: 5). Because she simultaneously described social problems such as poverty and litter, as well as crimes such as assault or theft, she established a problematical link between the so-called "poverty migration" discourse in Germany, on the one hand, and the closely related "gypsy-threat" narrative, on the other hand. What these two examples have in common is the reproduction of the manifestly racist perception of "gypsies" as a criminal threat in relation to the more general perception of "criminal migrants".

In what follows, I focus on the police narrative of the "gypsy threat" itself, on its function in police practices, and on the interrelated visual dimensions of the narrative—not only on the stereotype.

The Function of the "Gypsy Threat" Narrative for the Police

The narrative of a "gypsy threat" offers an easy way to explain crime as an "ethnic problem", and legitimizes the combating of this perceived security issue accordingly with supposedly adequate measures. There are at least two different police approaches to be analysed. The first assumes that it is constructive and helpful to fight crime through the collection of data about "the gypsies" by the police. This approach has been in use since the end of the nineteenth century, when the German police started to build databases about "gypsies". This police practice has continued, without interruption, in various forms right up to the present. While the legality of such practices is questionable, information about them is usually not available to people who do not work for the police. Sometimes the existence of these hidden practices is accidentally revealed, as was the case in 2016 when the Minister of the Interior for Saxony answered parliamentary questions about police databases. He revealed that the federal police still stored information about more than 2000 persons falling under the category of so-called 'changes residence frequently' [*'wechselt häufig Aufenthaltsort'*] (Sächsisches Staatsministerium des Innern 2016: 4), probably referring to persons who 'frequently change residence' [*'häufig wechselnder Aufenthaltsort'*], an expression that the German police have often used to disguise their references to gypsies (Stephan 2011). Civil society organizations have repeatedly tried to challenge—often with success—these problematic police practices since the 1970s. To do so, they have persistently had to investigate and protest until the institutions involved finally admitted their misconduct.[6] There are many other sources which hint at the existence of questionable police databases (End 2017). In 2013, for example, a headline of the German newspaper *Bildzeitung* stated that the 'Roma are the delinquents in seven out of ten burglaries or thefts' (Brücher and Xanthopoulos 2013). The article informed the reader that '[i]n Cologne, according to internal police statistics, 70% of the thefts from shops, pickpocketing, thefts of metal, and burglaries are committed by Romanian, Bulgarian and former Yugoslavian nationals – from Roma families'. This information suggests that internal police statistics about these matters do exist, particularly since police officers from Cologne and Berlin were quoted in similar ways in media reports from 2011 and 2012, respectively (End 2014: 266).

Another form of racialized data collection mentioned in several forms of media is the notorious practice of constructing family trees. These are based on tracing family relationships genealogically and using them in criminal investigations. This practice is especially prevalent in the case of so-called "grandchild trickery", (*Enkeltrick*) in which the perpetrator pretends to be a relative of the victims, who are usually elderly people, and misleads them in order to steal from them. Various forms of media have repeatedly reported that a police officer from Cologne, who specializes in investigating these criminal activities, has developed large family trees in order to understand better the structure of the "Roma clans" allegedly responsible for these crimes.[7] A police unit from Karlsruhe has also used a family tree, one that covers an entire wall of their office.[8] The unit presented this family tree at an international police conference (Brand 2015). The use of such genealogical data has neither been adequately disputed in police and political circles nor seriously investigated in academic ones to date, but in the light of their highly problematic historical context, questioning such police practices is a crucial first step to fundamentally analysing the kinds of racialization, securitization, and stigmatization that they entail. Romani and Sinti organizations have been criticizing these and similar police practices since the 1980s. By the mid-1980s, Romani Rose (1987: 151–52), the chairman of the Central Council of the German Sinti and Roma, had already stated that such files 'show that, by compiling family trees of Sinti and Romani families, the police have, up till now, maintained a deadly method from the times of National Socialism'.

The most common form of data collection relates to the "expertise" of individual police officers or units, which is neither stored nor printed, but only communicated internally (Feuerhelm 1987; Stephan 2011). There is some media coverage that points to the existence of this method. The award-winning documentary *The Big Theft* (2016) tells of an organized gang of pickpockets in Berlin. The supposedly "Roma" belonging of the suspects plays a significant role in this documentary, which ends with an interview with an officer from a special police unit who says: 'We have a new group once more… same ethnic group… same country… just organized differently…' (Bartocha and Sundermeyer 2016). The new investigation had only just begun, but the first thing he mentioned was the supposed belonging to the 'same ethnic group'. Many PPSs also hint at the circulation of such informal internal 'knowledge'. In one example, the PPS reads: 'The Romanians (Sinti) are an aggressive gang of beggars, currently staying in Hamburg with their parents. These persons are wanted for numerous offenses in Northern Germany' (PPS 2011b). In this case, as in others, the police investigators suggest that they have gathered information about the "Sinti/Roma" belonging of the suspects. It is therefore reasonable to suppose that this information has either been stored in files or in the form of the "expert knowledge" of individuals or a group working for the police.

In 2014, in a front-page story entitled *The burglars are coming*, the German weekly *Stern* suggested that police officers shared this 'knowledge' with witnesses. After a suspect was described as a 'Southerner' [*'Südländer'*] and an 'Indian', the police officer was quoted as telling the witness: 'We can speak openly…: gypsy' (Witzel 2014: 78).

When questioning these police practices, we have to ask why, in what ways, and on the strength of which legislation, the German police collect and store data on the basis of ethnicity. This trend is particularly worrying because practices of this kind have a dark legacy. They were already established at the time of the German Empire and were further radicalized and systematized under Nazi rule. The cases described suggest that such problematic bodies of knowledge, files, methods, and approaches still significantly shape police work today.

The second police approach consists not only of the secret collection of data but also of actively and publicly establishing and reinforcing the narrative of a general "gypsy threat". The police argue that it is their task to warn of crime risks, so another function of the PPSs, as well as of other media coverage, is to create awareness of this supposed threat among its audiences. This can be demonstrated through analysis of a typical press release about the general rise in burglaries (PPS 2011c). The release sought to raise awareness of this trend among citizens. It first claims that potential burglars spy on houses, citing the following example: 'Attentive residents in Alvesloe and Elmshorn called the police because there had been "beggars" at their doors, asking for money' (PPS 2011c). According to the witnesses, these 'beggars' seemed more interested in looking into their houses than in asking them for money. The press release states that the police checked on one so-called 'beggar' and claimed that he belonged to an 'ethnic minority' [*'ethnische Minderheit'*]. Directly after the description of this incident, the press release describes burglaries in a number of cities, as well as the goods stolen. It concludes by advising a 'healthy mistrust' of 'unknown people and cars in residential areas': 'Observations that seem suspicious should be reported to the police immediately' (PPS 2011c). This press release subtly links 'ethnic minorities' with burglaries and 'suspicious' sightings on the strength of checks performed on a single person who had not committed any crime. A press release such as this implicitly motivates people to call the police if they think they have spotted a "gypsy".

This invitation is made explicit in another example. The PPS in question describes a specific form of trickery, and draws upon racialized "knowledge" gathered by the police: 'According to police findings… the fraudsters are members of an ethnic minority from Romania' (PPS 2011d). The PPS continues: 'Therefore, the special department for cases of fraud is issuing a warning to citizens and asking for any information about where these two men, or other members of the ethnic minority, might have been seen'. As with these examples, many other PPSs end with warnings and invitations to call the police in the event of something suspicious happening. This is one of the main objectives of the PPS. The latter example explicitly spreads the message that all other PPSs—which, despite mostly reporting single, specific incidents, also communicate a generalized antigypsyist "knowledge"—implicitly convey: 'If you see a gypsy, please call the police'.

This second police approach amounts to racial profiling and in a wider context, to the discrimination against and persecution of the Roma, Sinti, and other groups and individuals regarded as "gypsies". To enact this function, it is also important for the police to tell their audience what and whom they should be looking for. This issue leads me to the next section, in which I analyse the visual regime which supports and co-constitutes the "gypsy-threat" narrative.

The Antigypsyist Visual Regime: The Apparent Visibility of Race

One starting point for my analysis of the general visual regime is Wolfgang Aschauer's (2015) work on the different ways of defining the Roma. He describes three forms of definition: the 'asocial gypsy', the 'ethnic-cultural gypsy', and the 'dark-skinned gypsy'. His approach is innovative, not so much in the way it introduces these terms but because of the argument that descriptions on the basis of racialized physical features not only still exist but are also the only way in which a liberal anti-discrimination approach can still mark an essentially "Roma belonging" while simultaneously avoiding ascriptions of social behaviour: if signifiers of "poverty" or "culture" are avoided, features like hair colour and complexion are the only characteristics by which "Roma" otherness can be marked (see also Surdu 2016). Irina Bohn, Franz Hamburger, and Kerstin Rock's (1993) study of articles from local media based on PPSs shows—interestingly—that the German police use each of Aschauer's definitions. They have analysed the characteristics of 'ethnic identification' found in their sample. Apart from the explicit mentioning of the Roma among the characteristics used, they found 'features of appearance' (both physical and clothing), 'features of group relation', 'features of lifestyle', 'features of behaviour' and 'features in specific situations' (1993: 176–78). On a theoretical level, we have to understand that this process of racializing groups and their definitions by means of physical features on the one hand, and social features on the other, might take new forms, depending on the time, place, and context, but this racial attribution does not imply that the process itself is new.

PPSs usually combine several of the features that Bohn, Hamburger and Rock (1993: 176) mention: 'These features can, in part, already be sufficient for a clear-cut ethnic identification. More frequently, however, we have observed a combination of several of these categories'. Commonly used examples of physical features are 'dark hair' or 'dark skin', also implicitly communicated via the description of 'Southerner' [*'Südländer'*] or 'Southern-European' [*'Südeuropäer'*]. In a press release from 2011, for example, labels of this kind have been combined:

> The couple could be described as follows: the woman was about 30–35 years old, a Southerner, apparently Sinti or Roma; the man was also about 30–35 years old, dark-skinned, also apparently Sinti or Roma. The alleged customs officers were described by the pensioner as men aged 30–35 years, with dark skin, apparently Sinti or Roma, both about 180 cm tall, and wearing black leather jackets. (PPS 2011e)

Similar descriptions can be found in media other than PPSs. For example, the *Stern* article mentioned includes similar descriptions. After the article has stated that several images were shown to a witness, she is supposed to have said: 'No, these are all Eastern Europeans. Don't you have any darker guys?' (Witzel 2014: 78) Such problematizations in police discourse have been influenced in at least two different ways by even more general visual regimes. First, labelling persons or groups as "black-", "dark-" or "brown-skinned" in police discourses is central to a long tradition of constructing and visualizing "gypsiness" which has prevailed since early modern times (Reuter 2014). Secondly, "otherness", as well as "evilness" and "deviance", has more generally been linked to non-whiteness (Rommelspacher 2009). In the case of "Roma" visualization, Aschauer argues, the focus on complexion has become even more important, as anti-racist policies do not want to reproduce racist assumptions based on supposedly specific "Roma" behaviour. Yet, according to his argument, since the reference to skin tone is required to articulate a regime of "otherness" and to legitimize "Roma" policies more particularly, the police have continued to reproduce such ambiguous forms of biological racialization (Aschauer 2015).

While Aschauer's analysis concentrates primarily on the role of skin tone and complexion, Bohn, Hamburger, and Rock also emphasize the importance of physical features such as hairstyles and clothing, something that is also relevant to my examination of PPSs. The references to "colourful skirts" [*bunte Röcke*], for instance, relate to a specific legacy of antigypsyist visuals, and, in PPS, they are usually combined with other racializing references. In a press release of May 2011, the female suspects are described as having 'deep black' hair and wearing 'colourful skirts' (PPS 2011f). Another PPS has already described the suspect in its title as wearing 'a colourful skirt' (PPS 2011g). The reference to "colourful skirts" alone is sufficient to trigger the image of a "gypsy woman". This underlines the racializing power of such images. Interestingly, the German Press Council has criticized the use of such qualifications. When, in 2009, a local news outlet wrote that they were not allowed to mention the ethnic background of suspects and wanted to use a police reference to their 'preference for colourful dress' instead (Borchard 2009), the Council reprimanded the journal for having hinted at the ethnic background of the suspects.

PPSs often combine different visual elements—physical appearance, clothing, hairstyle—reproducing an identifiable stereotype within a larger antigypsyist visual regime. One hairstyle regularly referred to in this way is a "bun" [*Dutt*]. This is an example of a visual description that is not part of a traditional "gypsy" image but an additional element, supposedly deriving from the intermingled context of "poverty migration" in which women with buns or headscarves have been regularly portrayed. It has, in any case, become a specific element of the visual police regime. In 2011, for example, references to suspects with a "bun" were used 25 times in the PPS of *News Aktuell*. With one exception, these references articulated a visual regime of a "gypsy threat" in which several qualifications—such as 'Sinti and Roma', 'traveller circles', 'travelling perpetrators', 'southern European', 'south-east European', 'dark complexion', and 'black', 'brown', 'dark brown', 'dark' or 'dark-blond hair'—were combined to establish a police discourse on property crimes—mainly trickery, burglaries and shoplifting (see End 2014: 256–59). Importantly, many of the features of appearance mentioned in these releases are highly gendered and visualize and racialize "gypsy women" in a way that is characteristic of more general and widespread antigypsyist visual representations of "women" and "children" (Reuter 2014: 105–10, 314).

Bohn, Hamburger and Rock (1993) describe three further categories of ethnic identification: 'features of belonging together', 'features of lifestyle' and 'features of behaviour'. The first two can be described more generally as supposedly social characteristics. PPSs regularly mention features such as "begging", "fortune-telling", "travelling", or "extended families" [*Großfamilien*], which further help to produce antigypsyist visual regimes. Just as is the case with physical features, these social characteristics themselves do not necessarily establish a clear-cut antigypsyist picture, nevertheless, in combination with other tactics, their use in police discourses usually supports the reinforcement of "gypsy" stereotypes. For example, the press release with 'colourful skirt' in its title includes references to a 'Southern' suspect who is described as a self-proclaimed 'fortune-teller' (PPS 2011g). Another revealing press release begins with the sentence 'Today at about 11:10, a group of five people, obviously members of an extended family, entered the post office…' (PPS 2011h). Since five people cannot 'obviously' belong to an 'extended family', this description is clearly loaded with meaning, and relies on traditional antigypsyist stereotypes. Such descriptions are not included because the police imagine that "extended families" can easily be identified; rather, these qualifications serve as keywords to evoke the whole visual regime constructed around the "gypsy threat".

The use of the final category mentioned by Bohn, Hamburger and Rock—'features of behaviour'—differs from that of their other categories. Whereas the latter build on broader and external contexts, the former category belongs largely to internal police discourses. Its use is the result of numerous police and related media discourses in which a specific local or contextual classification of crime has already been clearly established. Such a classification is usually supported and confirmed by police databases, genealogical data, and informal knowledge (see above). Consequently, building on such classifications, PPSs can avoid any explicit or encoded racialization while, nonetheless, effectively communicating the narrative of the "gypsy threat", and thus articulating the related visual regime:

> The reference to a specific 'group of perpetrators' which comes about here can be attributed to the structure and content of the underlying police press releases… As was already suspected, certain specific features of the crime and offender, previously labelled as typical, make possible a clear and unambiguous ethnic categorization of the suspects. It can be assumed that such a process of re-identification can occur on the basis of those press reports in which, though there is no direct ethnic labelling of the suspected offenders, certain content provided by the police is presented. (Bohn et al. 1993: 137)

To put it differently, after a period in which specific crimes, modes of procedure, or contexts have been explicitly racialized, it has become possible to skip such explicit labelling, although the racialized categorization continues to be communicated in the relevant circuits. This is clearly illustrated in the reporting of the so-called "grandson's trick" [*Enkeltrick*]. After police authorities had stressed for several years and on various occasions that this offence was being committed exclusively by "Roma", there was no further need to reproduce this racialization in new press releases in order to communicate that the perpetrators were "Roma", in order to rearticulate the narrative of a "gypsy threat" (End 2014: 267–71).

The examples above have demonstrated that the modes of crime associated with "gypsies" include several other forms of trickery. In some cases, the police have even invented specific terms to denote them, such as the "note trick" [*Zettel-Trick*] or the "glass of water trick" [*Glas-Wasser-Trick*]. A PPS from 2014 shows how such generalizations work in practice. It starts with a warning abouts the mentioned tricks in general and then describes a specific case. The suspects are described as 'all having a southern European appearance' and as 'Sinti or Roma' (PPS 2014). After describing the individual suspects as such, the PPS ends with an extensive general warning and description of all kinds of trickery, thus establishing a link between these crimes and the 'Sinti or Roma' mentioned at the beginning.

Bohn, Hamburger, and Rock (1993: 176) have argued that a final ethnic identification occurs through the mention of ethnicity itself. This also happens regularly in PPSs. These press releases usually describe a single crime involving one or more suspects or offenders and then explicitly mention that these supposedly all belong to a group of "Roma" or "Sinti". In a press release of April 2016, the police department of Frankfurt am Main mentioned a suspect and added that, according to a witness, they 'may have been a Sinti and Roma [sic]' (PPS 2016). This is a standard example of such a use, in which the police quote witnesses who claim that the suspects might have been "Sinti", "Roma", or "Sinti and Roma". There is often no explanation of why the witnesses believe this. Such PPSs implicitly suggest that it is possible to recognize "Sinti and Roma" by sight alone: 'Description of the offenders according to the claimant: both women looked like Sinti' (PPS 2011i). The idea that "Sinti" are easily recognizable by sight is based on the established visual regime of the "gypsy", obviously familiar to witnesses.

But it is not only witnesses who enact these forms of racialization, police forces themselves do something similar: 'The suspects spoke German without an accent, but potentially originate from circles of Sinti and Roma' (PPS 2011j). In this press release, the police themselves make the assessment of 'circles of Sinti and Roma'. Moreover, in this example, it is obvious that 'Sinti and Roma' is a signifier associated with "strangers", or non-Germans, as they are described in opposition to the German language. The idea of a 'circle' further adds up to this 'othering', establishing the idea of a separated world in which "the Sinti and Roma" live. Furthermore, this use suggests that this entire 'circle' is somehow related to crime (see also van Baar, Chap. 8, this volume). By mentioning "Roma", or "Sinti and Roma", the police conjure up the entire, previously established visual regime. This regime even seems to be somehow independent of individual examples as the following illustrates:

> Description of the offenders according to the claimant: both women looked like Sinti. 1.: straight blonde hair, about 20 to 30 years old, wearing trousers. Clothes were light-coloured. She was about 165cm tall. The face was rather longish. 2.: black curly shoulder-length hair, she was about 35–40 years old, dark skin-type, broad face and dark clothing. (PPS 2011i)

This statement is particularly remarkable as it includes descriptions of two different women who have not a single feature in common; in fact, they are described as exact opposites, but both nevertheless 'looked like Sinti'. This is a striking illustration of racializing mechanisms: racism has to be understood as a worldview that does not care about logical rigour or the need for self-reflection (Horkheimer and Adorno 1989: 196–209). Instead, it produces racist images—such as the typical appearance of "a gypsy"—which are widely accepted and understood, even though the actual description of the physical features of the suspects does nothing to help the establishment of such an image. The journalist Claudia Schumann quotes unnamed officers in a comment about the police mentioning 'the gypsy in police reports': 'Everyone can imagine a gypsy, the officers argue' (Schuhmann 2013). Thus, the antigypsyist visual regime has been widely disseminated, while, at the same time, it allows for huge flexibility and has the potential to widen, re-articulate, or actualize the definition of "gypsy" in order to incorporate new elements.

Code Words

A similarly flexible mechanism can be observed in the case of the code words that the police have introduced in response to protests from civil society organizations, especially the Central Council of German Sinti and

Roma in Heidelberg. These protests have led to a new type of police practice aimed at avoiding or circumventing accusations of racialization and racism. This practice can be understood as an encoding of the stereotypical terms that were previously in use. The practice had already started in the 1950s, when the German criminal police re-activated their so-called 'traveller divisions' (Rose 1987: 31–32). In those days, the decision-makers chose not to rename those police units publicly as 'gypsy divisions'. Such encoding continues to exist in German PPSs to this day. The strategy is aimed at communicating the same content to the recipients, while avoiding sensitive terminology and reducing the chance of possible allegations of racial discrimination. The majority of the recipients are journalists and other people who regularly read PPSs, and they have accordingly also become experienced in decoding them.

Apart from the use of the term "traveller" [*Landfahrer*] in police databases, as well as in other police communications, there are other codes that have historically been used to replace the explicit use of the term "gypsy" and continue to do so. In contemporary German PPSs, for example, the following labels are often used for administrative purposes: "daytime domestic burglars" [*Tageswohnungseinbrecher* or *TWE*]; "mobile ethnic minority" [*mobile ethnische Minderheit* or *MEM*] and those who "frequently change residence" [*häufig wechselnder Aufenthaltsort* or *HWAO*] (see Feuerhelm 1987; Stephan 2011). Following the official discontinuation of the use of the term 'traveller divisions' in the criminal investigation offices of the Federal Republic in the 1970s, various files that included one of these new labels were created to avoid, but nevertheless communicate, the signifier "gypsy". But even though the term "traveller" has also been discredited in administrative circles and databases, it is still in use in PPSs, as the following demonstrates: 'Bad Wildungen–Hundsdorf: Cash money stolen from an office – silver Mercedes with travellers flees' (PPS 2011k). The release continues: 'The quartet can be localized in the traveller circle'. This is a clear example of the avoidance of the term "gypsy" while communicating its meaning nonetheless.

The encoding *MEM* has been used in files and PPSs alike. 'According to witnesses, the wanted person could belong to a mobile ethnic minority' (PPS 2011l), reads just such a press release. This case is an example of police personnel who have translated the accounts of their witnesses. It is highly unlikely that the witnesses themselves described the perpetrators as members of a 'mobile ethnic minority'. Perhaps, the witnesses used the terms "gypsy" or "Sinti and Roma" and the police changed their statement to make it compatible with a norm of supposed political correctness. The police do something similar in the following release: 'According to the description given by the businessman, the persons appeared to belong to a non-sedentary ethnic minority' (PPS 2011m). In addition to the translation and the variation, this release is yet another example of how the police explicitly claim that "gypsies" have a specific appearance and accordingly articulate a specific visual regime of "criminal gypsies". The *MEM* encoding also illustrates well how such codes have evolved over time. As *MEM* became more readily understandable, a new and shorter version of the encoding could also be established: Descriptions, such as 'the victim of the robbery described [the perpetrators] as members of an ethnic minority' (PPS 2011n) or 'he happened to be a member of an ethnic minority' (PPS 2011c), are based on the establishment of the *MEM* code while simultaneously transforming it yet again.

The introduction and use of such ambiguous police labels can be seen as resulting in part from protests in Germany's post-war Roma and Sinti civil rights movement against institutional racism. More recently, it has become politically less and less acceptable to mention ethnicity explicitly in official police sources. In 2007, for example, during an examination of the national minority laws, officials of the state of Baden-Württemberg, in answer to questions from the Council of Europe, stated that '[o]f course, the terms "mobile ethnic minority" *["mobile ethnische Minderheit"]*, "gypsies" [*"Zigeuner"*], "traveller" [*"Landfahrer"*] or Sinti and Roma are not used in public reports of the police forces' (Advisory Committee on the Framework Convention for the Protection of National Minorities 2006). While it is clear that not all police press officers have implemented this political decision, this case nevertheless illustrates that the political authorities have been put under pressure. At the same time, there is an obvious lack of self-control in police institutions. Up to now, there has been no office or ombudsperson that has taken up the task of controlling police compliance with their own standards of non-discrimination. Sinti and Romani organizations are spending significant resources simply to guarantee that police forces act according to their own rules, not to mention their political efforts to combat the narrative of the "gypsy threat" within and outside police institutions. Most notably, the Central Council of the German Sinti and Roma in Heidelberg has criticized these and similar media mechanisms since the 1980s (Rose 1987; Zentralrat Deutscher Sinti und Roma 2010).

Conclusion

My analysis of several German police press releases shows that, to the present day, German police authorities exercise biased, racialized approaches to Sinti, Roma, and other groups and individuals whom they perceive as "gypsy-like". These approaches are based on the narrative of a "gypsy threat" that results in practices of securitizing those perceived as "gypsies". Common practices include the continued collection of ethnic data in various forms, as well as warnings to the general public of the alleged threat of "gypsy crime". This narrative is communicated through police press releases, but also through, for example, media interviews with police officers or spokespersons. The police press releases not only narrate a "gypsy threat" directly but also indirectly and more implicitly, by means of using alternative labels such as "Sinti" or "traveller", or descriptions of physical appearance and specific encodings that serve to mask direct instances of racialization.

I have also argued that this narrative is interwoven with a specific visual police regime of the "criminal gypsy", a sub-regime of the more general visual regime of "the gypsy". I have shown how this regime is aimed at a form of visual recognition of "the criminal gypsy", further supporting practices of racial profiling and social exclusion. Thus, not only has there been a continuation of practices of institutional discrimination but the German police have actively contributed to the re-articulation and perpetuation of a specific visual regime of "criminal gypsies" at the societal level.

Romani and Sinti organizations have opposed these discriminating police practices for a number of decades, but German police institutions have time and again developed new ways and mechanisms to maintain the narrative of a "gypsy threat" and its interrelated visual regime.

Notes

1. I put the term "gypsy" in double quotation marks here because I consider it to be a signifier of a racist construction; it is not used to describe real human beings. Throughout this chapter, this form of quotation is used for other signifiers of racist constructions as well. It is also used for self-designations, such as "Roma", if they are used as signifiers of racist constructions. This use is also in accordance with the practice of those movements in English-speaking countries in which some self-identify as 'Gypsies' and write the term with a capital G; see, for example, the terminology proposed by the National Federation of Gypsy Liaison Groups (Spencer 2012).

2. I use the term discourse in Foucauldian tradition as a description of a specific but flexible formation of ideology, knowledge and practices.
3. All translations from the German to the English are the work of the author.
4. Police press statements are quoted with the abbreviation PPS. For more detailed information, see the list of primary sources.
5. I want to thank my colleague Tobias von Borcke for making me aware of this publication.
6. Huub van Baar (2014: 38) remarks on something similar in the case of the French database "MENS" (*"minorités éthniques non sedentarisés"* ["non sedentary ethnic minorities"]) which was used illegally by the French police authorities to store information about "gypsies". This practice was discovered in 2010.
7. For the Cologne police officer, see End (2014: 269–71). Recently, van Baar (2014) and Kott (2014) have discussed similar cases of the use of family trees by the Dutch and Swedish police respectively.
8. This police unit in Karlsruhe has proudly presented its family tree in numerous TV documentaries (see, e.g., Brand 2015; Heise and Lehberger 2013).

Primary Sources

Bartels, E. 2016. Kriminalitätsentwicklung aus regionaler Perspektive – aktuelle Brennpunkte und ihre Bewältigung. Am Beispiel Duisburg. Available at https://www.bka.de/SharedDocs/Downloads/DE/Publikationen/Herbsttagungen/2016/herbsttagung2016BartelsLangfassung.pdf; jsessionid=F4BA8C45D9BB1C17763C2F2C536DF14A.live2292?__blob=publicationFile&v=3. Accessed 2 Aug 2017.

Bartocha, A., and O. Sundermeyer. 2016. Der große Klau. Die Mafia der Taschendiebe, *RBB*, March 22.

Borchard, H. 2009. Betrug im Namen der Tafel, *Offenbach Post*, August 20. Available at http://www.op-online.de/nachrichten/langen/betrug-namen-tafel-448759.html. Accessed 2 Aug 2017.

Brand, S. 2015. Bei Anruf Betrug. Die fiese Masche mit dem Enkeltrick, *SWR*, May 27.

Brücher, J., and G. Xanthopoulos. 2013. In Köln erwischt: Bei 7 von 10 Diebstählen und Einbrüchen sind Roma die Täter. *Bild.de*, March 6. Available at http://www.bild.de/regional/koeln/einbruch/bei-7-von-10-diebstaehlen-und-einbruechen-sind-roma-die-taeter-29386148.bild.html. Accessed 2 Aug 2017.

Heise, T., and R. Lehberger. 2013. Bei Anruf Betrug: Die Hintermänner der Enkeltrick-Masche, report for Spiegel-TV. *RTL*, December 8.

Kambouri, T. 2015. *Deutschland im Blaulicht*. München: Piper.

News Aktuell. 2014. NA-Presseportal. Die Recherche-Plattform von News Aktuell. Available at http://www.presseportal.de/polizeipresse/. Accessed 1 Feb 2014.

Polizei Baden-Württemberg. 2012. Presseportal Der Polizei Baden-Württemberg. Available at http://presse.polizei-bwl.de. Accessed 1 Aug 2012.

Polizei Bayern. 2014. Pressearchiv Der Polizei Bayern. Available at http://www.polizei.bayern.de/news/presse/archiv/index.html. Accessed 7 Apr 2014.

PPS. 2011a. Organisierter Taschendiebstahl: Kriminalpolizei Ludwigsburg führt bundesweites Ermittlungsverfahren, joint press release, State Prosecutor's Office Stuttgart and Police Directorate Ludwigsburg, December 16.

———. 2011b. Aggressive Rosenverkäufer, Polizeidirektion Itzehoe, Itzehoe-Heide, press release, September 21.

———. 2011c. Zahl der Dämmerungseinbrüche nimmt zu, Polizeidirektion Bad Segeberg, press release, November 17.

———. 2011d. Warnhinweis der Kriminalpolizei: Trickbetrüger unterwegs Bad Homburg und Kreisgebiet, Polizeipräsidium Westhessen – PD Hochtaunus, press release, July 29.

———. 2011e. Dreiste Bande betrügt Rentner – Polizei warnt vor Trickbetrügern an der Haustür, Polizei Bielefeld, press release, February 3.

———. 2011f. Tageswohnungseinbrecher waren unterwegs, Kreispolizeibehörde Rhein-Kreis Neuss, press release, May 19.

———. 2011g. "Wer sah Trickdiebin im bunten Rock?" Pressebericht des Polizeipräsidiums Südosthessen vom 05.09.2011, Polizeipräsidium Südosthessen-Offenbach, press release, September 5.

———. 2011h. Trickdiebstahl in Postagentur in Windberg, Polizei Mönchengladbach, press release, November 15.

———. 2011i. Einbrecher und dreiste Diebinnen, Kreispolizeibehörde Märkischer Kreis, press release, November 8.

———. 2011j. iPod und Bargeld aus Auto gestohlen, Polizei Korbach, press release, July 12.

———. 2011k. Bargeld aus Büro gestohlen – Silberner Mercedes mit Landfahrern geflüchtet, Polizei Korbach, press release, October 25.

———. 2011l. 60-jähriger Kradfahrer schwer verletzt; Rollerfahrer leicht verletzt; Brandstiftung?; Geschädigter setzt Belohnung aus; Einbrecher flüchtet ohne Beute u.a., Polizeiinspektion Cuxhaven-Wesermarsch, press release, May 25.

———. 2011m. Dreiste Diebe im Schmuckgeschäft, Kreispolizeibehörde Euskirchen, press release, August 30.

———. 2011n. Einbrüche; Graffiti-Täter ermittelt; Diebstahl im Schuhhaus; Kabeldiebstahl; Pavillon a.d. Gleisen; Bäume abgesägt; Führerschein in weiter Ferne; Ladendiebe gesucht; Vermisstensuche mit Polizeihubschrauber, Polizei Marburg-Biedenkopf, press release, July 26.

———. 2013. "Miese Betrugsmasche"; Täterduo erlangt mehrere tausend Euro Bargeld einer jungen Lüneburgerin; Polizei warnt vor sog. "Budscho-Phänomen", Polizeiinspektion Lüneburg, press release, July 1.
———. 2014. Trickdiebstahl eskalierte zum versuchten Raub, Polizei Mettmann, press release, January 16.
———. 2016. Handtaschenraub, Polizeipräsidium Frankfurt am Main, press release, April 20.
Schuhmann, C. 2013. Standpunkt: Der Zigeuner im Polizeibericht. *Main-Post*, October 15.
Witzel, H. 2014. Alle dreieinhalb Minuten. *Stern* 29: 74–82.

References

Advisory Committee on the Framework Convention for the Protection of National Minorities. 2006. Comments of the Government of Germany on the Second Opinion of the Advisory Committee on the Implementation of the Framework Convention for the Protection of National Minorities in Germany. Available at https://rm.coe.int/CoERMPublicCommonSearchServices/DisplayDCTMContent?documentId=090000168008f515. Accessed 2 Aug 2017.
Aschauer, W. 2015. Merkmale und Funktionen des Antiziganismus am Beispiel Ungarns. In *Antiziganismus. Soziale und historische Dimensionen von "Zigeuner"-Stereotypen*, ed. Dokumentations- und Kulturzentrum Deutscher Sinti und Roma, 110–129. Heidelberg: Dokumentations- und Kulturzentrum Deutscher Sinti und Roma.
Bohn, I., F. Hamburger, and K. Rock. 1993. *Die Konstruktion Der Differenz. Diskurse Über Roma Und Sinti in Der Lokalpresse*, unpublished report to the German Research Foundation.
Bonillo, M. 2001. *'Zigeunerpolitik' im Deutschen Kaiserreich 1871–1918*. Frankfurt am Main: Peter Lang.
Brähler, E., O. Decker, and J. Kiess, eds. 2016. *Die enthemmte Mitte: Autoritäre und rechtsextreme Einstellung in Deutschland*. Gießen: Psychosozial.
Busch, I. 2011. Wanderleben revisited: "Zigeuner"-Mythos und Repräsentation von Roma im National Geographic Magazin. In *Inszenierung des Fremden: fotografische Darstellung von Sinti und Roma im Kontext der historischen Bildforschung*, ed. S. Peritore and F. Reuter, 223–258. Heidelberg: Dokumentations- und Kulturzentrum Deutscher Sinti und Roma.
End, M. 2014. *Antiziganismus in der Deutschen Öffentlichkeit. Strategien und Mechanismen medialer Kommunikation*. Heidelberg: Dokumentations- und Kulturzentrum Deutscher Sinti und Roma.
———. 2015. Comment on Jan Selling, "The Conceptual Gypsy. Reconsidering the Swedish Case and the General". In *Antiziganism. What's in a Word?* ed. J. Selling et al., 132–136. Newcastle upon Tyne: Cambridge Scholars Publishing.

———. 2017. Antiziganistische Ermittlungsansätze in Polizei- und Sicherheitsbehörden. Heidelberg: Zentralrat Deutscher Sinti und Roma. Available at http://zentralrat.sintiundroma.de/download/6809. Accessed 3 Apr 2018.

Feuerhelm, W. 1987. *Polizei und 'Zigeuner'*. Stuttgart: Enke.

Fings, K. 2008. "Rasse: Zigeuner". Sinti und Roma im Fadenkreuz von Kriminologie und Rassenhygiene 1933–1945. In *'Zigeuner' und Nation*, ed. H. Uerlings and I.-K. Patrut, 273–309. Frankfurt/Main: Peter Lang.

Greußing, F. 1979. Das offizielle Verbrechen der zweiten Verfolgung. In *In Auschwitz vergast, bis heute verfolgt*, ed. T. Zülch, 192–198. Reinbek at Hamburg: Rowohlt.

Horkheimer, M., and Th.W. Adorno. 1989 [1944]. *Dialektik der Aufklärung*. Frankfurt am Main: Fischer.

Kott, M. 2014. It Is in Their DNA: Swedish Police, Structural Antiziganism and the Registration of Romanis. In *When Stereotype Meets Prejudice: Antiziganism in European Societies*, ed. T. Agarin, 45–75. Stuttgart: Ibidem.

Lucassen, L. 1996. *Zigeuner: Die Geschichte Eines Polizeilichen Ordnungsbegriffes in Deutschland 1700–1945*. Köln: Böhlau.

Patrut, I.-K. 2014. *Phantasma Nation: 'Zigeuner' und Juden als Grenzfiguren des 'Deutschen' (1770–1920)*. Würzburg: Königshausen & Neumann.

Reuter, F. 2014. *Der Bann des Fremden. Die fotografische Konstruktion des 'Zigeuners'*. Göttingen: Wallstein.

Rommelspacher, B. 2009. Was Ist eigentlich Rassismus? In *Rassismuskritik. Band 1*, ed. C. Melter and P. Mecheril, 25–38. Schwalbach: Wochenschau.

Rose, R. 1987. *Bürgerrechte für Sinti und Roma*. Heidelberg: Zentralrat Deutscher Sinti und Roma.

———. 2008. Die Aufarbeitung der Geschichte des Nationalsozialismus als Chance für die rechtsstaatliche Behandlung von Minderheiten. In *Das Bundeskriminalamt stellt sich seiner Geschichte*, ed. Bundeskriminalamt, 125–142. Köln: Luchterhand.

Sächsisches Staatsministerium des Innern. 2016. Kleine Anfrage des Abgeordneten Valentin Lippmann, Fraktion BÜNDNIS 90/DIE GRÜNEN. Drs.-Nr.: 6/4861. Thema: Personengebundene Hinweise (PHW) in polizeilichen Datenbanken. April 29. Available at http://edas.landtag.sachsen.de/viewer.aspx?dok_nr=9306&dok_art=Drs&leg_per=6&pos_dok=0&dok_id=undefined. Accessed 2 Aug 2017.

Spencer, S. 2012. To be a Gypsy and not be a "gypsy". That Is the Question. Available at http://www.nationalgypsytravellerfederation.org/uploads/3/7/5/2/37524461/to_be_a_gypsy_and_not_be_a_gypsy_that_is_the_question.pdf. Accessed 2 Aug 2017.

Stephan, A. 2011. Das BKA und der Umgang mit Sinti und Roma – von "Zigeunerspezialisten" in der Amtsleitung und "Sprachregelungen" bis zur

Sachbearbeiterstelle "ZD 43-22". In *Schatten der Vergangenheit*, ed. I. Baumann et al., 249–285. Köln: Luchterhand.

Surdu, M. 2016. *Those who Count. Expert Practices of Roma Classification*. Budapest: CEU Press.

van Baar, H. 2014. The Emergence of a Reasonable Anti-Gypsyism in Europe. In *When Stereotype Meets Prejudice: Antiziganism in European Societies*, ed. T. Agarin, 27–43. Stuttgart: Ibidem.

Wagner, P. 2007. Kriminalprävention qua Massenmord. Die gesellschaftsbiologische Konzeption der NS-Kriminalpolizei und ihre Bedeutung für die Zigeunerverfolgung. In *Zwischen Erziehung und Vernichtung*, ed. M. Zimmermann, 379–392. Stuttgart: Steiner.

Zentralrat Deutscher Sinti und Roma, ed. 2010. *Diskriminierungsverbot und Freiheit der Medien*. Heidelberg: Zentralrat Deutscher Sinti und Roma.

Zimmermann, M. 1996. *Rassenutopie und Genozid. Die nationalsozialistische 'Lösung der Zigeunerfrage'*. Hamburg: Christians.

CHAPTER 13

Roma Securitization and De-securitization in Habsburg Europe

Marija Dalbello

Central Europe has been a theatre for Roma securitization for centuries.[1] As a concept of shared history rather than a firmly bounded territory, Central Europe provides a site for studying the particular climate of insecurity associated with strangers and minorities—Roma minorities in particular—in a historical perspective. In the Habsburg realm, for strangers to be recognized as being 'safe' or having value, they had to belong to a *Volk*—a people—and be productive subjects of the Empire. The Danubian Roma were constructed as subjects of the Habsburg Empire through a discourse of security rather than through their contribution as connectors in an Empire built upon migrations and settlements or as representing the itinerant links between the East and the West. As a nomadic people, they were perceived as unsafe outsiders or criminalized through assignations of vagrancy and theft. I explore the image and the inter-texts in a broader

---

The author would like to thank Anselm Spoerri for reading drafts of this manuscript and the three editors of this volume for their invaluable feedback, which greatly strengthened the argument. Earlier versions of some of the arguments have appeared previously in presentations (Dalbello 2010, 2015).

M. Dalbello (✉)
Rutgers University, New Brunswick, NJ, USA
e-mail: dalbello@rutgers.edu

explanatory discourse of securitization following Lene Hansen's work on visual securitization (2011b) and the normative-political potential of de-securitization (2011a). The practices of visual securitization by which the normative securitization discourse was being challenged and enacted in practices of securitization and de-securitization reveal how images participated in the public constitution of threats and how a securitizing actor engaged visuality to produce a response in the discourses which defined the public sphere. The portrayal and stigmatization of the Roma as vagrants can be interpreted in the context of the development of capitalism and in the attempts of the state to discipline its workforce through subordination to measures intended to ensure their control and sedentarization, masked by claims of insecurity for the non-Roma.

Securitization originates from mechanisms which emphasize insecurity, identify threat, and organize thinking and the material consequences by which the reduction of threat can be achieved. In this model, de-securitization is the disappearance of the problematizing of the phenomena involved in terms of security threats. By contrast, diffusion of threat, conditional to it being able to generate a dialogic reciprocity with those who socially embody a threat, is a strategy distinct from the complete removal of threat, and the implications of this distinction can inform current securitization policies. The diffusion, rather than the removal of threat, and the dismantling of the conceptual and actual mechanisms of securitization, relies on building trust through an empathetic outlook or by adhering to mutually beneficial 'truces'. Diffusion is thus a constructivist process in the realm of epistemology, empathy, and policy, involving co-construction of the state and the citizens.

Dating from the end of the nineteenth century, the historical case presented in this chapter explores an argument around de-securitization in the sense of diffusion, rather than removal of threat; specifically, I follow the trajectory of 'change through stabilization' (Hansen 2011a: 539–540) as a core strategy of Archduke Joseph Karl Ludwig of Austria (1833–1905), the main 'de-securitization' actor in this historical case. He was a member of the House of Habsburg and a scholar of the Romani language. First, I show how the construction of Roma as the Volk (people) can be seen as a mechanism to start a process of de-securitization that meant presenting the condition of their becoming subjects of the Habsburg Empire by analysing an entry that he wrote for a popular illustrated encyclopaedia, *Die österreichisch-ungarische Monarchie in Wort und Bild*.[2] Next, I focus on the reformist project of the Roma settlement on his family estate, a practice of de-securitization enacted by this member of the social and intellectual elites, who was embedded in the international network of Orientalist scholars of the Gypsy Lore Society (GLS) and in a circle of Central European philologists.

I follow W.J.T. Mitchell (2005) in my reading of visuality. He suggested that visual culture cannot be limited to the visual but engages a range of sensory responses. Lene Hansen (2011b: 51) points to the inter-textual and inter-visual constitution of visual securitization for public consumption. Accordingly, for this author, visuality encompasses representational elements circulated in texts, symbols, and actions, as well as the sites of the production and consumption of representations, in particular all relations that control visibility or invisibility and which have the power to shape organizing frames and modes of seeing. This case is rooted at the nexus of security and visuality, but it exceeds the graphic nature of representations and the optical field.

Securitization Practices

In a long history of nomadism and state power, the Roma have been shaped as a 'historical' people in Europe through practices of securitization. Their assimilation, expulsion, or extermination were linked to these constructions. Although the dominant strategies of managing the 'threat' of the Roma as subjects in Europe's various imperial realms varied, they continued to define the marginality of the Roma as subjects in the authoritarian Eastern European socialist states that succeeded them (Barany 2002: 354–355). Nomadism, including the mass movements of workers, has continued to be of particular concern for state power in high modernity. Judith Okely, writing about the British Roma, suggests that it was the 'specific ethnic boundaries' tied to the 'ideology of travelling' maintained by the Roma that were at the core of struggle in which they were 'seen as lawless' as opposed to the attempts of the state to discipline them as 'wage-labour in the occupations approved by the state' in the service of a capitalist workforce (1983: 34–36). In turn, the repressive state 'has attempted to control, disperse, convert or destroy them' (1983: 238). Others (Barany 2002; Lucassen et al. 1998) have shown how the modern state throughout Europe has exercised the stigmatization of the Roma minorities through governmental policies. Historical documents mapping the migrations of European Roma have consistently shown that the Roma have been treated as a threat historically and across geographical contexts, with documented instances of their criminalization and persecution (Barany 2002; Lucassen et al. 1998). The 'solutions' for the control of nomadism, and the attitudes towards minorities and religions, have varied across Europe and its Empires.

Habsburg Policies and 'Common' Securitization Strategies

Charles VI's (1711–1740) decree was aimed at the extermination of the Roma within his domain. His successor, Maria Theresa (1740–1780), issued four 'Gypsy decrees', the purpose of which was forcible sedentarization (Barany 2002) through measures of assimilation. For instance, she forbade the use of the term 'Gypsy' and decreed that they should be renamed 'New Peasants'. Furthermore, she ordered the Roma to settle and pay taxes; she forbade them to use their own language, to leave towns without official permission, or to marry other Roma, and she ordered the separation of Romani children from their parents in order to educate them in state schools and foster homes (ibid.: 93–95). Maria Theresa's son and successor, Joseph II (1780–1790), instituted a system of 'monthly reports on Gypsy lifestyles from local authorities, permitting the Roma to visit fairs only in special circumstances, and banning nomadism and traditional Gypsy occupations' and 'emphasized improvements in Gypsy education and health and directed the Roma to attend religious (Roman Catholic) services weekly' (ibid.: 94). These policies framed the attitudes towards the Roma even in the century which succeeded the assimilationist policies of the absolutist rulers. Aimed at civilizing the 'savage' Roma through education, containment policies do not present an image of a 'gemütlich' Empire. Zoltan Barany (2002: 94–95) views these crude efforts at social engineering as bearing typological similarities to the strategies 'of the East European social states two centuries later… of expulsion and deportation' as a common strategy.

These policies were aimed at making the Roma imperial subjects and removing the idea of 'threat' by invisibilizing them through an organized programme of forced assimilation. Instead of deporting the Gypsies to the colonies, as did other European monarchs, the Habsburg rulers articulated 'rationalist' approaches intended for the improvement of the 'Gypsy problem' by making them conform to the ideals of an absolute monarchy (ibid.: 93) and focused on the strategy of elevating the Roma 'into the ranks of the "civilized" citizens' in order for them to be 'useful to the state' (Bright 1818: 540). Royal edicts were often rationalized as appeasing anti-Roma sentiment among local populations. In reality, the practices and treatment of the Roma were pluralistic, internal migrations building on the possibilities of economic cooperation between the Roma and the non-Roma, with the local population relying on a range of services and products which the Roma were able to provide through their crafts (Mayerhofer 1988).

Representations: Stereotypes and Their Role in the Visual Securitization of the 'Gypsy'

The securitization discourse manifests itself in the realm of representations and traditions, especially in the persistence of a 'Gypsy' stereotype, and set of Gypsy characters in some Central European folk customs and in carnival masks, folk theatre, and oral traditions which reveal the inscriptional and transmissive power of the memory systems that supported shared structures of thought around the Roma as typified outsiders. The euphemistic image of the unwanted outsider is preserved in the character of the 'cunning Gypsy', an underdog trickster who outsmarts and outwits his opponents, creating the association with borderline criminality that visualizes a pre-existing stereotype of the Roma. These stereotypes are found across Europe in cultural texts and reveal an aspect of 'othering' that takes the shape of 'an entertaining enemy' in popular culture (Tremlett, Chap. 7, this volume) and a whole range of narration and storytelling about 'Gypsy life' and gnomic genres (Dalbello 1989).

As an abstracting device and a key to how they were perceived as a threat, the stereotypes focus on the idea of a Gypsy character who is uncontrollable, melancholic, iconoclastic, and unbounded, a metaphor for freedom from the social institutions that represents a counterpoint to social control. The 'Gypsy' stereotypes mediate tensions between those at the centre of society and those at the periphery and are a form of incorporation as society's outsiders.

These stereotypes feed the securitization discourse which shapes the images and sensations characteristic of the limited ways of 'seeing' and 'imagining' the Roma in terms of the negative (cheating) and positive (romanticized) clichés disseminated through popular iconographies and storytelling. The securitization discourses depend on a chain of intertextual relationships, including the stereotypes, which maintain the suspicion of strangers and define the 'hypervisibility' of the Roma due to their supposed criminality, deviancy, excesses, or vulnerability.

De-securitization Practices

The de-securitization of Roma in the context of the integrative reformist programmes attempting a diffuse de-securitization, rather than the replacement of threat consistent with the political culture of the multicultural Empire, is discussed next.

Roma as People in the Encyclopaedia of the Habsburg Empire

The popular encyclopaedia of the Austro-Hungarian monarchy, *Die österreichisch-ungarische Monarchie in Wort und Bild* (hereinafter *Wort und Bild*), epitomizes an official programmatic publication which circulated representations of the Empire and its people (Volk) (Dalbello 2010). An artful combination of dynastic historiography and of natural and human geography, it mirrored and embodied the liminal identity of the Empire as an expression of its political culture, thus delineating a cultural and political territory involving what Larry Wolff (2010) calls 'organic work' through the Habsburg imperial framework, that is, the shared system of information operationalized by the military and bureaucracy. This system could create and operationalize the 'natural ecological domains' within the expanse of the Empire and allows for an understanding of the encyclopaedia as a strategy of imperial assimilation, a machine for inventing representations. The dimensions of circulability and inter-textuality in visual securitization, that is, the capacity in the visual and the textual to 'legitimize' a particular range of actions, are emphasized by Hansen (2011b: 54), epitomized in this lavishly produced and impactful encyclopaedia created by teams of 'experts' and written in an accessible style. Structured to reflect the spatial organization of the Empire and to present a 'fantasy of the empire' as an 'imagined community' (Anderson 1983), the project blended scholarship, patronage, and propaganda. As a regime of representations, it epitomized the ethnic diversity and the inter-weaving of history and fantasy common to Habsburg political culture (Ingrao 2000). The individual entries in *Wort und Bild* had a role in the articulation of forms of visuality, visibility, and the shaping of the public perceptions of both the self and others within the Empire, in order to 'sharpen attention' and create ambiguities which could bring about a specific course of action and generate discourse, rather than replicating positions in the discourse (Hansen 2011b: 54, 58).

The Discursive and Visual Context of the Zigeuner *in* Wort und Bild

The only space in *Wort und Bild* dedicated to the Gypsies, a liminal Volk in the natural and physical geography of the Empire, can be found in the last volume of the 'Ungarn' series (23 (6): 565–575). Its author was Archduke Joseph himself.

'Zigeuner in Wort'
His depiction starts by focusing on those 'familiar strangers' with the invocation of identifying stereotypes:

> Who has not seen in the territory of our fatherland the travelling bands on their miserable horses pulling their carts from village to village? Who doesn't know those brownish strangers who, at the edge of villages or towns, live a miserable existence in their mud dwellings? Who has not felt a moving response in their heart when hearing our *'new Hungarian'* musicians ['neumagyarischen', emphasis original] play? Who has not danced this *'fresh'* ['frischen', emphasis original] Hungarian dance Csárdás to their rapid beat? Surely, everybody has noticed how the dark-olive brown, longish face of these halfway Hungarians ['dieser Häfte Ungarns'] differs from all other European people, and their dark and ever sparkling eye, the beautifully shaped but thick red lips of their mouth, the dishevelled black curly hair, the slender agile appearance, their fine featured hands and feet and their ever happy and humorous temperament. (*Wort und Bild* 23 (6): 565)[3]

The characterization of Roma as 'brownish strangers' is marked through visual features emphasizing their distinctiveness from 'all other European people'. An empathetic feeling, mixed with the recognition of their 'familiar strangeness', is then modulated by their vitality when the observer describes their charming disposition and their beauty and sensuousness. He relies on Gypsy stereotypes to direct the way in which the Roma are to be imagined and on an empathetic attitude in the rhetorical questions directed to the reader. The Roma are presented as developing subjects of the Habsburg Empire in their role as assimilated Hungarian Gypsy musicians and through another Hungarian stereotype, the dance of Csárdás, as an evocation of hybridity and belonging.

They are 'halfway Hungarians' and thus not completely integrated into society. The reader is asked to imagine them through their embodied presence. Their familiarity encompasses a strangeness in the imagery that emphasizes and relishes contrasts, sensualizing the reader's gaze as they contemplate the familiarity/strangeness of 'luscious' lips, 'unkempt' and uncontrollable hair, and evoking the idea of unbounded freedom, of a life outside society and its norms. These Orientalist and racialized representations characterize the Roma in terms of disruptive mobility and a sense of not being able to care for themselves—outlining the childlike, disorderly, and playful qualities of the Gypsy as a Volk. While using evocative and embodied iconography to stir an empathetic vision, difference is socially constructed with rhetorical strategies that reinforce racialization and exclusion and which are consistent with historical stereotypical representations and the ideology and imagery of the Romantic era. In this entry, the text and the images come 'from a source endowed with authority... of the socially and institutionally powerful' and that 'institutional location' is an important dimension in considering this text and the visualizations in creating a discourse about the Roma as a Volk (Rose 2016: 214–215). The act of seeing the images (in the encyclopaedia) reiterates a historical visual regime of producing Roma stereotypes.

The author then shifts from seeing the Roma as already well known as a nomadic people and an itinerant link between the East and the West. He frames their speech as a monument to nomadic assimilation and hybridization and the result of their passage through various zones. He presents this argument by reporting on subjective hearing: 'when [one] hears them speak, their familiar tunes will play in [one's] ear, and whoever understands the language of the Gypsies will understand this and that word' (*Wort und Bild* 23 (6): 566). It was easy for him to hear these linguistic forms in Roma speech because of his interest in their language and its Indo-European roots, an important dimension for the philological scholarship of that time. He brings up a familiar trope of Roma origin which frames them as a historical people with a 'homeland', thus establishing them scientifically as a historical Diaspora in order to domesticate their nomadism. This suggests their representation as a people, but not as a nation, and does not imply either their assimilation or the justification of rigorous settlement policies. Instead, remaining nomadic would be their 'natural' historical disposition—nomadism as a classification that may render them 'valuable' and 'useful' because of the way in which they transmit culture. Introducing the historical origin and justification of dispersal through migration and a subsequent topology of settlement is a 'way of localizing' tactic, a typology localizing the 'Hungarian' Roma and circumscribing their capacity to be defined in terms of a particular nation and place of origin and thus attaching significance and meaning to nomadism (*Wort und Bild* 23 (6): 566). The focus on origins and migration topologies securitize inasmuch as the 'foreign' origin of the Roma is mobilized to justify regulation, thus giving a legalistic basis to previous attempts at regulating them. But, paradoxically, this also gives a legalistic basis to their privileges and past agreements with the authorities. In various attempts to de-securitize the Roma, the Archduke then goes on to practice selective memory (or omission) further on in the text.

For example, he mentions the policies of various Habsburg rulers in his entry and focuses primarily on the Holy Roman Emperor Sigismund of Luxemburg, who gave the Roma free passage at the time of the migrations in the fifteenth century, but he glosses over the more consequential methods of Maria Theresa and Joseph II. Thus, as he establishes the legalistic basis for understanding their right to a nomadic life and settlement, he plays down one of the most controversial historical dimensions shaping Roma securitization. Further, still into the text, he presents a distribution of 274,940 Roma in categories based on their 'level' of nomadism/organized settlement: Roma who are settled and sedentary; those who stay at a certain location for a certain period; and Roma who are on the move (*Wort und Bild*, 23 (6): 568–569). He analyses their regional distribution and provides other data about settlement and conditions of life, including the fact that 70% of Roma settlements have no access to schools. Documenting the topology of Roma settlement in order to present a categorization is in keeping with the administrative and bureaucratic approach to the discourse of securitization and with the way in which the authorities engaged in the surveillance of the Habsburg Roma. While the categorizations conform to the ways in which the authorities viewed the migrant Roma, the terminology paradoxically shifts the discourse of disordered migration to the 'level' of settlement, which gestures towards assimilative processes having been successful in rendering the Roma more sedentary. Through these typologies, which demonstrated that at least half of the Roma were sedentary, he challenges the existing regimes of visuality and the stereotyping of the Roma and shows that they can be imagined as a Volk and not just as nomadic imperial subjects. He presents a number of ambiguities; however, while he frames nomadism in terms of a privilege—as a decreed and regulated relationship between the authorities and the Roma groups—he also shows that sedentarization policies have not resulted in their elevation to subjects of the Empire with, for example, the right and access to education. He used this entry to contest and challenge official views by making visible the present condition of the Roma. The Archduke, a member of the Habsburg dynasty and an elite class, exercised his political influence from the position of a philanthropic actor. He characterized the Roma as being in need of becoming subjects of humanitarian-like intervention and of protection.

These tactics of resisting certain ways of seeing the Roma challenge their securitization as part of a project of constructing disciplined and eligible subjects of the Empire. Nomadism jeopardized the state project because the state could not keep track of its subjects. Thus, the Archduke revealed the limitations and the failures of the state in its responsibility to a people. Rather than employing non-stereotypical representations, he uses racialized stereotypes to engage an existing normalized regime of visuality but opens a dialogue about the Roma as actual imperial subjects. He reproduces these frames of seeing simultaneously, bringing the outsider in. The prevailing representation of the Roma as outsiders is thus softened through categorizations which introduce different structures of settlement to normalize them and thus diminish the 'hypervisibility' of the uncategorized. The representations allow for imagining their vulnerability—a danger around the ambiguity inherent in portraying those being 'at risk' as also 'risky'—because the stereotype does not serve to conceal or obscure their poverty. The phrase 'strangers who at the edges of villages or towns, live a miserable existence in their mud dwellings' merely expresses their destitute condition and not the moral deficiency or representation of deviance generally associated with nomadism.

With the *Wort und Bild* entry, the Archduke presents statements that could potentially disrupt the dominant ways of understanding and seeing the Roma in political and public debates, media and visual culture. In representing the Roma as imperial subjects, this entry is an artefact of political communication which has the effect of their de-securitization. The strategies of visualization in this entry establish the idea of the *Zigeuner* as something to be disseminated and replicated by the method of 'organic work' of the imperial information system and presents a blueprint for imagining the Roma as a Volk within the monarchy with its network of interconnected subjects of a unified, if trans-national (trans-ethnic), state.

'Zigeuner in Bild'
The illustrations in the *Wort und Bild* entry are entitled: *Zigeunermädchen* (The Gypsy girl), *Wanderzigeuner* (Nomadic Gypsies), *Zeltzigeuner und Zigeunerin* (Tent Gypsy man and woman), *Lager von schnitzenden*

Zigeunern (A settlement with Gypsies carving), and *Zigeunerhütten am Dorfende* (Gypsy huts at the edge of town). The source image for the engraving of The Gypsy girl was a painting or drawing by Archduke Joseph's daughter, Archduchess Maria Dorothea of Austria (Fig. 13.1). The photographs for the illustrations of a tent Gypsy man and woman were taken by the Archduke and are from the Alcsuth estate collection (Fig. 13.3). One of the settlement images was attributed to Johann Greguss (Fig. 13.2) and the other two could be stock images from Morelli, an engraving institute producing images on a large scale (Figs. 13.4 and 13.5). The iconicity of settlements is meant to illustrate spatial position

Fig. 13.1 *Zigeunermädchen* (von Ihrer k. und k. Hoheit Erzherzogin Maria Dorothea). *Gypsy Girl.* Creative Commons licence by Austria-Forum (Bilder: *Kronprinzenwerk*, Band 23: 565). (Note: The painting is autographed 'María' and the engraving is signed 'Morelli G.F.I.')

Fig. 13.2 *Wanderzigeuner* (von Johann Greguss). *Nomadic Gypsies.* Creative Commons licence by Austria-Forum (Bilder: *Kronprinzenwerk*, Band 23: 567). (Note: The engraving is signed, 'Pásztori' (a personal name or a location in the Győr-Moson-Sopron area))

and textures. The portrait images—the photographs of tent Gypsy man and woman from the Archduke's archive or a drawing of a Roma child by his own daughter—are examples of how the Archduke perceived the Roma and how he chose to illustrate this entry. They encode a personal way of seeing and the visual construction of the Roma as subject.

The uniform aesthetic effect of the illustrations depends on their flattened visual texture. They produce detailed yet impersonal images suited to the categorizations of the encyclopaedic approach. When based on photographs, they reduce their complexity (since photographs capture even the slightest movement) and their indexical nature. The reduced surface of a photograph emphasizes and forefronts the image as an idealized shape, suitable for showing typologies of genotypes and settlements conveying abstracted qualities. The images represent the Roma genotypes, with curly hair, mud huts, and the places of social marginality, which they inhabit at the edge of society and close to nature. The optical, distant vision 'with an imaginary universal value and scope' (Deleuze and Guattari

Fig. 13.3 *Zeltzigeuner und Zigeunerin* (nach Photographien in der Alcsuther Sammlung Seiner k. und k. Hoheit Erzherzog Josef). *Tent Gypsy man and woman.* Creative Commons licence by Austria-Forum (Bilder: *Kronprinzenwerk*, Band 23: 571). (Note: The engraving is signed, 'Morelli G.F.I.')

2003: 494) reinstates the haptic of the photograph or a painting via the gravure. Thus, the 'nomadic' haptic corresponding to a close-up vision is in tension with the optically distant vision—each creating a different kind of space; one is dynamic (in process, in parts) and the other static (classifiable, presents the whole). The converted haptic (nomadic) close-up vision generates a rationalized and ordered distant vision. The visuals are consistent with stereotypes, but they support those representations by

Fig. 13.4 *Lager von schnitzenden Zigeunern* (Johann Greguss). *A settlement with Gypsies carving.* Creative Commons licence by Austria-Forum (Bilder: *Kronprinzenwerk*, Band 23: 573). (Note: The engraving is signed 'Morelli G.F.I. Mésés K sc.')

Fig. 13.5 *Zigeunerhütten am Dorfende* (Johann Greguss). *Gypsy huts at the edge of town.* Creative Commons licence by Austria-Forum (Bilder: *Kronprinzenwerk*, Band 23: 574), unsigned

which the Roma can be conceptualized as a Habsburg *Volk* and are consistent with classificatory points in the text.

The text goes on to describe a school for Roma children in Alcsuth, a testimony to the Archduke's efforts (from an assimilationist position) to settle the Roma on his estate, an educational programme 'that produced good results', and which concludes with the assertion that teachers must be fluent in Romani and 'have more reliable knowledge about our Gypsies' (*Wort und Bild* 23 (6): 568). Further, he calls for critical reform in the administration regarding the Roma question, pointing to a mismatch between the legislation and the 'cultural habits' of the Roma. In this entry, he conforms to the existing categorizations by means of stereotypes, then confronts negative stereotypes, introduces factual statements and empathetic propositions, and presents a programme of what I understand as de-securitization.

The approach that Archduke Joseph used was consistent with the approaches advocated by the cosmopolitan network of amateur philologists (and Orientalists) affiliated with the *Gesellschaft für Zigeunerforschung* (GfZ) and the British GLS, in which he was also active.[4] The GLS presented their views, research, and news, which also involved pro-Roma lobbying.[5] As a reformist 'development' programme, the work of the Central European GfZ continued the legacy of the GLS. Archduke Joseph was a patron, member, and contributor to the society's journal.[6] His role as a Roma protector, in addition to his activities as philologist, was in accordance with that part of the manifesto of the GfZ that emphasized not only the scientific but also the social side of the endeavour. He reported at length on the results of his philanthropic project of assimilation. From an ethnographic point of view, he presented a programme of socioeconomic assimilation while framing it as preserving the 'native' culture. In this sense, the project was deeply ambiguous. While his activism was consistent with the policy of assimilation because it advocated for a change of culture, he practised it in a unique way, founding a refuge for the nomadic Roma on his estate to bring them 'inside' society and challenging the prevailing discourse of Roma 'as a threat', a strategy of diffusing threat based on 'soft', rather than 'hard', assimilationist principles. The characteristics of his agenda of assimilation and his strategy of counter-securitization can be read from the various reports about the Alcsuth colony, by which he also gave visibility to the Habsburg Roma.

Sites and Modes of Seeing: Archduke Joseph's Project of Roma Settlement as Strategy of De-securitization

On the Alcsuth estate, taken over by his family in 1819, Archduke Joseph created a settlement to provide a sanctuary for nomadic Roma. By 1891, his Alcsuth estate hosted 36 Roma families (81 men and 96 women). The residents had to observe rules outlined in a code called the Regulation for the Gypsy settlement in the Domain of Alcsuth (Habsburg 1896b). The nine rules were drawn up by the Archduke himself and defined the settlers' obligations with regard to dwellings, freedom of movement, keeping order in the colony, and the instruction of children. It also defined terms for their remuneration and prohibited theft. The code was one of the documents from the colonization archive maintained by the Archduke.

His logic as an agent of de-securitization was nevertheless locked within securitizing terms: because the Roma were 'different', they were seen as a danger, revealing the programme's inherent tension. He challenges the then mainstream approach to the Roma, presents them as co-constituting the Empire, and suggests ways of incorporating them on their own terms in a comparable way to more sedentary people. Nevertheless, his approach is paternalistic and rooted in the scientific racism of his days. A cynical interpretation might frame it as an exploitative project which profited from their labour and saw them as exotic 'noble savages'.

He relates his experiences with the Roma who settled on his estate in the aftermath of legislation which made them homeless:

> When several municipalities from across the Danube forbade the travelling tent-Gypsies from keeping horses and also confiscated their horses and carts when they had a chance, without finding any place for them to stay, it was only natural that they came to me knowing that they would always be welcome... All the families knew me. They had already spent many rough wintertime periods when they were surprised in their travels [by the harshness of the winter] on my properties where they received a place to stay and food. The moment the snowstorm was over they had already disappeared. Now they were forced to stay. (Habsburg 1893: 3)

The Roma colony, which was founded in the aftermath of a wave of anti-Gypsy policies that threatened their livelihood and reinforced their marginality, was built on the existing good relationship that the Archduke had maintained with groups of travelling Roma passing through the area.

Not only do we learn from the notices that he published about the Alcsuth colony (ibid.: 3–8) that the Archduke allowed the Roma to live and work on the estate but also we learn how he created conditions for sedentarization involving shelter in exchange for labour and controlled settlement. He offers close and involved commentaries, their tone is intimate, personal, and paternalistic. While the encyclopaedic entry 'revealed' and marketed the Roma as a *Volk* for the popular audience of *Wort und Bild*, the descriptions in the *Ethnologische Mitteilungen* were intended for the fellow ethnographers and philologists who were discussing the requirements for the ethnographic science which they were developing and the Indo-European origin of Romani. The observations were ethnographic in the sense that they would combine close observation and detail with interpretation. The descriptive accounts were aimed at visualizing the findings of his 'social experiment'. The modes and sites of seeing cast the Archduke in the roles of initiator, participant, and observer of the process. In 'the information about the Gypsies residing in Alcsuth', his tone is that of a guardian; he refers to them as 'my Gypsies' and, in an 1892 letter, addresses them in Romani, 'Munré lačhé čhavoralé!' ('My dear children!'), indicating a relationship that is not equal, even though it is affectionate and implies care (Habsburg 1896a: 57). The example of the 'monetization of work' being a 'threat' for the Roma calls for the Archduke's intervention:

> Because Gypsies cannot handle money, they obtain food from an alimentation depot. They receive clothes from a warehouse at a lower cost. The amount will be regularly subtracted from their pay, so that they can become accustomed [to economizing]. Women and children can, for now, obtain cloth for free. We will make sure they learn to sew. They will also learn how to bake bread. Each person capable of work will get an annual stipend of 400 crowns, and this amount will be paid weekly. We will make sure that they use their money for the right purpose, and do not spend it on brandy.
> (Habsburg 1896b: 105–106)

The references to acts of indulgence and excess in his account point to a common securitization discourse in which the Roma are seen as a threat to themselves, unable to take care of themselves, and in need of guidance. While he explains their resilience, he approaches and employs science as a cure. When reporting on the request of the Roma to visit the baths in Budapest, which he declined because of a cholera outbreak in Budapest at the time, he also includes the narration 'of why cholera became afraid of the Gypsies' (ibid.: 5). He presents the argument that social isolation protects them, in contrast to the case of settled Roma being decimated by the cholera, while the tent-Roma were not (ibid.: 5–6). The Roma are presented as engaging in hazardous and potentially self-harming practices:

> They lived in tents and they had a particular dislike for other types of dwellings, even during the hardest winter. They didn't know how to bake bread, and they didn't learn it with me. They prepared their *bokhál'i* from fine flour and they kneaded it into hard dough which they baked in hot ashes, and it was very good. Their favourite food was meat, and they would not hesitate to eat even old *Aasfleisch* which most probably they cooked in vinegar. When they had been residing in the colony for a few months, a cow died of anthrax, and she was buried deep in the ground because we knew our people. And, for three days and nights, there was a guard. On the fourth night, when the guard had retired, they dug up the cow and had a very happy meal. A boy was stung by a fly and got sick in his nose and throat with anthrax. He was operated on in a Budapest clinic and recovered fully. (ibid.: 4)

By focusing on the removal of threats from the Roma, he fabricates insecurities assigned to their own practices. Keeping them safe from threat echoes the sanitary concerns about outsiders and what they may bring to the settlement. Thus, the Roma are crystallized both through their representation as threatening others—'risky'—and threatening themselves—'at risk'—an ambiguity inherent in these representations.

His description of the Roma's ingenuity with metalwork, if given the proper tools, was in contrast to the futility of forcing them to do agricultural labour. In the case of metalwork, the Roma were able to scale up from tinkering to the production of metal tools for the entire estate. He also relates the partial success of their involvement in 'the harvesting of beets, loading up manure, or picking up of stones, where both sexes participated, [which] worked pretty well', unlike digging and construction, which 'occurred with a great deal of difficulty and complaining of how much their back hurts'. He takes the opportunity to theorize about the social structure and political organization of the familiar Roma bands, their unstable leadership structure, and kinship system. When focusing on labour issues, his approach stands in sharp contrast to the brutality of the methods used by the authorities in their process of securitization. And yet, while he recognizes the inability of the authorities to engage the perspective of the Roma, insofar as his own project was based on Roma assimilation and improvement, it shared the same inability to engage the Roma perspective fully.

The accounts in which the Archduke describes his encounters with the Roma refer to an entire sensory repertoire:

> Their clothing always consisted of minimal and torn up pieces and children lacked adequate clothing. Their customary smell of smoke could not be mistaken. The typical black hair with dark skin colour is roughly the case for a third of them. The others can have shadings all the way to bright blond with white skin, but all of them had very curly and unkempt hair. For the men as well as for the women, there are very few that can be called really beautiful. (ibid.: 3)

In the mediation of the visual, 'a sense of things' (Mitchell 2005: 257) in this representation conveys a range of sensory inputs that delineate visuality by references to their unmistakable smoky smell together with the optical perception of the shadings of skin colour and the jarring blondness, as well as the unkempt hair and ragged look. The specificity of the image and sensual immediacy in portraying the Roma are evocative (Hansen 2011b: 55–56) and ground the picturization in the subjective vision of the Archduke through his reported observations. The light skin colouring and blond hair are explained by social exclusion—since Roma do not mix with other populations. This, according to the Archduke, can be explained by their membership in 'a higher caste and that they are not meant to work, since in India the higher castes have lighter skin colour and don't work' (Habsburg 1893: 6). The Archduke thus uses 'sharpened attention' (Hansen 2011b: 53) to inter-visually and inter-textually construct an empathetic depiction of the Roma phenotypes. He also emphasizes their poverty and the children who 'lacked adequate clothing'. Contributing to essentialist disputation on the Indian origin of the Roma was an ambiguous move with regard to the Roma representation, having the potential to enable agency and self-articulation (van Baar 2011: 15). These representations matched the ideologies of scientific and romantic racism of the GLS which idealized otherness but maintained exclusion. His reference to 'mixing' with other populations and 'social exclusion' which then (as now) characterized the Roma as outsiders to European society could not integrate difference within the European plurality of people.

The Archduke intervened and acted as a protector in response to an external threat, the forced military service which had infringed on the habitual Roma way of life in the settlement in another segment, and in which he acted as a mediator between the authorities and the Roma

(Habsburg 1893: 5). The threat of conscription was the result of the Roma abandoning their nomadic practices and becoming visible to the state. The account also gives a sense of the political processes and tensions, the shifting loyalties in the colony, and friction with the Roma leaders, but also of his power. For instance, he notes: 'to those [among the settled Gypsies] who were removed on the wish of the administration, I restituted the old right to have a horse and a wagon, and because of this I am certain of their many future visits' (ibid.: 8).

According to the Archduke, the Roma elected him as their leader, which was a great honour and sign of acceptance. He ensured the protection of their rights within the bounds of the estate, even though that meant an exchange of labour for pay, and he commented on those who stayed more permanently, who 'work quite well now as coachmen and they are now part of the destiny of fixed pay and rigours' (ibid.: 8). The Archduke was an active participant in the relationship with the Roma who visited him or lived on his estate. In addition to being their protector, and gaining several honorary titles from the Roma as their leader, he also inhabited a participant role through ritual kinship—as godfather to newborn Roma children, something which was a sign of respect reserved for wealthy members of Roma communities. Gaining trust in the communities in which they studied is a trope that occurs in the writings of Roma researchers at that time. One of the markers of being an insider was the 'stealing test', which the Archduke mentioned in this account of when the Roma settled on his estate. References to such 'tests' of trust are found in the accounts of other Gypsyologists', including Heinrich von Wlislocki, for whom this meant being an accepted outsider. The 'stealing test' is connected to Roma criminalization; by this surprising turn, it becomes a marker of trust and feeling safe for the outsider (Gypsyologist), a gift of reciprocity.

It was important for the Archduke to show that the Roma trusted him and that they liked him, reporting that, during his absence, the Roma would wait for him on his doorstep (ibid.: 3). Even though they were closely observed, interacted with, and referred to as 'my children' or 'my Gypsies' by the Archduke, the Roma are not individualized or personalized. The accounts were not addressed to them and the Roma presence is distant, although, in some contemporary ethnographic reports, the visibility of the Roma as narrators offers a resonance of the Roma voices regarding the Archduke's project.

Roma Visibility in Oral Narrations

In the legends and anecdotes collected by GfZ practitioners, the visibility of the Archduke's 'philanthropic' activities was reflected in the oral narrations circulated by the Roma. Anton Herrmann (1893: 112), for instance, presented the following findings from his fieldwork:

> With some Gypsy tribes, Archduke Joseph has become almost a mythical character thanks to his studies, human colonization, and peaceful treatment of Gypsies not only in Hungary but also abroad. Anyone who is engaged in a serious study of Gypsies hears similar anecdotes and legends among Gypsies that concern His Highness and protector. The stories reported here were recorded on 24 May 1891 in southern Hungarian village of Bezdan (H. v. Wlislocki), according to the telling of a travelling Bosnian Gypsy Petar Karčić, and they refer to His Highness. The name Josipo (Joško) is a Slavic form, which appears in these stories, and Kučela is probably the place where His Highness lives, that is Alcsuth.

In the story, Archduke Joseph appears as Josipo. The story is a theophany, a genre of oral storytelling that involves the sighting of rulers from the near past. It also refers to the 'promised mythical land' that the Roma considered their domicile, in which legend is mixed with Roma folkloric tradition:

> Gypsies wanted to go to their King Joseph. Their old mother tried to dissuade them by telling them – 'in the town of Kučela you constantly need to work with the spade. I am telling you, this is not for you'. The Gypsy men did not listen to her and they went there. It was the land of the Gypsies. King Josipo told them: 'my dear sweet Gypsies, in my country lives a big Gypsy and she has six horns and each day she eats a man. My dear men, she will devour you all. And I will cry, cry, my sweet Gypsies, and I will not have any more men.' And Old Ćurko told him: 'My black king, I am not afraid. I will go to this big woman and I will eat her, I have big teeth.' (Herrmann 1893: 113–114)

Kučela may be a homonym for Alcsuth, and the Archduke self-reported that the Gypsies have given him the honorary title of *Vojwoda* (Duke). The narrators assume subject positions in these narratives, which are often merged with Romani traditions. The Archduke's excellent knowledge of the Romani language and their way of life could not simply be the product of armchair ethnography. While these legends were in oral circulation, their appearance in scholarly journals is significant in maintaining an image of the Archduke.

Through the core ambiguity of his interventions in shaping representations of the Roma and their practices, and through the programme of settlement, the Archduke points, at least to some degree, at how a diffuse de-securitization of the Roma, rather than replacement of threat, could be imagined in late nineteenth-century Habsburg Europe.

The modes and sites of seeing that Alcsuth provided had potential and offered a way of seeing the Roma on their own terms as a *Volk* of the Empire. Their circulability and inter-textuality in visual securitization were interfering with the securitization practices of local authorities and the state but had not shifted them or had any impact on the broader perceptions of Roma nomadism. This approach was fraught with the ambivalence inherent in the utopian dimensions of the refuge as a site for the removal of the threat to the Roma through their removal into an artificial society.

Conclusion

This historical depiction of securitization and de-securitization in Habsburg Europe forefronts the activities of Archduke Joseph in the realm of representations of the Roma, including the new sites for the production and consumption of representations and relations that control Roma visibility and invisibility. By circulating the idea of 'Gypsies as a *Volk*' in *Wort und Bild*, he created the text to produce something other than the usual frames and modes of seeing. He believed that the inclusion of Gypsies as a *Volk*, as a historical and territorialized people in Habsburg Europe, could lead to a better understanding of the condition of the Roma as a people of the Habsburg realm. The ethnographic approach that Archduke Joseph practised as a philologist was matched by his philanthropic activities with regard to the Roma. By organizing a colony for them on his estate, he created a new site for granting visibility to the Habsburg Roma—as potential citizens (the *Volk*), 'safe', and having value in their own right—and shared his insights with the GfZ community. It is extraordinary and exceptional that this project also surfaces in Roma narrations in a positive, albeit ambiguous, light.

In my view, his efforts to understand and his close study of the Roma demonstrate the ambivalence and the limits of charitable efforts, but they are nevertheless not to be dismissed as a practice. As an intellectual figure, the Archduke had land, influence, political power, respect, and education, as well as access to the modes of dissemination and marketization of the ideas and ideologies of the state. His scholarship and activism thus provide more than a historical understanding of the work of a single individual. His approach was compatible with the beliefs of some of the early researchers of Romani languages in the cosmopolitan networks that connected the Roma with Orientalist scholarship and philanthropy in Europe.

Colloquially, one could characterize the Archduke's activity as not only 'talking the talk': he was 'walking the walk' of what I call 'diffuse de-securitization' at a time when attempted eradication and forceful assimilation defined the practices of securitization affecting the nomadic Roma. The Archduke practised the politics of difference and compassion along humanitarian lines, but he also operated consistently within the strands of the official political culture of a multicultural Empire which emphasized plurality in unity. In this way, he acted along the grain of Habsburg imperialism. Unlike 'diffuse de-securitization', the 'hard' assimilationist approaches did not acknowledge the politics of difference (plurality) and aimed rather for the politics of non-identity or similarity, echoed by one-way processes in which a 'threat' label is de-assigned or taken away as evidence of de-securitization. In order for the conditions necessary for belonging through difference to be achieved for the subjects and objects of securitization discourses, and in order for their status as a social threat to be removed, these conditions have to be acceptable to them as well. In contrast to the mainstream approaches identifying 'othering' as exclusion from citizenship, I argue that construction of 'othering' within a plurality of a secured place for Roma ethnicity as a minority—insofar as the legalistic dimensions regulating similarity/difference as a liminal category are accepted through a social contract—can provide a basis for self-articulation and Romani agency. In line with recent reflections on Roma historiography and a reading of the eighteenth-century legacies which established such constructions of the Roma along the lines of an ambiguous enactment of ethnicity (van Baar 2011: 107–49), I chose to interpret the Archduke's conduct and his problematization of the Roma within the ideology of difference which he thought might bring about a minority self-articulation. In this de-securitization, however, 'their movement out of security' (Hansen 2011a: 526) on the sites of the family estate and in visual inter-image and inter-texts, his de-securitizing politics were limited by the philanthropic ambiguities that defined this project, even though it challenged the then dominant forms of Roma securitization.

The Archduke's conception of the Roma as a *Volk* encapsulates elements of the ideologies possible within a pluralistic setting of the Empire. His own membership in the elites enabled his protection of the groups of Danubian Roma on his estate, sharpening attention and circulating new positions for seeing the Roma. Radically ambiguous, his project shared both the romantic racism of the GLS and scientific racism (Acton 2015: 1192) with the cosmopolitan network of contemporary Gypsyologists and those characterizing the normative for reformist projects at the turn of the nineteenth century. It also shows that clear separation of de-securitization from securitization may not have been possible from the positions inhabited by these historical actors. In the reading I give here, the historical case contributes to an understanding of the potential of reformist programmes of this period and the construction of visual de-securitization. Founded on the scientific racism of its period in its ambivalent application, this case stands apart from anti-Gypsyism and the racist fantasies and obsession with Roma Aryan origin (Acton 2015: 1196) which accompany the programmes of Roma 'othering', exclusion, and extermination in the ensuing decades of the twentieth century. Its difference has been enacted by discursive and non-discursive means, in the ways in which the Archduke illustrated his experience with the Roma from within an assimilationist perspective that he constructed as a de-securitizing actor. That he did produce a change, and that his discourses turned into practices, becomes evident in the Roma narratives about the Archduke and his estate.

Notes

1. The terms 'gypsy' or 'Gypsy' are used only as far as they reflect usage in the historical texts quoted in this essay. In all other instances, the term 'Roma' is used, despite this usage being anachronistic when dealing with historical terminology.
2. This 24-volume encyclopaedia—also referred to as *Kronprinzenwerk*—was published by the Imperial and Royal Court State Printing office (1886–1902) under the sponsorship of Crown Prince Rudolf.
3. Translations from German are by Anselm Spoerri, Melita Matulić, and Marija Dalbello.
4. The *Gesellschaft für Zigeunerforschung* (GfZ) was active from 1893 to 1905 in Budapest and was the counterpart of the Gypsy Lore Society (GLS) (founded in 1888), which ceased its activities during this period, resuming them in 1907. The GfZ published materials on Gypsy studies in the *Mitteilungen zur Zigeunekunde*, also known as *Ethnologische Mitteilungen*

aus Ungarn. The GfZ was under the protection of Archduke Joseph, and its members were active for a decade and until his death in 1905 (Dalbello 2015).
5. The group outlined a programme of descriptive study, comparative research, and improvement of the status and human rights of the Gypsies and other 'people who are called vagrants'. The group emphasized internationalism and cosmopolitanism and founded its own journal, the *Journal of the Gypsy Lore Society* (Dalbello 2015).
6. This programme encompassed the descriptive study of Roma from the territory of Austria-Hungary.

REFERENCES

Acton, T. 2015. Scientific Racism, Popular Racism and the Discourse of the Gypsy Lore Society. *Ethnic and Racial Studies* 39 (7): 1187–1204.

Anderson, B. 1983. *Imagined Communities*. London: Verso.

Barany, Z. 2002. *The East European Gypsies*. Cambridge: Cambridge University Press.

Bright, R. 1818. *Travels from Vienna Through Lower Hungary*. Edinburgh: A. Constable.

Dalbello, M. 1989. Prilog bibliografiji o Romima (Ciganima) u SFR Jugoslaviji. In *Međunarodni naučni skup Jezik i kultura Roma,* ed. M. Šipka, 429–499 (Sarajevo, 9–11.VI 1986). Sarajevo: Institut za proučavanje nacionalnih odnosa.

———. 2010. Liminal People, Liminal Places, and the Borderlands, Conference Paper Presented at *Society for the History of Authorship, Reading and Publishing*, Helsinki, August 17–21.

———. 2015. The Fantastic Historiography of Gypsies and People In-between and on the Edges of Empires and Their Permanent Liminality, Conference Paper Presented at *Historians and the Margins: From North America to Former Empires*, Université Paris 13, June 18–19.

Deleuze, G., and F. Guattari. 2003 [1980]. *A Thousand Plateaus*. London: Continuum.

Habsburg, Archduke Joseph Karl Ludwig of Austria. 1893. Mitteilungen über die in Alcsuth angesiedelten Zelt-Zigeuner, *Ethnologische Mitteilungen aus Ungarn*, Bd. 3 (1893), Heft 1–12, Budapest: Buchdruckerei Mezei Antal, 3–8.

———. 1896a. Ein zigeunerischer Brief, *Ethnologische Mitteilungen aus Ungarn*, Bd. 5 (1896), Heft 1–3, Budapest: Buchdruckerei E. Boruth, 57.

———. 1896b. Normativ für die Ansiedlung der Zigeuner in the Alcsúther Domäne, *Ethnologische Mitteilungen aus Ungarn*, Bd. 5 (1896), Heft 4–10, Budapest: Buchdruckerei E. Boruth, 105–106; 231–232.

Hansen, L. 2011a. Reconstructing Desecuritisation. *Review of International Studies* 38 (3): 525–546.
———. 2011b. Theorizing the Image for Security Studies. *European Journal of International Relations* 17 (1): 51–74.
Herrmann, A. 1893. Zigeunersagen u. dgl. über Erzherzog Josef, *Ethnologische Mitteilungen*, Bd. 3, Budapest: Buchdruckerei Mezei Antal, 112; 113–114; 165.
Ingrao, C. 2000. *The Habsburg Monarchy, 1618–1815*. Cambridge: Cambridge University Press.
Lucassen, L., W. Willems, and A. Cottaar. 1998. *Gypsies and Other Itinerant Groups*. Basingstoke: Macmillan.
Mayerhofer, C. 1988. *Dorfzigeuner*. Vienna: Picus.
Mitchell, W.J.T. 2005. There Are No Visual Media. *Journal of Visual Culture* 4 (2): 257–266.
Okely, J. 1983. *The Traveller-Gypsies*. Cambridge: Cambridge University Press.
Rose, G. 2016. *Visual Methodologies*. London: Sage.
van Baar, H. 2011. *The European Roma: Minority Representation, Memory, and the Limits of Transnational Governmentality*. Amsterdam: F&N.
Wolff, L. 2010. *The Idea of Galicia*. Stanford, CA: Stanford University Press.

Index[1]

A

Active labour-market policies, 11
  public works, activation, 11
  workfare programmes, 93
Activism, 106, 299, 307
  activists, 8, 15, 77, 102, 180n2, 183, 189, 191, 200, 209
Acton, Thomas, 193, 308
Agency, vi, 5, 7, 21, 22, 48, 52, 53, 64n3, 123, 183, 194, 256, 303, 307
Ahmed, Sara, 236, 237, 247, 250
Alcsuth colony, 299, 301
Anti-ghetto, 14, 92, 97–99, 108
Antigypsyism, 22, 140, 161–164, 166, 167, 180n2, 193, 256n1, 300, 308
  reasonable, 95, 140, 167, 169, 179, 245
Anti-policies, 161–170, 175, 179
Aradau, Claudia, 4, 8, 31, 58, 117, 240

Arendt, Hannah, 8, 33–38, 40n3, 40n4, 62
Asociación Comisión Católica Española de Migraciones (ACCEM), 217–219, 227n17, 227n18

B

Balzacq, Thierry, 2, 53, 117, 140, 221
Barany, Zoltan, 183, 287, 288
Bigo, Didier, 2, 3, 29, 53, 67, 70, 117, 140, 142, 146, 151, 168
Biopolitics, 17, 18, 169, 173–175, 186, 192, 194, 201, 223
  of development, 160
Border(s)
  bordering, 30
  crossing, vi, 47, 48, 60
  external, 46, 54, 55, 57, 60, 61, 63

---

[1] Note: Page numbers followed by 'n' refer to notes.

Border(s) (*cont.*)
  internal, 9, 46, 54, 55, 57, 60, 61, 63, 76
  national, 37
  politics, 9, 46, 61
  practices, vii, 57
  regime(s), 46, 48, 54, 57
  securitization of, 9
  spectacle, 237, 246, 255
Brenner, Neil, 123, 124
Brown, Wendy, 10, 47

C
Çağlar, Ayse, 8, 31, 59
Campi nomadi, 58, 233, 245
Charles the Sixth, 288
Citizenship
  abject, 35, 39, 39n1
  EU, 5, 6, 9, 29, 31–34, 37–39, 57–60, 192, 221
  second-rank, 18
  technologies of, 5
Class, 10, 13, 14, 21, 59, 60, 93, 115–131, 145, 162, 183, 192, 198, 219, 248, 254, 294
Cluj, 115–131
Coercion, 40n2, 52, 132n1, 225
Commodification, 7, 13, 106
Community, vi, 16–19, 21, 29, 30, 32, 36, 48–51, 56, 60–63, 95, 104, 108, 109, 127, 129–131, 141–143, 146–151, 159, 160, 162, 164, 171, 174, 175, 177–178, 186, 188–190, 195–202, 213, 219, 221, 224, 235, 247, 249, 253, 255, 304, 306
Copenhagen School, *see* Securitization
Council of Europe, 18, 184–190, 195, 199, 201, 277
  mediation programmes (ROMED), 18, 184

Counter-conduct, 9, 68, 69, 74, 75, 77, 78, 82
Counter-narratives, 4
Criminalization, vii, 7, 29, 30, 38, 94, 101, 102, 105, 126, 208, 240, 245, 288, 304
Crisis
  financial-economic, 6, 123
  'migrant'/'refugee', 165
Critical security studies, 2–4, 115, 117, 139
Cultural studies, 139–141

D
Dalbello, Marija, 4, 7, 19, 22, 289, 290, 308n3, 309n4, 309n5
De Certeau, Michel, 9, 68, 82
De Genova, Nicholas, 7–9, 12, 31, 36, 37, 40n4, 48, 83n3, 104, 209, 220, 237, 246
Debord, Guy, 235, 246
De-humanization, 166, 247
De-politicization, 14, 91, 94, 101, 163, 165, 166, 184, 203
Deportability, 31, 32, 35, 209, 210, 220
  undeportability, 35
Deportation
  'soft', 19, 208–210, 220–222, 224
  and 'voluntary' return, 19, 209, 210, 220, 224
De-securitization, 4, 8, 21, 22, 46, 64, 163, 177, 286, 290, 293, 294, 300, 306–308
  as change through stabilization, 286
  diffuse, 307
  normative dimension of, 4, 286
  See also Securitization
Development
  biopoliticization of, 17, 18, 173–175, 186, 190–194, 200
  human, 17, 173, 174

programmes, 16–18, 162, 168, 173, 175, 184, 192, 299
and underdevelopment, 16, 19, 160, 170, 174, 175, 183–185, 192–194, 202, 224
Developmentalism
de-developmentalization, 18, 159, 160, 171, 172, 177
institutional, 16, 18, 160, 170, 184–186, 223
postcolonial, 16, 170, 172
Die österreichisch-ungarische Monarchie in Wort und Bild, 290
Discrimination, v, vii–ix, 15, 32, 48, 57–59, 96, 122, 127, 138, 141, 142, 152n2, 163, 164, 166, 167, 177, 187, 193, 270, 276, 278
Dispositif, 70–74, 117, 118, 128, 130, 131, 132n1
Duffield, Mark, 16, 173–175, 184, 185, 191, 194, 200, 201, 223

E
End, Markus, 22, 161, 262, 263, 267, 272, 274, 279n7
Entertainment, vii, 15, 137, 139, 141, 142, 149, 151
Escobar, Arturo, 16, 171, 184, 185, 193
Essentialization, vii, viii, 18, 20, 38, 141–146, 180n3, 265, 303
Ethnicity, 10, 23n1, 98, 151, 268, 274, 277, 307
Ethnography, 22, 111n4, 253, 255, 299, 301, 304–306
digital, 21, 235
Eurocentrism, 171, 184, 193
methodological, 16
European Commission, 18, 36, 57, 176, 184, 203n3
Europeanization, 54, 159
of Roma representation, 9, 16, 38, 159, 184, 186, 194

European Parliament, 64n3, 84n7, 166
European Union (EU), ix, 5, 9, 12, 15, 29, 31–33, 36–38, 45–46, 54, 55, 57, 71, 107, 148, 169, 191
border regime of, 45, 54, 56, 57
citizenship (*see* Citizenship)
as a political project, 5, 39, 54, 166
Roma Framework, 194, 203n3, 226n4
Evictability, 32, 58, 104, 127, 209, 210, 220
Eviction, 5, 13, 14, 19, 29, 30, 39, 48, 68, 72–75, 78, 104, 115, 116, 118, 119, 121–131, 142, 176, 210, 211, 216, 217, 219, 221

F
Facebook ©, 234–239, 241–244, 248–250, 257n2, 257n10
Fassin, Didier, 17, 70, 72, 76, 168, 209, 223
Fear, 101, 107, 109, 140, 148, 150, 218, 235, 250, 251, 255
Fekete, Liz, 30, 36, 40n4, 127
Ferguson, James, 160, 170–172, 176–178, 180n1, 180n3, 184, 185, 193
Foucault, Michel, 11, 68, 70, 78, 83, 93, 117, 140, 141, 174, 192, 252
France, 6, 9, 12, 57, 67–83, 105, 190, 191
Fraser, Nancy, 185

G
Gender, 10, 13, 115, 141–146, 162, 192, 198, 226n10
Gentrification, vii, 13, 115–131
Germany, 34, 45, 57–60, 190, 262, 265, 266, 277

Gesellschaft für Zigeunerforschung
    (GFZ), 299, 305, 306,
    308–309n4
Ghetto
    anti-ghetto, 14, 92, 97–99, 108
    ghettoization, 13, 29, 30, 96–99,
        105, 246
    hyperghetto, 14, 92, 97–99,
        101, 105
Gitano, 212, 215, 221, 226n4,
    226n11, 227n16
Goldberg, David Theo, 14, 92–97,
    99, 102, 107, 109, 110, 111n3
Governmentality, 17, 18, 173
    neoliberal, 10, 11, 111n1, 184, 199
    racial, 11, 198
Grill, Jan, 11, 30, 176
Gypsification, 33
Gypsy celebrity, 14, 138, 139,
    141, 146
Gypsy Lore Society (GLS), 193, 287,
    299, 303, 308, 308n4
Gypsy threat, 15, 22, 261–278

H
Habsburg Empire, 22, 285, 286,
    290, 291
Hall, Stuart, 140
Hansen, Lene, 4, 22, 236, 286, 287,
    290, 303, 307
Haptic, 241, 256n1, 297
Hate speech, 162, 166, 167, 249
Hepworth, Kate, 29–31, 221, 247
Herrmann, Anton, 305
Historiography, 171, 290
    Roma, 307
Holocaust, 166, 262, 263
Housing
    eviction, 14, 68, 72, 74, 104, 116,
        121, 127, 176, 217
    precarious, 83n1, 83n4, 84n15

Humanitarianism, 17–19, 164,
    207–225
Human rights
    ambivalence of, 58, 61–63
    critique of, 45
    liberal notion of, 62
Human security, *see* Security
Huysmans, Jef, 2, 3, 5, 54, 56, 117,
    140, 142, 144, 147, 169, 249
Hyperghetto, *see* Ghetto
Hypervisibility, 289, 294

I
Identity
    ethnic, 177
    national, 14, 63, 120, 122
Illegalization, 83n3
    of migration, 3, 32, 33, 56, 68
Inclusion
    obscene, 246, 255
    social, 16, 162, 163, 168, 172, 177,
        183–185, 190, 192, 194,
        198–200, 216, 221
Insecurity, v–x, 1, 2, 14, 21, 53, 54,
    60, 62, 74, 107, 140, 142, 144,
    147, 163, 178, 234, 236, 246,
    247, 249, 251, 253, 255, 256n1,
    285, 286, 302
Institutional developmentalism,
    see Developmentalism
Integration, v, vii, 36, 69, 72–74, 76,
    77, 82, 83, 84n15, 84n17, 106,
    108, 109, 116, 153n8, 166, 183,
    194–196, 200, 203n3, 208–212,
    215–217, 220–222, 224, 226n4,
    227n19, 262
    'failed' subject of, 19, 210–220
Intertextuality, 290, 306
Invisibilization, 8, 21, 91–110, 246,
    287, 306
    of racism, 14, 91–110

Irregularization, 3
  of migration, 6
  of the Roma, 3, 5, 9, 31–34, 58, 105, 177
Italy, 12, 20, 47, 57, 58, 61, 105, 242
Ivasiuc, Ana, 2, 12, 20–22, 54, 58, 64, 64n1, 94, 96, 105, 150, 169, 176, 178, 235, 240, 247, 248, 257n3

J
Joseph II, 288, 293

K
Kalir, Barak, 19, 208, 210
Kóczé, Angéla, 11, 13, 18, 30, 72, 191, 194, 203n2, 224, 226n7
Kovats, Martin, 186, 187, 191
Kreide, Regina, 2, 4, 6, 9, 62, 176, 220

L
Law, 6, 20, 31, 39n2, 49, 50, 52, 54–56, 58, 60, 61, 64n3, 68, 70–73, 75, 76, 78, 84n8, 84n12, 101, 125, 130, 151, 172, 210, 234, 240, 247, 277
Legros, Olivier, 4, 7–12, 69, 70, 72–75, 78, 93, 105, 177
Lentin, Alana, 93, 165
Lièvre, Marion, 4, 7–12, 69, 70, 77, 79, 83, 93, 105, 177
Life trajectories, 69, 76, 78, 80
Ludwig, Joseph Karl (Archduke of Austria), 22, 286

M
Marginalization, v, ix, 17, 32, 38, 60, 91–94, 96–98, 110, 116, 122, 131, 163, 177, 178, 185, 186, 197, 199, 203, 225

Maria Theresa, 288, 293
Marketization, v, vii, 3, 4, 10–15, 19, 20, 116, 118, 123, 307
McGarry, Aidan, 36, 91, 144, 162, 186, 190, 192
Media
  and 'Gypsy' images, 13, 15, 272
  social, vii, 21, 22, 233–256
Mediation, 18, 72, 183–203, 210–216, 224, 254, 303
  programmes, 18, 184–186, 188, 192, 195, 200, 202, 211–216
  (*see also* ROMED)
Messing, Vera, 11, 93, 149
Migrantization, 6, 31
Migration
  autonomy of, 7, 38, 39, 176, 212
  irregularization of, 6, 191
  securitization of, 19, 52–57, 207–225
Minoritization, 29, 32, 38, 39n1, 92
Minority self-articulation, 303, 307
Mireanu, Manuel, 12–14, 70, 123, 150
Mirzoeff, Nicholas, 21, 22, 235, 249, 251–253, 256
Mitchell, W.J.M., 236, 256n1, 287, 303
Mobility
  forced, 7, 10, 176, 207–225
  un/free, 12, 31, 32, 37, 39

N
Narrations, 144, 239, 289, 301, 305–306
  oral, 305–306
Nationalism, v, 2, 13, 95, 104, 119, 122, 234
Neighbourhood watch, 169, 254
Neoliberalism, 10–12, 14, 23n2, 92, 94, 96–99, 111n1, 119, 123, 124, 130, 173

Neoliberalization, 6, 10–12, 14, 15, 23n2, 91–93, 96, 99, 111n1, 173–175, 194
    racial, 11, 14, 92, 94, 173
Networks, 287
    activist, 15, 180n2
    cosmopolitan, 299, 307, 308
    institutional, 73
    international, 287
    kinship, 82
    repair, 175
    social, 82
    technological, 63, 253
Nomadism, 7, 20, 30, 38, 60, 287, 288, 292–294, 306
Nomadization, 7, 8, 104, 177, 220
    neo-nomadization, 30–31, 38
Normalization, 2, 6, 56, 59, 61, 83, 167, 192, 209, 225

O

Öjendal, Joakim, 223
Organization for Security and Co-operation in Europe (OSCE), 15
Othering, 20, 151, 212, 275, 289, 307, 308

P

Paris School, *see* Securitization
Pata Rât, 118, 121, 123, 126–131
Penalization, 94, 102, 105, 110
Pentecostalism, 177
Philanthropy, 70, 294, 299, 305–307
Picker, Giovanni, 199, 200
Picturization, 303
Police, 5, 17, 21, 22, 30, 34, 35, 64n3, 72, 76, 79, 99, 101, 102, 111n5, 117, 123, 125, 126, 128, 130, 131, 140, 147, 149, 150, 168, 175, 201, 214, 221, 226n13, 234, 242, 245, 256, 257n4, 261–278, 279n4, 279n6, 279n7, 279n8
Policing, 13, 21, 31, 32, 39, 48, 167–169, 185, 186, 236, 237
    informal, 21
Policy
    public, 173
    security, vi, 52, 67, 74–78, 168
Politicization, ix, 6, 8, 101, 165
Politics
    infra, 79
    of Roma (migrants), 9, 78–82
    security, 184
    ultra, 169
Popular culture, 14, 137–151, 289
Postraciality, 92–96
Post-socialism, 12–14, 118–121, 170–175, 183, 190
    and 'transition', 12, 120, 121, 194
Poverty, 11, 17, 18, 32, 60, 81, 98, 101, 102, 105, 131, 141, 150, 160, 161, 163, 164, 168, 170, 173, 174, 176, 178, 179, 186, 194, 217, 221, 223–225, 266, 270, 294, 303
Powell, Ryan, 12, 14, 97, 106, 129, 130, 173, 210
Power, 4, 8, 9, 12, 17, 21, 30, 34, 35, 46, 47, 52, 63, 64, 74, 79, 96, 107, 117, 118, 140, 192, 194, 197, 202, 225, 236, 246, 252–255, 272, 287, 289, 304, 307
Practices
    charitable, 306
    daily, 78, 83
    discursive, 70, 236
    of informal policing, 21
    non-discursive, 2
    police, 22, 99, 261–278
    self-harming, 302

Precariousness, v, ix, x, 5, 9, 14, 69, 71, 83n2, 91, 93, 94, 107, 120, 121, 124, 127, 130, 131, 139, 150, 161, 217, 225, 246
Privatization, 13, 14, 55, 104–106, 108, 119, 125, 194
Problematization, 4, 5, 16, 19, 57, 60, 92, 105, 141, 159, 184, 223, 271, 307
Protection
 ambiguity of, 15, 306
 minority, 16, 172
 politics of, 17, 169, 174, 249
Protest, viii, 8, 64, 131, 145, 146, 169, 233, 234, 247, 267, 276, 277
Public order, 5, 46, 59, 63, 70, 71, 99, 100, 111n5, 140

R
Race, 10, 13, 14, 21, 92, 94, 95, 106, 115, 116, 121, 132n2, 152n2, 160, 162, 166, 173, 180n3, 192, 254, 270–275
Racialization, 6, 14, 29, 70, 92–94, 99–105, 110, 111n3, 121, 129–131, 132n2, 160, 161, 163, 164, 170, 173, 176–179, 191, 192, 203, 226n11, 261–278, 292
 of poverty, 160, 170, 176, 178, 179
Racial profiling, 270, 278
Racism
 and antigypsyism, 95, 140, 160, 161, 262, 265, 266, 278n1, 308
 anti-Roma, 10, 14, 18, 91–110, 160, 161, 167, 179
 institutional, 162, 166, 277
 neoliberal, 92, 94, 105
 and Romaphobia, 160
 scientific, 193, 300, 308

Rancière, Jacques, 246
Reality television, 137, 142, 151
Reason
 domestic, 82, 83
 state, 67–83
Red Cross, 217–219, 227n17
Refugees, v, 1, 6, 8, 29, 31–33, 37, 38, 39n2, 45–47, 51, 52, 54–57, 59, 63, 64n3, 150, 165, 168, 169, 227n18, 299, 306
Representation
 exoticizing, 20
 operational, 21
 Orientalist, 177, 292
 racializing, 292
 of Roma, 16, 38, 138, 159, 184, 264
 stereotypical, 19, 292
 visual, 235, 256n1, 261–278
Resistance, viii, 4, 8, 9, 61, 68, 75, 131, 132n5
 tactics of, 68, 74, 294
Return, 19, 32, 33, 59, 75, 76, 163, 176, 187, 207–225
 'voluntary' (see Deportation)
Rights
 human, 9, 15, 17, 32–34, 36–38, 45–64, 64n3, 103, 141, 166, 169, 172, 183, 187, 188, 190, 194, 195, 197, 199, 203, 216, 309n5
 minority, 4, 6, 15, 16, 160, 162, 172
Right to escape, 6–8, 176
Risk
 at risk, vii, 11, 19, 22, 168, 208, 214, 215, 223, 294, 302
 'risky people', 168
Romania, 9, 12, 14, 59, 68, 71, 75, 76, 78–81, 83n4, 107, 115–131, 138, 188–190, 195, 201, 207–209, 214–217, 225, 269

Romani language, 286, 305, 307
Romaphobia, 161
ROMED, 18, 184, 186–192, 195–203, 226n7

S
Scott, James, 79
Securitization
  of borders, 9, 45, 46
  Copenhagen School, 2, 52
  and de-securitization, 4, 8, 22, 285–308
  dialectics of, 2, 60, 61
  of migration, 3, 5–10, 29, 36, 37, 52–57, 67, 105, 147, 207
  Paris School, 2, 53
  policy, 53, 286
  of public order, 140
  of societies, vii, 8, 12, 47
  of urban space, 14, 115, 118, 122, 124, 129, 130
  visual, 22, 286, 287, 289, 290, 306
Security
  demands, 131
  human, 3, 11, 17, 100, 162, 168, 174
  and insecurity, 1, 21, 53, 54, 234, 246, 255
  national, 2, 3, 191
  public, 60, 100, 131
  social, 5, 11, 59, 168, 221
Security-development nexus, 15–17, 19, 160, 164, 168, 175, 208–210, 221, 223–225
Security-marketization nexus, 10, 14
Security-mobility nexus, 3, 8
Security-visuality nexus, 19, 21
Sedentarism, 7, 20, 30, 277, 279n6, 293
  methodological, 30
Sedentarization, 286, 288, 293, 301
  policies, 293

Segregation, 20, 38, 48, 93, 97, 105, 107, 110, 163, 176, 177, 179, 200, 236, 251
Sigismund of Luxembourg, 293
Skeggs, Beverley, 145, 150
Slovakia, 12, 14, 92, 98–105, 108, 109, 111n5, 148, 150, 201
Social workers, 78, 82, 104, 202, 208, 211, 213, 214, 216, 219, 220, 222, 224, 225
Spain, 12, 57, 69, 71, 80, 105, 177, 207–225, 226n4
State, 29, 30, 33–35, 37, 47–54, 56, 63, 116, 207–209, 212, 215, 216, 218, 220, 222–225, 261, 286, 287, 294, 304, 306, 307
  reason, 67–83
  statelessness, 33, 35, 38
State socialism
  fall of, 10, 12
  transition, 12
Stereotypes, 7, 22, 46, 122, 139, 145, 178, 179, 198, 236, 266, 272, 273, 289, 291, 292, 294, 297, 299
Stern, Maria, 223
Stigmatization, 38, 97, 99, 102, 105, 106, 109, 110, 121, 139, 166, 268, 286, 287
  territorial, 102, 107
Strategies, 22, 30, 68, 75, 116, 177, 192, 194, 203n3, 218, 221–223, 287–289, 292, 294
Surdu, Mihai, 183, 264, 270
Surveillance, 5, 56, 58, 61, 100, 109, 131, 149, 164, 207, 208, 211, 213, 218, 222, 223, 225, 233, 234, 247, 252–254, 265, 293

T
Tactics, 4, 9, 68, 77, 78, 82, 273
Text/image, 22, 296

Theodore, Nik, 123, 124
Threat, vi, 1–6, 13–15, 17, 20–22, 46, 48, 52, 59, 60, 63, 64, 70, 71, 74, 76, 105, 107, 110, 116, 117, 124, 125, 132n1, 139–149, 151, 167, 168, 191, 208, 209, 213, 215, 221–225, 240, 247, 249, 261–278, 286–290, 299, 301–304, 306, 307
Tremlett, Annabel, 13–15, 139, 140, 142, 289
Tyler, Imogen, 142, 145, 146, 148, 151

U

Ultra-politics, 169
Underdevelopment, 17, 163, 168, 174, 175, 178, 179, 223
United Kingdom (UK), 12, 14, 57, 92
Urban space, 14, 115, 118, 119, 122–124, 130, 131, 208

V

van Baar, Huub, 3, 5, 7, 8, 11–14, 16, 18, 21, 30–32, 36–38, 39n1, 54, 56–59, 68, 70, 76, 93–96, 100, 104, 111n1, 111n4, 127, 129, 130, 140, 141, 179n1, 180n2, 180n3, 184, 186, 191–194, 208, 209, 220, 221, 223, 224, 245, 275, 279n6, 303, 307
Vermeersch, Peter, 21, 70, 94, 105
Vincle, 214, 215, 226n9
Vincze, Enikő, 121, 123, 127, 128, 130, 132n2, 221
Violence, v, vii, viii, 15, 30, 39n2, 72, 75, 77, 94, 104, 122, 124, 128, 140, 142–144, 166, 171, 178, 193, 203, 209, 220, 224, 225, 240, 247, 249, 250, 255
Visibility, 94, 236, 252, 264, 270–275, 306
 hyper (*see* Hypervisibility)
 and invisibility, 94, 306
Visuality
 complex of, 21, 235, 236, 251–253
 complex of securitarian, 22, 235, 251–255
 regimes of, 19, 21, 22, 94, 167, 293
 vigilant, 21, 235, 251, 254, 255
Visual regime, 22, 264, 270–275, 277, 278, 292
'Voluntary' return, 19, 207–227
Von Wlislocki, Heinrich, 304
Vrăbiescu, Ioana, 7, 11, 12, 19, 71, 93, 105, 164, 174, 210, 216, 221

W

Wacquant, Loïc, 14, 92, 94, 97–99, 107–109, 129, 246
Walters, William, 5, 35, 163–165, 169, 255
Welfare, 11, 36, 37, 100, 101, 105–107, 109, 124, 127, 139, 146, 151, 171, 194, 208, 218, 222
Western Europe, 3, 5, 20, 98, 178, 261
Wolff, Larry, 290

Z

Zero tolerance, 101, 163, 179
Žižek, Slavoj, 169

CPSIA information can be obtained
at www.ICGtesting.com
Printed in the USA
LVHW06*0910280518
578630LV00002B/5/P